Future Crossings

Series Editor

Hugh Silverman

PHILOSOPHY, LITERATURE, AND CULTURE

Future Crossings
Literature between Philosophy and Cultural Studies

Edited by
Krzysztof Ziarek
and
Seamus Deane

NORTHWESTERN
UNIVERSITY PRESS
EVANSTON
ILLINOIS

Northwestern University Press
Evanston, Illinois 60208–4210

Copyright © 2000 by Northwestern University Press. Published 2000. All rights
reserved.

Printed in the United States of America

ISBN 0-8101-1791-6 (cloth)
ISBN 0-8101-1792-4 (paper)

Library of Congress Cataloging-in-Publication Data

Future crossings : literature between philosophy and cultural studies /
edited by Krzysztof Ziarek and Seamus Deane.
    p. cm. — (Philosophy, literature, and culture)
Includes bibliographical references (p.).
ISBN 0-8101-1791-6 (alk. paper) — ISBN 0-8101-1792-4 (pbk. : alk. paper)
    1. Criticism—History—20th century. 2. Literature, Modern—History and
criticism—Theory, etc. I. Ziarek, Krzysztof, 1961- II. Deane, Seamus, 1940-
III. Title. IV. Series.
PN94 .F88 2000
801'.95—dc21

                                  00-010761

Contents

Part III. Modernity, Nationalism, and Cultural Difference

Acknowledgments

The idea for this book originated at the 1996 annual meeting of the American Comparative Literature Association, which Krzysztof Ziarek organized at the University of Notre Dame. The conference was entitled "Literature between Philosophy and Cultural Studies." We decided to use this theme as the subtitle of the current volume of essays.

Some of the texts included here have appeared previously in other publications. Elizabeth Grosz's essay is reprinted from "Thinking the New," in *Becomings: Explorations in Time, Memory, and Futures,* edited by Elizabeth Grosz. Copyright © 1999 by Cornell University. Used by permission of Cornell University Press. Joan Brandt's "The Politics of *Différance*" is adapted in part from Brandt's *Geopoetics: The Politics of Mimesis in Poststructuralist French Poetry and Theory.* Copyright © 1997 by the Board of Trustees of the Leland Stanford University. Used by permission of Stanford University Press. A shorter version of David Lloyd's "Counterparts" was published in *Burning Down the House: Recycling Domesticity,* edited by Rosemary Marangoly George (Boulder, Colo.: Westview Press, 1998). Finally, an earlier version of Joseph Kronick's "Between Act and Archive" appeared as a portion of chapter 3 of his book *Derrida and the Future of Literature* (Albany: State University of New York Press, 1999).

We would like to thank Erich Hertz, Harry McCandless, and Tom Butler for their help with preparing the manuscript of this collection for publication. Special thanks to our editors at Northwestern University Press, Susan Harris and Theresa Biancheri, for their support of this project and editorial advice.

Acknowledgments

Introduction

Krzysztof Ziarek and Seamus Deane

Literary studies are at present constituted as a site of interaction between various disciplines, a field conceived in terms of multiple and often contending interests and approaches: from cultural studies, poststructuralism, and deconstruction to feminism, ethnic studies, and postcolonial criticism. Many positions along the spectrum of discourses that make up literary studies are themselves far from "pure" or homogeneous; they are often hybrid, comprising or combining various orientations. Notwithstanding this plural and heterogeneous character of contemporary literary studies, it is possible to identify the main rift around which many of the contestations occur: it is the well-known divide between cultural studies and theory, the latter being often identified with poststructuralist criticism. The label "theory" is obviously broader and more diversified than that, yet what is most often contested under that name are indeed deconstruction and/or poststructuralist theories. Some of the distinctive traits of poststructuralism include: critique of reason as foundational or universal, decentering of the subject, problematization of reference and meaning, and undermining of totalizing narratives; while cultural studies advocate focusing on mass and popular cultures and concentrate on the analysis of the wealth of historical and cultural material. At their extreme, cultural studies renounce theory as narrow and elitist or accuse it of aestheticism and indifference to cultural reality and social practice. On the other hand, "theory" regards cultural studies as lacking theoretical acumen and philosophical "depth," which are exchanged for the descriptive richness of the historicist approach. These are obviously caricatures but they have, nonetheless, some currency in contemporary debates within literary studies. In reality, many of the most interesting approaches—for example, certain trends in feminism or postcolonial studies—are located between the poles of these polemics and complicate the picture of the apparently sharp and unbridgeable divide between philosophical approaches and cultural criticism.

One way of opening a critical and productive dialogue between philosophical approaches and cultural studies, which we briefly explore here, is to examine the different forms of the critique of aesthetics produced by the various approaches within those broadly sketched orientations. Cultural studies has among its aims the demystification of aesthetic ideology; the revelation of the political and controlling purposes behind and within the various hierarchies that distinguish "high" from "low" and "major" from "minor" in the various arts; and the assertion that there is, within the concepts of "disinterestedness" and even of "distance" upon which so many traditional approaches to aesthetic judgment are based, a specific and local agenda that has the (bogus) claim to universality as its central aim. There is clearly in such studies a determination to specify the context(s) of any particular work and to extend the notion of culture to include the mass audience and the popular culture which the Frankfurt School, especially Adorno, regarded as belonging to the sphere of commodification, in which critical thought has been successfully stifled. But so long as criticism is understood to be engaged in the revelation of what is concealed, it remains loyal to a central element of the Enlightenment heritage toward which it is in other respects suspicious or fearful. Given as it is to archival accumulation, heterogeneous particulars, and the internal coherences of local situations, cultural studies goes to great lengths to avoid any synoptic diagnosis that might be tainted with the ambition to be totalizing. This is often admirable and salutary, but it is also a position that is sometimes vulnerable to banalization, especially when, as Thomas Docherty has argued, the defense of specific cultural formations degenerates into a dispute between political correctness on the one hand and the defense of the canon on the other.[1]

There is Culture and there are cultures, and while some communities *have* culture, others *are* a culture. No matter how the debate between these terms is conducted, it will always have among its terms of reference the State, the nation, the institutional power that validates what culture is or what cultures are and thereby, in legitimating them, also finds a way of legitimating itself. Culture with a capital *C* is, of course, suspect; it wears an imperial, Eurocentric air. In the plural, cultures can both claim independence from the singular version and deny legitimation to systems of power—most of them imperial or colonial—that refuse to recognize their otherness, their particularity and their own intrinsic legitimacy. Unsurprisingly, then, postcolonial studies bear a strong relation to and may even in some ways be the source of and be sourced in cultural studies. Colonized cultures, more than any others, know the disempowering effects of reproducing the culture of the external power in an effort toward assimilation; they also know the profound aftereffects of having had one's own culture derided or denied, especially when this has been done with and through a certain complicity on the part of the victims; and finally they know that the assertion of a cultural identity and specificity runs the danger of reduplicating the oppression it earlier experienced if it claims for itself anything more than a legitimacy that pertains only to itself. One way out of this impasse—mostly associated with Gayatri Spivak—is to refuse the legitimating activity of culture itself. By virtue of such a denial, culture is removed from the servility toward the State, economic, and commercial power, which is part of its recent history in the nineteenth and twentieth centuries. But even then, there is still the question of the relationship of emergent nationalisms to forms of culture that have been compelled, for good reason, to redesign themselves as always symptomatic of that nationalism's authenticity. In such cases, culture, posed as traditional, is often in fact cosmetic. This further intensifies the recurrent anxiety about the relationship of nationalism to modernity; in that endless debate, culture very often is used as the means to legitimate a certain antimodernity within nationalism, thereby leading again to the schism between culture as regressive redemption from the forms of progress and development that modernity and the State have come to represent.

In the United States, such debates have a valency quite different from that which they would have in Africa, Asia, South America, or Europe. For in the United States, the central institution within which such debates are conducted is the university, and the various versions of multiculturalism that are discussed there rarely refer to the State, most especially to its imperial role; the American academy, as Bruce Robbins has pointed out, is closer to the marketplace than it is to the State, hence the constant recourse to the professional expert with a specific function that is different from the more generalized function of the intellectual in its non-American form.[2] There is, as a consequence, in American cultural studies debates an air of professionalism that is often taken to be an indication of its removal from political actualities. Professionalism as such is, in most important respects, an already depoliticized condition. This is an issue that could only be properly addressed in a detailed history of the migration of cultural studies from Europe to the United States, of postcolonial studies and their migration to the United States from various parts of the decolonized world, and a recognition that both these migrations are also intertwined with the history of the migration of cultural theory from post–World War II Europe into the radically different ethos of the United States and its unique version of the university in its relation to the State. One consequence of this would be the redrafting, in American terms, of those aesthetic questions which have "distance" and "disinterestedness" among their governing terms. Professionalism, like many aesthetic theories, depends upon the prior establishment of a distance from the objects of its inquiry, even if it thereafter goes to great and sometimes ingenious lengths to abolish it.

Two further points need to be made here. Although European intellectual debates provide the material for almost all of these essays, the interpretations are rooted in an American, or American-based, understanding and absorption of these debates. The European influence is decisive, however, in relation to the question of the aesthetic. For it is this question that governs the linkages that are traced in this volume between cultural studies and deconstruction. At its simplest, it is a question that embraces the putative contrast between approaches that are predicated on distance from the actual and on immersion within it. That is, as we have said, a contrast that has at the very least implicit effects on an understanding of the disagreements between cultural studies and deconstruction. In Europe—excluding the United Kingdom—the contrast is not so sharp nor so divisively understood, largely because European versions of the aesthetic have been much more profoundly altered by the ambition

and desire to understand its interconnections with the political. This desire has amounted to a necessity at least since the Second World War and
the horrors of the Holocaust, but it was already evident in the writings
of Lukács in the twenties and was also of course—although not in its
most distinguished phase—one of the central debates in Revolutionary
and in Stalinist Russia.

There is, therefore, a recognition in these essays that "cultural studies," however defined, and by whatever definition it gives to art or to
literature, cannot escape the question of the aesthetic, either by diminish-
ing its importance or by treating it as something of a historical relic from
the past. The idea of the aesthetic has indeed many authoritarian elements in its history and is inescapably bound up with a version of the
wholly autonomous subject that may now appear to be little more than
one of the potent but lost fictions of a bygone era. But the aesthetic
necessarily remains as an issue which has not had any theoretical formulation within the field of cultural studies, even though, it seems to us, it is
badly in need of that in order to begin the process of recognizing rather
than remaining oblivious to its own historical conditions and condition-
ing. This is all the more timely and important, precisely because of the
professionalism already mentioned, the situating of this and related questions within the American academy. For the academic perspective is, of
its nature, already involved in the problematics of distance and immersion, disengagement and commitment. These are terms that belong both
to the political and to the aesthetic fields. They are traditionally related,
but their relationship is now clearly in need of redefinition by those
whose experience equips them so well for the completion of that task. In
the redefinition of that relationship, we will see the European experience
incorporated and reinterpreted within the American context.

The very idea of "cultural studies" defines literature as determined
primarily by its being a part of the broader phenomenon of culture and
thus as both warranting and requiring that literary works be read together
with and in terms of other sectors of cultural production and their material and social conditions. Perhaps the most important contribution of
cultural studies is the thorough contextualization of literature: it is not
just a question of interrogating the suspect claims to the distinctness
of the aesthetic sphere but of conducting an exhaustive study of literature as part of cultural and social organization, as coextensive with the
material and discursive relations of power operating in particular historical and social contexts. Literature becomes read as an element of an
extensive sociocultural, and thus material and political, organization of

forces—a welcome strategy that undercuts the idea of a narrow disciplinary study of literary works and, from the outset, frames the question of literature in culturally and politically important terms: relations of power, gender, race, class, nationalism, and so on. For cultural studies, the production of art and literature is never simply a matter of aesthetic creation but becomes an avenue of articulating—establishing, solidifying, or contesting—the predominant social and discursive relations.

In this broader context of the study of culture, art becomes an institution among many, often a "less" important part of social life, secondary to politics, labor, and other social questions and their articulations in mass or popular culture, which claim a much wider audience than "high" art. One of the fallouts of this approach, however, is the fact that, if literature retains any distinct status, it is often articulated in terms of a politically and socially suspect separation of the aesthetic sphere, which conceals the fundamental dependence of art on society, and its existence as coextensive, and often complicit, with established relations of power. In this context, art is denied any autonomy, an autonomy which, contrary to Gramsci's or Adorno's explanations, becomes mistaken for separation, for the idea of "unworldly" art—indifferent and disinvested from the social reality in which it exists. Examining the critique of aesthetics in cultural studies in "Aesthetics and Cultural Studies," Ian Hunter raises precisely the question of whether aesthetics can be subsumed within a more general notion of culture and explained in terms of relations between culture and society. He disagrees with the idea that aesthetics is a partial domain, separated from "the driving forces of human development—labor and politics," and shows how Weber and Foucault propose a broader notion of aesthetics as a political/practical domain of "the unfolding of all that we might become."[3] What needs to be added to Hunter's discussion is that this different approach to the limits of the aesthetic he describes is an integral part of a much broader modern philosophical critique of aesthetics, initiated by Nietzsche, that in fact calls into question the Schillerian ideal of aesthetic cultivation, with which Hunter's essay (mis)aligns Foucault. While this tradition clearly departs from the narrow notion of art and the aesthetic—of art as essentially *aesthetic*—equally important to it is the critical potential evident in art's "resistance" to the idea of culture and institution.

Philosophical critiques of modernity in the twentieth century—from Heidegger and Adorno to Derrida, Lyotard, Irigaray, post-Heideggerian thought, and poststructuralism—foreground the question of aesthetics and often gather their critical impetus from the consideration of art and literature. Notwithstanding their many differences, what they have in common is the growing sense of the historical exhaustion of aesthetics and the inadequacy of the aesthetic categorizations of art. This idea of an impending "end" of art—in a way, a continuing reflection and response to Hegel's claim about the death of art—is a corollary of the critique of metaphysics initiated in different ways by Nietzsche, Heidegger, and Adorno, and continued by such thinkers as Foucault, Levinas, Deleuze, Derrida, and Irigaray. In *Beiträge zur Philosophie,* published in 1989 but written between 1936 and 1938, Heidegger links the end of aesthetics with the critique of the metaphysical notions of representation and objectivity: "The question [of the origin of the work of art] stands in innermost connection with the task of the overcoming of aesthetics and that means at the same time of a specific account of beings as objectively representable."[4] The end of aesthetics has a philosophical and cultural significance, as it is paired with the demand to rearticulate experience through a critique of metaphysical conceptuality, beyond the governing structures operative in the technological organization of life in modernity. Discussing how the aesthetic determination of art may be coming to an end, and with it "the categorization of the 'fine arts' that accompany it, and with these a whole aesthetic feeling and judgement, a whole sublime delectation," Jean-Luc Nancy remarks that art has a duty to put an end to "art," that is, to Art conceived in aesthetic terms, in order to present "the singular plural of obviousness—of existence."[5]

The contemporary philosophical critiques of aesthetics raise a two-tiered question about the aesthetic understanding of art. On the one hand, they call into question the idea of art as belonging to a separate sphere, to an aesthetic domain of experience, disconnected from everyday life; that is, they displace an aesthetic which posits art as absolutely *different* from, and thus *indifferent* to, other spheres of life. On the other hand, Continental thought articulates the need of a further, and somewhat different, critique of aesthetics, one that calls into question the ideas of experience, presence, history, representation, and production that operate in cultural critiques of aesthetics. The corollary of the rethinking of art as "aesthetic" is the problem of the status of the work of art, of its role and distinctness vis-à-vis the concepts of the object, aesthetic experience, production, institution. Three issues in particular are worth mentioning here: the idea of how art *works,* the question of aesthetic experience, and the relation between art and its material and cultural conditions of production. First, Continental critiques question the viability of the notion of an "art object": for Heidegger and Lyotard, the work of art has to be thought as an event; Derrida sees it in terms of "writing"; Blanchot as *dèsoeuvrement* or "unworkness"; Foucault as a critical attitude toward contemporary reality. Second, thinkers like Heidegger and Derrida explicitly call into question the idea that our relation to art can be interpreted in terms of the subject-object paradigm or explained through the category of aesthetic experience. They read the work of art as foregrounding the historicity of experience, as reformulating experience in terms of its futurity: always "out-of-joint," never self-identical or self-coincident—an approach that distances art from the notion of the subject and the idea of a private aesthetic experience.[6] Finally, for Adorno, modernist art rebels against the idea of representation and the ideology of aestheticism, but it also insists on maintaining a negative distance from its own conditions of production and reception: "Art is the social antithesis of society, not directly deducible from it."[7] Art is indissociable from social life and culture but is also distinct from it: it exceeds the cultural idea of art, and this is why Adorno repeatedly emphasizes the paradox of art's autonomy: "Art is autonomous and it is not; without what is heterogeneous to it, its autonomy eludes it" (*AT* 6). Although artworks are "afterimages of empirical life," they separate themselves from the empirical and discursive patterns of identification and the paradigms of meaning which articulate their contemporary reality. This distance or excess allows art to negate and reinvent "the categorial determinations stamped on the empirical word" (*AT* 4-5) and thus to call into question art's determination by the social and material conditions of its production.

In the context of the philosophical critiques of aesthetics, the question of literary studies becomes also the question to what extent literature and its study functions as part of cultural critique. What the Continental critiques of modernity allow us to see is that the critique of the idea of a separate aesthetic domain does not automatically mean that literature can be fully explained and theorized within the optics of the study of culture. Thinkers as different as Heidegger, Adorno, Derrida, and Irigaray would agree that art cannot be unproblematically equated with the notion of a cultural phenomenon or an object of cultural production, because art inverts and puts into question those very categorizations. Their writings raise the question of the very conceptuality that "produces" the idea of art as a cultural phenomenon and explains the "work" performed by art in terms of cultural and institutional effects and inscriptions. In Adorno's aesthetic theory, art clearly arises from the material conditions of its production, from its cultural milieu and within the institutional forms and critical practices that regulate it. But what makes art art, what is "artistic" about it, cannot be fully or exclusively accounted for in materialist or cultural terms, for these very terms are inverted and revised in art. They are not simply "critiqued," superseded, or replaced with alternative terms that are still operative *within* the horizon of culture and available discourses: rather, art puts into question the entire cultural/discursive edifice that makes it possible.

Adorno suggests that the paradox of art is that it is both *less* and *more* than praxis: "Art, however, is more than praxis because by its aversion to praxis it simultaneously denounces the narrow untruth of the practical world" (*AT* 241). By being simultaneously more and less than praxis, art contests the specific constitution of praxis and social relations. We could add that what makes art "interesting" and "critical" is precisely the possibility that it is "more" or *otherwise* than its aesthetic *and* cultural significations, that it contests the theorizations of art in terms of cultural-historical context and institutional status. We have to keep in view how art contests the cultural idea of art, how it takes to task the very conceptuality on which culture relies for self-definition and for determining art as its part or sector. To formulate this question more carefully, we should ask whether the cultural critique of aesthetics breaks with what could be seen as a correlate of metaphysics and aesthetics: the idea that art exhausts itself as a cultural phenomenon. The departure from a certain ideology of the aesthetic may not be enough, if a trace of aesthetics, and a very powerful one, subtends the very categorization of literature as a cultural phenomenon. As cultural criticism questions and loosens the "aestheticized" notion of art and allows us to show art's entanglement with materialist, historical, and discursive conditions of social life, it comes up against the categorization of art and literature as a cultural phenomenon and a social institution.

What cannot be forgotten is how art—certainly modern art and its "avant-gardes"—undermines positivistic discourse and its two symmetrical branches: assertion and critique. Commenting in his interview "This Strange Institution Called Literature" on the critical function of literature, Derrida points to modern texts (Joyce, Blanchot, and Celan, among others) that "operate a sort of turning back, they *are* themselves a sort of turning back on the literary institution."[8] They remark an excess of language, which makes it difficult and problematic for the institution of literature to identify itself, and which demonstrates how literature always dissimulates and complicates what it shows, never simply re-presenting or critiquing and negating it.[9] Art is often "more" than what it asserts and works "otherwise" than how it critiques. It poses a continuous challenge to the positivist trends of philosophical and cultural analyses. But it also calls into question decontextualized, abstract analyses of the "idea" of art, distanced from considerations of cultural and social reality. What we have described as the double question at the "end of aesthetics" problematizes both the aesthetic idea of art together with the notion of aesthetic experience and the parameters and stakes of the move "beyond" aesthetics into the cultural context of art: of the reading of literature from within institutional-discursive parameters of culture. As necessary and important as this "cultural" reading becomes at the end of aesthetics, the "philosophical" stakes and limits of such a reading should also be interrogated. This other perspective disquiets the very idea that the study of culture and institutional analysis "accounts" for art; it is a perspective that, in fact, will hold open the idea of "cultural studies" to questioning not only on its own terms, from within "culture," as it were, but also from the *without* which, as Adorno and Heidegger suggest, art itself marks— the without which perhaps marks art *as art.*

This problematic concerns the ways in which the idea of art as a sector of culture or cultural activity already presupposes what might be called a *cultural* view of art, a view that, as Heidegger suggests at the end of "The Question Concerning Technology,"[10] we need to keep interrogating "philosophically" to see whether it circumscribes and "misrepresents" what art does, fitting it into its own terms of analysis. Thus, some of the questions that philosophical critiques of aesthetics raise might be formulated as follows: To what extent does the change in the view of literature from *aesthetic* to *cultural* effect a departure from the *metaphysical* understanding of the work of art? Though it is never simply aesthetic, is the form that literature takes cultural to begin with? Is the idea of art as cultural production a form of the "containment" of art's significance, even if it is certainly different from the one perpetuated under the guise of aesthetic experience? What philosophical critiques, after Heidegger and Adorno, prompt us to reconsider is the extent to which the constitution of art as a cultural phenomenon, coincident with its production, functions, and discursive inscriptions, continues to repeat the metaphysical conceptualization of art. In our view, this question is as fundamental to cultural studies as the issue of deconstructing metaphysics is to philosophical critiques.

The questioning of the idea of literature as a cultural phenomenon (and thus of culture itself), to which philosophical revisions of aesthetics lead, has to be kept distinct from the idea of positing a discrete sphere of aesthetic experience. The charges of "aestheticism" or "formalism," all too readily invoked in this context, misunderstand and distort the stakes of such critiques. To say that literature questions its location as a cultural phenomenon does not mean that literary work transcends culture toward a separate aesthetic sphere, independent of the historical and material conditions that shape culture. It does mean, however, rethinking the idea that literature's relations to social reality and experience can all be explained or theorized within the optics that posits literature as *in essence* a social-cultural phenomenon. Against this supposition, Adorno's work thematizes art's "intervention" in terms of the negative of the social and the empirical, Heidegger writes about the critical displacement and transformation in art of "our accustomed ties to world and earth . . . all usual doing and prizing, knowing and looking"[11]—a transformation of everyday social and cultural relations—and Foucault sees art as critical of everyday social praxis. Philosophical criticism approaches, as it were, the other side of the question posed by cultural critique: can art exceed its cultural formation, in a manner that is not reducible to the idea of aesthetic experience as "separate" from other spheres of life? This questioning takes art beyond the scope of aesthetics but also toward the limit of the categories of culture and institution. It is, one could hazard, not an escape from the institutional, historical, and discursive framing of art and literature but, precisely, its result. It is a "reaction" of art to its own cultural situatedness, a reaction that questions what literature is, and how it might be, "in excess of" what is thematized of it in terms of aesthetic and cultural analyses. Through a rigorous attention to the social and historical conditions of its production, art performs in excess of those inscriptions and marks an opening toward the future—a futurity that underpins and "virtualizes" experience.

In *Aesthetic Theory,* Adorno locates this "excess," the critical social force of art, not in thematic or representational concerns but in what he calls art's form: "Among the mediations of art and society the thematic, the open or covert treatment of social matters, is the most superficial and deceptive"; and "[r]eal denunciation is probably only a capacity of form, which is overlooked by social aesthetic that believes in themes" (*AT* 229, 230). This excess can be explained neither aesthetically, philosophically, nor culturally. What Adorno proposes is certainly not formalism but an understanding of art as making its intervention or "critique" by way of exceeding the cultural, social, and discursive parameters which obtain at a particular historical moment or location from which art arises. At stake in such an approach is what we would like to call, merging Adorno's and

Heidegger's terms, the *social figure* of art. This figure exceeds and undoes the opposition between form and content: it is neither a matter of thematic social criticism nor of "purely" formalist experimentation. But this idea of the *figure of art* also questions the aesthetic, the philosophical, and the cultural notions of art. The work of such a figure extends, on the one hand, beyond aesthetic-philosophical ideas of representation, beauty, or judgment and, on the other, beyond the notion that art can be fully explained and subsumed within a more general notion of culture and its relation to society. It is a figure that mediates between cultural and philosophical critiques, because its social "significance" lies as much in contesting the idea of the aesthetic as in questioning the concepts of the social and the cultural.

It is possible to think about this social figure as a "second-degree" critique of aesthetics, a questioning that uncovers another layer of metaphysical conceptuality, that manifests itself in thinking art as "essentially" a cultural phenomenon. We could say that this approach "intensifies" the critique of aesthetics, raises it a notch to another degree. At the same time that it submits itself to cultural critiques, it keeps interrogating the very ideas of culture and critique. Rather than concluding that cultural studies, however defined, constitute an "advance" over poststructuralist thought, that they somehow supersede its concerns, we need to keep the critique of aesthetics in this double movement, in the tension between "cultural" readings and "philosophical" perspectives. These critiques of art and literature, undertaken from different locations and with a different conceptual armature by poststructuralism and cultural studies, need to be kept in play precisely in their *difference.* It is the difference between these approaches that brings into focus the possibility of the critical status of art as a product of culture that undoes and exceeds its own position and origin. It is in the cross between cultural and philosophical critiques that the future of literature (and literary criticism) comes into view, as an examination and contestation of the very nature and limits of literature, as a reflection on the character of the *work* that takes place in literary texts and its transformative — "futural" — relation to experience, culture, and history. In this critical crossing, what comes into the open is not only the future of literature but also, as Joseph Kronick suggests, the futurity of writing, which is itself related to a futurity or virtuality that Elizabeth Grosz's reading of Bergson diagnoses as the temporal structure of matter and experience. In its explorations of the intrinsic futurity of experience, and the cultural dislocations produced by it, modern literature itself demands such a crossing of perspectives, a mutual engagement between the philosophical and the cultural approaches.

Future Crossings suggests that the study of literature in the contemporary context is characterized by this betweenness: it is located between philosophy, in particular philosophical critiques of modernity, and broadly conceived cultural studies. As part of culture and its institutions, literature interacts with an array of cultural, social, and political issues, both inflecting them through its prism and finding itself influenced, even contested, by them. But literature also finds itself part and parcel of the ongoing philosophical and theoretical debates about the status of modernity, debates that have made, and for very good reasons, aesthetics and modernism one of the most important sites for reevaluating modernity in its political and cultural dimensions. This historical, cultural, and philosophical context makes literature and its study into an interdiscursive space, which exists and reinvents itself between various discursive formations.

One of the most telling instances of this in-betweenness of literature is examined in *Future Crossings* in the essays by Herman Rapaport and David Lloyd, in which the idea of the national poet or of the national character is subjected to a searching critique. The presence of a national idea or ideal in literature institutes the possibility of writing a national literary history. Yet such a history is always surrendering itself, at crucial moments, to the notion of a universally human dimension in literature which both sanctifies the national and also, in important respects, contradicts it. A philosophically based critique of this vexed and yet standard relationship lies at the heart of the best postcolonial commentary. The distinction between the national and the universal is at its most effective, paradoxically, when one is identified with the other. This has been a strategy adopted by the most powerful of colonizing cultures; it is in colonized areas of the globe that this identification has been most resisted and endured. It is also in these areas that an effective critique has been developed—in Algeria, India, the West Indies, and Ireland, among others—with important consequences for both the philosophical and literary traditions that have leaned so heavily on this distinction and have produced through it such hegemonic assent.

There is definitely a dearth of books that address the intersections and contestations between philosophical approaches to literary studies and cultural criticism, especially ones that, like *Future Crossings,* approach the issue from multiple perspectives: feminism, cultural studies, poststructuralist theory. Rather than simply providing an overview of the contested areas and the points of intersection between poststructuralism and cultural criticism, this collection addresses the question of the future(s) of literary studies. It approaches this problem through three sets of issues, which correspond to the three parts into which the essays have been arranged. The first part explores the parallels in understanding literature and experience in terms of their intrinsic futurity, that is, through their continuous differentiation and realignment, their latencies and virtualities, which keep reframing the question of literature. It also addresses the intrinsically interdiscursive and interdisciplinary character of the study of literature, which, visible most clearly in the debates within feminism, renders problematic any rigid division between theoretically nuanced approaches and the "richness" of cultural and "experiential" criticism. The essays in the second part of this book address the cultural implications of deconstruction and poststructuralism, in particular, the effects that a certain opacity and unpredictability intrinsic to difference has upon our understanding of community, politics, and ethics. The third set of essays focuses on the question of literature in relation to modernity, nationalism, and cultural difference.

Although the essays assembled here are consciously heterogeneous to reflect the variety of approaches and the contested nature of literary studies, they are framed by a fundamental revision of the concepts of future and the new, and the effects this rethinking has in opening up the study of literature as a site of differentiation, latency, and unpredictability. The collection starts by interrogating the very idea of the future—not only as an issue of time but also as the question of the very concepts of object, matter, history, and identity in the versions in which they inform current debates about literature and culture. Grosz's essay, "Thinking the New," which opens the collection, critiques the often uninterrogated concept of the future as it is employed not only in cultural/literary studies or philosophy, but also in the sciences. The understanding of time and future is crucial because it determines how experience, history, materiality, and textuality—key notions in contemporary polemics—are conceived in various approaches to literary studies. If being is futural, in the process of constant actualization of its latencies, opening itself anew to divergences and differentiations, then the notions of the literary text and the (con)text of culture also need to be reconsidered from within their "present" and as already being differentiated by the unpredictable, "unthought" future. The essays gathered here explore some of the effects of such a reconceptualization of history and identity: in feminist studies (Alice Gambrell); in how we conceive of politics (Joan Brandt); in the question of identity in reaction to the idea of Europe (Rodolphe Gasché); in the relation between ethics and aesthetics (Dorota Glowacka); in the debate about literature and nationalism (Lloyd, Rapaport); in the understanding of literature as archive and/or invention (Kronick); and in rethinking the self-legitimating narratives of modernity (Andreas Michel, Gilbert Chaitin).

The essays gathered in the first part, "Remembering the Future," illustrate the importance of the notion of futurity in opening up and resignifying the discursive and cultural divisions operative in academic discourses: between the humanities and sciences, theoretical and materialist approaches in feminism, theory and popular culture, and between the singularity and the repetition intrinsic to literature. To the extent that difference, or openness to otherness, marks the critical stakes of both cultural studies and philosophical reflection, the issue of the future, of the futurity and unpredictability intrinsic to experience and language, cuts across conceptual barriers and polemics and revises the very terrain on which such critical encounters take place: matter, identity, history, experience, culture, and so on. In "Thinking the New: Of Futures Yet Unthought," Elizabeth Grosz undertakes a rethinking of the notion of time, and thus of numerous assumptions about identity, history, and origin, that is accepted not only by philosophy and cultural studies but also by the sciences. She proposes to think futurity neither in the language of consumer capitalism (novelty for its own sake) nor in the language of science (the language of determinism), but instead in terms of difference, that is, as the latencies or virtualities, "the divergent resonances," within the present. Exploring a kind of "anarchization" of the future, Grosz draws attention to convergences between "new science," especially biology, and the movements of difference within the humanities. Focusing on Deleuze's reading of Bergson, Grosz questions the rigid divisions between vitalism and mechanism, organic life and inorganic matter, and, finally, between matter and information. Bergson's opposition between the possible and the virtual allows Grosz to make a crucial distinction between the concretization of the possible as a preprogrammed or planned change and the actualization of the virtual, which involves the creation of heterogeneous terms, divergence from the virtual, multiple differentiations, and unpredictability. Such actualization is not limited to the sphere of the human or the realm of consciousness but extends through organic life to inorganic matter and even to information. The concept of the virtual thus becomes central in reimagining the future in terms of production and differentiation that are open to the unexpected and other, thereby making impossible a closed conceptualization of self, origin, or change. In the end, Grosz suggests that we need to revise not only the conception of time in cultural studies, philosophy, or the sciences but also the very concepts of object and matter, which should be opened to differentiation.

Joseph Kronick's "Between Act and Archive: Literature in the Nuclear Age" describes Derrida's discovery of an affinity between the rhetoric of nuclear war and literature. Nuclear war is "a monstrosity," an event that cannot be understood because it is absolutely singular, it has never happened, and, were it to happen, it would leave no remains. It is wholly other. Yet there is no singular that, despite its claim to absolute uniqueness, can be understood or represented if it is not linked to iterability. In literature, an absolutely new, unique, invented text needs the sanction of the reader. The inaugurating signature needs a countersignature. Although the text is first, the countersigning reading second, this secondariness of the reader (reading) conditions the inaugurating text. For literature is an institution that is always preceded by the countersignature of the reading audience that both receives it and inaugurates it. Yet the literary work is also pure invention, the absolutely singular. That doubleness of singularity and institutionalism enables us to see Derrida's placement of literature as something that, lacking essence yet having presence, suspends the metaphysical foundations on which it depends. It places its philosophical possibility in parentheses, thus distinguishing itself from philosophy and revealing its alliance with the nuclear threat that never arrives and is yet always here.

Alice Gambrell's "Remembering Women's Studies" presents a retrospective examination of the history of women's studies by focusing on the condition of working between various discursive formations intrinsic to feminist scholarship. Looking at the complexity of the historiographical debates currently under way in feminist studies, Gambrell questions the status of the opposition between theory and the experiential/historical richness of cultural criticism, an opposition rendered problematic in the recent critiques of what Jane Gallop has called the "progress narrative" of feminism from the monolithic tendencies of women's studies in the 1970s to more nuanced theoretical readings of "feminist theory." Two second-wave formulations of female betweenness from the mid-1970s, Gayle Rubin's "The Traffic in Women" and June Jordan's "On Richard Wright and Zora Neale Hurston: Notes Toward a Balancing of Love and Hatred," serve as examples of the "complicated metacommentaries on the institutional status of feminist scholarship" and its defining polarities already evident in the earlier phase of women's studies. Gambrell argues that the conflicts between theory and historical recovery are, in fact, a constant in academic feminism, except that now they are embedded in "full-blown institutional operations." Rereading the past of women's studies in terms of the interdiscursive negotiations performed by Rubin and Jordan, Gambrell calls for defining a future space for feminist scholarship between the academic and discursive formations, a move she sees as vitally important in view of the current changes in the American university system.

In "The Dissolute Feminisms of Kathy Acker," Marilyn Manners reads the intersections of Acker's texts with both feminist theory/philosophy and popular culture as instances of Acker's "dissolute" treatment of the boundaries of feminism. Acker's "dissoluteness" is a dual operation: first, as a strategy of self-ironization and, second, as a parodic reinscription, citation, and even "plagiarism" of the figurations of femininity in theoretical texts (Irigaray, Kristeva, Cixous) and popular culture (Madonna). Constantly questioning and rewriting the boundaries of what is discussed under the rubric of femininity and feminism, Acker's recent fiction (*Pussy, King of the Pirates* and *My Mother: Demonology*) focuses on reconstructing myths and rewriting the feminine imaginary, though in a manner quite different from the feminist theory Acker is fond of appropriating. Acker's irreverence and "textual debauchery" playfully "startles 'theory' out of its delusions of coherence and mastery" and evolves a unique form of feminist writing that combines autobiography and poetic and theoretical statements with parody, popular culture, pornography, and "punk grrl 'lyricism.'"

The second part of *Future Crossings*, "Deconstruction and Culture: Community, Politics, Ethics," illustrates new directions that deconstruction opens for thinking the constituent elements of culture: politics, ethics, and identity. The revisions the three essays offer—from rethinking the philosophical, political, and ethical strictures of the idea of Europe to rethinking politics and ethics in terms of figures of otherness—proceed from a rethought notion of difference, whose intrinsic unpredictability and opacity mandates a critical reappraisal of the ideas and practices constitutive of the spheres of ethics and politics. These revisions are examples of how the deconstructive rethinking of difference and relation in terms of an exposure to an unpredictable future and otherness sets out to rework the cultural and experiential schemas that underlie the notions of community, ethics, or politics. In "Feeling the Debt: On

Europe," Rodolphe Gasché develops Derrida's rethinking in *The Other Heading* of the philosophical idea of "Europe" in terms of openness and responsibility to the Other. He argues that Derrida's approach to the idea of "Europe" arises as a reaction both to the concept of a reactivatable and unshakable identity and to the nostalgia for lost greatness which motivates the New Right's formulations of European identity. Unwilling to reject the idea of "Europe" altogether, Derrida reformulates the tensions between singularity and universality which underpin philosophy and European identity in a manner that allows him to explore how "the idea of Europe might still harbor critical possibilities that until now have not been actualized." Those possibilities arise from the status of identity itself, especially from the way in which identity is constituted through a double set of differences: external differences from other identities and other headings and an internal difference that, itself of a different order than identity, remains also other than non-identity. This order other and prior to the opposition of identity and non-identity questions binary sets of oppositions and forces open the interlocked programs of Eurocentrism and anti-Eurocentrism. The potential that Derrida reads in "Europe" lies in acknowledging not only the possibility of the other heading for Europe but also of the other *of* the heading, and thus a recognition of what remains unpredictable, unanticipatable, still to come. Juxtaposing Derrida's discussion of the openness intrinsic to the idea of "Europe" with the closure implicit in Heidegger's claim in *What Is Philosophy?* that Europe "identifies" itself through a fundamental feeling, or *Stimmung,* of attunement to Being, Gasché concludes that "Europe" can be understood not only as an acknowledgment of the debt to the Other but as "the demand for universal responsibility to and for the Other."

In response to criticism proffered by Fraser, Critchley, and others, Joan Brandt's "The Politics of *Différance: Tel Quel* and Deconstruction" rearticulates the political import of deconstruction, arguing that the undecidable logic of *différance* contains distinctly political possibilities. The singularity of deconstruction's understanding of politics comes from the fact that undecidability not only opens the possibility for assuming responsibility for action but also mandates a rethinking of the philosophical precepts upon which our notion of political actions relies. To make this point, Brandt examines the political climate of the late 1960s and early 1970s from which deconstruction's interrogation of the conventional notion of the political emerged. She underscores the moment of Derrida's separation from *Tel Quel* as signaling an approach to politics different from the dialectical and hierarchical oppositions which structured the politics of *Tel Quel.* In the case of *Tel Quel,* it was precisely the failure to assume "responsibility to otherness"—so critical to Derrida's thought—in the radical interrogation of "literary ideology," representation, and meaning that led to an increasingly doctrinaire application of Marxist and Freudian theory and had "disastrous political consequences." By contrast, Derrida's *différance,* irreducible to a dialectic, underscores the "problematical nature of the hierarchising oppositions upon which *Tel Quel's* and indeed all conventional conceptions of the political depend." It is the incompletion and openness to otherness in Derrida's *différance* that "constitutes our ultimate defense against the political acts of exclusion and intolerance."

Dorota Glowacka's "Ethical Figures of Otherness: Jean-Luc Nancy's Sublime Offering and Emmanuel Levinas's Gift to the Other" redraws the boundaries between ethics and aesthetics, pointing to the ethical significance of the deconstructive critique of the circular economy of exchange and the subject's self-reflective closure. The moments of convergence between Levinas and Nancy suggest the possibility of thinking the limit of the aesthetic inscribed in the sublime as having ethical significance. Focusing her argument through Levinas's critique of Western thought, Glowacka points to the entrapment of the other in the world of mimesis and suggests that the issue of representation is always an ethical issue. In spite of Levinas's often hostile remarks about aesthetics, Glowacka suggests a parallel between Levinasian ethics and Nancy's rethinking of the aesthetics of the sublime or Blanchot's "writing of the disaster": between the ethical gesture of offering the world to the other and the sublime as the offering of an impossible, receding totality, questioned and interrupted by unpresentable otherness. Since Levinas appears to consider only the aesthetics of the beautiful, Glowacka argues that there is a possibility of another aesthetics—that of the sublime—an aesthetics inflected through ethics, where art's relation to the other will no longer be formulated as representation but as bearing witness.

The essays in the final part of *Future Crossings,* "Modernity, Nationalism, and Cultural Difference," explore the intersections between cultural and philosophical critiques of difference, in particular their importance for rethinking the narratives of modernity and national community. It is perhaps in the arena of the formation of identities and cultural differences, and their relation to the possibilities and strictures presented by modern rationality, that the diverse orientations within cultural studies and philosophical approaches speak most directly to one another. The contributions by David Lloyd and Herman Rapaport start from different locations, the first examining Irish nationalism and the temperance movements and the second questioning the philosophical implications of the idea of self-positing. Both authors, however, show how aesthetics is implicated in the construction of national identity but also serves as a venue for exposing and resignifying the mechanisms of identification that regulate such constructions. Using Joyce's story "Counterparts" from *Dubliners* as a key text, Lloyd's essay "Counterparts: *Dubliners,* Masculinity, and Temperance Nationalism" interrogates the relationships between nationalism and modernity. He shows how Irish nationalism refigured itself against some of the colonial stereotypes, particularly that of the "feminine" Celt, and how the counterdiscourse of "masculinity" was ambiguously developed to assert the Irish capacity for self-government and, simultaneously, to indicate a particular hostility to the modernity that it also wished to capture for itself. This contradictory tendency is exhibited in the temperance movements that sought to overcome the problems of drink and alcoholism in Ireland and in the countermovements that identified drinking and pubs as a means of rejecting the dulling and alienating disciplines of capitalism and modernity. Yet this resistance is inescapably allied with a form of dependence, as manifested in Joyce's story and generally throughout his work. It is this mixed relation that lies at the heart of the Joycean aesthetic and of the Joycean analysis of nationalism's bivalve relationship to autonomy and dependence. It can be explicated as an assertion of difference that does not overcome dependence, and in rhetorical terms, as a distinction between a rigorous mimesis and symbolism. In Joyce's mimetic practice, the incorporative desire of the symbol is refused; so too is the realist representation of the actual. Instead, he produces a counterpart world in which another possibility, neither organized symbolism nor pure contingency, exists as an alternative to both.

In Rapaport's "Of National Poets and Their Female Companions," the relationships between Friedrich Hölderlin and Susette Gontard and between William and Dorothy Wordsworth are taken as exemplifications of a problem in "self-positing." In their addresses to these women friends, the poets reveal a consciousness of self that can never be wholly self-identical; it needs to acknowledge, through an intimate interlocutor, an alterity in self-consciousness which is never separable from it. This dilemma produces a conflict that characterizes the relation between the isolated subjective self and the historical subject; and this relation is reinscribed as that between the poet and the national community. Yet it is a relation that is effected across a break or caesura. The political and the personal are split, yet that split seeks to present itself as a national issue or destiny. The argument runs, to some degree, counter to Derrida's commentary on Heidegger.

Gilbert Chaitin's and Andreas Michel's essays reappraise the role of rationality in the constructions of modernity, specifically in relation to the problem of otherness and cultural difference. Chaitin's essay, "Lacan with Adorno? The Question of Fascist Rationalism," engages with Lacan's reading of Kant as an attack on the Enlightenment's version of formal reason and the alleged role of Kant's thought in the formation of modern fascism. In "Kant with Sade," Lacan attacks Kant's ethical formalism and his failure to take historical realities into sufficient account. Kantian universality can justify a general principle of evil as well as of good. Houston Stewart Chamberlain adopted many elements of Kant's thought to his own fascist and anti-Semitic purposes. The relationship between the anti-Kantianism of Adorno and Lacan and Chamberlain's adoption of Kant is effected in the concept of sacrifice and the role of the Other. The sadism at the heart of Nazism is controlled by the presence of this Other, which is comprehensible as a version of God or Reason, but is also historically embodied in the idea and actuality of the Führer. The relationship of the Enlightenment to fascism is thus acknowledged as a historical reality, as a philosophical continuity, and yet, also, as a profound aberration.

In his essay "Postmodern Investments: Lyotard and Rorty on Disenchantment and Cultural Difference," Michel argues that Lyotard's postmodern and antipolitical discourse retains a faith in, or at least a wish for, human emancipation. Despite the apparent contradictions in Lyotard's position, this remains true. It does not seem to fit with his repudiation of metanarratives nor with his sense that modernity has promised a utopia that it has failed to deliver. Although, at first sight, Richard Rorty's pragmatism would seem to have the advantage over Lyotard's attempts to reject imperialism and foster cultural difference, it is ultimately the case that Rorty's acceptance of the existing state of affairs is also an acceptance of existing power relations. It is therefore an enclosed pragmatism that blandly accepts the disenchanted modernity to which Lyotard seeks an alternative. That alternative may be the production of a new grand narrative in which resistance to modernity is sustained through the quest for justice, a quest that would threaten if not abolish the smugness of the rhetorical "we" which is the foundation of a purblind pragmatism.

The essays gathered in *Future Crossings* highlight several "crossing points" where the interests and investments of cultural studies and philosophical critiques of aesthetics and experience meet: the question of the institutional character of art and literature, literature's dependence on and autonomy from society, the viability and limits of the aesthetic under-standing of art, and the ideas of origin and transformation, to name a few. The essays suggest that the future of literary studies is linked to the idea of futurity and its impact on how we think the material, cultural, and aesthetic factors operating in literature. Such a future is bound to a re-thinking of experience and identity, and thus of culture and literature, in view of an intrinsic openness and unpredictability which structure both the material sphere and discourse as they re-form and virtualize them-selves in ways that exceed ideas of fixed or fully determined origin and that defy programmable and predictable changes and transformations. To think the future of literature in relation to the complex of material, aes-thetic, and cultural issues is not just to "imagine" what will become of literature and literary studies in the future but to explore, "here and now," the effects that the futurity of experience has on what literature is and how we read it. But that, one might say, already directs literature toward a different future and imagines what will come of it.

Futurity is neither an idea nor a condition but the idea of a condition. Its effects operate both retrospectively and prospectively, not only desta-bilizing canonized versions of the past but also opening that past to a different conception of the future. It retrieves the past in a manner com-parable to those practiced by various national revival groupings; like them, it also has within it the trace of a utopian moment that is shadowed forth in such a retrieval. Where it differs from such revivalisms is in its philosophical self-awareness. It questions the very conditions on which such complex cultural operations are founded. It is this constant turning upon itself, this persistent refusal to allow the infiltration of assumed distinctions—like that between national and universal—that makes the quest for a possible future or futures so restless. It does not seek to re-hearse the opposition between "theory" and "material conditions" but to find ways of imbricating these together. In such a project, it is inevitable that literature should be confronted by philosophy, for in the received views of each we see that very opposition embodied. The aim of the essays in our collection is to transgress the boundaries that have sepa-rated these fields and to demonstrate that, in doing so, the fields them-selves undergo a reformation that reveals the intimacies and interdepen-dencies that always existed between them. In that sense, the challenge to philosophy by literature, or to literature by philosophy, transforms it-self into a revelation of the assumptions that separated them and the issues that connect them. Ultimately, they come to form a discursive alli-ance that bears within it the possibilities of a future that was always there but which is now undergoing a process of liberation. The wall has come down, and with it a new series of possible worlds emerges.

Notes

1. Thomas Docherty, "Tragedy and the Nationalist Condition of Criticism," *Textual Practice* 10, no. 3 (1996): 479–505.
2. Bruce Robbins, *Secular Vocations: Intellectuals, Professionalism, Culture* (London and New York: Verso, 1993), 213–20.
3. Ian Hunter, "Aesthetics and Cultural Studies," in *Cultural Studies*, ed. Lawrence Grossberg, Cary Nelson, and Paula A. Treichler (New York and London: Routledge, 1992), 348, 349.
4. Martin Heidegger, *Beiträge zur Philosophie: Vom Ereignis*, vol. 65 of *Gesamtausgabe* (Frankfurt am Main: Klostermann, 1989), 503. Translation quoted from Robert Bernasconi, *Heidegger in Question: The Art of Existing* (Atlantic Highlands, N.J.: Humanities Press, 1993), 102.
5. Jean-Luc Nancy, *The Muses*, trans. Peggy Kamuf (Stanford: Stanford University Press, 1996), 38.
6. This critique of the idea of aesthetic/private experience operates in Heidegger's reading of "preservation" in "The Origin of the Work of Art"; see Heidegger, *Basic Writings*, 2d ed., ed. and intro. David Farrell Krell (New York: HarperCollins, 1993), 192–93. Hereafter cited as *BW.*
7. Theodor W. Adorno, *Aesthetic Theory*, trans., ed., and intro. Robert Hullot-Kentor (Minneapolis: University of Minnesota Press, 1997), 8. Hereafter cited as *AT.*
8. Jacques Derrida, "'This Strange Institution Called Literature': An Interview with Jacques Derrida," in *Acts of Literature*, ed. Derek Attridge (New York and London: Routledge, 1992), 41.
9. See Derrida's discussion of how literature exhibits and remarks the excess of language over the concept(s) of literature in ibid., 48.
10. See Heidegger's remarks about thinking art non- or post-aesthetically in "The Question Concerning Technology," *BW* 340–41.
11. This remark from "The Origin of the Work of Art" indicates the critical force of art's figure (*Gestalt*), *BW* 191.

Part I

Remembering the Future

The opposition holding between the being and its becoming can only be valid when it is seen in the context of a certain doctrine according to which substance is the very model of being; but it is equally possible to maintain that becoming exists as one of the dimensions of the being, that it corresponds to a capacity beings possess of falling out of step with themselves, of resolving themselves by the very act of falling out of step . . . [B]ecoming . . . is one of the dimensions of being, a mode of resolving an initial incompatibility that was rife with potentials.
—Gilbert Simondon, "The Genesis of the Individual"

Thinking the New

Of Futures Yet Unthought

Elizabeth Grosz

It is the question of the new I would like to address, however hesitatingly and schematically, in the exploratory space of this brief paper. This concept of the new entails many complications and perplexities. It involves, among other things, exploring the "nature" of time, the precedence of the future over the present and past, and the strange vectors of becoming that a concept of futurity provokes. This paper will argue that unless we develop concepts of time and duration which welcome and privilege the future, which openly accept the rich virtualities or latencies, the divergent resonances, of the present, we will remain closed to understanding the complex becoming that engenders and constitutes both nature and culture.

I want to set out some of the intellectual ingredients necessary for conceptualizing futurity or temporal openness. Not in those terms so favored by advertising slogans and funding applications—the language of avant-gardism, of innovation for its own sake, the slavish cult of supersession, the devotion to redundancy and perpetual updating (the language of consumer capitalism); nor in the language of classical science—in which the future is tied to and limited by our understanding of the past and present (the language of determinism); but in the more paradoxical and less saleable language of difference indicated, though not always in those terms or in the same ways, in the writings of Nietzsche, Bergson, Deleuze, Derrida, Irigaray, and others.[1] My project, of which this is a beginning fragment, is to think temporality and futurity, in all their richness, as modalities of difference.

This project of conceptualizing temporal relations in terms that emphasize the openness of the future is informed by and feeds into various philosophical and scientific accounts of (the interchangeability of) materiality and information. If becoming can be understood as the condition not only of human existence or life in general but is extended to matter itself, then perhaps concepts of matter and meaning (and their inherence in the sign, or their separation in physics)—the conceptual underpinnings of identity, representation, and repetition that govern philosophical, historical, and scientific thought regarding temporality—can be problematized and a more open-ended materiality and becoming conceived.

The concept of the new raises many anxieties. While it is clear that newness, creativity, innovation, and progress are all terms designated as social positives, the more disconcerting notion of unpredictable, disordered, or uncontainable change, which lurks within the very concept of the new, seems to disconcert scientific, philosophical, and cultural ideals of stability and control. Predictable, measured, regulated transformation seems a social prerequisite; but upheaval, the eruption of the event, the emergence of new alignments unpredicted within old networks seem to threaten to reverse all gains, to position progress on the edge of an abyss, to place chaos and disorder at the heart of regulation and orderly progress. How is it possible to revel and delight in the indeterminacy of the future without raising the kind of panic and defensive counterreactions that Foucault envisages a supervising, regulating power needs in order to contain unpredictability, the eruption of the event, the emergence of singularities, and the realignments of power?[2]

Current preoccupations with social change or upheaval, with the notions of transformation, revolution, transvaluation, or with the deconstructively flavored language of writing as trace or iteration, or identity as performative, all rely on assumptions about the nature of time, change, and the future which are commonly unspoken. The relations between identity, subjectivity, textuality, signification, and materiality are implicated in how we understand and live time.

This preoccupation with the new can be readily transcribed into many other terminologies, each with its own political genealogy and its own specific anxieties. Instead of the production of the new, the concept of revolution could be substituted. Is the concept of revolution so tied to a set of weary discourses that, within their terms, it can now only mean "predictable transformation," transformation which follows a predesignated path, innovation within legitimized parameters, that is, controlled and regulated metamorphosis (whether the rule of the proletariat, the equalization of relations between the sexes, or racial integration)? Or does it involve the more disconcerting idea of *un*predictable transformation—mutation—upheaval in directions and arenas, with implications or consequences, that cannot be known in advance?

This is a most disconcerting and dangerous idea: everyone seems to revel in the idea of progress, development, movement, but the very political discourses that seem to advocate it most vehemently (Marxism, feminism, postcolonial and anticolonial discourses, the discourses of antiracism) seem terrified by the idea of a transformation somehow beyond the control of the very revolutionaries who seek it, a kind of "anarchization" of the future. If the revolution can carry no guarantee that it will improve the current situation, ameliorate existing conditions, or provide something preferable to what exists now, what makes it a sought-for ideal? What prevents it from blurring into fascism, into reaction or conservatism?

Must we accept a more internal relation to the structures of corporate capitalism, global racisms, or even local government regulations, that is, to the structures which dominate the present, than the more politically comfortable position of outside opposition? Instead of directing ourselves to the new, perhaps we should focus on living with, and negotiating our way through, the complex and ambiguous structures we inhabit now (as a kind of Foucauldian pragmatism implies);[3] or instead, should we give more impetus and weight to reclaiming the concept of futurity, wresting it from the tired discourses and ritualized practices that surround its associated struggles, despite whatever anxieties and uncertainties this may entail?

Though they are common preoccupations of certain of the natural sciences (physics and certain branches of biology in particular), the nature of temporality or duration, and thus the relations between past, present, and future, have remained elided or unexplored within the humanities and social sciences. Nonetheless, philosophy and cultural studies have made a number of assumptions regarding time, movement, and change. Underlying these conceptions of change are various commitments to upholding the values of predictability and stability, or to reveling in the idea of the unpredictable, that need careful analysis and reconsideration.

Moreover, it is significant that one cannot contain temporal conceptions to those explicitly focused on. Conceptions of each of the three temporal modalities (past, present, and future in all their conjugative complexities) entail presumptions regarding the others that are often ill- or un-considered: how we understand the past, and our links to it through reminiscence, melancholy, or nostalgia, prefigure and contain corresponding conceptions about the present and future; the substantiality or privilege we pragmatically grant to the present has implications for the retrievability of the past and the predictability of the future; and, depending on whether we grant to the future the supervening power to rewrite the present and past, so too we must problematize the notions of identity, origin, and development.

For example, implicit in the very procedures of conventional forms of historical research, whether it is the history of ideas or the history of events that is at stake, is an understanding of the past as an inert, fixed, finalized set of events, processes, or things, which are in some sense capable of carrying their past status into the present form, that are capable of being "read" through from the past, seen as a trace. As David Hume recognized, the presumption that the past provides us with the means for understanding the present—the underlying assumption regarding the nature of most historical research—is circular: it must assume what it seeks to prove (that the present is like the past, and the future is like the present). The past can provide us with lessons to learn, with an anticipation or possible projection of things to come, only on the assumption of its fundamentally repetitive character, its cyclical or developmental form, its telos. The past can only be of relevance insofar as it can be revivified and enlivened through its links to the present (and ideally, the future). Otherwise the past remains dead, inert, lacking in significance, lacking the force to propel itself into the present.[4] Not the haunting, inhabiting spectre but the decomposing corpse.

The ways in which we consider the past to be connected to and to live on through the present/future will have direct implications for whatever conceptions of futurity, the new, creativity, production, or emergence we may want to develop. If the past constitutes a remnant, a ghost or mode of haunting the present, this is only insofar as we can no longer consider the present itself as fully self-present. The present can be seen, through this inhabitation, which is as unavoidable as it is problematic, as a mode of differing or differentiation.

This is not to suggest that the relations between the past and present, or between the present and future, that is, relations of progress or directionality, are only bound, or given their direction, by scientific laws, be they relations of causality as in classical science or relations of statistical probability as in contemporary science. On the contrary, the extent to which one remains committed to determinism is precisely the degree to which one rejects the open-endedness of the future.[5] In seeking an open-ended future, one is not required to affirm that misnomer "free will" but to acknowledge the capacity of any future eruption, any event, any reading, to rewrite, resignify, reframe the present. It is to accept the role that the accidental, chance, or the undetermined play in the unfolding of time. It is this open-endedness that Derrida affirms through his understanding of the power of iteration;[6] and that contemporary biology has designated through the notion of emergence, which is neither free nor determined but rather both constrained and undecidable. Moreover, it is precisely such a notion of open-endedness that contemporary physics, especially in its flirtations with biochemistry, seems to have put in place of the emphasis on determinism so powerful in classical physics.[7] And finally, it is such a notion that leads Deleuze to seek in Bergson the notion of duration or becoming, as we shall see shortly.

How can difference be affirmed in the realm of temporality, where even the pretension to identity seems to be automatically undone, where any equation $A = A$ is always already impossible? To ask this question is to raise the issue of production, creation, innovation, or even surprise: how is production or creation, as opposed to reproduction or re-creation, repetition or identity, possible? To pose the question in these terms is to raise the question of difference in the place of identity, and becoming in place of being. What terms might be more appropriate as a mode of embrace of the new? Or what may amount to the same thing—how to *think*, which always belongs to the new, the productive? How to think differently, in terms other than those which prevail, given that thinking, engendering the new, is more painful than failure, more terrifying by far than the habitual or the expected? How to conceive of a present inherently open to its unpredictable rewriting by the future, that is, to think an open, or *emergent,* future?

We cannot but be impelled toward the future (if such directionality makes any sense);[8] we live perpetually on its horizon.[9] The question is whether we can develop conceptual tools and resources that will enable us to understand and accept without panic the unpredictability of the new; whether we can think in terms quite other than those postulated by the presumptions of causality, repeatability, and control of experimental conditions and results; whether we can maintain a science or a knowledge that itself engenders and accepts the new. Without some conception of a new and fresh future, struggles in the present cannot or would not be undertaken or would certainly remain ineffective. And without new modes of knowing, knowledges themselves may contribute to this lack of effect.

What kind of difference must it be to differ not only from itself and what is other (difference as divergence, as the breakdown or failure of identity) but also to differ from its own differing: in short, to diverge in (at least) two directions at once? How are we to think the idea of direction or trajectory without being able to anticipate a destination?

It is this idea, direction without destination, movement without prediction, that is so intriguing about the current researches regarding genetic algorithms, biological emergence, cellular automata, and the formulation of programs and computer simulations of animal and insect behaviors that is described by the label "artificial life." There seem to be some convergences between the "new sciences" and the movement of difference within the humanities.[10] What these scientific discourses make clear is that the unpredictability of daily and cosmological life can be duplicated and rendered indiscernible from the ways in which a computer program exhibits emergent properties that are inherently unpredictable for its programmers or present users. The evolution of life itself, from the simplest organic forms to complex sentient beings, seems to parallel the inherent openness of the future, and indeed the openness of the structure of matter itself.[11]

Much of contemporary physics is impelled closer toward the interests and presumptions of biology, which has also been transformed in the process: their mediation is to a large extent a function of the privilege granted to the random and the unpredictable in both discourses. Biologists are not prepared to accept a simple subsumption of the principles of biology to those of physics and chemistry; instead they have insisted on the boundaries and conditions specific to the nature of biology. In doing so, physics has been forced to accept that certain of its well-known presumptions (entropy, to mention the most obvious) need reconsideration in the light of biology (which breaches the principle every minute of the day). The more closely physics comes to providing modes of mathematical modeling for biological processes, the more committed both disciplines must be to the power of the random and the event, to contingency and openness. In other words, the possibilities of convergence between these two sciences seem to depend to some extent on the translatability or interchangeability of mathematical languages of the type preferred in physics with the logical and computer languages and programs now to some extent guiding biological modeling. This convergence or proto-translatability seems possible because otherwise incommensurable disciplines share a certain core commitment to chance and randomness that may allow them to be rendered more capable of comparison. The biological notion of evolution seems to have provided the means by which biology has opened itself to futurity and thus aligned itself with certain notions of indeterminacy in contemporary physics.[12]

Can the new be reformulated in more "postmodern," or even "post-human" terms, where it is recognized as a trope of self-maintenance as much as an aspiration for the future? Should we focus too strongly on the question of the new, the future, we lose sight of the day-by-day struggles which provide the conditions under which the terms, categories, and concepts necessary to think and to make the new can be developed; but should we direct ourselves largely to the pragmatics of day-by-day struggles, we risk remaining locked within their frame, unable to adequately rise above or displace them, stuck in the immediacy of a present with no aspirations to or pretensions of something different, something better.

To think the new requires, entails, at least *some* commitment to and use of the past and the present, of what prevails, is now or once had been, of what is familiar or has been known, the self-same. The terms by which something can be judged new irreducibly involve recognition, re-cognition of the old, such that the new can be re-cognized as departing from it. How can the new be understood except as a departure from the old and thus in the terms of the old? If to think or understand the new is always to do so in existing terms, then to think the new may ultimately prove impossible.

Is knowledge inherently opposed to the future? While it may be true that certain modes or forms of knowing or thinking are incapable of thinking or knowing the new, the future, or becoming, nevertheless there is no inherent or essential opposition between them. But this does not mean that other modes of knowing, other forms of thinking are incapable of knowing the new. It is only if thinking is itself part of the provenance of the new—which clearly involves a new account of what thought is—that thinking can be an appropriate modality for dealing with the future, for coping with and producing the new.

This is the reservation expressed in the opposition between knowledge on the one hand and, on the other, the immersion in temporality and futurity posited in the writings of some of Bergson's disciples, even if not by Bergson himself. In Minkowski's analysis of lived time, for example, he raises the question "How do we live the future, independent of and before all knowledge?" (*LT* 79). Where memory and perception, the past and the present, are in play, the concerns of epistemology can be somehow addressed; but where it is a matter of futurity, of life and the direction forward, somehow knowledge can only function as a mode of resistance to the play of vital forces, the élan vital: "As for memory, it always concerns recorded events or things heard. It is much closer to knowledge than to life and consequently can occupy only a secondary place in an analysis of lived time" (*LT* 80).

Futurity is not amenable to exact prediction (except within the most experimentally contained and limited contexts). Indeed, for Minkowski, it is the outsideness, the fundamental alienness, of futurity to knowledge that is part of the awe and mystery, part of the *hold* that the future has over us as living subjects who are inevitably propelled forward:

> We look at the future and we see it in a broad and majestic perspective stretching out to lose itself in the distance. This majesty approaches the mysterious. But this mystery is as indispensable to our spiritual life as pure air is to our respiration. It makes of the future a reservoir of eternal and inexhaustible forces without which we could not continue to live. (*LT* 81)

We need to affirm, along with Minkowski, the joyous open-endedness of the future, without, however, asserting that such an indeterminacy functions only in the realm of consciousness, or even life itself. Vitalism is the philosophical commitment to a specific life force, a life energy, which distinguishes the organic from the inorganic. As part of an ancient tradition within philosophy, vitalism is conventionally opposed to mechanism, the belief that objects, things, are composed of externally or mechanically connected atomic elements. Vitalism is committed to the belief that the organism is greater than the sum of its parts, while mechanism claims that the unity of the organism comes from its particular ingredients in their specific configurations. Where vitalism seems unable to think matter and its capacities for transformation adequately, mechanism seems unable to think the specificities and distinctive features of organic existence, the peculiar properties of life. This opposition prefigures and is to some extent undermined by the opposition and convergence between physics (the conceptual descendant of mechanism) and biology (which can be seen to be oriented more by at least certain elements of vitalism).

The opposition Bergson, Minkowski, and other vitalists[13] assume between the organic and the inorganic, between consciousness, or mind, and matter (or, in their terms, between duration and space), must be questioned while simultaneously being taken seriously. Bergson, Minkowski, and others have accepted, as few others have, the (perpetually impending) precedence of the future over the past and present; they have acknowledged and delighted in the uncaptured playing out of the forces of duration, temporal continuity, and eruption or emergence, and the coincidence of this movement with the surprise and openness of life itself. However, their commitment to vitalism, and their understanding of duration or becoming as the privileged domain of the lived, the experienced, remains limited in at least three respects:

1. The refusal to see spatiality as just as susceptible to the movement of difference as duration. If time has numericized and mathematized duration, then so too mathematization has rendered space itself a kind of abstraction of place or locus. Just as time is amenable to both flow and discontinuity (to de- and re-territorialization), so too is space. Space is no more inherently material than duration, and is no more the privileged domain of objects than memory is subjective and to be denied to spatial events: each is as amenable as the other to the disconcerting of difference, which in any case refuses such a clear-cut distinction between them.

2. Vitalism's refusal to accord to matter itself the indeterminacy and openness that it attributes to life. It is no longer clear where the boundary between life and non-life, between the organic and the inorganic, or perhaps even the virtual and the real, can be drawn. What is the status, for

example, of those strings of RNA which lie halfway between the organic and the inorganic and which we call
viruses? Are viruses self-reproducing organisms or are
they more biochemical programs? Does it literally matter
whether they are enacted in organic molecules or in a
software language? A virus has been regarded as a self-
replicating, evolving organism, whether it consists of RNA
molecules or computer-program code, whether its content is chemical or informational. There are striking analogies between biological and computer viruses such that
the latter may well qualify to be considered forms of artificial life. At the very least, they blur the boundaries between what is regarded as inorganic and what has an
organic-like life of its own. Viral infections of both biological and software form are programs (genetic or computing) that are injected into the body of a larger "cell" or application. The cell is thereby infected and converted into a
system for the production of many replicas or clones, and
possibly mutations. A computer virus is a small segment of
computer-program code (at its most simple, from 2 to 20
kilobytes) that is capable of copying its set of instructions
onto host programs, which, when executed, spread the virus further. Biological viruses are similar in their informational length (usually around 3 to 30 kilobase pairs) and
in their various capacities.[14] How can the line be drawn,
such that material objects are characterized by an inertia,
and by temporal self-containment (i.e., by being) that the
organic world enlivens (through becoming)?

3. The inability to realize that it is not simply matter, organic
or inorganic, but, more intriguingly and less straightfor-
wardly, information, at least information insofar as it is
bound up with a particular mode or organization of matter, that becomes, that expands itself as it is impelled to
the future. It is significant that although there seems an os-
tensive commitment to materialism within biology, as one
would expect, nevertheless, there seems a stronger commitment to the independence of information from matter.
Matter figures as significant only insofar as its particular
modes of organization can support the demands/require-

ments for the transmission and reproduction of information. It is the peculiar transmigration of matter and information that seems to mark the "materialist" commitments of contemporary biology and to provide a space in which the notion of "artificial life," life generated in simulated space, life generated through information, can gain not only a plausible but perhaps an inevitable role in biological modeling.[15] Becoming is what emerses both matter and information: it is for this reason that temporal modeling, though not prediction, is as possible in the spheres of social and cultural activities as in the domains of ethology, biology, physics, or genetics.[16] This is made abundantly clear in the ways in which information, in virtual space, in computing programs of various kinds, exhibits emergent properties even though it is difficult to ascertain exactly what their modes of materiality consist in.

While clearly I can do no justice to the resources that may make such a project of thinking the new feasible—Bergson, Deleuze, Minkowski, Derrida, the writings on artificial life, on molecular biology, and on contemporary physics—it is nonetheless very rare in the history of Western philosophy that time, or duration, is conceived outside the constraints of a mathematization of space. Indeed, since Einstein, time is conceived as *the* mode for the mathematization of space. It is largely Deleuze's reading of Bergson that has rescued the latter from the kind of oblivion dealt to once popular figures of yesteryear, who are often treated as little more than anachronistic amusements. Deleuze's reading of Bergson[17] has taken a very long time to have any impact on the reassessment of Bergson's work and on refiguring conceptions of time in literary, cultural, filmic, and scientific contexts. For the purposes of this paper, I will look at only a tiny fragment of Bergson's work, duration, and its links to the notion of virtuality, which will be of use to reconceiving becoming and the new.[18]

Deleuze focuses on a number of Bergson's key texts, primarily *Matter and Memory* (1988), *Creative Evolution* (1944), and *Durée et simultanéité* (1922), where Bergson develops a position, unique in the history of philosophy, that unravels in order to reconceive the hard-and-fast distinctions between objectivism and subjectivism, matter and consciousness, space and duration. Bergson poses a peculiar and unexpected combination of vitalist phenomenology, scientific pragmatism, and psychophysiological and biological materialism that makes his work difficult to classify. For the sake of convenience, Deleuze's reading of Bergson can be divided into three central components: the relation between matter and memory; an account of the relations between past, present, and future; and the distinction between the virtual and the possible. While all three are fascinating, it is only the latter I can discuss here.

Bergson claims that a distinction between subjective and objective (or duration and spatiality, life and the nonorganic) can be formulated in terms of the distinction between the virtual and the actual. Bergson suggests that objects, space, and the world of inert matter exist entirely in the domain of the actual. They contain no virtuality. Matter has no hidden latency, no potentiality, no hidden becoming. While there is more to matter than our images of it (a claim that rescues him from the unwarranted accusation of idealism with which he is continually charged), material objects are nonetheless of the same kind as our images.[19]

For Bergson, if everything about matter is real, if it has no virtuality, the proper "medium" or milieu of matter is spatial. While it exists in duration, while clearly it is subject to change, the object does not reveal itself over time. There is no more in it "than what it presents to us at any moment." By contrast, what duration, memory, and consciousness bring to the world is the possibility of an unfolding, a hesitation, an uncertainty. Not everything is presented in simultaneity. This is what life (duration, memory, consciousness) brings to the world: the new, the movement of actualization of the virtual, expansiveness, opening up. "Thus the living being essentially has duration; it has duration precisely because it is continuously elaborating what is new and because there is no elaboration without searching, no searching without groping. Time is this very hesitation" (*CM* 93).

Time is a mode of stretching, of protraction, which provides the very conditions of becoming, however haltering they may be. Time is the hiccoughing that expands itself, encompassing past and present into a kind of simultaneity. Both exist, they concur "at the same time."[20] But they do not exist in the same order: they function, not in terms of the possible/real relation but in terms of the relations between actual and virtual. Matter and the present are to be placed on the side of the actual, and mind or duration and the past on the side of the virtual.

In doing so, Bergson in effect displaces the dominance of the possible/real relation. The process of realization, that "movement" or vector from the possible to the real, is governed by the two principles of *resemblance* and *limitation*. The real exists in a relation of resemblance to the possible, functioning as its exact image, to which the category of existence or reality is simply added. In other words, the real and the possible are conceptually identical (since, as Kant argued, existence is not a quality or attribute). Realization also involves the process of limitation; the narrowing down of possibilities, so that some are rejected and others made real. The field of the possible is broader than the real. Implicit in the coupling of limitation and resemblance, Deleuze suggests, is a preformism: the real is already preformed in the possible insofar as the real resembles the possible. The possible passes into the real by a process of culling. Deleuze suggests that this relation entails a fixity: the real emerges as the given (rather than produced), though the possible could just as readily be seen as the "retrospective" projection of the real.[21] The possible is both more and less than the real. It is more insofar as the real selects from a number of coexisting possibles, limiting their ramifying effects. But it is also less insofar as the possible is the real minus existence.[22]

Realization is a temporal process in which creativity and the new are no longer conceivable. Making the possible real is simply giving it existence without adding to or modifying its conception. The question begs to be posed: Is the possible the foundation or precondition of the real, or does the real project itself backward to produce the possible? Is the real an image of the possible, or the possible an image of the real?[23] To reduce the possible to a preexistent phantomlike version of the real is to curtail the possibility of thinking emergence, the new, the unexpected, of thinking an open future not bound directly or strictly to the present.[24]

In *Difference and Repetition* (1994), Deleuze claims that there are at least three ways in which the virtual should be distinguished from the possible. First, existence, the acquisition of the status of reality by the possible, can be understood either as an inexplicable eruption or a system of all or nothing: either it "has" existence, in which case it is real, or it "lacks" existence, in which case it remains merely possible. If this is the case, Deleuze argues, it is hard to see what the difference is between the existent and the nonexistent: seeing the nonexistent is a possibility that retains all the characteristics of the existent. Existence is regarded as the same as the possible, and they thus function as conceptual duplicates. Existence or reality are regarded as simply the unfolding of a predesignated possible.[25] By contrast, for Deleuze as for Bergson, the virtual cannot be opposed to the real: it is real. It is through its reality that existence is produced. Instead of an impoverished real (the possible), the virtual can be considered more a superabundant real that induces actualization.

Second, if the possible is thought in place of the virtual, difference can only be understood as restriction and containment rather than as production. Where the possible "refers to the form of identity in the concept," the virtual "designates a pure multiplicity in the Idea which radically excludes the identical as prior condition." The self-identity of the image remains the same whether possible or real; it is precisely such an understanding of self-identity that the virtual renders unthinkable.

And third, while the possible is regarded as a mode of anticipatory resemblance of the real, the virtual never resembles the real that it actualizes. It is in this sense that actualization is a process of creation that resists both a logic of identity and a logic of resemblance to substitute differentiation, divergence, and innovation. While the concept of the possible doubles that of the real, the virtual is the real of genuine production, innovation, creativity. It is only actualization that engenders the new.[26]

The process of actualization is a process of genuine creativity and innovation, the production of singularity or individuation. Where the possible/real relation is regulated by resemblance and limitation, the virtual/ actual relation is governed by the two principles of difference and creation. For the virtual to become actual, it must create the conditions for actualization: the actual in no way resembles the virtual. Rather, the actual is produced through a mode of differentiation from the virtual, a mode of divergence from it which is productive. The process of actualization involves the creation of heterogeneous terms. The lines of actualization of virtuality are divergent, creating multiplicities, the varieties that constitute creative evolution. This is a movement of the emanation of a multiplicity from a virtual unity, divergent paths of development in different series and directions.[27]

The movement from a virtual unity to an actual multiplicity requires that there is a certain leap of innovation or creativity, the surprise that the virtual leaves within the actual. The movement of realization seems like the concretization of a preexistent plan or program; by contrast, the movement of actualization is the opening up of the virtual to what befalls it. In the terms of another discourse, actualization is individuation, the creation of singularity (whether physical, psychical, or social), insofar as the processes of individuation predate the individual and the individual is a somehow open-ended consequence of these processes. Individuation contains the "ingredients" of individuality without in any way planning or preparing for it.[28] Individuation is the alignment of virtualities, which make both being and becoming surprising, resonant with more than the present. Individuation is in no sense tied to the human: it is what characterizes cloud formations, the formation of crystals, and the currents of oceans, as well as the development of cells and the creation of individuals. Individuation is a radical excentering and self-exceeding, whether psychically, organically, or at the level of the nonorganic. This is what becoming is of necessity—a movement of differentiation, divergence, and self-surpassing (Simondon has described it as "falling out of step with itself"), actualization, of virtualities in the light of the contingencies that befall them.

Insofar as time, history, change, and the future need to be reviewed in the light of this Bergsonian disordering, perhaps the concept of the virtual may prove central in reinvigorating the future insofar as refusing to tie it to the realization of possibilities (the following of a plan), linking it instead to the unpredictable, uncertain actualization of virtualities. This point is not simply a semantic one: it is not a question of dumping the word "possible" and replacing it with "virtual" but of understanding the concept in an entirely different way, understanding the processes of production and creation in terms of an openness to the new instead of a preformism of the expected.

Bergson's conception of virtuality provides us with a way of seeing the future as bound up with the continual elaboration of the new, the openness of things (including life—here I must depart from Bergson to attribute the possibilities of becoming to the nonorganic or the quasi-organic as well as to life in its more traditional senses). This is what time *is* if it is anything at all: not simply mechanical repetition, the causal ripple of objects on others, but the indeterminate, the unfolding and the emergence of the new.

Time is intrication and elaboration. It would be a mistake to identify time with narrative form or structure. Narrativity is a modality of time; time does not conform to any particular form of narrativity. Rather than the unfolding of a narrative, or of a proposition, the model that Bergson himself develops, with great prescience in view of the current transformations and upheavals going on in biology and biological modeling, is more akin to the randomness of evolution, the unfolding of lineage and mutation. Elaboration is time's mode of acting, but an elaboration that frees up, undetermines, interrupts, and deflects rather than causes.[29]

The future is the order, the domain, of endurance. But what endures, what exists in time and has time as part of its being, whose being is dictated by duration, is not what remains the same over time, what persists, what retains the fundamentals of its identity, as classical philosophy maintains. Time is that divergence between what was (that is, what exists in a state of virtuality) and what is or is capable of actualization. The future is what endures, not as it is in itself, but as an opening up to becoming, to something other. This becoming infects not only beings in/as duration but, in Bergson's understanding, the world itself.[30]

Duration proceeds not by continuous growth, smooth unfolding or accretion, but through division, bifurcation, dissociation—by difference—and through sudden and unexpected change or eruption. Duration is a mode of infecting self-differentiation: difference is both internal to its function and its modes of elaboration and production, and is its ramifying effect on those objects located "within" its milieu. This means that not only must conceptions of time (in physics, biology, and philosophy as well as cultural studies and social theory) be opened up to their modes of differentiation; it also means that our very concepts of objects, matter, being—well beyond the concept of life itself—need to be open to the differentiations which constitute and continually transform them.

Notes

A version of this paper was published in *Becomings: Explorations in Time, Memory, and Futures,* ed. Elizabeth Grosz (Ithaca: Cornell University Press, 1999), 15–28

1. Because some of the material I rely on lends itself very readily to sloganeering and self-promotion (I am thinking primarily of the discourses surrounding chaos theory, artificial life, computer simulation and virtual reality, genetic algorithms, evolutionary biology and cellular automata, all of which have gained funding, publicity, and support through their [self-] representations as cutting-edge, innovative, cultural capital), I will concentrate here to a large extent on a philosophical rather than a cultural studies orientation, not because cultural studies is more prone to popularization—nothing, it seems, is inherently immune to recuperation—but because my own disciplinary training is more philosophical than literary or cultural. My goal is not to *sell* the new but to provide some of the terms by which to try to think it, or perhaps to understand why it can't be thought.

2. See Michel Foucault, "The Discourse on Language," in *The Archaeology of Knowledge,* trans. A. M. Sheridan-Smith (New York: Harper Colophon, 1972).

3. Such pragmatism, as Jean-François Lyotard argues, always retains something of a commitment to humanism, to negotiation with present contexts, to adjustment within existing constraints:

> Pragmatism, as the name suggests, is one of the many versions of humanism. The human subject it presupposes is, to be sure, material, involved in a *milieu,* and turned towards

action. The fact remains that this action is given a finality by an interest, which is represented as a sort of optimum adjustment of subject to environment.

See Lyotard, "Matter and Time," in *The Inhuman,* trans. Geoffrey Bennington and Rachel Bowlby (Stanford: Stanford University Press, 1991), 44. Hereafter cited as "MT."

4. Rethinking the relations between past and present, reconsidering memory as a form of production rather than a form of information retrieval, thus helps in reconsidering the ways in which the past has been represented in various historiographical methods, as well as in everyday and philosophical conceptions.

5. This position, now regarded as the causal theory of time, is committed to temporal irreversibility on the grounds of the irreversibility of causal relations and is represented perhaps most clearly in the writings of Leibniz and Kant. It is a position that has also been forwarded in the more contemporary work of Reichenbach and Carnap. See Adolf Grünbaum, "The Causal Theory of Time," chapter 7 of *Philosophical Problems of Space and Time* (Dordrecht and Boston: R. Reidel, 1973).

6. See Jacques Derrida, *Limited Inc.,* trans. Samuel Weber (Evanston: Northwestern University Press, 1988).

7. See Mercer, quoted in Yates, *Self-Organizing Systems: The Emergence of Order,* ed. F. E. Yates, A. Garfinkel, D. O. Walter, and G. B. Yates (New York and London: Plenum Press, 1987), 11. Hereafter cited as *SO.*

To the biologist as to the philosopher the great inadequacy of determinism is its inability to account for the appearance of novelty. Biology above all seems rich in new and more complex structures and functions; the rigid determinist must either deny the reality of these novel appearances or claim that they are somehow derivable from general laws. . . . The feeling grew that biology would have to choose either to follow physics and live with determinism or to strike out on its own. To many it seemed that biological phenomena were so different from physical that some element of indeterminism would have to be admitted. The schism thus established lasted well into this century and produced some notable debates. However, at the present time controversy has faded in perspective and a very different atmosphere prevails; physics and biology are together edging toward a unified theory. . . . The fact that the generation of mutational novelty . . . by the random or chance chemical modification of the informational molecules, which are the genetic store of organisms . . . underlies the evolutionists' stress on the creative contribution of pure chance and the impossibility of predicting the results of its intervention.

8.   In *Lived Time: Phenomenological and Psychopathological Studies*, trans. Nancy Metzel (Evanston: Northwestern University Press, 1970; hereafter cited as *LT*), Minkowski argues that the future has an inevitable pull and lived force that moves us out of the stasis of the past and the tangibility of the present. It draws us into its directionality, without reflection or assent (which is not to say that we cannot live this direction in a modality of nostalgia):

> The *élan vital* creates the future before us, and it is the only thing that does it. In life everything that has direction in time has *élan*, pushes forward, progresses toward a future. In the same way, as soon as I think of an orientation in time, I feel myself irresistibly pushed forward and see the future open in front of me. And this fact of "being pushed" has nothing passive in it. This does not mean that exterior forces compel me to look in front of me and to progress in that direction. . . it means that I tend spontaneously with all my power, with all my being, toward a future. (38)

9.   As Minkowski makes clear: "A spatial image is much too weak to express the power of the future, which has extension, grandeur, power in it. An image comes involuntarily to mind—that of the horizon, where, when our gaze turns to infinity, the sky blends with the earth" (*LT* 81).

10.   This burgeoning area contains many initial attempts to chart parallels between the sciences and humanities. See Arkady Plotnitski, *Complexity*, and the work of N. Katherine Hayles.

11.   Lyotard describes the refiguring of matter in contemporary technoscience as a fourth blow (following Copernicus, Darwin, and Freud) unsettling the privilege of the human. Matter can be seen to exhibit desire, if "desire" is understood as divergence and complexification. Proceeding beyond anthropomorphism, even if cells, stars, and chemicals cannot read or desire in one sense, they can in another:

> . . . in the current state of science and techniques, resort to the entity 'Life' to cover what I call, for want of a better term, desire [*conatus, appetitio* for others], i.e., the complexification which disavows—de-authorizes so to speak—all objects of demand in turn: resort to this term seems still far too anthropomorphic. To say that Life is responsible for the formation of systems such as the atom or the star or the cell or the human cortex or finally the collective cortex constituted by machine memories is con-

trary, as are all teleologies, to the materialist spirit. ("MT" 45)

12.   The convergence of biology and physics in the late twentieth century seems to rely on a lateral convergence rather than the more conventional model of subsumption (a model that has tended to privilege physics as the most notable and pure of the sciences). There are in fact a number of issues that seem to make possible the drawing together of these two disparate domains:

1.   Physics had to relax its hopes for strict determinism which had seemed to rule out the possibility of biological novelty, contrary to the facts of biological evolution and diversity.

2.   Both physics and biology had to strengthen their understanding that evolutionary, historical, irreversible processes in the macroscopic (including macromolecular) dynamics are not time symmetric, and small factors or fluctuations may have amplified effects, especially at bifurcation points where symmetry can easily be broken down.

3.   The uses of terms and concepts cast in the mold of information-communication metaphors that now dominate biological explanations have to be justified by accounting for information as a by-product or side effect of dynamics. . . . The dichotomies of structure and function, form and process, genotype and phenotype, biology and physics are seen to be variations on that of information and dynamics. (*SO* 625)

13.   It must be hastily added that while Bergson is commonly taken as the last full-blown vitalist, there is much in his work that mitigates such an understanding. Where he affirms vitalism in the face of the mathematization of nature, at the same time he seems to undermine it by asserting the interchangeability of mind and matter, their difference of degree: "[F]rom mind to matter there is but a fundamental difference of degree, which depends on the capacity to gather and conserve. Mind is matter which remembers its interactions, its immanence. But there is a continuum from the instantaneous mind of matter to the very gathered matter of minds" ("MT" 40).

14.   In "Computer Viruses—a Form of Artificial Life?" in *Artificial Life II,* ed. C. Langton, C. Taylor, J. D. Farmer, and S. Ramussen (Redwood City, Calif.: Addison-Wesley, 1992), Eugene H. Spafford argues that, according to the properties artificial-life scientists want to associate with the definition of life, a computer virus could qualify as life. Yet he concludes that this indicates a problem with the definition of life on which computer programs have re-

lied. He cites the following criteria, which he believes the computer virus satisfies:

1. Life is a pattern in space-time rather than a specific material object
2. Self-reproduction, in itself or in a related organism
3. Information storage of a self-representation
4. A metabolism that converts matter/energy
5. Functional interactions with the environment
6. Interdependence of parts
7. Stability under perturbations of the environment
8. The ability to evolve
9. Growth or expansion (741).

While noting, indeed arguing in favor of the analogy, Spafford is clearly disturbed at the implication that a hard and fast line may not be able to be drawn dividing life from its simulation, and at the very end of his paper he reasserts in somewhat dogmatic form exactly that which his own paper has helped problematize. He argues that "we must never lose sight of the fact that 'real life' is of much more importance than 'artificial life,' and we should not allow our experiments to threaten our experimenters" (744), when in fact his own arguments make it increasingly difficult to divide the experimenter from the experiment.

For more on the links between biological and computer viruses, see Andrés Moya, Esteban Domingo, John J. Holland, Richard Dawkins, and Andrew Ross, "RNA Viruses: A Bridge Between Life and Artificial Life," in *Advances in Artificial Life*, ed. F. Moran, A. Moreno, J. J. Mereko, and O. Chacón (Berlin: Springer-Verlag, 1995), 77.

15. In "Artificial Life," *Artificial Life*, vol. 4 (Redwood City, Calif.: Addison-Wesley, 1989), Chris Langton makes explicit the relative indifference of biological concepts of life to the specific modes of materiality to which it has up to now been confined:

> Certainly life, as a dynamic physical process, could haunt other physical material: the material just needs to be organized in the right way. Just as certainly, the dynamic processes that constitute life—in whatever material bases they might occur—must share certain universal features— features that allow us to recognize life by its dynamic *form* alone, without reference to its *matter.* This *general* phenomenon of life—life writ large across all possible material substrates—is the true subject matter of biology. (2)

Whenever the specificities of matter are regarded merely as "substrate," "ground," or "support" of a program, form, or idea, it seems that we return to the reign of Platonism and the profound somatophobia to which it gave rise. It is significant that Langton's conception of matter as substrate has been challenged, not entirely surprisingly, from the point of view of molecular biology, "according to which 'form' and 'matter' do not represent separate realms." See Claus Emmeche, "Life as an Abstract Phenomenon: Is Artificial Life Possible?" in *Toward a Practic of Autonomous Systems,* ed. Francisco J. Varela and Paul Bourgine (Cambridge, Mass.: MIT Press, 1992), 466.

16. For a current overview of the role of computer simulation and what have been called "artificial societies," see Nigel Gilbert and Rosaria Conte, eds., *Artificial Societies: The Computer Simulation of Social Life* (London: University College of London Press, 1995).

17. Gilles Deleuze, *Bergsonism* (New York: Zone Books, 1988). Hereafter cited as *B*.

18. These are clearly abiding concerns in Deleuze's writings, from his work on Hume, through his analysis of Proust and his understanding of the time-movement in his studies of cinema, to his more recent writings on thinking and philosophy. Outlining this trajectory would no doubt warrant a book-length study (maybe in another lifetime!).

19. As Bergson says in *Matter and Memory,* trans. N. M. Paul and W. S. Palmer (New York: Zone Books, 1988):

> There is in matter something more than, but not something different from that which is actually given. Undoubtedly, conscious perception does not encompass the whole of matter, since it consists, in as far as it is conscious, in the separation or "discernment," of that which, in matter, interests our various needs. But between this perception of matter and matter itself, there is but a difference of degree and not of kind, pure perception standing toward matter in the relation of the part to the whole. This amounts to saying that matter cannot exercise powers of any kind other than those which we perceive. It has no mysterious virtue; it can conceal none. (71)

20. As Deleuze says in *Bergsonism:*

> The past and the present do not denote two successive moments, but two elements which coexist: One is the present, which does not cease to pass, and the other is the past, which does not cease to be but through which all presents pass. . . . The past does not follow the present, but on the contrary, is presupposed by it as the pure condition without which it would not pass. In other words, each present goes back to itself as past. (59)

21. Deleuze writes:

> Everything is already *completely given:* all of the real in
> the image, the pseudo-actuality of the possible. Then the
> sleight of hand becomes obvious: If the real is said to re-
> semble the possible, is this not in fact because the real was
> expected to come about by its own means, to "project
> backwards" a fictitious image of it, and to claim that it was
> possible at any time before it happened? In fact it is not
> the real that resembles the possible, it is the possible that
> resembles the real, because it has been abstracted from the
> real once made, arbitrarily extracted from the real like a
> sterile double. (*B* 98)

22. See Henri Bergson, *The Creative Mind: An Introduction to Metaphysics,* trans. Mabelle L. Andison (New York: Citadel Press, 1992). Hereafter
cited as *CM.* According to Bergson,

> [o]ne might as well claim that the man in flesh and blood
> comes from the materialization of his image seen in the
> mirror, because in that real is everything to be found in this
> virtual image with, in addition, the solidity which makes it
> possible to touch it. But the truth is that more is needed
> here to obtain the virtual than is necessary for the real,
> more of the image of the man than for the man himself, for
> the image of the man will not be portrayed if the man is
> not first produced, and in addition one has to have the
> mirror. (102)

23. The processes of resemblance and limitation constituting realization, Bergson argues, are subject to the philosophical illusion which consists
in the belief that there is *less* in the idea of the empty rather than the full,
and less in the concept of disorder than order; whereas in fact the ideas of
nothing and disorder are *more* complicated than of existence and order:

> Underlying the doctrines which disregard the radical nov-
> elty of each moment of evolution there are many misunder-
> standings, many errors. But there is especially the idea that
> the possible is *less* than the real, and that, for this reason,
> the possibility of things precedes their existence. They
> would thus be capable of representation beforehand; they
> could be thought of before being realized. But it is the re-
> verse that is true. . . [W]e find that there is more and not
> less in the possibility of each of the successive states than
> in their reality. For the possible is only the real with the

addition of an act of mind which throws its image back into the past, once it has been enacted. But that is what our intellectual habits prevent us from seeing. (*CM* 99–100)

24. Bergson writes:

As reality is created as something unforeseeable and new, its image is reflected behind it into the indefinite past; thus it finds that it has from all time been possible, but it is at this precise moment that it begins to have been always possible, and that is why I said that its possibility, which does not precede its reality, will have to precede it once the reality has appeared. The possible is therefore the mirage of the present in the past; and as we know the future will finally constitute a present and the mirage effect is continually being produced, we are convinced that the image of tomorrow is already contained in our actual present, which will be the past of tomorrow, although we do not manage to grasp it. (*CM* 101)

25. See Deleuze, *Difference and Repetition,* trans. P. Patton (New York: Columbia University Press, 1994). Hereafter cited as *DR:*

Existence is supposed to occur in space and time, but these are understood as indifferent milieux instead of the production of existence occurring in a characteristic space and time. Difference can no longer be anything but the negative determined by the concept; either the limitation imposed by possibles of each other in order to be realised, or the opposition of the possible to the reality of the real. (211)

26. See Deleuze, *DR:*

Actualization breaks with resemblance as a process no less than it does with identity as a principle. Actual terms never resemble the singularities they incarnate. In this sense, actualization or differentiation is always a genuine creation. It does not result from any limitation of a pre-existing possibility. . . . For a potential or virtual object, to be actualized is to create divergent lines which correspond to—without resembling—a virtual multiplicity. The virtual possesses the reality of a task to be performed or a problem to be solved: it is the problem which orientates, conditions and engenders solutions, but these do not resemble the conditions of the problem. (212)

27. See Deleuze, *B:*

> While the real is in the image and likeness of the possible that it realizes, the actual, on the other hand, does *not* resemble the virtual from which we begin and the actuals at which we arrive, and also the difference between the complementary lines according to which actualization takes place. In short, the characteristic of virtuality is to exist in such a way that it is actualized by being differentiated and is forced to differentiate itself, to create its lines of differentiation in order to be actualized. (97)

28. In his "The Genesis of the Individual," trans. Mark Cohen and Sanford Kwinter, in *Incorporations,* ed. Jonathan Crary and Sanford Kwinter (New York: Zone Books, 1992), Gilbert Simondon, who has been so influential in much of Deleuze's writings, especially in *A Thousand Plateaus,* articulates the movement of becoming, not in terms of any substantive being but in terms of processes of individuation. Individuation is seen in terms of a series of states of metastable equilibrium; it is thus necessarily regarded in terms of becoming. Simondon may have succeeded in going a step further than Bergson in thinking the implications of movement as the internal condition of individuation or being itself:

> The concept of being that I put forward, then, is the following: a being does not possess a unity in its identity, which is that of the stable state within which no transformation is possible; rather, a being has a *transductive unity,* that is, it can pass out of phase with itself, it can—in any arena—break its own bounds in relation to its *center.* What one assumes to be a *relation* or a *duality of principles* is in fact the unfolding of the being, which is more than a unity and more than an identity; becoming is a dimension of the being, not something that happens to it following a succession of events that affect a being already and originally given and substantial. Individuation must be grasped as the becoming of the being and not as a model of the being which would exhaust his signification. . . . Instead of presupposing the existence of substances in order to account for individuation, I intend, on the contrary, to take the different regimes of individuation as providing the foundation for different domains such as matter, life, mind and society. (311–12)

29. See Bergson, *CM:*

> [T]ime is something. Therefore it acts. [T]ime is what hinders everything from being given at once. It retards, or rather it is retardation. It must, therefore, be elaboration. Would it not then be a vehicle of creation and of choice? Would not the existence of time prove that there is indetermination in things? Would not time be that indetermination itself? (93)

30. See Henri Bergson, *Creative Evolution,* trans. Arthur Mitchell (New York: Random House, 1944), 14:

> The universe *endures.* The more we study the nature of time, the more we shall comprehend that duration means invention, the creation of forms, the continual elaboration of the absolutely new. It is true that in the universe itself two opposite movements are to be distinguished . . . , "descent" and "ascent." The first only unwinds a roll ready prepared. In principle, it might be accomplished almost instantaneously, like releasing a spring. But the ascending movement, which corresponds to an inner work of ripening or creating, *endures* essentially and imposes its rhythm on the first, which is inseparable from it.

Between Act and Archive: Literature in the Nuclear Age

Joseph Kronick

When Jacques Derrida addressed the Cerisy-la-Salle conference devoted to his works, he chose as his title "On a Newly Arisen Apocalyptic Tone in Philosophy," as if to mark the occasion as one belonging to the discourse of crisis. His title refers to Kant's polemic against the "mystagogues" who threaten to destroy philosophy in their exaltation of inner feeling at the expense of reason and morality. Kant objects to those who rest the principle of morality on the feeling of pleasure or displeasure aroused by phenomena. Such a belief "concludes that the legislation of reason requires not only a *form* but also *matter* (content, purpose) as a determining ground of the will."[1] Kant warns that such a doctrine erases all morality because it necessitates that any action must follow upon the feeling produced by an object, which would do away with the principle of reason acting in accordance with the ideal. This doctrine of feeling makes morality follow upon the experience of an object, whereas Kant argues that the basis of morality rests upon belief in the supersensible, not the empirical (*RTP* 61).

The new German thinkers suffer from a "mistuning" (*Verstimmung*) of the head because they seek a "supernatural communication 'mystical illumination'" rather than listen to the moral law (*RTP* 62). Kant characterizes the moral law as an inner voice whose call comes from an unknown location. When we listen, he writes, "we are in doubt whether it comes from man, from the perfected power of his own reason, or whether it comes from an other, whose essence is unknown to us and speaks to man through this, his own reason." Rather than pursue this voice, he says, we should devote ourselves to the properly philosophical task of turning the moral law into clear concepts. When the law is personified, reason "is made into a veiled Isis . . . [which] is an *aesthetic* mode of representing precisely the same object." One can, he says, "use this mode of representation backward" to "enliven those ideas by a sensible, albeit only analogical, presentation, and yet one always runs the danger of falling into an exalting vision, which is the death of all philosophy" (*RTP* 71). Kant's anxiety over philosophy lies in his need to place the law beyond representation, beyond the voice that speaks in or to us. This law, which always remains the same, must be singular and repeatable, which means that if it is to be binding upon us, it must—this is what Kant resists—differ from itself in order to be what it is. There would be no law without this iterability (the principle that identity is conditioned by repetition and difference). Kant had difficulty grasping that the law is singular and unique when it should be universal, which it is. Like Kafka's man before the law, "[h]e had difficulty with literature."[2]

We can hear in Kant's warning of the death of philosophy an apocalyptic tone, a tone we seem to have grown accustomed to at the fin de siècle. Today, we now hear not only of the death of philosophy but of the death of literature as well. Yet I would argue that there is still a future for philosophy and literature; in fact, we might say that the future depends upon them. The irony of Kant's assuming an apocalyptic tone in a warning against the very same should alert us to the fact that the language of crisis destabilizes the very principles of transcendental and ontological critique. In demanding that we forgo a search into the source of the voice of moral reason, Kant offers to make peace with his adversaries. Yet in denouncing those who proclaim the end of philosophy, he has, as Derrida comments, himself marked "a limit, indeed the end of a certain type of metaphysics, [and] freed another wave of eschatological discourses in philosophy" (*RTP* 144). With all this talk of ends, we cannot help but ask if Derrida's apocalyptic tone is not a mark of the limits of deconstruction. Indeed, many critics have denounced deconstruction precisely as an eschatological discourse that offers no way out of the very limits it reveals in other philosophies. But Derrida does not come to pronounce an end (of metaphysics, of literature, of man), but rather he speaks of what is to come, the future, or what he calls the invention of the other, and it is on this basis that he makes his claim for the responsibility of deconstruction.

In two essays originally delivered as talks at Cornell University in 1984, "No Apocalypse, Not Now (full speed ahead, seven missiles, seven missives)" and "Psyché: Inventions of the Other," he gathers around the topic of the future the apparently opposing notions of absolute destruction and absolute invention, two events, we might say, that lie in the future. They are figures for the future, that is, of the unanticipatable, the surprising, the monstrous. I hope I am not doing an injustice to Derrida or am proceeding too hastily if I say that the notions of invention, destruction, the monstrous, the future, and literature entail one another. We can readily enough imagine nuclear apocalypse as a monstrosity, an event for which there is no proper name but is to come, perhaps. Invention, as well, projects forward and never takes place "without an inaugural event," a first time and a last time, a monstrous beginning susceptible to repetition.[3]

What Derrida calls "destruction" and "invention" are not opposing terms but tropes, catachreses, for the future. If the future, *l'avenir*, is what is to come, *à-venir*, it is not a repetition of the same but is something surprising, an event for which we are not prepared. Like invention, it is illegitimate; it disrupts a norm or the order of things. It is, in a word, monstrous, hence, a catachresis, "a violent production of meaning." Derrida speaks of his own work, and philosophy itself, as a catachresis, and it is this figure that makes philosophy literary, that is, a showing, or "monstration," of the other (*montre* means "to show" and is etymologically linked to *monstre*). Derrida says,

> I am trying to produce new forms of catachresis, another kind of writing, a violent writing which stakes out the faults and deviations of language; so that the text produces a language of its own, in itself, which while continuing to work through

> tradition emerges at a given moment as a *monster,* a monstrous
> mutation without tradition or normative precedent.[4]

Deconstruction shares with literature this status as an event not marked by an internal criterion but by its movement toward the other. Deconstruction and literature—and by "literature" I mean a particular kind of writing that does not necessarily coincide with belles lettres or the institution of "Literature"—produce monstrosities, a writing that grafts itself onto traditions (for a monster is, by definition, a kind of hybrid violating a norm) and beckons toward something new, something other.

The other is not to be thought on some anthropological basis—it is not other people nor is the other precisely some thing—the other is to come, which is not to say it is out-standing, as Heidegger said of death, but the other is, Derrida says, the only possible invention, "an event through which the future (*l'avenir*) comes to us" ("P" 46). Rather than speak of it as the "not yet" or what is "out-standing," we can say the other is impossible; it is "the invention of that which did not appear to be possible" ("P" 60). It is the condition of the future. For a future that is already known could not be a future, and so it appears as a monstrosity, which is always something new. But at the same time, a monstrosity means that a norm has been violated, and because the future would have to take the form of a monstrosity, it is turned toward a past that it dislocates. We can say that the future, like literature, is recognizable by its tone, its coming to us as something idiomatic or singular, as an other that unsettles the conditions of its coming. This is why there is no internal criterion to the literary "event," to borrow Derrida's term, no essence of literature. There is no idiom, no event, that can be pure; a singular event or work would find no place in the world. It must open itself to iterability, that is, "produce 'effects of generality,'" if it is to be experienced or read.[5] Hence, "the literary event is perhaps more of an event (because less natural) than any other, but by the same token it becomes very 'improbable,' hard to verify" ("SIL" 73). This can be called the "law" of experience: any experience as such must be singular, but to maintain this singularity the experience must permit itself to be effaced, carried away, or re-marked by generality. That is, singularity as singularity can only be experienced if it is open to the possibility of repetition. Without this level of ideality, the singular is not recognizable in a human world; it must be conditioned by an "original" doubling, fold, or re-mark that permits it to be what it is: singular and recognized as such. Therefore, the literary event is more an event than any other because it is the unnatural and necessary, the monstrous, event that promises itself as unique and as repetition. It institutes and transgresses. This is why we can say that the only absolute referent of literature is nuclear catastrophe because literature has always pointed to an ultimate referent, the absolutely singular that has no place in the world. This is the monstrosity of literature: it aspires to the condition of its own demise—pure invention is pure destruction. That literature should die of its own aims, fail to achieve the singularity of absolute presence, means that it has a future, a future dependent upon the other. Insofar as literature is where the undecidable relation to the other may occur, it is not necessarily poetry or fiction or what we traditionally call "literature" but the quasi-transcendental condition for the coming of the other. Thus, Derrida will say "deconstruction is itself a form of literature," which means that like literature it always engages the idiomatic.

It is a great mistake to confuse deconstruction with nihilism, or to accuse deconstruction of saying that we are imprisoned in language or cannot distinguish reality from its fictional representations (see "DO" 123). Deconstruction, like a certain kind of literary writing, is concerned with the impossible, but necessary, task of designating the other. Deconstruction, then, is not just another kind of writing but produces "what in fact looks like a discursive monster so that the analysis will be a *practical* effect, so that people will be forced to become aware of the history of normality."[6] If the future must be a monster, deconstruction welcomes it rather than tries to normalize it. It says *yes* to the future, promises itself to be responsible (for the other).

In the exergue to *Of Grammatology*, Derrida writes, "The future can be anticipated only in the form of absolute danger. It is that which breaks absolutely with constituted normality and can thus announce itself, *present* itself, only under the species of monstrosity."[7] The future announces itself as a monstrosity, an event "for which there is no self-presentation nor assured destination." The monstrous is a name for what has no name, for what is to come. It is to come precisely because it does not have the status of a present being, nor is it an object of knowledge. It would be a first event and a last, a destruction that leaves no remains, something like a nuclear apocalypse. Derrida uncovers an affinity between the rhetoric of nuclear war and literature that lies not in scenarios of mass destruction but in the anticipation of the wholly other, the only possible invention. The invention of the other addresses the problem of singularity and of an event to come, the "monstrosity" of an absolute referent, that which is without precedent and can be figured as nuclear catastrophe. This is not to say nuclear catastrophe is merely a trope for absolute destruction, but it is what allows us to think the absolute referent, the condition of all other referents.

The absolutely singular, that which is, properly speaking, unique, would never be accessible to the understanding or even presentable at all if it were not linked to iterability. On the basis of the formalizing power of iterability, the law that subjects singularity to generality, nuclear war, or absolute destruction, and literature, or absolute invention, are similar. What allows us to think the singularity of nuclear war, "its absolute inventiveness," or the possibility of a destruction that leaves no remainder, is the total destruction of the "juridico-literary archive," that is, of literature.[8] Deconstruction, as I have said, resembles a literary practice on the basis of the experience of invention and monstrosity rather than on some notion of style. This does not mean that deconstruction is more literary than philosophical, but it could be said, as Derrida suggests in an interview, that a performative text like *The Post Card* seeks to institute, let us say "invent," itself as unique, as an "inaugural performance" that simultaneously institutes a competency of the reader to countersign — that is, in confirming the signature of the other, a countersigning reading answers to the text's iterability. It acknowledges itself as arriving after the text, "[b]ut this absolute pastness was already the demand for the countersigning reading. The first only inaugurates from after, and as the expectation of, the second countersignature." This "incalculable scene," Derrida concludes, programs the history of literary criticism ("SIL" 70). The countersignature is neither a dialectical nor a temporal response. Nor can we call it metaleptic, if we understand this to mean transference or reversal. If "the first only inaugurates *from after*" the second, it does not merely follow the second but could be said to await a second that precedes it.

Literature, in its conventional sense, is dependent upon a written archive and positive law, but it cannot be reduced to the simple opposition between singular event and institution, act and archive. To sustain its status as act or invention, the literary work must come back toward the past, toward a set of conventions and laws that allows us to recognize it as unique. Therefore, act and archive meet in the literary work because it links the advent of the new with its reinscription in a system, in generality. This makes the literary work a first time and a last time, "an event that seems to produce itself by speaking about itself, *by the act of speaking of itself*" ("P" 29). Invention and destruction meet in the singular event that signs itself as unique and fails to coincide with itself; that is, it states its uniqueness in a discourse that projects forward the possibility of its repetition. It is not that literature only transgresses the institutions that stand in place, it reveals the precariousness of the same institutions that would define it. There is no natural essence of literature; literature is "inscribed on the side of the intentional object, in its noematic structure" ("SIL" 44). Having no internal criterion, no identity, literature would at once seem to be an exemplary institution because its existence is tied to a historically specific origin (in approximately the seventeenth century) and an institutional bulwark, the law (that is, copyright, licensing and printing laws, censorship, and so on).[9] On the other hand, the literary work exemplifies invention—it comes as a surprise, as a unique or singular event, the invention of a new institution. Yet this event is destined to betray its being as a new institution because it reveals itself as such: "it appears in an institutional field designed so that it cuts itself up and abducts itself there" ("SIL" 74). The new work, in other words, never arrives alone; it inscribes itself in a context and a genealogy. The new work, if it is to be read, institutes the conditions of its unique being and the possibility of response. It is better, therefore, to speak of the literary "event" than the literary thing or object on the grounds that literarity is "the correlative of an intentional relation to the text" ("SIL" 44). The literary event is not natural because it suspends the thetic or naive belief in the referent. At the same time, when we look for the essence of literature, that which the reduction is to lead to, we find no internal criterion to govern it.

If the new work must, as has often been said, instruct its audience on how to read, then the reader is invited, as Derrida says, to countersign. This recalls us to the notion that the possibility of the signature, its effect as a singular and reproducible event, is its iterability.[10] The signature is the operation of the text as a whole, "the whole of the active interpretation which has left a trace or a remainder."[11] The new work, the invention, appears already marked de jure by a time and place that opens the present of the signature, its assertion of a here and now, to a countersignature. Like juridico-political acts, the literary event consists in producing a law that transgresses the law or institution that it comes after and makes this law possible and impossible by virtue of its status as event. The literary event is a dividing/divisive act.

The event is a doubling signing, a countersigned signature or contract without exchange.[12] In other words, the event/invention irrupts within an already constituted field where, as something surprising and unanticipated, it "inscribes itself as act (action and archive)" (SS 54). The event is not outside the field—if it were, it would be an infinite other[13]—but designates, inscribes, or signs itself by giving itself to be read or countersigned. As something new, the literary event institutes itself in a chain of conventions (but not without altering these conventions), thereby ensuring its repeatability or legitimating it for the future. The literary event has the force of law: it is the injunction of the entirely other that I be responsible to that which is singular and different. It is, therefore, an impossible debt.[14] Literature is what gives us to think the entirely other, the unanticipatable other, "what is not inventable, and it is then the only invention in the world, the only invention of the world, our invention, the invention invents us. For the other is always another origin of the world and we are (always) (still) to be invented. And the being of the we, and being itself. Beyond being" ("P" 61). The event that watches over the future, an event that invents us, invents or affirms the coming of the other, would be the arrival of the other in the performative that unsettles its status or condition as a performative—unique and repeatable.

The other, according to Derrida, is not inventable but is the only invention of the world. It allows for the unanticipatable, an origin, still to be invented. We could call it an experience of the impossible, a first event that is also a last event, an absolute invention, an absolute *epochê*. It would not be the achievement of absolute knowledge, the Husserlian project of a "voice without *différance*,"[15] or what Husserl calls "consciousness free of all worldly being,"[16] but the experience of the precariousness of the event that goes by the name "literature" and whose possibility consists in the archivizing act. As act, literature produces "its constituted law" in the "discursive forms, 'works' and 'events' in which the very possibility of a fundamental constitution is at least 'fictionally' contested, threatened, deconstructed, presented in its very precariousness" ("SIL" 72). In other words, literature belongs to the law or the juridico-political production of institutional foundations—there would be no literature without institution—and at the same time, literature, in its fictionality, contests these laws.

This makes the literary event more an event than any other. Literature has this status by virtue of its having no identity, no essence. It consists in the act, the *epochê* of the referent. As that which produces and harbors its referent inside itself, literature allows us to think the absolute *epochê*, "the *epochê* of absolute knowledge" ("NA" 27). By virtue of its absolute dependence on the archive and its performative relation to the referent, literature is susceptible to the threat of total destruction, to nuclear holocaust. As we will see, nuclear catastrophe is thinkable only on the basis of that which has no referent outside itself; otherwise the possibility of continued existence or the capacity to be reconstructed still exists (see "NA" 26). I find it, therefore, a grave misunderstanding of Derrida to charge him with textualizing the threat of nuclear destruction. In asking us to recognize the link between nuclear catastrophe and the literary archive, he is not confusing the real and its simulacrum but is indicating that literary writing affords us the possibility of thinking that which is too commonly said to be unthinkable—absolute destruction of the world. The absolute end of meaning and truth, the "unthinkable" end of the world, is thinkable on the basis of fictionality, literature's *"being-suspended,"* its suspension *and* dependence upon meaning and reference. That is to say, absolute destruction is thinkable on the basis of the bracketing of the referent. The error of someone who charges Derrida with denying us the resources of distinguishing reality and fiction not only confuses fictionality with fantasy but misses the point that fictionality does not do away with reference to something outside of language. Literature's neutrality, its being without essence, means it is the place, the resource, where it becomes possible to think presence and absence, meaning and reference. Under the name of literature we experience the possibility of nothing—which is what a totally self-referential literature would be, if such a thing were possible—and therefore everything. To say, then, that absolute destruction is thinkable only within literature is to remind us that when we set ourselves the task of speaking about what constitutes the possible end of the world, we are speaking about the threat to absolute knowledge, the "absolute *epochê,"* which means we must recognize that any possibility of speaking about what is to come rests upon literature's condition as being at once an ideality (Derrida says that if literature were to resist a transcendent reading absolutely it would destroy the necessary referral function of the text—there would be no trace of the text) and the possible suspension of meaning. This is what gives literature its power to interrogate the categories of transcendental authority and absolute suspension that constitute the discourse and reality of the nuclear age.

I am describing what Derrida calls literature's provision of "'phenomenological' access to what makes of a thesis a *thesis as such*" ("SIL" 46). Derrida's career began with the acknowledgment of the necessary recourse to phenomenological language when speaking about literature, and in his first book, *Edmund Husserl's "Origin of Geometry": An Introduction,* he explicitly linked the question of invention to absolute destruction. Husserl had to introduce the concept of writing to ensure the ideality of meaning, and it was this need for an intraworldly existence of the idea that also led him to assert that the absolute annihilation of the world would modify but not touch the existence of consciousness (see *I* 110). Eidetic or transcendental description (that is, the ascertaining of essences rather than "facts") required the *epochê,* the bracketing or setting aside of the natural attitude (the spontaneous thinking, feeling, desiring that goes on as long as I face the world in my everyday attitude), but as Derrida notes in agreement with Eugen Fink, Husserl had to have recourse "to a language that could not itself be submitted to the *epochê—* without itself being simply in the world—thus to a language which remained naive, even though it was by virtue of this very language that all the phenomenological bracketings and parentheses were made possible." [17] In other words, phenomenology itself is not susceptible to thematization, the process wherein noetic-noematic experience is laid hold of in the *epochê* or reduction.

Literary critics have come under attack for assuming that literary language does not fall victim to the "blindness" of metaphysical language, but Derrida, in his thesis defense, writes of being "fascinated by the literary ruse of the inscription and the whole ungraspable paradox of a trace which manages only to carry itself away, to erase itself in marking itself out afresh, itself and its own idiom, which in order to take actual form must erase itself and produce itself at the price of this self-erasure" ("TT" 38). [18] These remarks suggest not that literature challenges metaphysics— quite the contrary—but that literary writing, a whole other thing than "literature," is that aspect of every text that puts phenomenology in crisis. As Rodolphe Gasché has written, insofar as literature is "characterizable only by its structure of bracketing," it "puts the transcendental authority and dominant category of being into question." [19] Indeed, it is only in approaching the question of literature through the phenomenological language of intentionality that we can approach anything like "nuclear criticism," the subject of a 1984 *Diacritics* colloquium and the stage for Derrida's delivery of "No Apocalypse."

If we accept that in Husserl, the theme of phenomenology is intentionality,[20] and that thematization takes up what is presented in the unthought or what he calls the natural attitude toward the world and makes it an object of consciousness, then Derrida's assertion that literature is what allows us "to think the uniqueness of nuclear war" must be taken up in phenomenological terms as the nonthematic condition for thought. In acknowledging that the Idea is never "the *theme* of a phenomenological description" but is determinable as the horizon of intuition, as the *End-*

stiftung that is infinitely deferred, Derrida concludes that "phenomenology cannot be reflected in a phenomenology of phenomenology."[21] If phenomenology aims at the thematization of the "unthematized structures of consciousness" (that is, to rise to the condition of a purely eidetic science) and is unable to thematize itself, then the claim that literature belongs to the nuclear epoch, "the *epochê* of absolute knowledge" ("NA" 27), means that literature affirms the unthematizable as the condition for the anticipation of the future as apocalypse without truth.

Nuclear war is, perhaps, the possibility of what has always been the defining condition of literature as the aleatory and unique event. It is the infinite horizon of what we call "literature": "nuclear war is the only possible referent of any discourse and any experience that would share their condition with that of literature" ("NA" 28). This statement may seem frivolous, or worse, to some, but it must be kept in mind that, here, "literature" is not belles lettres but what Derrida says takes place each time there is some trace, some minimal structure of referral to an other by which self-identity is maintained. Having no identity in itself, literature is characterized by this relation to the other. There is literature, or literature begins, everywhere and every time there is a trace. What is perhaps most difficult to grasp in Derrida's concept of literature is that it always is something else; which is to say, literature does not exist. We cannot say "literature is," but there is literature whenever there is some trace. Being without identity, "literature will have begun when it is not possible to decide whether, when I speak of something, I am indeed speaking of something (of the thing itself, this one, for itself) or if I am giving an example, an example of something or an example of the fact that I can speak of something."[22] To speak of examples is to speak of something, literature, for example, as such, without making it an object. As singular and general, the example stands in place of everything it would exemplify, but it never stands in place of itself. *Ulysses* may be an example of the novel as such and is, therefore, generalizable, but it is not an example of *Ulysses*. Literature bears witness to this impossibility of the law (of the example) to be the law. Therefore, literature can speak of anything without touching upon what it holds in reserve. Literature, in short, is always "something other than itself, an itself which moreover is only that, something other than itself" (*ON* 144 n. 14).

This is the apophatic principle of literature—it can only speak by not speaking of what it would speak (about). And this is the madness of literature—it is always beside itself; it always is, does, says something other than itself, such as speaking about (the possibility of) nuclear war.

Literature exists as something, but it is not as if literature existed in place of, to use our present example, the rhetoric of the nuclear age. This something is negativity. Literature takes place when it cannot be decided whether, when I speak of something, I am giving an example of speaking in place of something or I am speaking of something. Literature is not, but there is literature. It exists in the mode of being there, as the surprise of the event, absolute invention and absolute destruction. When Derrida denies that there can be a literature that refers solely to itself, he does so not on the grounds that literature is dependent upon some external referent but on the basis of the notion that being without identity, literature is always the response to the other; it never ceases referring to the other.

It would be an absurdity to take Derrida's deconstruction of the rhetoric of nuclear disaster as a refusal to confront the politics of deterrence and the threatening possibility of nuclear war. Insofar as nuclear war would be "an ultimate event," a final destruction, it is inseparable from fable. The "reality" of the nuclear age is constructed on the basis of something that has never happened, absolute destruction, but which is nonetheless there (I do not say "real" because it has not occurred and is, strictly speaking, something we speculate about [see "NA" 23]). In calling this possible event a "fable," Derrida is not saying it is identical with literature but that it shares with literature the suspension, the *epochê,* of the referent. For what is it we refer to when we speak of nuclear war but something that belongs to the realm of a signified but not a real referent? The absolute destruction promised by nuclear war would leave no remainder. And what is it then that allows us to think such an event, an event whose advent erases the possibility of its imagination? Literature, which by virtue of its character as trace is constituted by a remainder, a reserve that shelters the other, which is never subject to representation but which gives us the chance of saying everything.

Nuclear criticism, therefore, comes into view as the finite consciousness of the infinite capacity for a remainderless self-destruction. "'Nuclear criticism,'" Derrida writes, "like Kantian criticism, is thought about the limits of experience as a thought of finitude." The prospect of nuclear war, of a remainderless destruction, would be *"waged in the name of . . .* something whose name, in this logic of total destruction, can no longer be borne, transmitted, inherited by anything living," a "name of nothing," a "pure name" ("NA" 30–31; ellipsis in original). This war in the name of the name, a war of total destruction, while realizable by the technologies of the nuclear age, has always been the reason why wars are waged. It is war waged in the name of something that is more valuable than life. This ultimate event would be, Derrida says in his first missive, "a final collision or collusion" in which the differences of noetic and noematic would merge into one another. It would erase the difference between the "phenomenological and intraworldly" ("NA" 21).

The prospect of absolute destruction institutes the possibility of absolute consciousness, consciousness free from the annihilation of physical things—as Husserl proposed. As long as nuclear criticism is devoted to anticipating absolute or remainderless self-destruction, it conforms to Husserl's concept of historicity as the passage of sense. Nuclear catastrophe presents itself, makes itself available to thought, on the basis of its self-destruction before the truth, the name. Nuclear criticism remains bound to the notion that the destruction of phenomenological sense will be a destruction of ideal sense. To the extent that nuclear criticism anticipates infinite destruction, it is guided by the Idea of Reason.

Derrida's comparison of nuclear criticism to Kantian criticism ought to give caution to anyone who wishes to take up "nuclear criticism" as a regional discipline of deconstruction.[23] Insofar as nuclear criticism is a thought of finitude, operating within the poles of receptive being and infinite intellect, it is an attempt (the last?) to account for the concept of subjectivity and the existence of absolute consciousness. That is, to the degree that nuclear criticism is directed toward the future, it postulates a consciousness that will survive nuclear destruction.[24] It would be a mode of self-reflection, a turning back to the conditions of the world insofar as the world is to be grasped as the absolute referent, as what is there or given for experience.

"Such a criticism," Derrida writes, "forecloses a finitude so radical that it would annul the basis of the opposition and would make it possible to think the very limit of criticism. This limit comes into view in the groundlessness of a remainderless self-destruction of the self, auto-destruction of the autos itself. Whereupon the kernel, the nucleus of criticism, itself bursts apart" ("NA" 30). The opening of this kernel, this dehiscence, would bring into view the opposition between finite and infinite that sustains criticism as a discipline subordinate to philosophy. Within the terms of this opposition, we think the possibility of absolute destruction from an infinite perspective. Like Hegel's master, we wage war in the name of something more valuable than life itself, except that we must live on in order to enjoy our victory (see "NA" 30). Perhaps one of the most distinctive features of Derrida's argument lies in his revealing that the apocalyptic perspective assumes the vantage point of an infinite knowledge. As the only absolutely real referent, nuclear catastrophe is the ideal of pure presence, the real, rather than the signified, referent. A "remainderless self-destruction," a destruction without iterability, one that would leave no trace (of itself), is thinkable on the basis of presence.[25] It confirms the idea of the future as apocalypse, as revelation. Such a notion of absolute destruction belongs to the text of metaphysics and the epochality of Being. Erasure, however, belongs to the structure of the trace (*M* 23). If the trace "exceeds the truth of Being," then the disappearance of the trace of the ontological difference, the difference between Being and beings, would be fulfilled in the nuclear epoch. Our thinking of nuclear catastrophe is metaphysical insofar as it maintains, indeed fulfills, the opposition between presence and absence. Nuclear radiation would not be simply a metaphor of the trace left after the effacement of beings, the effacement of difference, but the threat of nuclear holocaust has been with us as long as the concept of presence, which is thinkable only in its opposition to absence. The concept of nuclear holocaust belongs to a concept of ideality and, therefore, to iterability and the effacement of the trace.

If iterability supposes that a "one time," such as a nuclear catastrophe, is already divided, then it undermines the opposition between finite and infinite upon which nuclear criticism rests. Nuclear criticism would be the completion of metaphysics according to the text of metaphysics. A criticism that holds "the groundlessness [*le sans-fond*] of a remainderless self-destruction of the self" up to view would be one that shows the only subject of criticism to be the effacement of the absolute trace, "the trace of what is entirely other [*trace du tout autre*]" ("NA" 28). Derrida's deconstruction points to a dehiscence, an opening, that displaces the oppositions between finite and infinite, and de facto and de jure, by reinscribing philosophical discourse in the general text, what Gasché calls "an intentionality without an intentum"; that is, the text displaces phenomenological intentionality with an intentionality that "cannot be *fulfilled* by a corresponding extraintentional referent" (*T* 281). Because nothing can exist outside the general text—there can be no extratextual referent, or nothing is without a context—the threat of nuclear catastrophe is thinkable only in terms of the destruction of that which has no referent outside itself, that is, literature. Literature gives us to think the totality of absolute destruction because it is without essence: as the trace that erases itself, it is the unthematizable. Literature is unique, the singular event, precisely because it is structurally conditioned through its being as suspended, its being-suspended. The epochal character of literature makes it totally dependent on the archive and, at the same time, it gives us to think the total destruction of the archive, which is to say, it gives us to think the formalizing power of philosophical discourse—of first times and last times, of invention and destruction.

We might ask, why "No Apocalypse, Not Now"? Nuclear war precipitates us toward "the uniqueness of an ultimate event, of a final collision or collusion" ("NA" 21). An "absolute acceleration" would leave no time for repetition, the very condition of presence, of consciousness, of historicity. The collision/collusion of the intraworldly, the totality of objects of experience, and of phenomenology, a science of essences, would mean that consciousness itself would undergo annihilation along with the world. Nuclear war, to the extent that it is not located in the world but has existence "only where it is talked about," might be called a fable, as Derrida argues, not in its conventional sense as a fictive narrative but as a "fabulous speculation," or what Husserl would call a pure object of consciousness ("NA" 23).

For Derrida, the nuclear age brings phenomenology to a crisis. Because phenomenology begins with the parenthesizing of the natural attitude—that is, the exclusion of the positing of the natural world in its actuality, of the world as it is given to experience—and distinguishes experiential sciences or matters of fact from eidetic science, which concerns universal essences, nuclear war, as a phenomenon that is both technical and rhetorical, leaves, as Derrida says, "no more room for a distinction between belief and science" ("NA" 24). Consequently, if Husserl's regressive inquiry (*Rückfrage*) should seek to establish the priority of ideal objects over the empirical determination of fact, then nuclear war is "fabulous" to the extent that it blurs any distinction between sense and actuality. Beyond the rhetoric surrounding nuclear weapons and its blurring of the distinction between belief and knowledge, the collapse of the difference between the phenomenological and the intraworldly puts in crisis the phenomenological parenthesizing of the natural attitude.

Whereas the neutralizing of the thetic or naive belief in the given world would provide access to the world as a pure object of consciousness, nuclear war does not sustain this distinction precisely because, like literature, it exists only once—that is, it has an ideal objectivity—*and* is finite.[26] There can be no essence of nuclear war, no absolute suspension of the natural attitude that is the condition of our talk of nuclear catastrophe. The reduction that goes under the name of nuclear war—the reality that comes to us as an event that is yet to happen—is a suspension of "reality." This is the fable of nuclear war. In the critical place of the nuclear age there is "[n]o truth, no apocalypse" ("NA" 24). We might say, there is no essence of nuclear war—it is textual both in the colloquial sense and the broader sense Derrida gives the term. Therefore, to say we cannot oppose *doxa* and *episteme* or the natural attitude and the phenomenological attitude means that the distinction between the idealization of anticipation, which authorizes the passage to the infinite Idea, and "ideation as an intuition of an essence" (*IOG* 134–35) can no longer be maintained. Creation and production, truth and simulacrum, are blurred. In other words, the distinctions that are predicated by phenomenological reduction are not dismissed but are "folded." We can no longer think in terms of opposition but must recognize that these "distinctions" have no distinct boundaries; they contaminate one another.

What announces itself in nuclear war—and so far, it has only announced itself—never gives itself as such, that is, in its essence. Derrida's title, "No Apocalypse, Not Now," echoes his statement, "there is no—or hardly any, ever so little—literature."[27] The threat of apocalyptic destruction, destruction without revelation, is echoed in the epochal character of literature. Literature belongs to the nuclear epoch to the extent it is exposed to destruction without revelation. In its character as the bracketing of transcendental authority, of Being, literature has not a real but a signified referent (cf. "NA" 23). If "literary writing has, almost always, and almost everywhere, according to some fashions and across very diverse ages, lent itself to this *transcendent* reading, in that search for the signified which we here put in question" (*OG* 160), it does not do away with transcendent reading altogether, just as it does not do away with literature, in its institutional sense, or philosophy. Derrida makes this point when questioned about this passage from *Of Grammatology.* Employing a phenomenological language, Derrida denies that

> literarity is . . . a natural essence, an intrinsic property of the text. It is the correlative of an intentional relation to the text. . . . There is therefore a literary *functioning* and a literary *intentionality,* an experience rather than an essence of literature (natural or historical). The essence of literature, if we hold to this word essence, is produced as a set of objective rules in an original history of the "acts" of inscription and reading. ("SIL" 44–45)

This phenomenological terminology reminds us of the instituted, posited, or thetic character of the text. Literature is at once an "instituted *fiction* but also a *fictive institution* which in principle allows one to say everything" ("SIL" 36). In addition to having a purely textual or linguistic existence, nuclear war is bound by a historically specific set of rules governing its discourse. Finally, there is the precarious position of the referent. Nuclear war, like literature, does not have a real referent. This does not mean it does away with reference nor that it can be reduced to the status of a mere fable. "One has to distinguish between the 'reality' of the nuclear age and the fiction of war. . . . 'Reality,' let's say the encompassing institution of the nuclear age, is constructed by the fable, on the basis of an event that has never happened (except in fantasy, and that is not nothing at all)" ("NA" 23). Nuclear war would be the epochal determination of the nuclear age: as the ultimate referent, nuclear war multiplies discourses, produces the set of rules by which this anticipated entirely-other, nuclear catastrophe, is set aside or determined. Nuclear war, we might say, gives us to think the thesis as such. As a fable, an invention, it is a nonthetic experience of the thesis. Nuclear war does not annul the positing that Husserl calls the natural attitude but sets it aside, parenthesizes it, to allow us to speak seriously about the fiction of absolute catastrophe. Whereas for Husserl the consciousness that is reached in the *epochê* would not be touched by the annihilation of the physical world, the absolute destruction of nuclear war is "real," if we can use this term to describe a fiction whose referent is contained within itself.

It is the possibility of a nonthetic experience of the thesis, the "naive belief in meaning or referent," that links literature and the nuclear age. The suspension of a thetic relation to meaning or the referent does not eliminate reference nor, as Derrida points out, does it constitute "the object as a literary object. . . . In any case, a text cannot avoid lending itself to a 'transcendent' reading. A literature which forbade that transcendence would annul itself" ("SIL" 45). Such a literature would be a chaotic literalness of defunct signs (see *IOG* 88). Yet by providing a nonthetic experience of the thetic, literature dislodges the moment of transcendental consciousness, the pure thought that would be unaffected by the annihilation of the world. Literature is the expression of consciousness as delay and, therefore, a displacement of the reflexive appropriation of the Logos in the reduction. The "fold" in the moment of transcendence is not annulment but a remarking or spacing that accounts for the experience of the transcendental. The fold "is not a form of reflexivity," if one means by it the movement of self-presence (*D* 270). The fold or folding back is a placing in reserve, a setting aside of Being in the margin or at the threshold of the text. It is a polysemic structure of "dehiscence, dissemination, spacing, temporalization, etc." (*D* 271). Characterized by

the fold, literature holds itself back and thereby resists the phenomenali-
zation that makes an intuition of the essence possible. "If there is no
essence of literature—i.e., self-identity of the literary thing—if what is
announced or promised as literature never gives itself as such, that
means, among other things, that a literature that talked only about literature or a work that was purely self-referential would immediately be
annulled" ("SIL" 47).

Derrida's denial of a purely self-referential literature has implications
for nuclear criticism. The fact that nuclear war has not occurred, that it
remains "just talk," is not nothing. The aporias of the nuclear referent—
it is a signified, not real, referent; it is an event that produces a real referent within itself—means that what goes by the name of nuclear war is
not confined or limited to known events but is constituted by an act that
is, structurally, the only possible referent of any discourse or experience
by virtue of its performative character as absolute invention and absolute
destruction. If a purely self-referential literature annuls itself, then literature allows us to think the total destruction of that which contains its
referent within itself. This, I must add, has nothing to do with apocalyptic
fantasies or fictions of nuclear holocaust but is a structural possibility of
literature, in Derrida's special sense of the word. He is, therefore, not
asking us to think of nuclear war in terms of futuristic scenarios but in
fundamental terms of what it means to desire the absolutely real. In de-
claring nuclear catastrophe the "only referent that is absolutely real," he
is, indeed, linking absolute destruction to absolute invention.

Derrida's warning, then, is directed not so much at the policy plan-
ners who believe the Western democracies must prevail if a nuclear war
is fought, but against the rationale of deterrence that ignores its connection to "a structure in which randomness and incalculability are essential"
("NA" 29). No, a throw of the dice does not abolish chance, nor does
a missile. Governments try to integrate chance into a calculable order,
forgetting that what is calculable belongs to the order of the same. To
prepare for the entirely other, what is to come, requires not an imper-
sonal calculus but an aleatory element that does not allow itself to be
encapsulated in some program. This sounds very much like a desire for
revelation, a God who can save us from ourselves, but if it is, it is not a
God whom we will recognize nor will He speak in one voice. For this
war can only be fought in the name of something that cannot be transmitted, a name beyond the name, an absolute name that is revelation itself.
Derrida exposes that beneath policy planning and even outright rejection
of nuclear armament in the name of life itself lies a belief in absolute

knowledge, the belief that absolute negation is, in fact, not only a possibility but something knowable and calculable. It is the purely self-referential act that annuls itself. In exposing the conditions that permit us to imagine nuclear holocaust without ever really imagining it, Derrida draws us back to time and its vicissitudes. No Apocalypse, Not Now.

A purely self-referential literature promises us the totality of that which is constituted in itself, constituted as producing its referent in and by itself. This would mean a literature indissociable from the nuclear epoch as "the absolute *epochê* . . . the *epochê* of absolute knowledge. Literature belongs to this nuclear epoch, that of the crisis and of nuclear criticism, at least if we mean by this the historical and ahistorical horizon of an absolute self-destructibility without apocalypse, without revelation of its own truth, without absolute knowledge" ("NA" 27). The experience of nuclear war would be the "experience of the nothing-ing of nothing that interests our desire under the name of literature" ("SIL" 47). In the self-referential work, literature (without essence) "experiences" itself as a nullity; it experiences the essential finitude wherein its relation to reference is suspended—that is, held back, neutralized, as having no essence of its own, dependent on something other than itself (cf. "SIL" 48).

Literature enables us to think the possibility of appearing (of Being), not in the sense of an a priori condition or as the phenomenological absolute but insofar as its status as writing or textuality suspends the relation to meaning or reference and thereby places it "on the edge of everything, almost beyond everything, including itself" ("SIL" 47). Having no standing in Being, having no "foundation outside itself[,] [l]iterature is at once reassured and threatened by the fact of depending only on itself, standing in the air, all alone, aside from Being" (*D* 280). Literature is characterized not by possessing an essence but by its setting aside or bracketing of essence of Being. As long as we think of literature conceptually, think of it as determined by the concept—preeminently that of mimesis in the sense of imitation—we are thinking it as (a) subject of/ to philosophy. Consequently, the special relationship Derrida claims for literature and nuclear war would not hold because literature would have its possibility for being outside itself. However, if literature, harboring its referent within itself, is aside from Being, without any foundation outside itself, it "gives us to think the *totality* of that which, like literature and henceforth in it, is exposed to the same threat [i.e., of total destruction]" ("NA" 27).

Were nuclear catastrophe to happen, there would be nothing—outside the text. Derrida's famous sentence "*il n'y a pas de hors-texte*" (*OG*

158) implies that because there is no essence of literature, it does not constitute a totality. As the *epochê* of the *epochê,* literature's function of setting aside allows for the experience of the natural attitude or thesis but is itself nonthetic. Literature is, in other words, fiction, a being-suspended that neutralizes the metaphysical assumptions it cannot totally escape ("SIL" 49). Literature is

> at once the exception in the whole, the want-of-wholeness in the whole, and the exception to everything, that which exists by itself, alone, with nothing else, in exception to all. A part that, within *and* without the whole, marks the wholly other, the other incommensurate with the whole. Which cuts litera-ture short: it doesn't exist, since there is nothing outside the whole. It does exist, since there is an "exception to every-thing," an outside of the whole, that is, a sort of subtraction without lack. (*D* 56)

Literature, then, is all *and* nothing at all. Having no essence of its own, "literature" is aside from Being; it is epochal in character and, hence, belongs to the nuclear epoch, the experience of the nothing-ing of nothing. This absolute destruction does not concern a formal struc-ture, called "literarity," which is "extended to any possible archive," but is literature's experience of "its own precariousness, its death menace, and its essential finitude. The movement of its inscription is the very possibility of its effacement" ("NA" 27). Literature and nuclear destruc-tion are bound by virtue of their relation to the absolute referent, the only real referent being that absolute catastrophe that would destroy the entire archive and all symbolic capacity. Both nuclear warfare, to the ex-tent that it belongs to rhetoric and still is to come, and literature share the space of an instituted fiction, a fictive institution ("SIL" 36). And like literature, nuclear warfare is not to come, in the sense that it may occur tomorrow or whenever, but has the status of a promise, a to-come (*à-venir*) that never arrives but is already here, like a "memory which pro-duces the event to be told and which will never have been present" ("SIL" 42). As what gives us to think this remainderless, a-symbolic destruction, literature is not merely fiction but what makes it possible to think what is necessary and impossible to think, the singular event of nuclear war. In asking us to think of a randomness and incalculability essential to all endings, Derrida disavows the logic of deterrence in favor of a more origi-nal and radical incalculability that prepares us, not for the coming of missiles, but for the coming of the other, the only possible invention. The future is the work of literature.

Notes

1. Immanuel Kant, "On a Newly Arisen Superior Tone in Philosophy," trans. Peter Fenves, in *Raising the Tone of Philosophy: Late Essays by Immanuel Kant, Transformative Critique by Jacques Derrida,* ed. Peter Fenves (Baltimore: Johns Hopkins University Press, 1993), 59. Hereafter cited as *RTP.* Derrida's address was first published, along with the proceedings of the conference, in *Les Fins de l'homme: A partir du travail de Jacques Derrida,* ed. Philippe Lacoue-Labarthe and Jean-Luc Nancy (Paris: Galilée, 1981).

2. Jacques Derrida, "Before the Law," trans. Avital Ronell and Christine Roulston, in *Acts of Literature,* ed. Derek Attridge (New York: Routledge, 1992), 213. Derrida argues that in literature, "the categorical engages the idiomatic. . . . The man from the country had difficulty in grasping that an entrance was singular or unique when it should have been universal, as in truth it was. He had difficulty with literature."

3. Jacques Derrida, "Psyché: Inventions of the Other," trans. Catherine Porter, in *Reading de Man Reading,* ed. Lindsay Waters and Wlad Godzich (Minneapolis: University of Minnesota Press, 1989), 28. Hereafter cited as "P."

4. Jacques Derrida, "Jacques Derrida: Deconstruction and the Other," interview by Richard Kearny, in *Dialogues with Contemporary Continental Thinkers: The Phenomenological Heritage* (Manchester: Manchester University Press, 1984), 123. Hereafter cited as "DO."

5. Jacques Derrida, "'This Strange Institution Called Literature': An Interview with Jacques Derrida," trans. Geoffrey Bennington and Rachel Bowlby, in *Acts of Literature,* ed. Derek Attridge (New York: Routledge, 1992), 62. Hereafter cited as "SIL."

6. Jacques Derrida, "Passages—from Traumatism to Promise," trans. Peggy Kamuf, in *Points . . . Interviews, 1974-1994,* ed. Elisabeth Weber (Stanford: Stanford University Press, 1995), 386.

7. Jacques Derrida, *Of Grammatology,* trans. Gayatri Chakravorty Spivak (Baltimore: Johns Hopkins University Press, 1976), 5; translation modified. Hereafter cited as *OG.*

8. Jacques Derrida, "No Apocalypse, Not Now (full speed ahead, seven missiles, seven missives)," trans. Catherine Porter and Philip Lewis, in *Diacritics* 14, no. 2 (Summer 1984): 26. Hereafter cited as "NA."

9. For the importance of law for literature, see "Des Tours de Babel," trans. Joseph F. Graham, in *Difference in Translation,* ed. Joseph F. Graham (Ithaca: Cornell University Press, 1985), 190–200.

10. For the relation of the signature to repetition, see Derrida's "Signa-

ture Event Context," in *Margins of Philosophy*, trans. Alan Bass (Chicago: University of Chicago Press, 1982), especially 327–30. Hereafter cited as *M.*

11.   Jacques Derrida, *The Ear of the Other: Otobiography, Transference, Translation*, trans. Peggy Kamuf, ed. Christie McDonald (1985; rpt., Lincoln: University of Nebraska Press, 1988), 52.

12.   Derrida writes of the contract and signature in *Signéponge/Signsponge*, trans. Richard Rand (New York: Columbia University Press, 1984), 48. Hereafter cited as *SS.*

13.   On the problem of the infinitely Other, see Derrida's "Violence and Metaphysics: An Essay on the Thought of Emmanuel Levinas," in *Writing and Difference*, trans. Alan Bass (Chicago: University of Chicago Press, 1978): "If one thinks, as Levinas does, that positive Infinity tolerates, or even requires, infinite alterity, then one must renounce all language, and first of all the words *infinite* and *other.* Infinity cannot be understood as Other except in the form of the in-finite. . . . The other cannot be what it is, infinitely other, except in finitude and mortality (mine *and* its)" (114–15).

14.   I draw upon Derrida's remarks on the thing and law in *Signéponge/Signsponge:*

> Thus the thing would be the other, the other-thing which gives me an order or addresses an impossible, intransigent, insatiable demand to me, without an exchange and without a transaction, without a possible contract. . . . I owe to the thing an absolute respect which no general law would mediate: the law of the thing is singularity and difference as well. An infinite debt ties me to it, a duty without funds or foundation. I shall never acquit myself of it. Thus the thing is not an object; it cannot become one. (14)

15.   Jacques Derrida, *Speech and Phenomena*, trans. David B. Allison (Evanston: Northwestern University Press, 1973), 102.

16.   Edmund Husserl, *Ideas Pertaining to a Pure Phenomenology and to a Phenomenological Philosophy. First Book: General Introduction to a Pure Phenomenology*, trans. F. Kersten (The Hague: Martinus Nijhoff, 1983), 116. See also section 49. Hereafter cited as *I.*

17.   Jacques Derrida, "The Time of a Thesis: Punctuations," trans. Kathleen McLaughlin, in *Philosophy in France Today*, ed. Alan Montefiore (Cambridge: Cambridge University Press, 1983), 39. Hereafter cited as "TT."

18.   The notion that literary writing must erase itself in order to produce itself can be fruitfully considered in the context of Russell's theory of types. See John Llewelyn's discussion of the theory of types and undecidability in "Responsibility with Indecidability," in *Derrida: A Critical Reader*, ed. David Wood (Oxford: Basil Blackwell, 1992), 75–80. The theory of types seeks to avoid the paradox of self-referential sentences (such as, "This sentence is

false") "by asserting that no propositional function can meaningfully take itself as argument" (75). Llewelyn exposes the limitations of this theory in a reading of Francis Ponge's "Fable."

19.   Rodolphe Gasché, *The Tain of the Mirror: Derrida and the Philosophy of Reflection* (Cambridge, Mass.: Harvard University Press, 1986), 259. Hereafter cited as *T.* Gasché's situating of Derrida's remarks on the being of literature within and against phenomenology is very important to my argument, as the ensuing discussion will show.

20.   See section 84 of Husserl's *Ideas:* "Intentionality is an essential peculiarity of the sphere of mental processes taken universally in so far as all mental processes in some manner or other share in it" (199). Intentionality is the property of consciousness to be the consciousness *of.* . . .

21.   Jacques Derrida, *Edmund Husserl's "Origin of Geometry": An Introduction,* trans. John P. Leavey Jr. (Stony Brook, N.Y.: Nicholas Hays, 1978), 137-38, 141. Hereafter cited as *IOG.*

22.   Jacques Derrida, "Passions," trans. David Wood, in *On the Name,* ed. Thomas Dutoit (Stanford: Stanford University Press, 1995), 142-43 n. 14. Hereafter cited as *ON.*

23.   Nevertheless, several works have appeared on nuclear war and criticism. Their major themes include the function of time, infinite deferral, and the rhetoric of deterrence. One of the better works is Peter Schwenger's *Letter Bomb: Nuclear Holocaust and the Exploding Word* (Baltimore: Johns Hopkins University Press, 1992). Christopher Norris has written on Derrida's essay "No Apocalypse, Not Now" on at least two occasions. In *Derrida* (Cambridge, Mass.: Harvard University Press, 1987), he treats it in the context of his overall argument that deconstruction is a critique of the "paradoxes in the nature of reason" (163). In *Uncritical Theory: Postmodernism, Intellectuals and the Gulf War* (London: Lawrence and Wishart, 1992), he is more critical of the essay, charging that it invites a blurring of the distinction between the actual and the simulated necessary for judgment (38-47). This criticism strikes me as more pertinent to a work like William Chaloupka's *Knowing Nukes: The Politics and Culture of the Atom* (Minneapolis: University of Minnesota Press, 1992) than as a proper assessment of Derrida's argument. Norris wishes to find in Derrida a radicalizing of Kant that continues the "critical engagement with the truth-claims and ethical values of Enlightenment thought" (*Uncritical Theory* 47). Norris narrowly interprets the phenomenological suspension of judgment as a relinquishment of accountability and misses the point that Derrida's deconstruction of the *epochê* situates the possibility of judgment in literature's being without essence.

24.   Richard Klein calls this godlike perspective the "nuclear sublime" after Frances Ferguson's article of this name (*Diacritics* 14, no. 2 [Summer 1984]: 4-10). He writes: "Nuclear Criticism denies itself that posthumous, apocalyptic perspective, with its pathos, its revelations, and its implicit reas-

surances; it supposes that the only future may be the one we project forward from the time when total nuclear war, for the time being, has not taken place" ("The Future of Nuclear Criticism," *Yale French Studies* 77 [1990]: 77–78). He goes on to say that what distinguishes this future would be the absence of a "posthumous perspective," the work of mourning (81). I believe he misreads Derrida to the extent that he treats the possibility of total destruction strictly within terms of a hypothetical or anticipatible future. The prospect of a future without repetition falls within the possibility of an origin without alterity: absolute absence is on a par with absolute presence.

25. Survival, however, is predicated upon iterability, the condition of the functioning of all language: "Iterability supposes a minimal remainder (as well as a minimum idealization) in order that the identity of the *self-same* be repeatable and identifiable *in, through,* and even *in view of* its alteration" (Derrida, *Limited Inc.,* trans. Samuel Weber [1977; rpt., Evanston: Northwestern University Press, 1988], 53). Hereafter cited as *LI.* Iterability both constitutes the ideality of truth and divides it. It is the condition of something being recognized in different times and places, *and* it deconstitutes the "thing" as *eidos* or essence (that is, as self-identical). Iterability is an impure "idea," "a differential structure escaping the logic of presence or the (simple and dialectical) opposition of presence and absence, upon which the idea of permanence depends" (*LI* 53).

26. In "The Origin of Geometry" (originally published in *The Crisis of European Sciences and Transcendental Phenomenology,* trans. David Carr [Evanston: Northwestern University Press, 1970]), Husserl defines ideal objects as a class of "spiritual products of the cultural world" that exist permanently for everyone, unlike either a mere psychic experience lying exclusively in an individual's mental space or a physical product, such as a tool, that is repeatable in exemplars. In a note he adds, "But the broadest concept of literature encompasses them all; that is, it belongs to their objective being that they be linguistically expressed and can be expressed again and again; or, more precisely, they have their objectivity, their existence-for-everyone, only as signification, as the meaning of speech" (reprinted as an appendix to Derrida's *IOG,* 160).

27. Jacques Derrida, *Dissemination,* trans. Barbara Johnson (Chicago: University of Chicago Press, 1981), 223. Hereafter cited as *D.*

Remembering Women's Studies

Alice Gambrell

For women artists, scholars, and public intellectuals during the second half of the twentieth century, the condition of working *between* discursive formations — marked in the subtitle of this volume — is a familiar one; it has given rise to a sizable portion of post-1945 feminist writing, activism, painting, cinema, and performance. During the early 1950s, filmmaker Maya Deren evoked this condition quite clearly at the start of the written account of her field research on Haitian *vodou*. There, Deren described how her own avant-garde cinematic practice had taken shape in the interstices of "a cinema tradition completely dominated by the commercial film industry on the one hand and the documentary film on the other."[1] Deren's Haitian film footage, she explained, was meant to enable her to complicate this too-stark polarity, to generate new forms and practices in the spaces between.

The critical and theoretical literatures of academic feminism from the last quarter-century are filled with examples of this same kind of interdiscursive negotiation, which might usefully be read as a kind of founding feminist gesture, one that has gained in power and complexity through frequent repetition and revision. To call this condition familiar, however, is not to say that it is transparently interpretable—a matter of hard-won experience that we therefore intimately understand, or a place that we can map from memory, having been there before. To the contrary, "between-ness" can signify either or both of two things: on one hand, a liminal no-man's-land, ungoverned and abundant with possibility, or, on the other, a sharply circumscribed, tightly delimited space between protest and affirmation, between the devil and the deep blue sea, between men. In Maya Deren's case, this doubleness can be measured in the distance that separates the textual inventiveness of *Divine Horsemen: The Living Gods of Haiti,* her published account of the successes and failures of her Haitian fieldwork, from the chastening specter of Deren's unedited Haitian film footage, which she stashed in a closet soon after her return to the United States, and whose finished version was assembled for viewers only posthumously.[2]

By considering the problem of a feminist intellectual past in the context of a volume focused on "future crossings," moreover, my own essay locates itself in a position of temporal betweenness that has become more and more insistent in contemporary academic-feminist writing on the problems entailed in remembering our own disciplinary history. Most often, in these recent instances, the distinction between remembering the past and inventing possible futures has been blurred; regarding "women's studies"—which I understand here as the interdisciplinary field of the study of women, institutionalized in the American academy during the early 1970s and largely superseded by "feminist theory" or "gender studies" during the 1980s—we have seen a richly volatile and self-conscious mixture of the two.[3] At the conclusion of her 1993 intellectual memoir "Decades," for example, Nancy K. Miller noted that,

> [h]aving arrived at this [end]point, I should now adopt a more
> confident, visionary tone and scan the cultural firmament for
> signs of things to come: portents for feminism in the nineties.
> But that would require that I feel either prepared to speak for

feminism, or willing, as I have been so often in the past, to
predict what its next moves might and should be. I seem instead to be more at ease reviewing (even teaching) the history
of a feminist past than imagining its future; waiting, as the decade unfolds, to see what the critical subjects we have created
in our students will bring about.[4]

Against her own stated intention that she would look backward, avoiding
all "portents" and "predict[ions]," Miller nonetheless did succeed, however inadvertently, in forecasting one of the major critical preoccupations
of the end of this present decade: the urgent effort to recall, to narrate,
and (even) to teach academic feminism's own recent past. Miller's retrospective glance propelled many of her readers into the future, in a play
of temporality that was articulated more explicitly by Deborah McDowell
in her near-contemporaneous essay titled "Transferences: Black Feminist
Discourse: The 'Practice' of 'Theory'" (1995). There, McDowell set about
to "determine what 'historical knowledge' of 'contemporary feminist theory' we are constructing at this moment." In the process, McDowell admitted to taking sequential "liberties" in order that she might go on to
"construe" what she called "the present as the future's past."[5] In other
words, by analyzing the way in which feminism's past is now being ener-
getically invented by critics and theorists, McDowell suggested as well
the paradoxical necessity of remembering the future, where the consequences of our current historiographical choices would bear themselves out.

I begin by refocusing the particulars of this collection's title, and by
resituating them within the context of some of the contemporary preoccupations of academic feminism, in part because they demonstrate, as
yet another decade turns, just how tightly enmeshed are the concerns of
feminist and more generally comparatist interpretive activities. The key
oppositional terms given here—"philosophy" and "cultural studies"—
have similarly strong reverberations within feminist discussion, where
the status, indeed the definition, of theory (read: "philosophy") has once
again become a problem, after a more or less problem-free decade defined by subtle and energetic feminist reengagements of canonical theoretical texts from a range of Continental philosophical traditions.[6] At the
same time, a new set of terms for critical approbation—most prominently, praise for "empirical" and/or "descriptive richness" (read: "cultural studies")—has arisen in recent feminist debate, terms that range in
their uses from methodological tool to marketing slogan.[7]

The persistent allure of these sorts of oppositions is surprising, given the complexity of the historiographical debates that are currently under way within the field of feminist scholarship. Although contemporary efforts by feminist critics to locate suitable forms for narrating our own institutional past have taken a number of forms, one broad and salutary area of overlap has emerged among them: a wide-ranging dissatisfaction with what Jane Gallop has called the "progress" narrative of academic-feminist history,[8] a narrative wherein the purported methodological vulgarities and monolithic tendencies of 1970s "women's studies" give way to a subtler, more theoretically nuanced, more culturally diverse brand of "feminist theory." Gallop has worked against this transparently self-serving tendency by turning her own attention toward both the unexpected subtleties of earlier texts and the blind spots that persist within later ones. Miller has worked toward developing a synthesis of earlier and later interpretive emphases, most influentially within her recent experiments with the form of the intellectual memoir. And McDowell has developed an episodic narrative form, one that enables her to focus tightly upon flashpoints of critical contradiction wherein the work of African American feminist critics has been (and continues to be) associated with the less-valued term in the "theory"/"practice" dyad, whose significances have shifted back and forth over the last twenty-five years.

What the passing away of the "progress" narrative has given rise to is a multivalent and sometimes volatile effort to reengage the changing relationships between particular, habitually invoked terms and techniques in order to mount a contrast between the recent past and the present: a monolithic "woman" versus a heterogeneity of "women"; the "experiential" versus the "theoretical"; direct political engagement versus the decline of public culture; outlaw status versus institutional approbation. In the readings that follow, as such, what I will be testing out is the utility of a fairly narrow hypothesis: that one way of approaching the difficult process of disciplinary retrospection is to look at how texts that emerged from this earlier cultural moment contain within themselves compressed and exceedingly complicated metacommentaries on the institutional status of feminist scholarship itself, including (and perhaps especially) commentaries on the aforementioned polarities which have defined academic feminism from its founding moments. To this end, I will focus on two second-wave formulations of female betweenness (both of them published in the mid-1970s, as their formulaic titles might indicate): Gayle Rubin's "The Traffic in Women: Notes on the 'Political Economy' of Sex" and June Jordan's "On Richard Wright and Zora Neale Hurston:

Notes Toward a Balancing of Love and Hatred." Above all, I mean to examine ways in which the heterogeneity of the category of "women" has marked the academic-feminist project from the start.

During the last half-decade, Rubin's essay "The Traffic in Women: Notes on the 'Political Economy' of Sex" has been most readily available in Karen Hansen's and Ilene Philipson's 1990 anthology *Women, Class, and the Feminist Imagination,*[9] where it can be located in a section titled "The Past: Socialist-Feminist Classics." For fifteen years prior to the publication of Hansen's and Philipson's volume, the essay's home was in Rayna Rapp Reiter's *Toward an Anthropology of Women*—a groundbreaking 1976 collection that by now is itself habitually referred to as a classic.[10] Before that, in 1974, a version of the essay appeared in *Dissemination,* an Ann Arbor journal described by Rubin as "obscure." Finally, in its earliest incarnations, it served as a 1972 honors thesis in women's studies at the University of Michigan, a project that grew out of a group-authored assignment for an undergraduate anthropology course Rubin had taken two years earlier. In fact, as Rubin recently explained in a published interview with Judith Butler, the essay began as an *appendix* to that undergraduate assignment, separated from the main text because, as Rubin recalls it, one of her classmates "was reluctant to include this wild stuff in the body of the paper."[11]

I make my way backward down the swerving bibliographical trajectory of "The Traffic in Women"—tracking the essay through its "classic," vanguard, "obscure," and "wild" incarnations—because the print history of the essay evokes in miniature so many of the difficulties encompassed in the task of remembering women's studies. On one hand, among many academic feminists (both those who worked to invent the field, and those who came along some time later, when the field had achieved a measure of institutional stability), there is a palpable ambivalence toward some of the purported methodological vulgarities of second-wave intellectual production; even when second-wave texts are treated respectfully, it is often a respect of the most tentative, qualified kind. Writing specifically about "The Traffic in Women" in 1991, Miller noted, slightly abashed, how in those earlier days she "found it hard to resist the appeal of the monolith"—that is, the monolithic category of "Women" identified in Rubin's title.[12] And Rubin herself, recalling in 1994 the global, transhistorical logic that fueled her analysis of kinship and the exchange of women in the "Traffic" essay, claims that, at the time, there was still a kind of naive tendency to make general statements about the human condition that most people, including me, would now try to avoid. When you read Lévi-Strauss or Lacan, they make pretty grandiose generalizations. Plus they never hesitate to call something *the* theory of this and *the* theory of that. . . . By the time I wrote 'Thinking Sex,' I wanted to make more modest claims. ("ST" 88)

And more recently, in 1999, Robyn Wiegman mapped out a series of powerful strategies for "enabl[ing] feminism to think beyond a solo gender paradigm *that has never been comprehensive enough.*"[13]

On the other hand, however—and again, this is the case for feminists from both sides of what tends to be configured as a "generational" divide—the 1970s are at least as often construed as a kind of golden age, when feminist commentary was provocative, uninhibited, at times distinctly glamorous. Thus, for example, we have Sandra Gilbert's 1998 essay "What Ails Feminist Criticism," which posited a series of "Edenic scenes . . . the story of feminist criticism in the paradise of a roused, indeed 'raised,' consciousness."[14] Or again, we have the October 1993 special issue of the *Voice Literary Supplement,* titled "The Waves: Feminists Ride Again," which was largely composed of celebrations of second-wave icons—Shulamith Firestone, Valerie Solanis, Erica Jong—from the perspective of a newly constituted third wave.[15]

I list these examples partly in order to illustrate the extent to which historiographical habits of mind tend to resist being categorized according to institutional "generations." More broadly, however, what I am looking for is a way of thinking through the difficulties of earlier forms of academic feminism in a late-nineties academic context, a problem that seems to me to be summed up neatly in the tentative opening phrase of Barbara Christian's recent memoir of her own intellectual coming-of-age: "If memory serves me right."[16] Most of all, I am seeking a retrospective position that is located somewhere between self-conscious disavowal and celebratory reimagining.

In "The Traffic in Women," Rubin lay the groundwork for a number of theoretical discussions that have continued up to the present time: particularly, what she calls her "refinement" of the notion of the "sex/gender system" ("TW" 76), but more generally, her against-the-grain readings of old-school social-scientific and psychoanalytic arguments about the function of female social subordination in the production of culture. Apart from the manifest theoretical content of Rubin's discussion, however, it is also possible to locate in her essay a variety of what McDowell

has called "strategies of emplotment" ("T" 94).[17] The most obvious emplotment—and the one most clearly responsible for the essay's "classic"
status—is Rubin's slow, dramatic spinning out of a feminist interpretive
method. Rubin locates crucial points of contact among a range of texts
by Lévi-Strauss and Freud—both of whom present some version, albeit a
version riddled with antifeminist presuppositions, of her broader argument about the "traffic in women" as a process or practice that enables
the consolidation of culture. Rubin describes her interpretive method,
early in the essay, as an "exigetical" undertaking; she then provides a
dictionary definition of "exegesis" as "'critical explanation or analysis;
especially, interpretation of the Scriptures'" ("TW" 75) and characterizes
her own readings, in her own words, as "freely interpretive" ("TW" 75).
(Thus, for example, psychoanalysis is transformed by Rubin from "an intricate rationalization of sex roles as they are" into "a feminist theory
manqué" ["TW" 89].) What is in many respects most compelling for contemporary readers of the essay is Rubin's painstaking early enactment of
a particular interpretive strategy that in future years would come to seem
inevitable—so much so that the extent of its utility is now being called
into question by some of its own major practitioners, including Rubin
herself.[18]

What Rubin's "exigetical" inventiveness helps to underscore is one of
the essay's slightly less obvious emplotments: the story of the transformation of scholarship on women from renegade activity into academic field.
In her opening paragraph, for example, Rubin notes that "[t]he literature
on women—both feminist and antifeminist—is a long rumination on the
question of the nature and genesis of women's oppression and social
subordination" ("TW" 74). She then goes on to present a corrosively iron-
ical list of hypotheticals, in which she proposes possible causes of wom-
en's subordination, along with their possible practical solutions. Thus,
she proposes modestly that "if innate male aggression and dominance are
at the root of female oppression, then the feminist program would logically require either the extermination of the offending sex or else a eu-
genics project to modify its character" ("TW" 74). What Rubin enacts in
this passage is a turning away from the chimerical search for first causes
and practical remedies, and toward what she calls an "alternative explanation" ("TW" 75), and, finally, more profoundly, what (toward the end of
the essay) she calls a "theory" ("TW" 100).

Cultural historian Deborah Gordon, in a vivid and insightful recent
essay that maps the methodological transition from an "anthropology of
women" to a "feminist ethnography," locates Rayna Rapp Reiter's anthol-

ogy, and more specifically Rubin's essay, at a historical pivot point when "the polemic edge" of earlier work on the "anthropology of women" became blunted.[19] Indeed, it is important to note that Rubin's essay concludes not with a turn toward political action, but instead with a turn toward further interdisciplinary work in the field that she has helped to open. "Eventually," Rubin writes in her final paragraph, "someone will have to write a new version of *The Origin of the Family, Private Property, and the State,* recognizing the mutual interdependence of sexuality, economics, and politics without underestimating the full significance of each in human society" ("TW" 107).

In a 1994 interview published in the journal *differences,* Rubin noted that in 1972 she was the very first women's studies major at the University of Michigan, where she patched together her coursework under the rubric of an independent honors major rather than from offerings set out in a stable, coherent curriculum. These days, of course, Michigan grants undergraduate and graduate degrees in the field, and Rubin's agenda-setting essay has been memorialized by Hansen, Philipson, and others as part of a canonical "Past." As such, it is tempting to read in the essay— not only in its contents, but also in its print history—a strategic emplotment of the transformation of a "wild," unruly "women's studies" into a more "refine[d]" and "modest" academic practice of feminist theory. I want, however, to resist that reading, despite the fact that (as Gordon has lucidly demonstrated) there is much in the textual and institutional records to support it, or some version of it. What troubles me, however, is the way in which such a reading reinforces a number of the interpretive polarities that in recent years have both enabled and limited cultural criticism of academic feminism's own past: authenticity versus demystification; empiricism versus theory; oppositional political engagement versus scrupulous self-interrogation; complicity versus resistance; the "monolith" versus the multiple. I want to suggest, instead, an alternative emplotment of "The Traffic in Women," and then, via a reading of some of June Jordan's contemporaneous work, to conclude by thinking through some of the problems entailed within that alternative.

The final sentence of Rubin's essay, as I have noted, proposes the necessity of a scholarly practice that works its way between and among a range of interpretive protocols: Marxism, psychoanalysis, anthropology, and what was then the nascent field of feminist theory. What Rubin suggests in these final remarks, as I have argued elsewhere with different emphasis, is that the problem of women's studies is largely a problem of *affiliation*—a problem that has to do with the intellectual formations to which one is attached, whether consensually or not.[20] The history of the composition of "The Traffic in Women" as an independent honors thesis written for a self-generated major comprises a vividly illustrative example of this. Rubin—working her way between and among departments and programs, making up a method as she went along—developed an improvisatory intellectual practice that dramatized the necessarily varied affinities and split affiliations that characterized so many of the early texts of feminist scholarship; in a late variant of Maya Deren's interstitial practice, Rubin dramatized her shifting but inevitable position between.

It is thus difficult to ignore the resemblance between her own activity—as a woman circulating among a range of distinct male-governed formations—and the forms of female "traffic" that she describes throughout her essay. Moreover, it is hard to imagine that Rubin—a reader so energetic in her pursuit of other theorists' blind spots—could herself have been blind to the distinctly local significance of her commentary. She makes this point herself, in fact, in a short stretch of remarks wherein she briefly abandons her habit of listing examples drawn from the anthropological literature and turns instead to her own, more immediate surroundings. She writes: "[I]f men have been sexual subjects—exchangers—and women sexual semi-objects—gifts—for much of human history, then many customs, clichés, and personality traits seem to make a great deal of sense (among others, the curious custom by which a father gives away the bride)" ("TW" 87). The gesture that Rubin makes here—her sudden shift from distant to local example—comprises an instance of what Clifford Geertz has described as textual "self-nativising"; this, according to Geertz, is a process of "juxtapos[ing] the all-too-familiar and the wildly exotic in such a way that they change places."[21] (Here it is useful to recall Rubin's 1994 remark about the mass of "wild stuff" that constituted the first version of "Traffic," which was banished to the appendices of her group-authored term paper.) The culture of the observer, as such, becomes the culture under observation.

"The Traffic in Women" masks its own self-reflexiveness behind a form of feminist universalism that Rubin, as I noted earlier in this essay, has since denounced. So her essay itself needs to be read exigetically—not as a "general statemen[t] about the human condition," but instead as a more narrowly focused meditation upon the conditions of its own composition. What remains to be examined, however, are certain other blind spots that I have not yet mentioned, and that are somewhat more resistant to the sorts of reading processes that I have thus far enacted.

For Geertz's phrase—"self-nativising"—begs a number of questions about the oft-remarked tendency among white feminist commentators during the seventies to describe their own social subordination by means of reductive analogies to the subordination of men and women of color. (Indeed, it should be noted here that some of the most compelling feminist cultural histories of the early 1970s to be produced in recent years look closely at the dynamics of cross-racial masquerade.)[22] Rubin, of course, fills her essay with global litanies of parallel forms of the subordination of women, noting their "endless variety and monotonous similarity, cross-culturally and throughout history" ("TW" 76). Perhaps more pointedly, Rubin makes a strategically crucial analogy, early in her essay, between Marx's commentary on the (male) "Negro slave" and her own analysis of the "domesticated woman." Rubin writes:

> Marx once asked "What is a Negro slave? A man of the black race. The one explanation is as good as the other. A Negro is a Negro. He only becomes a slave in certain relations. A cotton spinning jenny is a machine for spinning cotton. It becomes *capital* only in certain relations. Torn from these relationships it is no more capital than gold in itself is money or sugar is the price of sugar." One might paraphrase: What is a domesticated woman? A female of the species. The one explanation is as good as the other. A woman is a woman. She becomes a domestic, a wife, a chattel, a playboy bunny, a prostitute, or a human dictaphone only in certain relations. Torn from these relationships, she is no more the helpmate of man than gold in itself is money . . . and so on. What then are these relationships by which a female becomes an oppressed woman? ("TW" 75)

Notwithstanding the exigetical bravado displayed in this improvisation on a theme by Marx, Rubin here generates one of the more graphic examples in the literature of the second wave of the erasure of African American women from a discourse that posits race and gender as distinct, rather than overlapping categories (thus, the famous 1982 anthology title *All the Women Are White, All the Blacks Are Men, but Some of Us Are Brave*). This is notable enough in and of itself; however, what makes Rubin's gesture of exclusion all the more curious and complex is the fact that her essay, in its massively detailed presentation of data, is by no means an essay exclusively "about" white women; it purports, instead, to a more broadly cross-cultural scope.

In her more recent work, Rubin glosses these sorts of universalizing gestures and exclusionary analogies as the signs of more "naive" times. What would be more productive to consider, I think, would be the possibility that "Traffic" was itself shaped and determined in important ways by an anxious half-awareness of contemporaneous critical production by women of color, who in Rubin's essay are largely silenced by means of cross-cultural analogy, even as they serve everywhere as both empirical example and mirror image. Describing her exigetical technique, Rubin wrote that Freud and Lévi-Strauss "see neither the implications of what they are saying nor the implicit critique that their work can generate when subjected to a feminist eye" ("TW" 75). With scant need for paraphrase—only a shift of pronouns would be required—one might say much the same thing about Rubin around 1975. Indeed, to present-day readers (including Rubin herself), the essay is far too willing to generalize the global problematics of the "traffic in women"; in it, Rubin concentrates far more closely upon "sameness" than upon "variety." The essay maintains its resonance even now, however, as an elliptical commentary on the situation of feminist intellectuals in the American academy, attempting to do interdisciplinary work in a university context in which disciplinary boundaries were strictly maintained. Divided just as strictly then (as in many cases we remain) into tightly bounded categories of race and class and sexuality, feminist theorists also have much to learn from Rubin's essay by observing the dynamic of exclusion and incorporation that operates within it.

I have thus far treated Rubin's essay as a radiant dramatization of and metacommentary upon a pair of related historical circumstances: the interdiscursive negotiations performed by early students of women's studies as well as their veiled and often failed efforts to negotiate within the irreducibly diverse category of "women." While it would be tempting (and not unreasonable) to treat "Traffic" as unambiguous evidence of the monocultural exclusivity of much feminist commentary produced in the United States during the 1970s, I have tried as well to illustrate a slightly more complex dynamic at work in Rubin's essay: her staging of an encounter with Engels, Lévi-Strauss, Freud, and Lacan that is more profoundly an encounter with the quasi-fictional figure of the woman of color, who is both everywhere visible and nowhere audible in her essay.

My purpose is not by any means to rescue Rubin's mid-1970s universalism for readers in the present by pointing up its hidden complexities. It is, instead, to point up the ways in which the apparently monolithic "woman" of 1970s white-feminist commentary was herself split and divided, and to suggest how terse repudiations of the "naive tendenc[ies]" of white feminists of that phase might themselves work to obscure a somewhat more dynamic and varied historical and textual record. For an assumption that undergirds virtually every contemporary narrativization of the recent past of academic feminism is that it was not until a half-decade later, with the publication of the monumental anthologies *This Bridge Called My Back: Writings by Radical Women of Color* (1981) and *But Some of Us Are Brave* (1982), that feminists of color finally began to interrogate the unexamined whiteness of academic feminism, thereby propelling feminist scholarship into its next, more heterogeneous phase. I have no argument with claims about the importance or the wide-ranging and salutary influence of these two anthologies. What troubles me, instead, are the "chronopolitics" (McDowell's term; "T" 99) at work within their late placement in the timeline of academic feminism. This is a remnant of the discredited "progress" narrative, which recalls in pointed ways Johannes Fabian's influential analyses of the temporal equivocations so often involved in the construction of cultural "others." [23] (Robyn Wiegman has forcefully made a related point, criticizing disciplinary histories that enact a shift of emphasis from "the intentions of women of color to speak for themselves to the effects of their discourse on white women" ["CR" 378].) For both *Bridge* and *But Some of Us Are Brave* are composed in part of work written during the prior decade; both, moreover, position themselves both as statements propelling a monolithic feminism into a more diverse future *and* as sourcebooks granting access to a richly varied feminist past—a past that is too often ignored, even in the most progressive recent commentaries. In the case of *But Some of Us Are Brave,* in fact, some of the most compelling published documents are a series of syllabi for courses on "The Black Woman" taught by black feminist scholars during the years leading up to the volume's publication; the bibliographical addenda track the development of a field over the course of nearly two decades. Nonetheless, the reception histories of both books have blunted their considerable retrospective force—a force that highlights the development over time of a range of feminisms of color, prior to the early 1980s—and have instead cast the books solely in prophetic, forward-looking roles. [24]

I will now turn to June Jordan's essay "On Richard Wright and Zora Neale Hurston: Notes Toward a Balancing of Love and Hatred," reading it (as before, exigetically) as a particular commentary on the institutional conditions evoked so vividly, if indirectly, by Rubin's essay. For if Rubin's essay is impelled, as I have argued, by its muted interaction with the spectral figure of the woman of color, then Jordan's is impelled by its interaction with an equally spectral feminism. The appearance of Rubin's honors thesis in 1974 in *Dissemination* coincided with another crucial event—albeit to cultural historians an only slightly less "obscure" one—in the development of academic feminism: the publication of the August 1974 number of *Black World*. The journal featured on its cover a Carl Van Vechten photograph of Zora Neale Hurston, a writer who at that point was familiar only to a scattered collection of people in the know: patrons of secondhand bookstores in Harlem; college students enrolled in courses on "The Black Woman"; a small, aging readership who recalled Hurston's books from the thirties; and, finally, a community of scholars credentialized in more traditional areas who had been engaged for some time, largely on their own time, in the process of inventing a black-feminist counterpart to the nascent fields of "black studies" and "women's studies." That issue of *Black World* contained a special section devoted to the topic of "Black Women Image Makers," including an important essay of the same title by Mary Helen Washington, commentaries by Ellease Southerland and June Jordan on Hurston's career and her critical reception, and a withering critique by Alvin Ramsey of the 1974 television adaptation of Ernest J. Gaines's novel *The Autobiography of Miss Jane Pittman.*

Barbara Christian has discussed the *Black World* special issue as a mid-1970s testament to "the growing visibility of Afro-American women and the significant impact they were having on contemporary black culture"[25] and has offered various reasons—in particular, the marginal "academic" status of *Black World*—for its relative obscurity in the recent scholarly record.[26] To Christian's lucid analysis, I would add that the language of "image mak[ing]" elicits embarrassment from many contemporary feminist scholars, hearkening back as it does to the early-1970s "images-of-women" methodologies that in recent years, as Gallop has demonstrated, have become touchstones in narratives of the "progress" of feminist analysis from vulgarity to refinement, from literal-minded opposition to more nuanced theoretical engagement. It would be possible to argue, as such, that the white-feminist turn toward "theory" exemplified by Rubin's essay coincided with a more empirically grounded series of intellectual labors performed by African American feminist commentators; thus, as some cultural historians have recently suggested, we can observe the implicit racism of a "progress" narrative that continually characterizes the methodological emphases of black feminist critics as retrograde.[27] The "challenge," as Deborah McDowell has put it, is to create a "counter history," one that "resist[s] the theory/practice dichotomy" rather than consolidating it ("T" 103).

Neither Washington's nor the other contributors' commentaries on the deployment of the "image," in fact, can be fairly characterized as static, formulaic, essentialized complaints about the dangers of negative images—as "images-of-women" criticism now tends commonly to be understood. In fact, a highly complex metacommentary on the problems and processes of representation begins to spin itself out as early as the issue's cover, where Van Vechten, who was white Manhattan's semiofficial tour guide to the Harlem Renaissance, frames Hurston for the viewer's consumption, only to be answered in the pages of the journal by Washington's argument that African American women "have myth- and image-makers of our own who have done their job well,"[28] and whose work Washington proceeds to subject to strenuous, subtle analysis. June Jordan's article, on Hurston and Richard Wright, opens with two drawings: a delicately pretty, vaguely impressionistic Hurston juxtaposed with a severe, near-photographic Wright. The argument of Jordan's essay, by sharp contrast to the illustrations, comprises an effort to dismantle the conventional critical opposition between "affirmation" and "protest" that had theretofore dominated the critical reception of both writers and that finds its ironic visual rhyme in the two portraits. Ellease Southerland's account of Hurston's life and career, finally, is illustrated by a curious, little-known photograph of Hurston standing next to a publisher's display booth sponsored by the Federal Writers' Project, which financed some of Hurston's field research in the southeastern United States.

The distance marked by these visual and verbal texts is the distance between Hurston as object and as agent, as an image made and as one who actively makes (and even markets) her own image; different versions of Hurston are throughout the journal set against each other and against the contexts through which they were originally articulated. Finally, and perhaps most crucially, these pages in certain respects map the past and future development of African American feminist literary theory and criticism: in Washington's, Jordan's, and Southerland's articles, the archival activity of recovering a forgotten past is situated within and against a broader philosophical problematic, wherein the terms through which African American women have conventionally been represented are placed in constant, tense negotiation with a long tradition of black women's self-representation. Hardly a clear-cut matter of correcting mistakes—of replacing bad, white-authored lies with good, black-authored truths—the articles in the *Black World* special section maintain a steady focus on the determining hierarchies of American color while also engaging in a dynamic negotiation between archival and textualist, empirical and philosophical, methods.

One of the clearest and most complex enactments of this dynamic transpires in the course of Jordan's "Notes Toward a Balancing of Love and Hatred." Jordan's broad subject is the way in which the idea of "black art" was then being deployed within the American mass media; her preliminary argument is that Richard Wright's literary celebrity resulted in the erasure of Hurston's, an enactment of what she calls the "choose-between games" of African American literary fame, wherein—as the now-familiar argument goes—only one celebrity at a time is allowed to emerge into view. Jordan writes: "[W]e would do well to carefully reconsider these two, Hurston and Wright: perhaps that will let us understand the cleavage in their public reception and prevent such inequity and virtual erasure from taking place, again."[29] This "cleavage" she defines as an unnecessary polarization of their writing practice into two different tendencies: "affirmation," exemplified by Hurston, and "protest," exemplified by Wright. Jordan continues:

> *Native Son* (undoubtedly Wright's most influential book) conforms to white standards we have swallowed regarding literary weight: It is apparently symbolic(rather than realistic), "serious" (unrelievedly grim), socio-political (rather than "personal") in its scale, and not so much "emotional" as impassioned in its deliberate execution. ("ORW" 6)

On the whole, Jordan's argument is a plea for black multiplicity; she consolidates her position by demonstrating how Hurston's *Their Eyes Were Watching God* can itself be considered a species of "protest" novel, while *Native Son* carries within it its own brand of affirmation: according to Jordan's protodeconstructive formulation, Wright's novel "emphasizes the negative trajectories of that same [Hurstonian] want, hope and confrontation" ("ORW" 7).

These "negative trajectories" demonstrate the way in which Hurston's career takes shape in the blind spots generated by Wright's. What is an equally insistent "negative trajector[y]" within Jordan's own argument, however, is her frequent refusal to cast her argument in explicitly gendered terms. The "realistic," the "'personal,'" the "'emotional,'" the "affirmati[ve]": while all of these terms of critical disapprobation leveled against Hurston by the "mass media" are implicitly gendered, Jordan only intermittently makes this explicit. Instead, they tend to be cast by Jordan in terms of racial rather than racial-and-gendered problematics; they are symptoms of "plain craziness, plain white craziness we do not need even to discuss" ("ORW" 7).

Her article accrues its black-feminist force in large part by means of its placement next to Washington's very different essay, "Black Women Image Makers," which is much more direct than Jordan's in the gendering of its argumentative terms. What slowly emerges into view—in the course of the implicit dialogue between Jordan's essay and Washington's—is the interdiscursive formation of black feminist studies, working its way between women's studies and black studies and creating something different than the simple sum of its parts.[30] Hurston's work, according to Jordan, was "assessed [by critics] as sui generis, or idiosyncratic accomplishment of no lasting reverberation or usefulness" ("ORW" 7). Through Jordan's argument, the "sui generis" is recast, in more positive, productive terms, as an activity transpiring between discursive formations, as black feminist scholarship up to that point had in fact done.

Jordan's engagement with the problematics of gender takes the form of a "negative" argumentative "trajectory," due in part to her effort to dodge what she calls "the glare of white, mass-media manipulation" ("ORW" 4)—a turning away from whiteness and toward the rich diversities within blackness. Rubin's turn toward blackness, on the other hand, demonstrates the way in which anxieties over contemporaneous scholarly production by women of color exerted a determining if largely implicit effect upon early versions of white-feminist theoretical technique. These sorts of blurrings and ambiguities go a long way toward helping us to complicate the all-too-common notion that academic feminisms produced by women of color in the late 1970s and early 1980s constituted a belated response to the exclusions that were everywhere apparent within the now-"classic" texts of women's studies. Risking what is no doubt far too neat a formulation, I would further suggest—however provisionally—that these ambiguities might also enable us to resequence the chronology that undergirds this narrative: to see it, for the moment, the other way around, so that women's studies in its most widely known early forms begins to look more and more like the belated response of white commentators to challenges posed by women of color. In fact, by returning to my own point of departure, Maya Deren's *Divine Horsemen,* it is possible to see how processes similar to these were already being enacted, well before the invention of academic feminism as we now know it. For Deren's negotiations between the conventions of commercial and documentary film took shape in a process of her own immersion within Afro-Caribbean cultural forms, a project inspired by Deren's earlier work as an assistant to black choreographer-anthropologist Katherine Dunham, whose Haitian field research preceded Deren's by over a decade.

By foregrounding the problem of betweenness as a constituent of feminist intellectual activity—in the recent past *and* in the present—I have attempted to work my way around and (at times, of necessity) within the argumentative polarities that have governed many recent analyses of feminism's own recent past. What I finally have tried to accomplish with these neoexigetical readings of Rubin's and Jordan's essays, however, is not to enact a simple reversal of temporal priority, one that locates the woman of color at the point of feminist origin, but instead to develop an interpretive stance that enables an acknowledgment of the complexities *and* the reductivenesses of a diverse range of feminist writing that emerged during the early 1970s and before. Robyn Wiegman's 1999 call for "intersectional analysis" that "cit[es] the *multiple* histories of struggle by, for, and among women as necessary to the vitality of feminist critique" is very much to the point here ("CR" 370; emphasis added). And Rubin's contributor's note in the Reiter anthology is instructive as well: there, Rubin described herself as living in Ann Arbor, where, as she put it in 1976, she had already "survived many incarnations of feminist politics."[31] What matters here, I think, is that feminism not only affiliates itself in multiple ways; it is also itself multiple, and has been for some time.

Finally, to return to the broader questions posed by this present anthology: the tensions currently being generated within feminist studies by the opposition between "philosophy" and "cultural studies" might usefully be read as a revised form of Gayatri Spivak's mid-1980s arguments (made most influentially in her now-canonical essay "Can the Subaltern Speak?") about the relative utility of Derridean and Foucauldian analysis. In that essay, Spivak decried the "received idea" that "Foucault deals with real history, real politics, and real social problems [while] Derrida is inaccessible, esoteric, and textualistic."[32] Her criticisms of Foucault as well as her defense of deconstruction were located well beyond the limits of this specious opposition and were set within the context of Spivak's carefully calibrated performance of her own institutional situatedness and unsituatedness. Spivak's arguments might in turn be read as a recalibration of earlier debates—to some extent audible in both Rubin's and Jordan's essays—over whether "theory" was a useful complement to the practice of historical recovery that guided so much second-wave feminist scholarship; as I have shown in each case, however, neither Rubin's essay nor Jordan's can be made to conform comfortably with a historiographical scheme that (in Spivak's terms) seeks to divide "real history, real politics, and real social problems" from the "inaccessible," the "esoteric," and the "textualistic."

In the present moment, as such, we are witnessing the reemergence of a constant within academic-feminist debate, one that reconstitutes itself every few years, each time with a slightly different terminological or methodological tonality. I have attempted to show how by accepting the terms of this opposition, we simplify not only the intertwined significances of its constituent parts but also the history of academic feminism itself. What differentiates the present form of this conflict from those of the past, however, is the fact that its constituent parts can no longer be clearly encoded in the language of critical approaches, of methodological tendencies, or (perhaps especially) of proper names. Instead, "philosophy" and "cultural studies" are full-blown institutional operations, complete with departmental (or programmatic) status, faculty lines, complex infrastructures, and dozens of bewildered students waiting in the halls to meet with their advisors. With the shrinking availability of curriculum development funds at most American colleges and universities—and with an expanding tool kit of increasingly brutal strategies for enhancing academic institutional efficiency—the stakes of these old debates have once again changed. It is with some urgency, therefore, that we need to think hard about defining a series of productively conflictual spaces between philosophy and cultural studies, a process that can only be undertaken if we are willing to look hard at the mechanisms that have worked to keep them divided in the first place. The problems entailed in remembering women's studies provide a cautionary tale. By learning to reread the complicated interdiscursive negotiations performed by women like Rubin and Jordan, however, we might also be able to generate other models, other possibilities, for rereading the past, the present, and the future.

Notes

This essay began as a paper delivered in spring 1996 at the American Comparative Literature Association conference, whose topic was "Literature between Philosophy and Cultural Studies." My goal there was to transpose to the contemporary moment a series of arguments that I had made about modernism in my book *Women Intellectuals, Modernism, and Difference: Transatlantic Culture, 1919-1945* (Cambridge: Cambridge University Press,

1997). In its present form, the essay extends the book's claims about the institutional "emplotments" of Gayle Rubin's mid-1970s work by looking at Rubin's racial self-construction in "The Traffic in Women" and by juxtaposing her work to contemporaneous writing by June Jordan (see *Women Intellectuals* 27-29). Since 1996 the essay has benefited (in direct and in indirect ways) from the intellectual generosity and sympathetic criticism of many friends and readers, among whom I would like especially to thank Kathleen Biddick, Barbara Green, Janet Lyon, and the editors of the present volume.

    1.   Maya Deren, *Divine Horsemen: The Living Gods of Haiti* (1953; Kingston, N.Y.: Documentext, 1970), 5.

    2.   See Maya Deren, *Divine Horsemen: The Living Gods of Haiti* (1985), ed. Teiji and Cherel Ito (Cooper Station, N.Y.: Mystic Fire Video, 1990).

    3.   For a range of opinions on the problem of disciplinary naming, see the 1998 special issue of *differences* (9, no. 3) entitled "Women's Studies on the Edge."

    4.   Nancy K. Miller, "Decades," in *Changing Subjects: The Making of Feminist Literary Criticism,* ed. Gayle Greene and Coppélia Kahn (New York: Routledge, 1993), 42.

    5.   Deborah McDowell, "Transferences: Black Feminist Discourse: The 'Practice' of 'Theory,'" in *Feminism Beside Itself,* ed. Diane Elam and Robyn Wiegman (New York: Routledge, 1995), 94. Hereafter cited as "T."

    6.   For example, McDowell's aforementioned "Transferences" takes up the problematical definition of "theory" by examining how, as she puts it, "theory has been reduced to a very particular practice" that tends to result in the "exclu[sion]" of "black women and other critics of color . . . from the category of theory" (105). Elsewhere, in a charged exchange published as "More Gender Trouble: Feminism Meets Queer Theory" in a 1994 special issue of *differences* (6, nos. 2-3 [Summer-Fall 1994]), Elizabeth Grosz and Teresa de Lauretis debated the continuing utility of psychoanalysis to feminist and lesbian analysis. There, Grosz put the following question to de Lauretis:

> Is [feminist theory] a reading practice, a practice of interpreting patriarchal texts differently, affirming the capacity of every text (however phallocentric or patriarchal it may be) to be read otherwise? Or is it a practice of the production of alternative or different knowledges, whose goal may be either the production or revelation of 'new' objects using given investigative procedures or the development of different methodological procedures?

See Grosz, "The Labors of Love, Analyzing Perverse Desire: An Interrogation of Teresa de Lauretis's *The Practice of Love,*" *differences* 6, nos. 2-3 (Summer-Fall 1994): 275.

    7.   For example, see Judith Butler's interview with Gayle Rubin, "Sexual Traffic," *differences* 6, nos. 2-3 (Summer-Fall 1994): 91-93. Hereafter cited

as "ST." And in a back-cover blurb accompanying *Women Writing Culture,* ed. Ruth Behar and Deborah Gordon (Berkeley: University of California Press, 1996), Donna Haraway praises the volume for its empirical richness.

8.   Jane Gallop, *Around 1981: Academic Feminist Literary Theory* (New York: Routledge, 1992), 81.

9.   Gayle Rubin, "The Traffic in Women: Notes on the 'Political Economy' of Sex" (1975), in *Women, Class, and the Feminist Imagination: A Socialist-Feminist Reader,* ed. Karen V. Hansen and Ilene J. Philipson (Philadelphia: Temple University Press, 1991), 74–113. Quotations from the essay will be taken from this edition, hereafter cited as "TW."

10.   *Toward an Anthropology of Women,* ed. Rayna R. Reiter (New York and London: Monthly Review Press, 1976).

11.   My account of the essay's bibliographical history derives from Rubin's comments in "ST" 65.

12.   Nancy K. Miller, *Getting Personal: Feminist Occasions and Other Autobiographical Acts* (New York: Routledge, 1991), 125.

13.   Robyn Wiegman, "Critical Response: What Ails Feminist Criticism? A Second Opinion," *Critical Inquiry* 25 (Winter 1999): 376; emphasis added. Hereafter cited as "CR."

14.   Susan Gubar, "What Ails Feminist Criticism?" *Critical Inquiry* 24 (Summer 1998): 881.

15.   *Voice Literary Supplement* (October 1993). For a related case, see also the fashion layout "Free Angela," published in *Vibe* (March 1994): 52–59, which featured actress Cynda Williams in a series of reenactments of early-1970s photographs of Angela Davis; and Davis's response, "Afro Images: Politics, Fashion, and Nostalgia," *Critical Inquiry* 21 (Autumn 1994): 27–45.

16.   Barbara Christian, "Being the Subject and the Object: Reading African American Women's Novels," in *Changing Subjects,* 195.

17.   I use McDowell's terms here because they bear so closely on the subject at hand, but it's important to note that McDowell, in this context, is writing about explicit historical accounts of the history of academic feminism; Rubin's historiographical nuances, as I argue, are for the most part implicit. At least as pertinent here are James Clifford's comments on allegorical "emplotments" that disclose themselves in classic texts from the anthropological tradition. See Clifford, "On Ethnographic Allegory," in *The Predicament of Culture: Twentieth-Century Ethnography, Literature, and Art* (Cambridge, Mass.: Harvard University Press, 1988), 99.

18.   To trace the shifts in Rubin's own position, see "TW" 75: "[Freud and Lévi-Strauss] see neither the implications of what they are saying nor the implicit critique that their work can generate when subjected to a feminist eye." For her later reexamination of the "exigetical" method, see "Sexual Traffic" 92:

> I know this is a completely heretical opinion, but it is often
> more difficult to assemble, assimilate, understand, orga-

nize, and present original data than it is to work over a group of canonical texts which have been, by now, cultivated for so long by so many that they are already largely digested. There is plenty of "theory" in the best empirical studies, even if such studies often fail to cite the latest list of twenty-five essential authorizing or legitimizing "theorists."

19.   Deborah A. Gordon, "Conclusion: Culture Writing Women: Inscribing Feminist Ethnography," in *Women Writing Culture,* ed. Ruth Behar and Deborah A. Gordon (Berkeley: University of California Press, 1996), 435.

20.   See Gambrell, *Women Intellectuals, Modernism, and Difference,* 27–31.

21.   Clifford Geertz, "Us/Not-Us: Benedict's Travels," in *Works and Lives: The Anthropologist as Author* (Stanford: Stanford University Press, 1988), 106–7.

22.   For example, see Alice Echols, *Scars of Sweet Paradise: The Life and Times of Janis Joplin* (New York: Metropolitan Books, 1999). For a distinct but related discussion, see Tania Modleski, "The White Negress and the Heavy-Duty Dyke," in *Old Wives' Tales and Other Women's Stories* (New York: New York University Press, 1998), 80–100.

23.   McDowell's use of the term "chronopolitics," in fact, echoes Johannes Fabian's in *Time and the Other: How Anthropology Makes its Object* (New York: Columbia University Press, 1983), 144. Fabian's discussion of the temporal manipulations undergirding anthropological constructions of the "other," moreover, is further pertinent to our subject matter here. Thus, for example, Jane Gallop's richly ironized discussion of the so-called "primitive" moment of second-wave "images of women" criticism — "a heroic, simpler time," as Gallop puts it, "when we were bold but crude" — might be elaborated by means of Fabian's and McDowell's chronopolitical arguments. See Jane Gallop, "Writing about Ourselves," in *Around 1981,* 79.

24.   Two major recent anthologies should take us some distance toward ameliorating this situation: *Words of Fire: An Anthology of African-American Feminist Thought,* ed. Beverly Guy-Sheftall (New York: New Press, 1995), and *Chicana Feminist Thought: The Basic Historical Writings,* ed. Alma M. García (New York: Routledge, 1997).

25.   Barbara Christian, "But What Do We Think We're Doing Anyway: The State of Black Feminist Criticism(s) or My Version of a Little Bit of History," in *Changing Our Own Words: Essays on Criticism, Theory, and Writing by Black Women,* ed. Cheryl A. Wall (New Brunswick, N.J.: Rutgers University Press, 1989), 59.

26.   Two recent book-length studies of Hurston, though near-exhaustive in their research, fail to mention the *Black World* texts. Besides Christian's analysis, a rare prominent reference to them can be found in Ann duCille's

"The Occult of True Black Womanhood" (1994), reprinted in *Skin Trade* (Cambridge, Mass.: Harvard University Press, 1996).

27.   See Valerie Smith, "Black Feminist Theory and the Representation of the 'Other,'" in *Changing Our Own Words,* 40–41, and McDowell, "T" 104.

28.   Mary Helen Washington, "Black Women Image Makers," *Black World* (August 1974): 18.

29.   June Jordan, "On Richard Wright and Zora Neale Hurston: Notes on a Balancing of Love and Hatred," *Black World* (August 1974): 5. Hereafter cited as "ORW."

30.   Christian, in "But What Do We Think We're Doing Anyway," offers a broader context, arguing that "the conjuncture of the black arts movement and the women's movement" (61) created the conditions of possibility for the publication of the *Black World* special issue.

31.   Reiter, *Toward an Anthropology of Women,* 8.

32.   Gayatri Chakravorty Spivak, "Can the Subaltern Speak?" in *Marxism and the Interpretation of Culture,* ed. Cary Nelson and Lawrence Grossberg (Urbana: University of Illinois Press, 1988), 291.

The Dissolute Feminisms of Kathy Acker

Marilyn Manners

Near the beginning of Kathy Acker's 1993 novel *My Mother: Demonology,* an unidentified narrator says: "Most of my life, but not all, I've been dissolute. According to nineteenth-century cliché, dissoluteness and debauchery are connected to art."[1] This introductory revelation might serve as an ironic emblem for Acker's writing: it voices self-recrimination from an indeterminate source; it qualifies an already qualified assertion ("Most . . . but not all"); its many meanings bleed out into relations among text, writer, and reader. In one direction, the statement acknowledges some readers'—including feminist readers'—adverse reactions to Acker's "dissolute" inscription of pornographic sex scenes; in another direction, it self-reflexively suggests Acker's own disdain for and brutal destruction of nineteenth-century aesthetic "clichés," particularly, although not exclusively, what she calls "bourgeois linear narrative."[2] Further, there is no guarantee that these apt words are even Acker's own: her dissolution, in many senses, extends to rampant plagiarism of other texts—ranging from formulaic porn to Artaud to Kristeva. Such "debauchery," both textual and sexual, has been part of Acker's writing from its beginnings. It need not be seen, however—as it sometimes has been—simply as a corrosive, destructive, or even deconstructive enterprise (although it has been that too); nor can this dissoluteness be attributed to derivative, superficial, or banal writing (even, or especially, when her writing is most self-consciously derivative, superficial, or banal). Rather, Acker's "dissolute-ness and debauchery are connected to art" indeed. More than a simple strategy, Acker's dissolute writing is both a form of epistemology and a poetics.

Although Acker described her early work as a process of deconstruction, she spoke later about how she "started thinking about constructing rather than destructing-deconstructing-destructing"[3] in her writing. She also began to look to and incorporate classical Western myth, a revisionary practice which has itself become a traditional feature of feminist writing. Such interests on her part should not, however, have led anyone to anticipate a turn to convention, in any sense: Acker's writing—early and late, in deconstructive or constructive modes—remains as distant from probity or utopian feminist visions as from traditional linear narrative or character construction. In fact, Acker's renewed interest in myth provides an apt example of her writing's improper confusion, and profusion, of categories of all sorts. Although Acker studied as a classicist, and although she incorporates stories of Antigone and Andromeda, for instance, in her novels, her references to myth-making and her revision of Greek female figures bear little resemblance to other feminists' rewriting of classical Western mythology; instead, her reconstruction of these myths remains thoroughly dissolute. Acker's idea of myth encompasses using "non-accessible . . . [o]r not readily accessible language" (*2GZ* 3), such as the languages of dreaming and sex. She has explained that she's "just very interested in trying to access what goes through the mind say as you go through orgasm. And it wouldn't even make sense to say one could deconstruct that" (*2GZ* 3). Her writing, that is, traverses the troubled intersection between language and body, while eschewing visions of a pre- or extralinguistic body, or of a corporeally saturated feminine language. Yet Acker's writing has also regularly transgressed a perhaps even more well-regulated border, that between philosophical thought or theory (including feminist thought) and popular culture.

When Acker deploys mythological female figures, therefore, the graffiti-covered halls they roam are not likely to be those of Pompeii. Indeed, when Acker participates in immediately recognizable feminist discourses (as opposed to her use of pornography or her emphasis on passive female characters, which have taken many much longer to "read" as feminist), a mixture of "high" and "low" culture often characterizes her particular contribution. Whereas Cixous conceptualizes an emblematically beautiful and laughing Medusa, for instance, or Irigaray employs Antigone's narrative to illustrate women's place as guardian of the blood and as the ground which supports male subjectivity,[4] Acker's Andromeda wanders through an abbey set up for performance art, while remembering an early REM video,[5] and her Antigone rides a motorcycle and says to Creon: "I left your lousy world. Only a fool will now attempt to stop us girls" (*PKP* 182).

Further, Antigone—although she is useful for Acker as one in a long series of incestual yet Oedipal-triangle-destroying women—is merely one voice, one name in her chorus of pirate girls. Acker's Antigone is introduced as follows:

> *Hegel, or the panopticon, sees all, except for the beginning of the world. In that beginning, which is still beginning, there is a young girl.*
>
> *Her name's not important. She's been called King Pussy, Pussycat, Ostracism, O, Ange. Once she was called Antigone. . . .* (*PKP* 163; Acker's emphasis)

It would be foolish to argue, however, that Acker's mythological revisions have nothing whatsoever to do with those of Cixous or Irigaray. Her "I left your lousy world" echoes Cixous's "Not another minute to lose. Let's get out of here" in "Laugh of the Medusa";[6] and Irigaray's essay "The Eternal Irony of the Community" addresses Hegel on the subject of Antigone, noting that in Sophocles' *Antigone* "the privilege of the proper name is not yet pure."[7] Irigaray writes in the same essay that "at times the forces of the world below become hostile because they have been denied the right to live in daylight. These forces rise up and threaten to lay waste the community" ("EIC" 225); this statement could serve to summarize the first part of Acker's novel *Pussy, King of the Pirates,* in which women set fire to their brothel, inciting revolution and destroying the city and its environs (*PKP* 44). There are, furthermore, constant references in late Acker novels to both flying and fluidity—tropes certainly familiar to readers of Cixous and Irigaray.[8]

The improper intermingling so characteristic of Acker's written texts exceeds textual bounds, moreover. Acker's readers must not only learn to negotiate with the (heterogeneous, morsellated, dissolving) bodies of those texts themselves (as well as the relentlessly deglamorized bodies described within them); they have also had to confront the (text-in-process) body of the writer herself. Before her untimely death, Acker's own body could also be read as "sext," as Cixous termed it in the 1970s ("LM" 255). In Acker's words, "It's the text. It's the body, it's the real body, which is language, the text."[9] This included Acker's own tattooed, bodybuilding, shaved and bleached, motorcycle-riding, and labia-pierced body, that is, a body similar to those in the illustrations on the inside front and back covers of *Pussy, King of the Pirates*—a rendering which complicates even further any question of where the dissolution of bodies and texts begins and ends.

Furthermore, unless Acker's readers distance themselves and refuse to take the trip, they must consider the textual relation of their own bodies: "If there's this distance between the reader and the text, the reader's just an observer. I want the reader to come right into the text because that's the only way you can take the journey. . . . I know how to make the reader at least come along on the journey and enter into the text."[10] Although perhaps a bit optimistic here about her ability to entice all her readers "to come right into the text," Acker often spoke in similarly spatial and corporeal terms when discussing relations among writer/text/reader. Her ideal reader, therefore, is not merely affected or infected but becomes another kind of body-worker. What Acker has had to say about the parallel work of writer and tattooist might be transposed to the work of the reader as well:

> The process of tattooing for him [Acker's tattooist] is learning about someone's body, which is learning about someone. He's not going in there to re-make the body in terms of some model that's outside that body. It's the difference between listening and making. When you listen to something you're not imposing your shtick on whatever you're making. For me, it's like writing, using other texts the way I do now. . . . To learn to work a text is partly to learn to listen. ("CKA1" 4)

Acker's characteristically dissolute feminism changed in manifestation but not in effect over the course of the last twenty years. If Acker's "pornography" and passive or victimized female characters baffled or offended some feminists, she herself found a good deal to criticize in much feminist writing of the time. Of British feminist writers, for instance, she charged that "[i]t's diary stuff and the diary doesn't go anywhere, and there's not enough work with language."[11] In contrast, Acker explained her own constantly transforming writing project at length, sometimes describing it as a series of theoretical problems (for example, of identity or of language and the body); she also rejected conventional narrative from the beginning: "I came out of the poetry world, not out of prose, so I wasn't concerned with the traditional narrative or even narrative at all. I wasn't interested in telling a story, where you make up one or two fictional characters and tell about their relation to the world."[12] As Acker became more accepted by feminist readers—and as a feminist writer— her dissolution of feminism's (often unacknowledged) borders continued unabated, although the contours of her project may have shifted to mocking Kristeva's orientalism, deflating Cixous's universalizing pretensions, or muddying Irigaray's sometimes rather pristine fluidity.

To argue for entangled complexities within more recent Acker texts is not, however, to suggest that Acker's early texts were simple, although they have nevertheless sometimes appeared so. In the case of two early Acker novels, *Kathy Goes to Haiti* (1978) and *Blood and Guts in High School* (1978; pub. 1984), relative simplicity seems in fact to have led to some of their more obvious—and in one instance, graphically blatant— aspects being strangely ignored. These texts provide, therefore, particularly useful test cases of how we might best "journey" through ("DM" 15) and "listen to" ("CKA1" 4) her dissolute textual bodies.

Blood and Guts in High School is one of the many Acker texts which some readers have found both fascinating and difficult to "listen to." This novel opens with a certain "Janey Smith" who is ten years old: "Never having known a mother, her mother had died when Janey was a year old, Janey depended on her father ["Johnny Smith"] for everything and regarded her father as boyfriend, brother, sister, money, amusement, and father."[13] The novel has three separate endings: in the first, "[s]he dies" (*BGHS* 140); the text of the second closes with "Shall we look for this wonderful book? Shall we stop being dead people? Shall we find our way out of all expectations?" (*BGHS* 147); and in the third, we read that "[s]oon many other Janeys were born and these Janeys covered the earth" (*BGHS* 165).

This novel's character- and narrative-mocking beginning and ending might in themselves alert a reader to the hazards of reading literally; as Karen Brennan puts it, Janey is constituted "as a fluid entity-voice (not really a character) in Acker's novel."[14] Indeed, *Blood and Guts* is an early but full-scale dismantling of both the literal and the literate: Acker undoes, through excessive repetition, both Oedipal triangulation and the unbearable banalities of heterosexual "romance" in a text that contains almost forty pages of illustrations (some embedded "narratives" in their own right), a section of Persian poems, and entire pages of "text" that un-write themselves:

All this, and more, has not dissuaded some readers from literal-minded sense-making (particularly regarding Janey's incestuous relationship and submissive behavior), even though the novel itself contains an emphatic warning about the dangers of representation very early on: "If the author here lends her 'culture' to the amorous subject, in exchange the amorous subject affords her the innocence of its image-repertoire, indifferent to the properties of knowledge. Indifferent to the properties of knowledge" (*BGHS* 28).[15] *Blood and Guts in High School* was in fact banned in Germany on grounds of literalism regarding both content and form, as Acker has explained:

> I kept wondering where's kindersex in the novel at first. That's between Janey and her father. They didn't get it that it was a double play. They thought it was real. They took everything absolutely literally. Janey has sex with her father, that's kindersex. Then there's S/M, which is probably the most correct thing they came up with. . . . And then there's experimentality. ("DM" 19)

More perplexing, however, are readings which do not in the least insist on the literal, and which indeed perform exquisitely complex bodywork overall, but which nonetheless make an oddly selective "journey" through *Blood and Guts in High School*. In the course of several pages of discussion on drawings included in the novel, Karen Brennan carefully analyzes two of Acker's drawings of penises ("GE" 255–60; *BGHS* 8 and 14), and Gabrielle Dane, although in less detail, also refers to Acker's penis drawings as well as to "ODE TO A GRECIAN URN" (*BGHS* 63),[16] a sketch of a headless, bound, female body. What seems surprising, however, is that neither mentions, even in passing, two proximate, full-page drawings of female genitalia, "My cunt red ugh" (*BGHS* 19) and "GIRLS WILL DO ANYTHING FOR LOVE" (*BGHS* 62)—the latter in fact a facing-page of "ODE TO A GRECIAN URN." Even more strikingly, both essays nonetheless directly discuss issues which evoke their own omissions, as they call attention to "Acker's (scandalous) feminist aesthetic" ("HFP" 251), "try[ing] to express that for which no ready words exist" ("HFP" 248), "attempts to represent—textualize—the unpresentable" ("GE" 261), and Janey's "very disappearance from Acker's pages" ("GE" 250). Such incongruous neglect brings rather sharply to mind the continued relevance of Irigaray's exposure of "the non-visible, therefore not theorizable nature of woman's sex and pleasure" (*S* 139). Perhaps, as Kathleen Hulley has noted in a different context, "CUNTS made visible are blinding" indeed.[17]

Kathy Goes to Haiti evokes additional "blind spots" in feminist and gender-attentive readings of Acker. In *Kathy Goes to Haiti*, narrative development and character construction are much more conventional than is usually the case in Acker's work: Acker's protagonist Kathy remains Kathy throughout, without the vertiginous slippage into other personae and points of view so typical of Acker's other novels; the plot is also extraordinarily straightforward—with only a few stream-of-consciousness digressions and jarring leaps in continuity. Acker has explained that she wrote *Kathy Goes to Haiti* specifically as

> a parody of a porn novel. I tried to write the dumbest book I could. . . . It's a joke . . . to call it Kathy first of all. I wrote the novel really to make money—they were buying porn novels at the time. So I took the formula of the porn novel, and I made a structure, a mathematical structure. In this chapter we have psychology, and here we have this happen . . . and then I wrote it according to this structure. It was the most boring thing in the world to write. I tried to make the characters as dumb as possible, and I basically tried to make nothing happen. ("IRD" 281–82)

Kathy is, as promised, "as dumb as possible." Her dialogue ranges from the merely inane, "Oh goody. I'm so happy,"[18] to the dangerously foolish: "If you have love in your heart and live for other people, these people will have love in their hearts. I know I'm sounding soppy, but it's what I believe" (*KGH* 90).

Nonetheless, *Kathy Goes to Haiti,* whether acknowledged or even intended by Acker to be so, is not as dumb as it might look. This early novel also ruthlessly parodies conventional travel books and tourism, and Acker has in fact admitted that it is "also my version . . . of a travel journal."[19] Specifically, *Kathy Goes to Haiti* concerns white North American tourism in the Caribbean, as its opening lines suggest: "Kathy is a middle-class, though she has no money, American white girl" (*KGH* 5). *Kathy Goes to Haiti* follows its protagonist Kathy as "[o]ne summer she goes down to Haiti. She steps out of the American Airlines plane and on to the cement runway, her first example of Haitian soil" (*KGH* 5). From this ironic statement onward, Kathy serves as a parodic emblem of postcolonial relations as distilled in the tourist industry—whether she is sneaking always-inadequate food to beggar boys from a pension or serving as a sort of traveling Western-culture lending library—until, at the very end of the novel, she "turns around and walks outside into the sun. She's more dazed than before" (*KGH* 170).

Few critics—excluding Acker herself—have written on *Kathy Goes to Haiti* in any detail,[20] and for Robert Siegle, *Kathy Goes to Haiti* concerns itself primarily with gender and sexuality; Acker's depiction of the protagonist Kathy as a tourist in Haiti is therefore purely incidental, or useful only for emphasizing problems in male-female relations.[21] Siegle argues, for instance, that,

> [c]oaxed by her desires into sexual scripts that pain as well as please her, Kathy is drawn by necessity into mortal competition in order to survive emotionally. Haiti is a locale that shows an unsubtle version of the double bind that such a subject faces, its *local color* and *lush sexual undergrowth* used as the *Day-Glo accenting* to Acker's nascent reading of American culture. (*SA* 76; emphasis added)

Siegle's exoticized "Haiti" is, however, very hard to locate in Acker's *Kathy Goes to Haiti*. There, a reader is presented instead with Kathy's abysmal ignorance regarding U.S.–Haitian relations, while the (generally stable, sober, and omniscient third-person) narrator, on the other hand, periodically provides less naive information (including even a "New York 1950s cocktail lounge" called, significantly, the Imperial [*KGH* 38]). There, the most lyrical passage on the natural beauty of Haiti ends in the following manner:

> The roosters are crowing their lungs out and small goats are pissing on the sand and dry dust which covers everything and the pigs are rooting in the sand for whatever garbage the rising waves are leaving behind. . . .
> A group of eleven-year-old boys are sitting on a curb. Alex has two toothpicks, one long and one short, legs from rickets or polio and for the last two days has been running a fever. (*KGH* 101)

Acker's interwoven parodies of pornography and tourism (the latter crisscrossing issues of postcoloniality and ethnography) in *Kathy Goes to Haiti* bring to mind the numerous connections drawn between pornography and ethnography by Christian Hansen, Catherine Needham, and Bill Nichols, and one of their observations seems particularly pertinent in the present context: "The body itself looms as the 'star' of pornography and ethnography."[22] Acker's "ethnography" may be as unburdened by "stars" as is her "pornography," but "the body" in Acker's writing is indeed everywhere (in endless specific permutations) and nowhere (in coherent or universalizing form) to be found.

Siegle's elision of the postcolonial politics of *Kathy Goes to Haiti* allows disregard of the numerous complications of who is "victimizing" whom in power relations there; it also ignores the novel's exposure of the universalizing pretensions of whiteness. On the other hand, Colleen Kennedy's feminist critique both of Acker's use of pornography and of Siegle's praise of Acker does not directly discuss *Kathy Goes to Haiti,* except insofar as she claims that Acker "mak[es] these [victimized] characters reflections of herself (in two books the main character is actually named Kathy)."[23] Reading Acker's "dissoluteness and debauchery" quite literally, Kennedy concludes that "pornography written by women ultimately renders them victims of it" ("SS" 175). As she conflates author and protagonist, so too does Kennedy repudiate Acker's use of parody: "Clichés cannot be distinguished from their parody. To borrow from Toril Moi's analysis of Irigaray, 'the mimicry fails because it ceases to be perceived as such; it is no longer merely a mockery of the male, but a perfect reproduction'" ("SS" 183)[24]

Whether as a positive or negative touchstone, reference to Irigaray often seems strangely appropriate in discussions of Acker. Brennan at one point cites Irigaray's criticism of Lacan on the issue of women's pleasure, but in that context as well as in the present one, Irigaray's words seem strangely to wind back around to address Acker's readers—notably in these cases her feminist readers—as well: "The question whether, in his logic, they [women] can articulate anything at all, *whether they can be heard,* is not even raised. For raising it might mean that there may be some other logic, one that upsets his own. That is, a logic that challenges mastery" (quoted in "GE" 259; emphasis added). Acker herself has also "cited" and parodied (if rather respectfully) Irigaray's writing on logic and mastery, pleasure and the sex which is not one, Lacan and whoever else isn't listening:

> A man's power resides in his prick. That's what they, whoever they is, say. How the fuck should I know? I ain't a man. Though I'm a good fake lieutenant, it's not good enough to have a fake dick. I don't have one. Does this mean I've got no strength? If it's true that a man's prick is his strength, what and where is my power? Since I don't have one thing, a dick, I've got nothing, so my pleasure isn't any one thing, it's just pleasure. Therefore, pleasure must be pleasurable. Well, maybe I've found out something, and maybe I haven't.[25]

For academic feminists in particular, Acker's dissoluteness is perhaps especially fraught with hazard. Even beyond specific cases of inattention to significant details—such as the sex about which apparently nothing can be said (Brennan and Dane), content having to do with race, tourism, and postcolonialism (Siegle), or formal questions of representation (Kennedy)—academic feminists must especially concern themselves with fastidious focus and discipline. However "interdisciplinary" our interests or fields of study, we are not generally at liberty to pursue "a logic that challenges mastery," either in theory or practice. Yet, although Acker's wanton excesses and academic feminist discipline may indeed be ill paired, her dissoluteness provides more than vicarious thrills or voyeuristic peeks at an alternate episteme or fictional universe or "lifestyle." Her writing—with its deadpan, but insistent, inscription and parody of pornography and female victimization; its unraveling of assumptions about originality, a woman's voice, and "the" body; its dismantling of the universality of whiteness; and its admixture of theory and popular culture—might in many ways be seen as an extended interrogation of Anglo-American feminism, and certainly of any notion of a homogenous "feminism."

I want to look particularly now at the beginnings and endings of two late Acker novels, *Pussy, King of the Pirates* (1996) and *My Mother: Demonology* (1993). In these books she works on constructing, rather than deconstructing, as formerly, novels in which myths of witches and mothers and daughters, pirates and lesbian lovers take shape. Specifically, I would like to think about the dissolute form of these beginnings and endings, to examine how Acker constructed the friable borders of her textual bodies, writings which are called novels only for the sake of convenience.

Part I of *My Mother: Demonology* is preceded by an epigraph:

> My mother began to love at the same moment in her life that she began to search for who she was. This was the moment she met my father. Since my mother felt that she had to be alone in order to find out who she was and might be, she kept abandoning and returning to love.
>
> My mother spoke: (*MMD* 3)

Because of this introductory colon, the "I" speaker of the statement referred to earlier—"Most of my life, but not all, I've been dissolute"—seems likely to be "my mother," which leaves the speaker of the epigraph nonetheless unidentified. At any rate, the narration begins with the words: "I'm in love with red. I dream in red." For this narrator, red represents, among other things, "the color of wildness and of what is as yet unknown" (*MMD* 10). (And if we were reading the novel itself, we would be reading within its bright red covers.) I, "my mother"—if "I" is indeed she—has a mother of her own, moreover, a "great lady" (*MMD* 9) who "commands" her daughter to the point of imprisoning her (*MMD* 10) and who has a quite different relation to redness: "Mother just hates everyone who isn't of our blood. She uses the word *blood*. She hates everyone and everything that she can't control; everything gay, lively, everything that's growing, productive. Humanness throws her into a panic; when she panics, she does her best to hurt me" (*MMD*11). Ellen Friedman has said that

> *My Mother: Demonology* turns at the end suddenly quasi-mystical. Its last line has the narrator seeing "a reflection of [her] face before the creation of the world." Despite the fact that the narrator sees this reflection in a roll of toilet paper, the statement is the closest Acker has come to a discourse of inclusion, to a statement of individual identity in the world. Yet this hesitant, self-mocking affirmation is only a resting place at the end of a text whose tone is better summed up in its epigraph.[26]

The epigraph to which Friedman refers, however, is not the one I just cited, the epigraph ending in the words "My mother spoke:" (an epigraph which falls between the second title page of the book and the title of Part I). She refers instead to the epigraph which precedes both a title page and the table of contents but which comes after the book's first title page and its dedication ("to Uma"). Acker is nothing if not playful, yet the first epigraph of this novel takes up a different subject from the second and is playful only painfully:

> After Hatuey, a fifteenth-century Indian insurrectionist, had been fixed to the stake, his Spanish captors extended him the choice of converting to Christianity and ascending to Heaven or going unrepentantly to Hell. Gathering that his executioners expected to go to Heaven, Hatuey chose the other. (*MMD*, n.p.)

Among *My Mother: Demonology*'s false, repetitive, duplicitous beginnings, among its multiple titles and citations and sections, among Hatuey and Spanish executioners, among nameless daughters and mothers and the color red, the narrator says, a few pages in, "I told myself story after story. Every story is real. One story always leads to another story" (*MMD* 11). The first story of this novel, unless we take its dedication, or its title, to be the first story, is that of Hatuey.

Ellen Friedman does not say why she believes that this first epigraph "sums up" the "tone" of *My Mother: Demonology;* one can only suppose that she refers to the biting political irony of much of the novel. Nor does Friedman suggest what the relation between the novel's first and second epigraphs might be. Yet thinking the relation between these two epigraphs can be quite helpful when one encounters, for example, a section of the novel called "About Chinese Women" (*MMD* 80–81), a segment that plagiarizes Kristeva's book of the same name. Acker repeats one sentence of Kristeva's text almost exactly: "when a woman doesn't believe in God, she, like everyone else, validates her existence by believing in man" (*MMD* 80).

Half a page later, Acker revises a second statement. Kristeva's original (in English translation) reads as follows:

> Otherwise, I would have had to write the dizziness which, before China or without China, seizes that which is fed up with language, and attempts to escape through it: the abyss of fiction. However, that's not what I felt called upon to do here, where an imaginary 'we' is trying above all to understand what, in the various modes of production, has to do 'with women'—and not only to experience the general impossibility of this plural. Thus, a writing once more deferred . . .[27]

Acker abruptly rewrites this passage as: "I write in the dizziness that seizes that which is fed up with language and attempts to escape through it: the abyss named *fiction.* For I can only be concerned with the imaginary when I discuss reality or women" (*MMD* 80; emphasis in original).

The most obvious point to be drawn here is that Acker shifts Kristeva's elaborate and anxious concern over standing at the edge of the "abyss of fiction" into a plunge into that abyss. But also, in between the two Kristeva plagiarisms I have cited, Acker adds:

> Since they were all Chinese, I couldn't communicate with any of them.
> There were times when I thought, I shouldn't be here.
> (*MMD* 80)

It is difficult not to hear in this statement echoes of Jamaica Kincaid's indictment of colonialism and slavery, tourism and racism in her work *A Small Place:* "There must have been some good people among you, but they stayed home. And that is the point. That is why they are good. They stayed home."[28] Many might also be reminded of Spivak's critique of Kristeva (in "French Feminism in an International Frame") in which she not only skewers Kristeva's reading of Chinese women as nameless masses or Kristeva's refusal to examine her own positionality, but also charges her with a sloppy reading of the figure of Electra.[29] This brings us, rather dizzily, back to Acker herself, since most of her texts contain some version of an incestuous Electra figure. But Acker does not stop playing with Kristeva there. She also takes Kristeva's Chinese women, described as "full-blown, even buxom . . . always with oval contours" and parodically deflates Kristeva's lyrical and exoticizing image: Acker's Chinese women become fat maids wielding meat cleavers who regard the narrator "the way one gazes at an object that is so other it can't be human" (*MMD* 81).

The end of *My Mother: Demonology* harks back both to this segment and to the beginnings of the novel: "my face before the creation of the world" is not simply reflected in a roll of toilet paper but in a "roll of white toilet paper [which] was covered with specks of black hairs" (*MMD* 268). It would be disingenuous to ignore two closing references to color in this novel so saturated with color from cover to cover. "Black" and "white," while not strictly referential here, serve at least a doubled purpose: racial politics permeate this text from its first epigraph regarding Hatuey's choice of hell over continued proximity to the Spanish, and that epigraph plays off against references to sexuality, desire, and identity in the second epigraph ("My mother . . ."), references which are transformed at the end of the novel to anonymous pubic hairs. But whereas the issues raised by the epigraph concerning "[m]y mother" are carefully analyzed in readings of Acker's work, the issues raised in the Hatuey epigraph are too often neglected—as are any possible relations between the two.[30] Despite this neglect, however, the intersection of the politics of race and colonialism, on the one hand, with the politics of sexuality and gender, on the other, has been an important element in Acker's work at least since her 1978 novel *Kathy Goes to Haiti* (which is equal parts scurrilous parody of porn and scathing parody of white tourism in the Caribbean).

Acker's novel *Pussy, King of the Pirates* also ends with an overt reference to black and white: "Ange and I grabbed all the money we could and got into the rowboat that was hidden by the two, the white and the black, stones" (*PKP* 276). *Pussy, King of the Pirates,* like *My Mother: Demonology,* has more than one beginning; in this case, the first, a preface, opens with the death of the father (*PKP* 3), while the second, the first chapter, opens with the death of the white world (*PKP* 28). In the sequence leading up to the novel's end, the pirate girls begin to fight each other, and "[w]ater mixed with air and earth. . . . It looked as if the end of the world was the same as its beginning" (*PKP* 240). A bit later:

> Water was all over the place, had already flooded the world, there was no more ground.
> This was the realm of continual ecstasy.
> Now everything was wet, dripping with it. Dank and rotten. This world was never going to stop. . . . They [the pirate girls] were still very dirty and exceedingly smelly. (*PKP* 251)

Yet, for all the references to "the world of mud" (*PKP* 241), the cave in which the pirate treasure is finally found is "a large, airy place, with a little spring and a pool of clear water" (*PKP* 275). This idyllic cave echoes Ange's mother's box—from whence both Ange and the treasure map came. Here, in the cave, conflict ends, and we would seem to find an atypically utopian ending to this novel—except that things are not in fact so clear-cut. Ange and O, after all, grab all the money they can in a novel, as well as a corpus, which consistently rails against acquisition. There also remains ambiguously indeterminate pirates' blood, associated both with the realm of death and with the realm of female sexuality. Further, the treasure map which comes from Ange's mother's box contains a segment referring to James Baldwin's writing, which shows "what it's like to be a black man in our society" (*PKP* 260). Nor does the novel end when the narrative ends; rather, there follows "A Prayer for All Sailors," which itself ends with the line, "For your lips have been stained by blood" (*PKP* 277). The "Prayer" is then followed by a map of pirate island ("pas sang rouge"); this map comes with instructions, among them an invocation to dive into perfectly blue water so that you will look like the pirates, that is to say—though these instructions fail to mention it—filthy and slimy and bloody.

The doublings of these novels' beginnings and endings cannot simply be read as yet another hall of mirrors, however dirty or distorted. Indeed, we are far from the realm of mirrors altogether: mirrors with their frozen, reflecting surfaces and their replication of the Same (see Irigaray, especially *Speculum*). Acker's late novels are instead texts of accretion which confound both beginnings and endings, while nonetheless constructing what she calls "mythical magic" ("CKA1" 2) among all their elements: intra-, inter-, and extratextual, even, if you like, extraterrestrial: "Antigone decided to celebrate this day . . . by changing her name to Angelique, who used to be some whore, because she told us, she was currently talking to an angel" (*PKP* 273). Acker, like Irigaray, has written extensively through and of tropes of the elements: earth, air, fire, and especially water—water with its amniotic fluidity, its relation to the flow of blood and of language. Yet both also became interested in such unexpected figures and strategies as angels and the possibility, if not the promise, of happy endings. In Irigaray's terms, "A sexual or carnal ethics would require that both angel and body be found together. This is a world that must be constructed or reconstructed."[31] One must remember that these angels and other possibilities in no way imply a transcendent escape from the material, the fleshy, or the messy—and that in the realms of either sex or politics, or even messier yet, in both at once.

Given Acker's increasing popularity with academics, her recent greater, and warmer, reception among feminists, and her nearly cult status in some quarters (such as the World Wide Web or cyberpunk), it can be quite bracing to encounter the hackles she still raises in others, particularly in more mainstream popular media, where, for example, a character from *My Mother: Demonology* has been dubbed "full of anger and shallow references to academic feminist philosophers."[32] Indeed, snide implications that Acker is nothing more than a slightly talented literary poseur may bring to mind something like the treatment often served up to Courtney Love (of the band Hole, and, if this identification is still necessary, widow of Kurt Cobain):

> To read the novel [*Pussy, King of the Pirates*] . . . is to be constantly reminded that Acker's self-consciously postmodern soup would be much more effective in other media—as a video game, a graphic novel or cartoon, a multimedia CD. . . . Acker invokes many literary touchstones . . . but you find yourself thinking that this pushing of the novelistic envelope has been done better, and more originally, by others.[33]

The clichéd notion of "pushing the envelope" is virtually synonymous with Madonna, of course, and Acker herself "self-consciously" smashed the icon of "originality" for years: "I now wonder where the idea or the ideology of creativity started. Shakespeare and company certainly stole from, copied each other's writings. Before them, the Greeks didn't bother making up any new stories. . . . Nobody *really* owns nothing."[34] These critics describe fairly accurately Acker's particular recipe for "postmodern soup" (self-conscious, angry, plagiaristic, and so forth); indeed, it is precisely her dissolute project itself which garners disapproval. It would not be entirely inappropriate, however, to take a clue from readings that characterize Acker as "shallow," unoriginal, or "postmodern," if only because they force recognition of the enormous distance so often still maintained (whether or not articulated) between high and low culture, theory and cultural production, originality and mimicry, the serious and the playful.

If there are links (and many think there are) between Acker's writing and Irigaray on fluidity and multiplicity and mimicry or Cixous on "writing the body" and theories of the maternal and feminist hysteria, I would argue that Acker's writing takes full part in that feminist theoretical process—rather than that Acker is merely influenced by, or heir to, a certain theoretical discourse operating in another realm or, more likely, another level. That is to say that feminist genealogies do not develop in strictly linear fashion but rather undulate and intermingle, so that sometimes Cixous, for instance, seems to make more sense, though not for more mastery, when read back through Acker—or for that matter, through Courtney Love. In the same vein, Acker's work serves as an impressive reminder that there exists no stable hierarchy ranging from theory (down) to literature and (finally) popular culture. To put this somewhat differently, it seems more productive, and accurate, to consider Acker not simply an appropriate target for the "application" of Cixous's theory but rather to consider Acker as an active contributor to theoretical discourse, including feminist thought. I can, in fact, only second Acker on this general point because she suggested it herself often enough—if somewhat less directly and more humbly—although she also underscored the differences between her writing and theory as such: "I don't talk through theory, I talk through fictional process. There's a different sort of language" ("CKA1" 2).

Acker has not, of course, been the only one engaged both in a theoretical feminist process and at the same time in the production of a more "popular culture." If Courtney Love's shifting personae sometimes sound like sisters to Acker's Janey Smith ("I tell you everything / And I hope that you won't tell on me . . . Pee-girl gets the belt / It only makes me cry . . . I've got a blister from / Touching everything I see"), Love also renders Cixous's maternal metaphor in a wide range of shades of "white ink" ("LM" 251) that undo "the" universalized maternal (much as Acker dismantles "the" universalized female body): "Your milk is so sick / Your milk has a dick / Your milk has a dye . . . Your milk is so mean / Your milk turns to mine / Your milk turns to cream."[35]

When Acker performs what Friedman calls "an audacious rendering of Cixous's writing the body,"[36] she similarly takes it elsewhere quite graphically:

> Everytime I talk to one of you, I feel like I'm taking layers of my own epidermis, which are layers of still freshly bloody scar tissue, black brown and red, and tearing each one of them off so more and more of my blood shoots into your face. This is what writing is to me a woman. (*ES* 210)

These lines are spoken by a character named Abhor, said to be (on the first page of the text and by the other major character/narrator of *Empire of the Senseless,* Thivai) "my partner, part robot, and part black." Abhor's parody of "writing the body" is layered over a parody of Thivai's/Tom Sawyer's irritatingly ludicrous "rescue" of Abhor/Jim, inscribing, alongside references to tattooing, a racial positionality markedly absent in Cixous. "Black brown and red" function at least doubly in this passage: they underscore the missing specificity of "the" body-which-is-written, problematizing the universalized "body"; they also mark a body which is both painful writing and painfully written upon, and that in a text "dedicated to my tattooist" (Acker has said, "That's what tattooing is for me, it's myth" ["DM" 21]). Gender, furthermore, blurs messily as Acker plagiarizes her own pornography with a reverse money shot: "my blood shoots into your face."

Kathy Acker wrote theory in a dissolute mode characterized by a tattooed pirate's brew of autobiography, textual "appropriation," poetry, parody, pornography, essayistic prose, nonlinear fiction, (feminist, poststructuralist, postmodern, and posthuman) theoretical statements, political proclamations, punk grrl "lyricism," and myth. She was also a very good listener. That Acker would have taken up and deployed the stereotypical model of the "good woman" as "good listener" underscores once again her connections with other feminist theorists, and Irigaray's use of mimicry might come first to mind here:

> One must assume the feminine role deliberately. Which means already to convert a form of subordination into an affirmation, and thus to begin to thwart it. . . . To play with mimesis is thus, for a woman, to try to recover the place of her exploitation by discourse, without allowing herself to be simply reduced to it. It means to resubmit herself . . . to 'ideas,' in particular to ideas about herself, that are elaborated in/by a masculine logic, but

so as to make 'visible,' by an effect of playful repetition, what was supposed to remain invisible: the cover-up of a possible operation of the feminine in language. It also means 'to unveil' the fact that, if women are such good mimics, it is because they are not simply resorbed in this function. *They also remain elsewhere. . . .*[37]

Acker was one of the many women recently engaged in highly improper projects of mimicking, mocking, and otherwise disrupting ("these Janeys covered the earth," according to Acker). Although her writing and overall cultural production are otherwise quite different, Trinh T. Minh-ha's description of reactions to her own theory, for example, has a good deal to say to Acker's writing, including the issue of mimicry as the excessive repetition of the same old thing:

The mixing of different modes of writing; the mutual challenge of theoretical and poetical, discursive and 'non-discursive' languages; *the strategic use of stereotyped expressions in exposing stereotypical thinking;* all these attempts at introducing a break into the fixed norms of the Master's confident prevailing discourses are easily misread, dismissed, or obscured in the name of 'good writing,' of 'theory,' or of 'scholarly work.'[38]

In the hands of a writer such as Trinh, "theory" is itself broken up, startled out of its delusions of coherence and mastery. Her writing provides, therefore, one of the many answers to Irigaray's question, *"Isn't the phallic tantamount to the seriousness of meaning?"* (*TS* 163; Irigaray's emphasis). If we listen carefully enough, we will hear Acker also answer: "The dead cock was no longer leading us, 'cause we were back at the edge of the water" (*PKP* 275).

Notes

1. Kathy Acker, *My Mother: Demonology* (New York: Pantheon, 1993), 8. Hereafter cited as *MMD.*

2. Kathy Acker, "A Conversation with Kathy Acker," interview by Benjamin Bratton, *Speed* (http://www.arts.ucsb.edu:80/~speedPast/1.1/acker.html): 1-5, esp. 5. Hereafter cited as "CKA1."

3. Kathy Acker, interview in *Varieties of Violence,* a special issue of *2gz* (formerly *Girls Review*), 1, no. 1 (Spring 1995): 3. Hereafter cited as *2GZ.*

4.   Luce Irigaray, *Speculum of the Other Woman,* trans. Gillian C. Gill (Ithaca: Cornell University Press, 1985), 214-26. Hereafter cited as *S.*

5.   Kathy Acker, *Pussy, King of the Pirates* (New York: Grove, 1996), 185. Hereafter cited as *PKP.*

6.   Hélène Cixous, "The Laugh of the Medusa," trans. Keith Cohen and Paula Cohen, in *New French Feminisms: An Anthology,* ed. Elaine Marks and Isabelle de Courtivron (New York: Schocken, 1981), 255. Hereafter cited as "LM."

7.   Luce Irigaray, "The Eternal Irony of the Community," in *Speculum of the Other Woman,* 214-26. Hereafter cited as "EIC."

8.   There is a growing body of critical writing which closely links Acker's writing to that of Irigaray, Kristeva, and especially Cixous: hysterical feminine writing and writing the (female) body, for example, have both been discussed, in passing and at length, in relation to Acker's work (Martina Sciolino, Ellen G. Friedman, Gabrielle Dane, Karen Brennan).

9.   Kathy Acker, interview by Rebecca Deaton, *Textual Practice* 6, no. 2 (Summer 1992): 280. Hereafter cited as "IRD."

10.   Kathy Acker and Sylvere Lotringer, "Devoured by Myths," in *Hannibal Lecter, My Father* (New York: Semiotext[e], 1991), 15. Hereafter cited as "DM."

11.   Ellen G. Friedman, "'Now Eat Your Mind': An Introduction to the Works of Kathy Acker," *Review of Contemporary Fiction* 9, no. 2 (Summer 1989): 37-49.

12.   Kathy Acker, interview by Lisa Palac, *On Our Backs* (May/June 1991): 19.

13.   Kathy Acker, *Blood and Guts in High School* (New York: Grove Weidenfeld, 1978; first published London: Pan Books, 1984), 7. Hereafter cited as *BGHS.*

14.   Karen Brennan, "The Geography of Enunciation: Hysterical Pastiche in Kathy Acker's Fiction," *boundary 2* 21, no. 2 (1994): 263. Hereafter cited as "GE."

15.   The original text copied here is Roland Barthes, *A Lover's Discourse: Fragments,* trans. Richard Howard (New York: Hill and Wang, 1978), 9. Acker changes the masculine pronouns and repeats the final phrase.

16.   Gabrielle Dane, "Hysteria as Feminist Protest: Dora, Cixous, Acker," *Women's Studies* 23 (1994): 249-50. Hereafter cited as "HFP."

17.   Kathleen Hulley, "Transgressing Genre: Kathy Acker's Intertext," in *Intertextuality and Contemporary American Fiction,* ed. Patrick O'Donnell and Robert Con Davis (Baltimore: Johns Hopkins University Press, 1989), 182.

18.   Kathy Acker, *Kathy Goes to Haiti in Literal Madness* (New York: Grove, 1988; first published by Rumor Publications in 1978), 7. Hereafter cited as *KGH.*

19.   Cited on the Kathy Acker, *Kathy Goes to Haiti* homepage as from the introduction to Acker's *Young Lust* (http://euro.net/mark-space/bkKathyGoesToHaiti.html).

20.   One exception is Terry Engebretsen, "Primitivism and Postmodernism in Kathy Acker's *Kathy Goes to Haiti*," *Studies in the Humanities* 21, no. 2 (December 1994): 105–19. While usefully discussing the representation and subversion of primitivism in the novel, Engebretsen also insists that "[f]inally . . . the novel is interested in the psychology of Kathy's relationship with Roger—a relationship conditioned by her primitivist assumptions—rather than in historical and political analysis of the situation in Haiti" (118 n. 4).

21.   Robert Siegle, *Suburban Ambush: Downtown Writing and the Fiction of Insurgency* (Baltimore: Johns Hopkins University Press, 1989), 72–76. Hereafter cited as *SA*.

22.   Christian Hansen, Catherine Needham, and Bill Nichols, "Pornography, Ethnography, and the Discourse of Power," in Bill Nichols, *Representing Reality: Issues and Concepts in Documentary* (Bloomington: Indiana University Press, 1991), 220.

23.   Colleen Kennedy, "Simulating Sex and Imagining Mothers," *American Literary History* 4, no. 1 (Spring 1992): 176. Hereafter cited as "SS."

24.   Toril Moi, *Sexual/Textual Politics: Feminist Literary Theory* (London: Methuen, 1985), 142.

25.   Kathy Acker, *Empire of the Senseless* (New York: Grove, 1988), 127. Hereafter cited as *ES*.

26.   Ellen G. Friedman, review of *My Mother: Demonology* by Kathy Acker, *Review of Contemporary Fiction* 14, no. 1 (Spring 1994): 213–14.

27.   Julia Kristeva, *About Chinese Women*, trans. Anita Barrows (New York: Marion Boyars, 1977), 160.

28.   Jamaica Kincaid, *A Small Place* (New York: Plume, 1988), 35.

29.   Gayatri Chakravorty Spivak, "French Feminism in an International Frame," in *Other Worlds: Essays in Cultural Politics* (New York: Routledge, 1988), 139–40.

30.   An exception is C. Jodey Castricano's "If a Building Is a Sentence, So Is a Body: Kathy Acker and the Postcolonial Gothic," in *American Gothic: New Interventions in a National Narrative*, ed. Robert K. Martin and Eric Savoy (Iowa City: University of Iowa Press, 1998). Castricano's essay, which appeared after my own essay was completed, carefully examines *Empire of the Senseless* in light of both postcolonial theory and feminism.

31.   Luce Irigaray, *An Ethics of Sexual Difference*, trans. Carolyn Burke and Gillian C. Gill (Ithaca: Cornell University Press, 1993), 17.

32.   Kate Wilson, review of *My Mother: Demonology* by Kathy Acker, *Entertainment Weekly* (1 October 1993): 50.

33.   Chris Goodrich, review of *Pussy, King of the Pirates* by Kathy Acker, *Los Angeles Times Book Review* (24 March 1996): 10.

34. Kathy Acker, "A Few Notes on Two of My Books," *Review of Contemporary Fiction* 9, no. 2 (Summer 1989): 33.

35. Courtney Love and Hole, "Softer, Softest," on *Live Through This* (BMI, 1994).

36. Friedman, review of *My Mother: Demonology,* 213–14.

37. Luce Irigaray, *This Sex Which Is Not One,* trans. Catherine Porter (Ithaca: Cornell University Press, 1985), 76. Hereafter cited as *TS.*

38. Trinh T. Minh-ha and Judith Mayne, "From a Hybrid Place," in *Framer Framed* (New York: Routledge, 1992), 138; emphasis added.

Part II

Deconstruction and Culture

Community, Politics, Ethics

Feeling the Debt

On Europe

Rodolphe Gasché

Husserl has argued in *The Crisis of European Sciences* that for Europe to have a distinct identity, a being that is truly its own, it has to reactivate its teleological beginning in Greece, that is, in the absolute idea that marks the birth of the European spirit.[1] What causes this inborn idea in European humanity to be absolute is that it is concerned not with a geographical, national, ethnic, or religious entity but with humanity's struggle to understand itself. Yet, we may ask, by what nature of certainty can Husserl establish this idea? What kind of judgment leads him to the assertion that this idea alone can guarantee European identity, if not even confirm identity in general? Since, as Derrida has put it in *The Other Heading,* Europe's "self-identification as repetition of itself" is based on "repetitive memory" and "anamnestic capitalization,"[2] the idea of Europe must have all the characteristics of ideality, if it is not even the idea of ideality itself. Undoubtedly, for Husserl, the certainty of the idea in question, is a cognitive certitude, apodictably intuitable, as is also evident from the theoretical style and ductus of *The Crisis*.[3] By contrast, in several of the attempts recently made in France and Italy to salvage the philosophical idea of Europe, for all its ideological and historical datedness—an effort that is also clearly intent on disputing the New Right's formulations of European identity—the idea in question is no longer seen as something that European humanity possesses as an always reactivatable, and unshakable, knowledge about itself. But before even hinting at what this novel conception of Europe might be, and especially at what its status is, if, indeed, it is not an assured cognitive truth, I should emphasize from the outset that these attempts at securing a future for the idea of Europe did not arise because of some nostalgia for a lost greatness. Neither did they seek to rescue the old idea of Europe by opposing to its discredited expansionist and universalist conception a "new" model of European identity, based on cultural self-sufficiency and a nervous nationalism, as has been the case with the French New Right. Rather, the attempt to rescue the philosophical concept of Europe derives first from the insight that this endeavor is a more politically efficient way of combating the old idea of Europe, as well as of resisting its new nationalist version in the New Right, than would be an outright rejection of the idea of Europe itself. Moreover, is Europe not responsible for the idea of Europe and for all that has been done and thought in its name? Can Europe simply turn away from this responsibility in search of another identity, as if it did not matter that it had thought of itself as an idea? However, to acknowledge this responsibility entails the abandonment of any attempt to save what of the old Europe is bound to come to an end, since the desire to protect it from the decadence and decline of its former values not merely forfeits the possibilities of Europe—its future—but by this desire Europe, as Massimo Cacciari has noted, "betrays itself, its own *etymon*."[4] Hence, if the mentioned attempts to rescue the idea of Europe persist in not discarding this notion outright, it is due to a feeling that, as a philosophical idea, the idea of Europe might still harbor critical possibilities that until now have not been actualized. Europe, it is felt, is not comparable to a content whose form could be thrown away like an empty shell, once extracted and realized. Unwilling to set aside a concept before all its resources have been tapped, the thinkers involved in reassessing the philosophical concept of Europe have argued that this concept is not necessarily outdated; that, indeed, it still harbors critical potential; and in particular, a potential for Europe itself whose past has been intimately linked to this idea that it had of itself.

In the context of this reassessment, the theoretical, and hence knowable, idea of Europe is replaced by a feeling for Europe, by a felt European identity. Among those who have taken it upon themselves to explore a possible critical potential for the idea in question, Jacques Derrida admits that in *The Other Heading: Reflections on Today's Europe* he has been speaking "with names (event, decision, responsibility, ethics, politics— Europe) of 'things' that can only exceed (and *must* exceed) the order of theoretical determination, of knowledge, certainty, judgement, and of statements in the form of 'this is that,' in other words of the *present* or of *presentation*" (*OH* 81). For Derrida, "Europe" is thus not, first and foremost, a theoretical issue. The opening sentences of the book describe the imminent and unique crisis of Europe today, as one in which one no longer knows what the name "Europe" refers to and what the identity of Europe is. But this failure to know what the idea of Europe is about, and the actual impossibility of discursively establishing its meaning, is not seen as something fatal. It might well be an opportunity, if not even a chance. As Derrida suggests, "the very old subject of European identity," with its "venerable air of an old, exhausted theme," might still "retain a virgin body," a body that in spite of all theorizing about it has been left uncharted (*OH* 5). It should not, therefore, come as a surprise if Derrida, having established himself as an old European, although not quite by birth, opens his discussion of the idea of Europe, and of European identity, by confiding a feeling to his reader. This feeling is made instantly and explicitly into the "first axiom" of his text. By definition, an axiom is a fundamental statement requiring no proof, since it is considered either to be self-evident or to implicitly contain the definition of its own terms; thus, the axiom serves as the premise for a series of statements. Here, however, it is a feeling, rather than a proposition, that is postulated, and made into an axiom; a feeling, of course, that is not a private feeling but one that is, or might be, shared by "we Europeans." It is the paradoxical, if not aporetic, feeling that "we are younger than ever, we Europeans, since a certain Europe does not yet exist," but, at the same time, "already old and tired," "already exhausted." Derrida's second axiom is an axiom in the stricter sense, since it formulates an intelligible necessity rather than a feeling. According to this second postulate, *"what is proper to culture is not to be identical to itself."* This axiom does not stipulate that a culture would have no positive identity whatsoever or that to have one would be a mystification. On the contrary, it establishes that a culture has identity only on condition of its being non-identical to itself, of its being in "difference *with itself* (*avec soi*)." This constituting difference of a culture *with itself* is double in kind. Identity presupposes, first of all, an external difference. This is a difference with itself that derives from identity's continual reference to the identity of other cultures over and against whom any self-identity is established. These other cultural identities, as identities of the Other, can simply be different from the one of European culture, but they can also be identities that stand in a relation of opposition to European identity. Yet since *avec soi*, in addition to meaning "with itself," also means "at home (with itself)," or *chez soi*, Derrida makes use of this "strange and slightly violent syntax" to maintain that for cultural identity to be possible, it must be further divided by an internal difference, a self-difference that "would gather and divide just as irreducibly the center or hearth [*foyer*] of the 'at home (with itself)'" (*OH* 9–10). This internal difference is the difference of any identity not from the state of non-identity from which it had to be wrenched, but with a "state" anterior to the difference of identity and non-identity. The difference in question opens all identity to its divergence and is the necessary condition under which a center or hearth can be gathered and made to relate to itself. Up to this point in his text, Derrida has spoken of cultural identity. But with his statement that "there is no self-relation, no relation to oneself, no identification with oneself, without culture, but a culture of oneself *as* a culture *of* the other, a culture of the double genitive and of the *difference to oneself* [*à soi*]" (*OH* 10), Derrida extends the axiomatic law in question to identity in general, to what is properly one's innermost own. The second axiomatic law thus states that the inmost own, which is in this case the cultural identity of Europe, is *per essentiam, sine essentia.*

As Derrida recalls in *The Other Heading,* Europe has always understood itself as a head and heading, both geographically and spiritually. But if the second axiom establishes a law for all identity formation, then Europe's self-identification as a head and heading presupposes the double difference with and to oneself. More precisely, what follows from this law is that if Europe wishes to understand itself as a head and a heading, it is incumbent upon it, first of all, to recall, to remember, and *reactivate* the other already constituted identities thanks to which it is, in distinguishing itself from them, what it most properly and truly is. If all identity necessarily presupposes a relation to a constitutive external difference, then in order to be itself, Europe cannot ignore what Derrida calls "the other heading," or, given that all cultures presuppose "an identifiable heading, a *telos*" (*OH* 17-18) toward which they move, Europe cannot ignore "the heading of the other" (*OH* 15). Without relating to the trace of the other heading within the heading that is most properly its own, Europe as a head and heading would in all rigor cease to be an identity. It would achieve absoluteness. In Jean-Luc Nancy's terms, it would become fully immanent to itself, and death would thus become its truth.[5] Commenting on the title *The Other Heading,* Derrida remarks that in addition to suggesting a change in direction and destination, the expression "the other heading"

> can mean to recall that there is an other heading, the heading being not only ours, but the other, not only that which we identify, calculate, and decide upon, but the *heading of the other,* before which we must respond, and which we must *remember, of which* we must *remind ourselves,* the heading of the other being perhaps the first condition of an identity or identification that is not an egocentrism destructive of one self and the other. (*OH* 15)

However, identity also requires the internal difference which, while continuing to divide identity, also makes it possible for identity to gather itself into its own. This difference within which identity collects itself is a difference with something that is altogether of a different order than identity, and hence something other than non-identity. The internal difference that divides all identity is a difference with identity in general, with that which is conceived in terms of the identifiable, and which, consequently, also precedes the thought, or concept of the non-identical. Derrida, therefore, continues: "But beyond *our heading,* it is necessary to recall ourselves not only to the *other heading,* and especially to the *heading of the other,* but also perhaps to the *other of the heading,* that is to say, to a relation of identity with the other that no longer obeys the form, the sign, or the logic of the heading, nor even of the *anti-heading*— of beheading, of decapitation" (*OH* 15). For Europe to be what it most essentially is—a head and heading—it must recall that without which it could not constitute itself at all, and which for this very reason affects it most fundamentally—the other heading—and recall itself to it. But it must further recall, and recall itself to that which, while not being its opposite—headlessness, and a drifting without direction—is no longer of the order of the head and of a heading, but is the very thing from and thanks to which the binary oppositions of heading and the other heading, of self and other, of identity and non-identity, can distinguish their meaning. With this openness of the question of European identity (and ultimately of any identity) to a "constituting" difference of identity of the order of the other *of* identity, hence also of non-identity, Derrida forces open the interlocked and predictable programs of Eurocentrism and anti-Eurocentrism, to acknowledge something that is no longer of the order of the concept of Europe, or of its opposite, but is, in some way, presupposed by this concept. What, then, is this "other *of* the heading?" one might ask. In distinction from the differences that constitute identity externally and that can be qualified in terms of the non-identical, and in further distinction from any previously constituted identities—"the other headings"—whether or not they stand in a relation of opposition to it, the other *of* the heading is structurally impossible to identify. It is neither identical to itself nor non-identical. The question *what is* the other *of* the heading must remain a question; it "should remain, even beyond all answers," Derrida remarks (*OH* 16–17). Indeed, the other *of* the heading, or, more generally, the other *of* identity, is but the place or trace in the heading, or in the identical, of that which cannot be calculated according to the logic of identity and non-identity, but to which this logic, in order *to be what it is,* must necessarily refer (in a mode of referring that is not simply one of negation) as its "undeterminable" other.

The exposition of the second axiom, according to which "what is proper to culture is not to be identical to itself," has thus laid bare an intricate system of reference which is constitutive of identity in general. This system of structural exigencies, without which no identity can get off the ground and remain in its distinctness, considerably complicates the traditional conceptions, including Husserl's, of what comprises Europe's specificity. Much more than just the origin, as Husserl still thought, needs to be reactivated in order for Europe to gain an innermost own. If Europe is to have an identity, "it must be equal *to itself and to the other*" (*OH* 45); in other words, it must meet the "impossible" requirement to respond at the same time to the two contradictory demands in question. At this point, let me then recall the first axiom, according to which Derrida felt that the idea of Europe, although old and tired, could still hold some potential. Indeed, as the second axiom spells out, when that which is most proper to Europe opens onto other already constituted headings, but especially onto the other *of* the heading, that is, onto what is unpredictable, unanticipatable, uncalculatable (and hence thwarts all programs), in short, onto the future, then the concept of Europe, it is felt, encounters, perhaps, a chance.

The identity of Europe, defined as a head and a heading, is not without the double difference, the external, but also the internal difference that presupposes a "relation" to the other *of* the heading. Thus the question of the identity of Europe is a very old question, not merely because it has been posed since antiquity but, more fundamentally, because as an identity Europe is dependent on something older than itself, older than an "itself," and in relation to which its difference has had to be negotiated from the very beginning. But Derrida claims that although "this question is also very old, as old as the history of Europe, . . . the experience of the *other heading* or of the other *of* the heading presents itself [today] in an absolutely new way." What Derrida intimates here is that the necessary structural, that is, intelligible, conditions under which European identity is constituted are today experienced, and felt, in a radically singular way. With this proposal, the first axiom is further specified. Derrida asks:

> And what if Europe were this: the opening onto a history for which the changing of the heading, the relation to the other heading or to the other of the heading, is experienced [*ressenti*] as always possible? An opening and a non-exclusion for which Europe would in some way be responsible? For which Europe *would be,* in a constitutive way, this very responsibility? As if the very concept of responsibility were responsible, right up to its emancipation, for a European birth certificate? (*OH* 17)

Undoubtedly, Europe has in the past repeatedly posed to itself the question of its own identity, its conceptual nature, its inherent telos, its difference and relation to the other heading, and even to the other of the heading. But compared to past discussions and reflections on this question, the new, and absolutely new experience of European identity consists not only in the fact that it is a *felt* (*ressenti*) identity but also in the fact that this feeling is about the *always possible* change of that identity. More exactly, since the experience in question concerns the constituting traits, the structural conditions of possibility of European identity itself, it is the feeling that precisely those traits that secure its identity in the first place are also responsible for the possibility of this identity's change. Indeed, given that these conditions of possibility are such that they include a reference to the other of Europe—the other headings and the headings of the other—as well as to an other that is no longer categorizable in terms of self-identity and this identity's others, the inscription of such otherness in identity necessarily opens it to a possible alteration. What is felt "today," thus, in a feeling of the moment—the always possible "changing of the heading, the relation to the other heading or to the other of the heading," in short, that identity can only be achieved on the condition that it is always, necessarily and structurally, exposed to possible change—is, at the same time, a transcendental experience (of sorts) of the conditions of all identity, and its limits.[6] Differently put, this feeling which registers an essential debt to the other heading, and the other of the heading, a debt so essential that the possibility of change is intrinsically tied into the positivity of identity, hence, that an element of unpredictability is inevitably part of identity, is the "new" felt identity of what it means to be European. Unlike the responsibility of European humanity to its inborn telos, and to the idea of a universal rational essence of mankind, the new experience of identity to which Derrida refers is marked by an essential insecurity. Furthermore, the responsibility that comes with this transcendental experience is not a responsibility for anything inborn, but rather for openness and non-exclusion, not only to the other, to other concepts or horizons, but even to the other of the concept and the horizon, without which no self-identity is thinkable.[7]

As I have intimated, Derrida's recasting of the notion of European identity as a feeling of an identity that in an essential manner implies an openness, and a debt toward the other heading and the other of the heading, addresses the shortcomings of the Husserlian conception of what is most properly Europe's innermost own. It is a feeling of identity that assumes responsibility for everything identity implies. Commenting on this new experience of the constituting difference of European identity as an affirmative experience of the always possible change (precisely insofar as identity is owed to the Other, and [if I may say so] to the Other *of* the Other) of these seminal differences without which there can be no identity whatsoever, Derrida writes that this experience "presents itself in an absolutely new way, not new 'as always' [*comme toujours*], but newly new" (*OH* 17). As an absolutely new experience, it is a truly singular experience and not a variation on the old ways in which Europe has questioned the conditions of its identity. But if this experience is so new, why still call it by the old name "Europe"? What necessity compels retaining this designation to identify something never identified under the name of "Europe," something entirely new? Does not Derrida make it amply clear that "that which seeks or promises itself *today*, in Europe," is not given, "no more than its name, Europe being here only a *paleonymic* appellation" (*OH* 30–31). Is it because "Europe" has essentially something to do with identity itself? Is it because what is in question here is the possibility of an effective intervention, and reshaping, of what hith-

erto has been meant by identity? If the new experience, and the responsibility in question, are still named "Europe," is it not, first, because of Europe's legacy as far as the thought of universality is concerned? Is it not
because of what "we, Europeans," "recall (to ourselves) or what we promise (ourselves)," as Derrida writes (*OH* 82)? Precisely because Europe has
been the name for the concept or idea of universality—of an innermost
own rationality of mankind—it is incumbent upon Europe to assume the
responsibility to and for the felt openness and nonexclusion that all
claims to identity, willingly or not, imply. But there is still another reason
why this responsibility should still be called by the old name "Europe," a
name synonymous with universality. Indeed, to use the name "Europe"
as a denomination for the responsibility in question is to engage the Europeans, first and foremost, in that responsibility. Calling it by that name is
a performative, a first singularization of this responsibility, one that is
binding and that calls on Europeans to respond to its call insofar as they
are Europeans, that is, the inheritors of a mode of thinking that sought
universality from the start. But to designate this universal responsibility
by that name is also to emphasize that it articulates a feeling that no
longer pretends to speak in the name of the Other, and on his or her
behalf. However, if it is true that this responsibility concerns the European first and foremost, it does not follow at all that the identity that it
confers would merely consist in Europe's turning in on itself. No withdrawal into any particularity takes place here. Rather, the felt responsibility, that is, its extreme singularization (because felt) of a universal respect
for the Other, radically commits the European. Finally, even if the feeling
of such a universal respect excludes making demands upon the Other,
this does not in any way diminish the universal sweep of the European's
singular responsibility. An experience as the one described not only ap-
plies to Europe. But the responsibility that it articulates does not tolerate
summoning the Other to act accordingly. It allows even less to impose
this responsibility upon the Other.

Before further exploring the necessities that tie "Europe" to this responsibility, in other words, before explicitly taking on the question of
universality and singularity in *The Other Heading,* I return to the experience in which the identity of Europe is established by way of the feeling
of the always possible changes of the constituting traits of identity itself
and which I have qualified as transcendental. How can Derrida lift a feeling, a mere feeling, one would like to add, to such heights and make it
do what, according to Husserl, properly belongs to the competence of
reason? Undoubtedly, in the history of philosophy, certain *pathe* have

been shored up and freed from their intrinsic irrationality, and thereby granted a philosophical status beyond the merely private one that is normally associated with them. One thinks, for instance, of admiration in Descartes, respect in Kant, love in the early Hegel. One is especially reminded of the kind of feeling that, according to Plato and Aristotle, is at the origin of philosophy itself—the feeling of wonder. If, hereafter, I shall seek to clarify Derrida's referral to a transcendental feeling of sorts via a somewhat long digression through a text by Heidegger, it is because that text not only seeks access to the essence of philosophy from the singular feeling of the *thaumazein,* but because it also determines philosophy as an essentially Greek approach, in short, as synonymous with Greece, and to some extent with Europe as well. Understood this way, Europe exists first, although only implicitly so in Heidegger's text, as, and in accord with, a certain state of mind.

In *What Is Philosophy?* Heidegger argues that although "sentiments, even the finest, have no place in philosophy," a feeling or, more precisely, a mood or state of mind (*Stimmung*) characterizes philosophy and philosophizing at its most fundamental level. This fundamental disposition or affection by which philosophy moves and concerns us (*uns be-rührt, uns angeht*) is of the order neither of "that which is usually called feelings and emotions, in short, the irrational," nor of rational thinking, but is prior to this distinction and is a transcendental disposition of sorts as well (*WP* 27).[8] By confronting Heidegger's elaborations on the state of mind which is coeval with philosophy, and which is thus also coeval with the West or Europe,[9] with Derrida's understanding of the new feeling concerning European identity, I hope to show, first and foremost, that in *The Other Heading* Derrida stages a critical debate with Heidegger's notion of *Stimmung* and the latter's claim that such a disposition is what properly constitutes the specificity of philosophy, and hence also of Europe, or the West.

Heidegger reasons at the beginning of his text that any response to the question "What is philosophy?" requires an attunement to what specifically resonates in that word but also to what is implied by a question such as this, a question that asks "what is." Without such an attunement, the answer not only remains exterior to what is in question and to the questioning mode; it also remains exterior to the questioner rather than concerning him or her expressly, and in depth. The answer, therefore, demands not only that one "hear the word 'philosophy' coming from its source . . . the word ['philosophy'], as a Greek word," but also that the question that inquires into the whatness of something be heard as an "originally Greek question" (*WP* 29, 39). I will take up, one after the other, Heidegger's expositions on the original meaning of the word *philosophia* and on the intrinsically Greek nature of the question itself:

1. According to Heidegger, "the word *philosophia* tells us that philosophy is something which, first of all, determines the existence of the Greek world [*Griechentum*]. Not only that—*philosophia* also determines the innermost basic feature [*innersten Grundzug*] of our Western-European history" (*WP* 29). Essentially, philosophy is Greek because "in origin the nature of philosophy is of such a kind that it first appropriated [*in Anspruch genommen hat*] the Greek world, and only it, in order to unfold" (*WP* 31). It is Greek not primarily because its factual emergence dates back to sixth-century Greece, but because the Greeks were the first to answer its claims and to make its idea the basis for the singular existence of the Greek world. Indeed, it is the response of Greece as a whole to the idea of philosophy that endows Greece with its singular firstness and makes philosophy a Greek thing. Philosophy is Greek to such an extent that even the fact that it has been guided and ruled since the Middle Ages by Christian conceptions does not make it Christian in any way. No religious faith nor authority of any other kind can change philosophy's originary Greekness. A non-Western philosophy is a contradiction in terms, philosophy and the West being exchangeable notions, Heidegger holds. He writes: "The statement that philosophy is in its nature Greek says nothing more than that the West and Europe, and only these, are, in the innermost course of their history, originally 'philosophical'" (*WP* 31). Greece itself was the first to embody this ideal, and Europe is "philosophical" at least inasmuch as the innermost trait of its intellectual history is concerned. Heidegger's only supporting argument, echoing Husserl's elaborations in *The Crisis*— that the development of the sciences is proof of Europe's "philosophical" nature and destiny—provides a first clue as to what the word "philosophy" implies. Indeed, if the modern sciences' ability "to put a specific imprint on the history of mankind upon the whole earth" and to inaugu-

rate "ages" of the world (*Weltalter*) is interpreted as proof of their stemming "from the innermost Western-European course of history, that is, the philosophical" (*WP* 33), then the "philosophical" becomes intimately linked to a concern with humanity and the world as a whole. Philosophy, then, is the theoretical and practical assumption of a responsibility for the concerns of mankind as such, and for what is of the order of the whole earth, the whole world. Consequently, philosophy's original Greekness consists in nothing less than the fact that this singular nation conceived of itself and acted in accord with universal principles, principles that transcended Greece as a particular nation and people. Only in this sense, Heidegger concludes, can the philosophical—the word *philosophia*—be said to "appear on the birth certificate of our own history" (*WP* 35).

2. Undoubtedly, questioning is not the sole privilege of Greece and the Western world. But what then is the supposedly specifically Greek mode of questioning? *Ti estin,* "what is it," inquires not only into the *whatness* of a singular thing; it also gives "an interpretation . . . of what the 'what' means, in what sense the *ti* is to be understood" (*WP* 39), Heidegger explains. As is obvious from the dash that in the German title of Heidegger's book—*Was is das—die Philosophie?*—both separates the question "what is" from that which is being questioned, "philosophy," and also simultaneously gathers these two parts together, the question "what is" inquires into something distinct from the singular subject of the question, something that is of the order of the universal rather than of the singular. The Greek question, a question that (by way of its form) already contains its answer, postulates an engagement of the universal in the singular something. It interprets the singular, its whatness, from a dimension that is, in principle, recognizable by all at all times, even though it may have received very different determinations throughout the history of philosophy. The specificity of the Greek questioning mode thus resides in its asking after the meaning of the whatness of something singular, and

that in distinction from this singular thing is universally shareable. Further, the form itself of the question *ti estin* makes it a question pertinent to everyone as well. By virtue simply of its form, it can claim universality. Hence, to ask the question "What is it—philosophy?" is to ask a Greek question both in form and content. "We ourselves belong to this origin even when we do not mention the word 'philosophy.' We are peculiarly [*eigens*] summoned back into this source and are re-claimed for and by it as soon as we not only utter the words of the question, 'What is philosophy?' but reflect upon its meaning," Heidegger remarks (*WP* 39). In short, for Heidegger as for Husserl, this responsibility for and to universality, not merely as a theme but as a form as well, in other words, universal answerability, is the proper heritage of the Greek tradition, the "innermost basic feature" of what Europeans can claim most properly as their own. To be European is to be Greek, and to be Greek means to be concerned not with oneself but with what is to be universally predicated of all; more precisely, to be Greek means to be concerned with things as they present themselves, with their what-ness *in propria persona,* before the arrival of any concealing interpretation, resulting from factors such as customs and beliefs, traditions and traditionalisms. Furthermore, to be Greek is not only to be concerned with what is relevant to humanity at large; it is also to be concerned with it in a form capable of universal validation.

Before evoking what resonates in the word *philosophia* when heard with a Greek ear, Heidegger makes, and I quote his own words, "a statement of principles": to "listen . . . to the words of the Greek language . . . [is to] move into a distinct and distinguished domain . . . [because] the Greek language is no mere language like the European languages known to us. The Greek language, and it all alone, is *logos*" (*WP* 45). Greek is distinct from all known European languages in that it is hardly a language to begin with, if language is thought to be constituted by signs and to be idiomatic in nature. By contrast, in the Greek language, language *is* in an immediate fashion what it names; its names *are* the *whatness* of things. Heidegger holds: "What is said in it *is* at the same time in an excellent way what it is called. If we hear a Greek word with a Greek ear we follow its *legein,* its direct presentation [*Darlegen*]. What it presents is what lies immediately before us. Through the audible Greek word we are directly in the presence of the thing itself, not first in the presence of a mere word sign" (*WP* 45). With the Greek language one is thus in the direct presence of the whatness of a thing or concept. It is a language transparent to a point that its words, by directly presenting the very essence of something, are indistinguishable from what they name. Not only does this language postulate that all particular things have their universal concepts, but as the language *of* conception and conceptualization, rather than of some particular idiom, it is a universal language, universality as language itself. In sum, the Greek language is a language that breaks with Greek as an idiom, that executes the essence of language, in order to say and exhibit things as they are originally in themselves, that is, before their universally sharable whatness becomes clouded by the sedimentations and interested coverings-up of particular idioms, including that of Greek itself.

Philosophia as a Greek word is, then, the direct presentation of what it names! Authorized by the Heraclitean use of the word *philosophos,* Heidegger defines the originary Greek meaning of *philosophia* as speaking in accord, in harmony, with the *logos* that gathers everything that is into its Being. And he adds that *philosophia* arises at the moment when "the fact that being is gathered together in Being, that in the appearance of Being being appears," becomes "the most astonishing thing for the Greeks" (*WP* 49). This immediate accord alone, this harmony, or correspondence with the *logos*—an accord coextensive to the feeling of astonishment—describes the properly Greek meaning of *philosophia.* *Philosophia,* it follows, is a double accord, not just of thought and Being but of thinking and feeling; more precisely, of a thinking anterior to "philosophy" and the isolated *pathos* of astonishment. Indeed, Heidegger claims that thinking becomes "philosophy" as soon as this original harmony is lost—as soon as thinking, no longer in accord with Being, becomes *episteme theoretike,* that is, the search for what in Aristotle's words is forever and forever missed, namely, the search for what is being—and this claim only underscores the prerational, pretheoretical, precognitive nature of a thinking that is originally inseparable from a certain kind of feeling, a feeling ennobled by the "fact" (a "fact" of universal bearing) that provokes it.

Significantly enough, for Heidegger, the thinking/feeling of *philosophia* is not yet a thinking that questions. Thinking enters the questioning mode characteristic of philosophy only at the moment when the initial accord no longer prevails, when thinking becomes a "yearning search for the *sophon,* for the 'One (is) all'"; or, more precisely, when "the being in Being . . . becomes the question, 'What is being, in so far as it is?'" (*WP* 53). The philosophical questioning mode "what is" (*ti estin*) betrays already a loss of access to Being itself and is thus derivative from the lost accord that had been achieved in *philosophia.* Thus, it is not so much the question *ti estin* as it is the thinking/feeling of *philosophia* in harmony with the *logos* and with a "fact" of universal sweep, which is specifically Greek. This thinking/feeling alone, indeed, deserves to be truly called Greek. But at the same time, every mode of thought, whether it is a declaration of the loss of *philosophia,* an attempt at rescuing it, an all-out attack on it, or even a deliberate ignoring of it, depends for its intelligibility on this original harmony of a thinking that is not yet thinking (in that it is not yet distinct from feeling) and a feeling that is not yet feeling (that is, in distinction from thinking), which is in harmony with Being and which thus remains inherently Greek—that is to say, European, or Western. This is all the more the case for a discourse in the philosophical questioning mode, one that asks "what is," and singularly, "What is philosophy?" An answer to this question, if there is to be one, can, therefore, "only be a philosophizing answer which, as a response, philosophizes itself" (*WP* 65). Such an answer requires that the philosopher be attentive to what has been lost and to what it is that, by its loss, provokes the question in the first place. A philosophical answer is, therefore, not a reply to a question in the form "what is." It presupposes, instead, a displacement of the questioning and answering mode. A philosophical question, in Heidegger's terms, must cor-respond (*ent-sprechen*) to what is in question, or more precisely to what in the question addresses the philosopher. He writes: "If this cor-respondence is successful for us, then, in the true sense of the word, we respond to the question, 'What is philosophy?'" (*WP* 69). Response demands here a prior listening to that which has already avowed itself to us, and of which the question into the whatness is only, as it were, a negative, in order for the response to become a cor-respondence. "In such a correspondence we listen from the very outset to that which philosophy has already said to us, *philosophy,* that is, *philosophia* understood in the Greek sense" (*WP* 71). What, then, is the nature of this cor-respondence?

Resuming his discussion of the role of "fine sentiments" in philosophy, Heidegger writes:

Philosophia is the expressly accomplished correspondence which speaks in so far as it considers the appeal of the Being of being. The correspondence listens to the voice of the appeal [*Stimme des Zuspruchs*]. What appeals to us as the voice of Being evokes [*be-stimmt*] our correspondence. "Correspondence" then means: being de-termined [*be-stimmt*], *être disposé* by that which comes from the Being of being. *Dis-posé* here means literally set-apart, cleared, and thereby placed in relationship with what is. Being as such determines speaking in such a way that language [*Sagen*] is attuned [*sich abstimmt*] (accorder) to the Being of being. Correspondence is necessary and is always attuned [*gestimmtes*], and not just accidentally and occasionally. It is an attunement [*Gestimmtheit*]. And only on the basis of the attunement (*disposition*) does the language [*Sagen*] of a correspondence obtain its precision, its tuning [*Be-stimmtheit*]. (*WP* 75-77)

If in the correspondence of *philosophia* express attention is given to the voice of the appeal or avowal of Being, correspondence is determined by that voice, "affected" by it, as it were, and granted a voice itself. In correspondence, the voice of Being, by avowing itself, not only opens up the space for a possible addressee and respondent; it attunes the addressee's speaking as well, by tuning it to Being's own voice. A correspondence thus achieves an accord, an accord which is, first and foremost, a *Gestimmtheit,* a mood, sentiment, disposition, or state of mind. Heidegger concludes:

As something tuned and attuned [*ge-stimmtes und be-stimmtes*], correspondence really exists in a tuning [*Stimmung*]. Through it our attitude is adjusted sometimes in this, sometimes in that way. The tuning understood in this sense is not music of accidentally emerging feelings which only accompany the correspondence. If we characterize philosophy as tuned correspondence, then we by no means want to surrender thinking to the accidental changes and vacillations of sentiments. It is rather solely a question of pointing out that every precision of language [*Sagens*] is grounded in a disposition of correspondence, of correspondence, I say, heading the appeal. (*WP* 77-79)

The disposition in question is an essential (*wesenhaft*) disposition. It is neither of the order of sentiments, in the sense of irrational counterparts of thinking, nor of the order of intellectual adequation to things;

rather, already presupposed by such orders, this disposition precedes the classical distinction between feelings and rational thought. In all rigor, attunement (*Stimmung*) is not a feeling. It precedes feeling, just as much as the accord that it brings about between saying and the voice of Being precedes rational thinking, and thus precedes any propositional definiteness and determinateness.

To characterize philosophy by this essential disposition of correspondence is, for Heidegger, an insight that refers back to the early understanding of philosophy in Greek thought as belonging "in the dimension of man which we call tuning (in the sense of tuning and attunement)" (*WP* 79). Indeed, Heidegger holds that, according to Plato and Aristotle, the fundamental *pathos* of wonder, or astonishment, is not only the starting point of philosophy but also the mood that "carries and pervades philosophy" at all times (*WP* 81). Every single moment of philosophizing reactivates this special "feeling" in which "we step back, as it were, from being, from the fact that it is as it is and not otherwise," to face, in a fascination of sorts, Being, the Being of being itself. Yet what one is drawn to in the retreat from beings, is something that extends beyond all particular beings, is Being itself—in traditional philosophical language, a universal shared by everything that is. Being, as Heidegger puts it in *Being and Time,* is "*the* transcendens *pure and simple*."[10] The feeling that retreats and is drawn to this "universal" is, as it were, universal as well. Tuned and attuned to Being as the *transcendens* pure and simple, it is by right a feeling ennobled by this *transcendens,* a feeling unlike all other feelings.

From what I have just said, I retain that *philosophia* is, first and foremost, a cor-responding attunement to Being itself. As an attunement to Being, *philosophia* is thus something essentially Greek, or rather is that which alone merits to be called Greek. Greekness is understood here no longer as the essence of Greece in an empirico-historical or sociocultural sense. Greekness is but the ennobling ability of a people (the Greeks, for example) to break with, and depart from, itself as a particular nation in time and space. Europe, or the West, insofar as its innermost basic features are Greek, is thus to be understood according to that same qualification. At its most elementary, Greece, or Europe, is, for Heidegger, and in distinction from Husserl's understanding of Europe as rooted in a rational idea, nothing but a universally sharable feeling—even though Heidegger does not speak of universality, the term having too traditional and humanist connotations—about the enigma of Being.[11] This tunement and attunement to Being, named Europe, or the West, sets Europe not only necessarily apart from other cultures that have not raised themselves, by concerning themselves with *the transcendens* pure and simple, above their particularity, but from itself as well. Yet even though this attunement to Being and its openness makes Europe different from itself, and should, in principle, prevent it from closing itself upon itself, this difference with and to itself inevitably tempts Europe to cultivate this difference for its own sake. For Derrida, this temptation is not absent from the writings of Heidegger, as his reference in *The Other Heading* to "the vigilant sentinels of being" shows. These sentinels, in the name of Being, guard the border that the difference between self and other creates within Europe or the West, so that the latter's identity should not be exposed to other conceptions of universality, or to the other of universality (*OH* 26). Attunement to Being, that is, to the difference which, according to Heidegger, makes all the difference, can also become a powerful incentive to remain at home, entrenched in cozy and smug self-sufficiency. How, then, are we to distinguish Derrida's reference to a feeling that is constitutive of the identity of Europe from Heidegger's elaborations on a fundamental attunement? Is not Derrida's call to reactivate the debt to the Other, and also to the other *of* the heading, an attempt to open the fundamental disposition or attunement, an attempt to complicate the always alluring tendency to turn the difference with and from self caused by the concern with Being into a self-achievement? Could the reactivation of this debt have been conceived of specifically in order to address the possibility that the difference with itself, which is at the heart of Europe's idea of universality, can also always become a means for self-closure; a possibility that seems to have escaped the vigilance of the vigilant sentinel of Being? In this case, however, the feeling that pervades *The Other Heading* is entirely different from any previous notion of feeling. It is less fundamental than Heidegger's fundamental attunement, but it is at the same time indebted to, and doing justice to, other headings; which is still to say nothing of that which eludes the logic of identification altogether, the other *of* the heading.

In order to begin answering these questions, it is not without significance to remark upon the thoroughly different tone of Heidegger's and Derrida's discussion of feeling. Compared to Heidegger's solemn, if not pompous, seriousness, Derrida's approach to the subject maintains a certain ironic distance, and, as is evident from the first axiom of the book, plays on a self-irony regarding his own undoubtedly earnest identification with what is European. It is an irony motivated by a particular tension; namely, that as a European one can subscribe to what "Europe" has stood for and still promises only by also looking elsewhere. But this difference in tone is indicative of a much deeper difference in concern. Undoubtedly, the feeling Derrida calls "Europe" is a feeling that is also universalist in its sweep. But unlike *Stimmung,* which is the fundamental attunement to Being, Derrida's "Europe" is a feeling which acknowledges that, however insuperable the thought of Being may be, Being as a "universal" is indebted to, and limited by, other universals (and possibly by the opposite of the universal), and even by something other than the universal and the nonuniversal. It articulates a feeling concerning both the limits and the always possible alteration of what precisely it is that remains necessary in order to secure something universal, and to identify this universal as such. There is no question here of substituting one universal principle for another, or for the opposite of universality, but rather of recognizing (by way of feeling) that any universal principle is what it is in demarcation from other, possibly opposite principles, including the opposite of a principle, and from something that eludes the fundamental difference between the universal and the particular. In short, the sentiment evoked in *The Other Heading* takes on the Heideggerian conception of *Stimmung* to demonstrate that however legitimate the appeal to Being is in determining the essence of *philosophia,* and simultaneously of Europe, this very appeal presupposes both a relation and an indebtedness to the Other, neither of which may be overlooked or discounted. This felt debt changes the *Stimmung* from top to bottom. The recognized debt to the Other includes the debt to what has been called the other *of* the universal, without thereby rephrasing that other as a particular; and what is felt to have universal pertinence under the name of "Europe" commits the European, first of all, to that debt.

One problem has been left in abeyance, and it concerns Europe's claim to being a head and a heading in the first place. In his discussion of the ongoing debate among European nations about the possible site for a capital of European culture, Derrida notes that what is at stake is "not only the predominance of a national language, tongue, or idiom, but the predominance of a *concept* of the tongue or of language, a certain idea of the idiom that is being put to work" (*OH* 46–47). Undoubtedly, this discussion betrays the fierce struggle between the European nations for control over European culture and for national hegemony in the domain of European culture. But, as Derrida writes, "national hegemony is not claimed—today no more than ever—in the name of an empirical superiority, which is to say, a simple particularity." Indeed, national hegemony "claims to justify itself in the name of a privilege in responsibility and in the memory of the universal and, thus, of the transnational—indeed of the trans-European—and, finally, of the transcendental or ontological" (*OH* 47).[12] The point made here is that Europe's claim to be a head and heading is not merely an expression of what it undoubtedly has been, namely, a region characterized by its factual technological superiority and its cultural arrogance, but is a further expression of its inherent drive for hegemony. All claims in this regard take for granted a superiority of Europe; and they are justified, as Derrida points out, not on empirical but on universal grounds. Yet why would this be so? Could it have to do with the fact that all hegemony claims, whether made by Europe or by anyone else, presuppose a prior self-identification; and could it be that any identity claim is a claim to some superiority?

Derrida puts forth the argument that universality, and the difference it makes—particularly in the case of Europe—is a value that cannot be surrendered without condoning the worst violence; therefore, he claims, one must subscribe to the logic of capitalization and maximization by which universality is brought about. At the same time, one must not fail to look for something other, which means not only "for what is already found outside Europe . . . [but] to the to-come of the *event,* to that which *comes,* which comes perhaps and perhaps comes from a completely other shore" (*OH* 69). After making these points, Derrida returns to the question of the relation of universality and singularity. Universality as a *value* implies singularity, Derrida maintains; it is, necessarily, the universal of singulars and must therefore embody itself in exemplary fashion within the singular. Conversely, Derrida explains that any

> self-affirmation of an identity always claims to be responding to the call or assignation of the universal. There are no exceptions to this law. No cultural identity presents itself as the opaque body of an untranslatable idiom, but always, on the contrary, as the irreplaceable *inscription* of the universal in the singular, the *unique testimony* to the human essence and to what is proper to man. (*OH* 73)

What this means is that, in every instance of self-identification, wherever a singularity seeks to identify itself it must make the claim that its singularity represents in exemplary fashion the universal values of humanity. In the case of Europe, the conception it has had of itself as a head and a heading is a response to this inevitable requirement for a consolidated identity to begin with. In addition, wherever and whenever self-identification takes place, which is to say, not only in the case of Europe but in every case, then the claim for a special responsibility to the universal is made. "Each time, it has to do with the discourse of *responsibility:* I have, the unique 'I' has, the responsibility of testifying for universality. Each time, the exemplarity of the example is unique" (*OH* 73). To illustrate the generality of this formal law, according to which no self-identification is possible without taking charge of the universal and putting oneself in charge of it, Derrida refers to a "personal impression" of Valéry, according to whom the French *believe* and *feel* that they are "*men of universality.*" Notwithstanding the subjectivity of the impression, and the subjectivity of the phenomenon itself, the belief and feeling in question are, according to Valéry, "constitutive of the essential or constitutive traits of French consciousness in its 'particularity.'" The French, as it were, feel themselves into what they are by believing, as Valéry phrases it, that they "specialize in the sense of the universal" (*OH* 74). Identity, the identity of a singularity—in this case, Frenchness—is thus constituted by the feeling on the part of the French that they exemplarily represent humanity, or the universal. But Derrida holds that the paradox "is not reserved for the French. Not even, no doubt, for Europeans" (*OH* 75). Because of the formal law linking all self-identification of a singularity to universality, this feeling of specialization within the universal may well be—"paradox of the paradox" (*OH* 75)—a universal feeling. If this is so, then the implications of this paradox must be drawn out with care.

From this final paradox, it follows that all claims ("all the propositions and injunctions") by any self-identifying singularity, which are, as we have seen, claims to universality, are inherently divided and de-identified. Indeed, if all singularities such as nations can and even *must* claim this status as "men of universality," then any identity, any heading, any superiority "is related to itself not only in gathering itself in the difference *with itself* and with the other heading, with the other shore of the heading, but in opening itself without being able any longer to gather itself" (*OH* 75). Any exemplary embodiment of universality, any exemplary responsibility to and for what is common to all humanity, presupposes an openness to the Other, and the Other *of* the Other, to the point where all successful gathering into a closed and undivided self-identity becomes impossible. Far from implying that all gathering is therefore an illusion or mystification, this opening is precisely the condition of the possibility of gathering. Only *from* the other's identity and claim to a privileged representing of universality, as well *from* the other *of* identity and universality, do the exemplary embodiment and the responsibility to and for universality become meaningful in the first place. To conclude, it is, therefore,

> *necessary* to take note of this [namely, that everything in the position of a head or heading, a limit or concept, is indebted to the other head and heading, and to what is other to this order of things or concepts], which means *to affirm in recalling,* and not simply to record or store up in the archives a necessity that is already at work anyway. It has begun to open itself onto the *other shore of another heading.* . . . Yet it has at the same time, *and through this even,* begun to make out, to see coming, to hear or understand as well, the other *of* the heading in general. More radically still, with more gravity still—though this is the gravity of a light and imperceptible chance that is nothing other than the very experience . . . of the other—it has begun to open itself, or rather to let itself open, or, better yet, to be affected with opening without opening *itself* onto an other, onto an other that the heading can no longer even relate to itself as *its* other, *the other with itself.* (*OH* 75–76)

I recall that, for Derrida, "Europe" today is the experience, or sentiment, of this necessity that all claims to identity and universality require nonexclusion and an opening to the Other, the non-Western; but also to what is still strictly to come, hence not calculable, hence other than the opposition of the Western and the non-Western. It is the limit-experience of the constitutive de-identifying traits, without which there can be no identity, concept, limit, or horizon. Defined in these terms, "Europe" is the idea of responsibility itself. Indeed, as the recalling-experience of the traces of the Other in identity—of their reactivation—"Europe" could be understood as an identity responding to, affirming, and reaffirming the Other from which it draws the possibility of (being) itself. "Europe," in what constitutes it most properly, could thus be construed not only as a thankful acknowledging experience of the debt to the Other but as the demand for universal responsibility to and for the Other. This experience of "Europe," its singular feeling that any identity must at heart be that of a responsibility to and for the Other—a feeling of universal scope—still merits being called "Europe," because the name "Europe" has always meant a head and a heading. It is what could still make Europe potentially different, and put it ahead of itself, in the position to no longer be itself.

It might make Europe different from itself if it were understood to name and embody the universal demand that justice be done to the Other. As a demand for openness, universally, this feeling is not only a demand that Europe not close itself and not make itself comfortable in its difference with itself and others. It is the demand made upon the Europeans above all, that is, upon those who have seen themselves ahead, to seek their identity in opening and nonexclusion, and in abiding universally by the limits to which all responsibility, even a responsibility to and for responsibility itself, remains indebted.

Notes

1.   The following text is a chapter of a book-length study in progress on various attempts to probe the philosophical resources of the concept of Europe in the face of the senile reactivation of the cosmopolitan idea of peaceful coexistence, or the return to isolationist and nationalist values, that have marked the ongoing debate on Europe.

2.   Jacques Derrida, *The Other Heading: Reflections on Today's Europe,* trans. P.-A. Brault and M. Naas (Bloomington: Indiana University Press, 1992), 12, 19. Hereafter cited as *OH.*

3.   Edmund Husserl, *The Crisis of European Sciences and Transcendental Phenomenology,* trans. D. Carr (Evanston: Northwestern University Press, 1970).

4.   Massimo Cacciari, *Gewalt und Harmonie: Geo-Philosophie Europas,* trans. G. Memmert (Munich: Carl Hanser, 1995), 170.

5.   Jean-Luc Nancy, *The Inoperative Community,* trans. Peter Connor, Lisa Garbus, Michael Holland, and Simona Sawhney, ed. Peter Connor (Minneapolis: University of Minnesota Press, 1991), 12.

6.   At the risk of the always possible reinscription into a classical problematic of precisely that which Derrida's text seeks to displace, I shall call this singular feeling, because it is also one about conditions of possibility, a transcendental feeling, as it were. I make this claim in order to demarcate this feeling from what one ordinarily understands by that term and to emphasize its singularity. Needless to say, Derrida's texts question the possibility of the distinction between the empirical and the transcendental, but such de-transcendentalization does not, for that matter, seek a return to the ontic, the empirical, the historical, or the relative. What is at stake for Derrida is not the necessity of the distinction but rather the possibility of its absoluteness. The point Derrida makes is that a transcendental experience occurs in a singular experience, and in the case of the conditions of European identity, moreover, in a mode that is not cognitive but rather of the order of sentiment.

7. See, for instance, *OH* 78–79, where Derrida speaks of the duty of "tolerating and respecting all that is not placed under the authority of reason" and the necessity to respect even "whatever refuses a certain responsibility."

8. Martin Heidegger, *What Is Philosophy?* trans. W. Kluback and J. T. Wilde (Estover: Vision Press, 1989). Hereafter cited as *WP.*

9. "The often heard expression 'Western-European philosophy' is, in truth, a tautology," Heidegger claims (*WP* 29–30).

10. Martin Heidegger, *Being and Time,* trans. J. Macquarrie and E. Robinson (London: SCM, 1962), 63.

11. Undoubtedly, Heidegger's reservations regarding the concept of universality go much deeper. Unlike the rational idea of Husserl, an idea that can, and must claim universality, the thought, or feeling of Being, though not anti-universal, implies a displacement of that concept, and conceptuality.

12. The same is valid for singling out and imposing one language as the language of European culture. On philosophical and conceptual grounds, rather than on the basis of any empirical or even pragmatic superiority, one might justify placing one language ahead of all the others as the representative of a more promising idea of language. In other words, a language's superiority can be justified only on the grounds of its greater ability to reach beyond the national, the idiomatic; that is, on the grounds that its conceptual range extends beyond the particularity of its idiom to include the implicit responsibility for and to what is universal that comes with that greater range. It is a superiority that presents itself, in short, that makes claims for itself, and answers to the claims it makes.

The Politics of *Différance*

Tel Quel and Deconstruction

Joan Brandt

In spite of a number of studies that make a compelling argument in favor of the political implications of deconstruction's interrogation of politics (not to mention the many works in which Derrida himself addresses this question), there are those who have remained and will no doubt continue to remain unconvinced that such an interrogation is anything more than a retreat from the political itself.[1] Nancy Fraser is, of course, one of the first critics who comes to mind in this particular context,[2] but a more recent work by Simon Critchley, which makes a strong case for the ethical dimensions of deconstructive thought, conceived in the Levinasian sense as an opening to the alterity of the Other, argues that deconstruction fails when it comes to translating the undecidability of that ethical relation into a course for political action.[3]

Joan Brandt

In an effort to respond to the criticism proffered by Fraser, Critchley, and others, this essay argues that it is precisely this relation to otherness inscribed in the undecidable "logic" of *différance* and supplementarity that not only constitutes what Critchley describes as the "ethical moment" within deconstruction but contains distinctly political possibilities as well, possibilities for assuming our political "responsibility to act" while rethinking the philosophical precepts upon which our concepts of political action are grounded.[4] In order to make this point, I consider the question of the political from a more historical perspective by examining the highly charged political climate of the late 1960s and early 1970s out of which deconstruction's interrogation of conventional notions of the political emerged. For what has up to this point received little attention from those who characterize poststructuralism's, and particularly deconstruction's, "privileging" of language as an apolitical textualism or a perverse kind of nihilism is that those who are usually assembled under the "poststructuralist" label (as if they were part of a monolithic theoretical "movement") responded to the turmoil surrounding the student uprisings of May 1968 in very different but nevertheless "political" ways, with some, such as the members of the *Tel Quel* group, becoming increasingly militant and others, such as Derrida, resisting the revolutionary rhetoric of those caught up in the political frenzy of the period.

Just why deconstruction and *Tel Quel*, whose interests were initially quite similar, moved in such different directions is a question that, I believe, is worthy of consideration, because it has political repercussions that are still being felt today. Indeed, the struggle that continues to be waged by Derrida, Kristeva, and others to find new ways of thinking about the political can be traced to that highly volatile period of the sixties when the more revolutionary aspects of Marxist theory were gaining an increasingly strong hold upon many French intellectuals, particularly upon those associated with *Tel Quel*, the avant-garde French journal to which Derrida was also an early contributor. Founded in 1960 by Philippe Sollers in an effort to challenge the major literary currents of the early postwar years, *Tel Quel*, in fact, became a powerful intellectual force in the late 1960s, when it served as a vehicle for the dissemination of many of the ideas of the newly emerging French theorists and literary writers, including such innovative thinkers as Foucault, Barthes, Derrida, Kristeva, Lacan, and Althusser.

While these writers were joined in a common effort to call into question the principles of identity structuring traditional notions of language,

148

literature, philosophy, and politics, it should be remembered that there were those who became increasingly alienated by the political radicalism that began to emerge at *Tel Quel,* where a failure to assume a certain "responsibility to otherness" was to have devastating political consequences. Attacked and even ridiculed for its naive utopianism and its increasingly doctrinaire tendencies, the *Tel Quel* collective came to be repudiated by its own members. Openly criticizing, in 1981, the "romantic vision" that prevailed during *Tel Quel*'s politically militant period of the late 1960s and early 1970s, Philippe Sollers denounced the idea of a collective effort, claiming not only that the collectivity itself could be just as oppressive as the social order it opposed but that its goal of accomplishing social revolution through a revolution in language was an "illusion" that had structured the activities of many of the avant-garde groups of the twentieth century.[5]

What began as a radical interrogation of "literary ideology" and related notions of representation, meaning, author, reader, and the literary work of art degenerated into a doctrinaire application of Marxist/Freudian theory in an effort to revolutionize language and the literary text. Believing that capitalist ideology is embedded in Western representational discourse and traditional literature, whose logic of meaning works to suppress difference and heterogeneity and thus to preserve the fundamentally constricting and repressive structures dominating almost every aspect of Western bourgeois culture, the group argued that by formulating a revolutionary textual practice that would bring to the surface those material, heterogeneous forces that have been traditionally repressed, it would be possible to undermine the objectivist, capitalist ideology embedded in Western discourse and thus help to achieve by indirection a transformation of the social order and its repressive laws as well. What occurred, however, in the course of its effort to implement its revolutionary poetic practice and theory was the constitution of a collective that became itself increasingly restrictive. Through its insistence upon conformity, upon a common identification with its revolutionary ideal, the *Tel Quel* collective came to embrace, both in its discourse and in its very structure, the exclusionary logic it sought to oppose. Instead of the spirit of openness and exploration that seemed to prevail during the early days at *Tel Quel,* when the journal and its collaborators were receptive to a wide range of divergent views, there now seemed to be one major theme that came to dominate, at least in the *Tel Quel* editorials. That was their adherence to a revolutionary Marxism as it intersected with Freudian theory. It led first of all to a rapprochement with the French Communist

Party, then to a rejection of the Party's "bourgeois" politics and a turn toward Maoism, and ultimately precipitated bitter feuds with anyone who refused to adopt a common practice and whose "discourses" were "contrary to the Marxist/Leninist line."[6]

Indeed, the politics at *Tel Quel* and the seemingly endless flow of strident editorials demanding a strict adherence to its particular interpretation of Marxist/Leninist doctrine led not only to a paradoxical reinstatement of the very tactics, behavior patterns, and thought processes of the oppressive linguistic and socioeconomic systems it had initially hoped to contest, but also to the constitution of a binary vision of reality that could not help but insinuate itself into *Tel Quel* theory. For the oppositional, objectifying, and therefore "capitalist" logic that grounded *Tel Quel's* polemics also structured its notion of the "revolutionary" text. It required that the closed, essentially readable product of the literary tradition be seen as diametrically opposed to the open, "unreadable" process of textual production. *Tel Quel's* politicization of the literary text, which stemmed from the unquestioned belief in its revolutionary capacities, indeed raised a number of difficulties for *Tel Quel* theory, not the least of which was the assignment of a certain "essence" or specificity to the structures it was working against, assuming a quality of cohesiveness that was taken to be intrinsic both to the traditional literary text and to the social system of which it is a part. As a result of this, however, the group had to uphold the very concept of language, with its premises of unity and meaning, that it had set out to undermine.

This problem is particularly evident, I would argue, in those places in Kristeva's writings where, in the course of her elaboration of a materialist theory of language which provided the basis for the literary activity of the members of the *Tel Quel* group, she posits a distinction between the discourses of poetry, which render the ungrammaticalities of semiotic rhythms and intonations particularly explicit, and the discursive operations of normative language. The problem here is not so much Kristeva's claim that poetic language brings to the foreground the "undecidable character of any so-called natural language [which] univocal, rational, scientific discourse tends to hide"[7] as it is her tendency to forget the undecidability inhering in *all* forms of discourse when she stresses the unsettling, disruptive, indeed revolutionary potential of the "poetic" and of the semiotic processes with which it is linked. For normative discourse, in this case, particularly when it is tied to the formation and socialization of the speaking subject, acquires a coherence and uniformity that allows it to perform a strictly repressive role. Indeed, it seems incontrovertible that the process of politicization at work at *Tel Quel* informed Kristeva's reading of the literary text as well, leading her away from her more radical interrogation of the representational assumptions structuring all traditional notions of language and literature (and from the possibility that the resistance to closure actually functions within representation itself) toward a more conservative conception of language which places the cohesive structure of representational discourse in opposition to its more aberrational, unstructured, indeed, "poetic" manifestations. For Kristeva believed at the time that it was by means of the modern, "polyphonic" literary text, whether in the form of Céline's scatological narrative and its "vision of the abject" or the "poetic language" of Sollers's *Nombres,* with its meaningless repetition of sounds and rhyme, that the repressed heterogeneity often associated with the maternal phase could be *restored* to discourse, thus wedging an opening in the closures constituted by the literary and philosophical tradition.[8]

This particular view of the traditional text informs Kristeva's and *Tel Quel*'s misreading of Derrida's notion of *différance* as well. As a notion that refers to the spatio-temporal movement within language that both generates and defers meaning, Derrida's *différance* was initially valued by *Tel Quel* for its capacity to function as a kind of unconscious infrastructure of language, working in conjunction with Marxist and Freudian theory to disrupt capitalist/patriarchal institutions whose authority depends upon traditional notions of the sign and its assumptions of absolute presence. What formed, however, the basis of an alliance between *Tel Quel* and Derrida also contributed to the eventual break between the two. Not only did the journal criticize Derrida's refusal to embrace revolutionary Marxism,[9] at which time Derridean theory came to be referred to as *"le gla-gla précieux derridien"* (affected Derridean gobbledygook),[10] but Kristeva, in a far less polemical way, began critiquing the dissolution of the thetic in Derrida's grammatological project:

> [G]rammatology denounces the economy of the symbolic function and opens up a space that the latter cannot subsume. But in its desire to bar the thetic and put (logically or chronologically) previous energy transfers in its place, the grammatological deluge of meaning gives up on the subject and must remain ignorant not only of his functioning as social practice, but also of his chances for experiencing *jouissance* or being put to death. Neutral in the face of all positions, theses, and structures, grammatology is, as a consequence, equally restrained when they break, burst, or rupture: demonstrating

disinterestedness toward (symbolic and/or social) structure, grammatology remains silent when faced with its destruction or renewal.[11]

The possibility for political action is undermined by Derrida's theory because his term *différance,* according to Kristeva, which turns the Hegelian notion of negativity into a positive or affirmative concept, provides no notion of the subject as agent of social change. Negativity, in this case, becomes "drained of its potential for producing breaks" and thus fails to account for the splitting that produces the speaking subject. "[S]ince *différance,*" Kristeva writes, "neutralizes productive negativity, it is conceived of as a *delay* [*retard*] that comes *before* . . . the sign, *logos,* the subject, Being. . . . In this way the trace dissolves every thesis . . . it can do so because it grasps the formation of the symbolic function preceding the mirror stage and believes it can remain there, even while aiming toward that stage" (*RPL* 142–43).[12] Recognizing, however, that Derridean grammatology would "undoubtedly not acknowledge the pertinence of this psychoanalytic staging [*stadialité*], which depends on the categories and entities of beings" (143), Kristeva reveals that her revolutionary project is, in fact, dependent on such distinctions and categories. Not only do transgressive strategies require a notion of the subject for their conceptualization and implementation, but such strategies would indeed become worthless if there were no way to theorize the linguistic and social constraints that are meant to be transgressed. This is, in fact, what is implied in Kristeva's critique of deconstructive analyses of Husserlian phenomenology:

> [S]uch "deconstructions" refuse (through discrediting the signified and with it the transcendental ego) what constitutes one function of language though not the only one: to express meaning in a communicable sentence between speakers. This function harbors coherence (which is indeed transcendental) or, in other words, social identity. Let us first acknowledge, with Husserl, this thetic character of the signifying act, which established the transcendent object and the transcendental ego of communication (and consequently of sociability), before going beyond the Husserlian problematic to search for that which produces, shapes, and exceeds the operating consciousness (this will be our purpose when confronting poetic language). Without that acknowledgement . . . any reflection on significance, by refusing its thetic character, will continu-

ally ignore its constraining, legislative, and socializing elements. (*DL* 131)

In seeking to preserve the position of the subject by acknowledging its constraining, legislative power, Kristeva also aims to safeguard a place for those heterogeneous elements that are meant to break down the boundaries that the subject imposes, for it is her view that deconstruction's denial of the thetic constitutes a denial of heterogeneity as well. Indeed, if *différance* is a movement that always "precedes" the sign and subject, if, that is, there is no subject that has been saved from "foundering in inarticulable instinctuality" (*RPL* 148), then there can be no thought of the semiotic heterogeneity in which the differential movement of the trace supposedly takes place. Consequently, and more importantly, without the possibility of "experiencing" semiotic heterogeneity and its drive-related effects, there can be no affirmation of its transgressive capabilities:

> Although it begins by positing the heterogeneity in which *dif-férance* operates, doesn't grammatology forget this heterogeneous element the moment it neglects the thetic? Doesn't it indefinitely delay this heterogeneous element, thus following its own systematic and philosophical movement of metalanguage or theory. Indeed grammatology seems to brush aside the drive "residues" that are not included in the *différance* toward the sign, and which return, heterogeneous, to interrupt its contemplative retention and make language a practice of the subject in process/on trial. (*RPL* 143–44)

While *différance,* in this case, seems paradoxically to have acquired the constraining capabilities that Kristeva previously claimed it lacked, and thus to have reinstated a notion of the thetic in a theory that presumably dissolves such possibilities, Kristeva's point is to show that grammatology, in failing to account for the subject *and* for its "object," heterogeneity, thus undermines any possibility of a political role for Derrida's notion of *différance.* In making this argument, however, she not only moves *différance* out of the realm of heterogeneity by linking it more closely to that of the symbolic, but she shows once again that her own and *Tel Quel's* revolutionary strategy is dependent on the preservation of these two categories and on the logic of contradiction which allows one to "subvert" the other. If, therefore, as Toril Moi has stated, Kristeva's "insistence on the *reality* of the drives" is what "forces her to oppose

Derrida's grammatological project" (*KR* 16), if, that is, she posits the existence of "nonsymbolized," "nonsymbolizable," "nondeferred energy charges," which *différance* as a process of deferral or "symbolic becoming" has presumably "effaced," it is for the principal reason that in order for instinctual heterogeneity to maintain its status as a radically disruptive force, it must be preserved as an unmediated space of pure drive uncontaminated by symbolic structurations (including those of *différance* itself). It depends as well on a logic of negation whose potential for instituting the break between the semiotic and the symbolic is not only what constitutes the subject but also what allows it to be put "in process/on trial."[13] This is why Kristeva believes that the revolutionary potential of the Derridean project is still unrealized. While she clearly affirms that project at the outset of her argument, claiming that it is "the most radical of all the various procedures that have tried, after Hegel, to push dialectical negativity further and elsewhere," she finds that its range is still too limited, that it must be pushed even further to a point where the unleashing of heterogeneous "energy discharge" within the movement of *différance* itself brings about a full realization of its disruptive capabilities:

> This instinctual heterogeneity—neither deferred nor delayed, not yet understood as a becoming-sign—is precisely that which *enters into contradiction with différance* and brings about leaps, intervals, abrupt changes, and breaks in its spacing [*espacement*]. Contradiction can only be the irruption of the heterogeneous which cuts short any *différance*. . . . The return of the heterogeneous element in the movement of *différance* (symbolic retention, delayed becoming-sign-subject-Being), through perception and the unconscious (to use Freudian categories), brings about *the revolution of différance* [my emphasis]: expenditure, semantico-syntactic anomaly, erotic excess, social protest, jouissance. (*RPL* 144)

Différance has thus been radicalized or even "heterogenized" by Kristeva's reworking of Derrida's notion. As a form of "erotic excess," or *jouissance,* it becomes an instrument of "social protest" and is thus made to work in much closer conformity with *Tel Quel*'s revolutionary program. This effort to push Derrida's grammatological project in a more explicitly political direction had been made in an even more concrete and direct way several years earlier in an interview, published in *Positions,* between Derrida and two members of the *Tel Quel* group, Jean-Louis Houdebine and Guy Scarpetta.[14] Here, some of the questions raised on the theoretical level by Kristeva were placed in the context of Derrida's commitment to Marxism. The interview showed that points of divergence, even at a time when Derrida was still expressing his "solidarity" with the *Tel Quel* group (*P* 78), were becoming increasingly apparent as the interviewers grew more insistent in their effort to pin Derrida down on the question of dialectical materialism. Anticipating the questions raised later by Kristeva in *Revolution in Poetic Language,* they confronted Derrida directly on the issue of heterogeneity as it relates to both Marxist theory and Derrida's own texts. They objected that, despite the many points of convergence between Derrida's notion of "writing" and the "materialist text," there was not only a curious lack of explicit reference to Marxist theory in Derrida's work, and most particularly in his essay "La Différance," which was first published, interestingly enough, by *Tel Quel,*[15] but also a reduction of the "motif of heterogeneity" to a "theme of spacing," whereby the "differences" articulated in Derrida's analysis came to lose their radicality by becoming merely another variant of the Lacanian symbolic.

Claiming that it is the very logic of Lacanian categories (certain aspects of which Kristeva will also embrace) that his work calls into question, Derrida insisted that the movement of *différance* as *dissemination,* as that which remains irreducible to a single unity of meaning, is what actually "resists . . . the order of the 'symbolic'" just as it undermines the possibility of any hypostatized notion of "heterogeneity" as the "symbolic's *simple* exterior" (*P* 84–86). Consequently, when Houdebine pressed Derrida further on the question of the text and its relation to dialectical materialism whose logic, as Houdebine defined it, is to be "articulated on the basis of the conceptual series 'matter' (that is, an irreducible heterogeneity in relation to a subject-meaning)/contradiction/struggle of the contraries . . . in the process of their transformation" (*P* 60), his comments elicited from Derrida the following response:

> It is not always in *the* materialist text (is there such a thing, *the* materialist text?) nor in *every* materialist text that the concept of matter has been defined as absolute exterior or radical heterogeneity. I am not even sure that there can be a "concept" of an absolute exterior. If I have not often used the word "matter," it is not, as you know, because of some idealist or spiritualist kind of reservation. It is that in the logic of the phase of overturning this concept has been too often reinvested with "logocentric" values, values associated with those of thing, reality,

presence in general. . . . In short, the signifier "matter" appears to me problematical only at the moment when its reinscription cannot avoid making of it a new fundamental principle which, by means of theoretical regression, would be reconstituted into a "transcendental signified." . . . It then becomes an ultimate referent, . . . or it becomes an "objective reality" absolutely "anterior" to any work of the mark. . . . I do not believe that there is any "fact" which permits us to say: in *the* Marxist text, contradiction *itself,* dialectics *itself* escapes from *the* dominance of metaphysics. (64–65, 74)

It seems clear, then, that Marxism, or a certain reading of Marxist theory which posits the "triumph of materialism"[16] and the hierarchical oppositions matter/meaning, same/other, outside/inside, homogeneous/heterogeneous upon which such a position rests, could itself be subject to a deconstruction of its precepts in Derrida's view—although Derrida himself had up to that point never engaged in a lengthy critique of Marxist theory (or of *Tel Quel,* for that matter) and claimed that he would rather avoid contributing to the attacks so prevalent in the late 1960s directed at groups on the left. This does not mean, however, that the motif of "irreducible heterogeneity" (which for Houdebine "constitutes the materialist motif *par excellence*") had been banished from the Derridean notion of *différance.* On the contrary, if the motif can be interpreted as a "radical alterity" that undermines and displaces such oppositions, Derrida's own work could, as Derrida himself indicates, be considered "materialist" (*P* 64). In this sense, however, Derrida's argument goes further than that of *Tel Quel* by showing in what way the spacing that Houdebine and Kristeva find too closely associated with "linguistic differences" is not only compatible with the motif of heterogeneity but is also what undermines the "purity" of such concepts as heterogeneity itself. For it could be argued that Houdebine's version of heterogeneity, which he defines, citing Kristeva, as that which is "without meaning, outside and despite it" (*P* 74), ceases, in this case, to be heterogeneous; it becomes instead self-identical, uncontaminated by those "linguistic" elements that presumably remain outside its borders. Consequently, when Derrida speaks of "radical alterity," it is not to assume a similar position of pure exteriority whereby heterogeneity as a hypostatized "Other" would ultimately be subsumed under a notion of the Same, but to point to an otherness that inhabits the self-identical, not as the result of some subversive or transgressive act but as an alterity that has always been internal to any closed structure, be it linguistic or otherwise.[17]

This inscription of otherness within the self-same is indeed what is indicated by Derrida's notion of *différance,* with which the notion of spacing is associated. As a movement within language that generates and is, at the same time, drawn into the play of differences that ultimately constitutes meaning, *différance,* although it precedes the production of meaning, cannot itself be looked upon as an absolute point of origin or causative agent, for it exists only as an operation that produces differences and is, therefore, continually caught up in the very process it has set in motion. The origin or source of signification, in this case, does not remain outside language but becomes a function within the differential movement of language itself. *Différance* as spacing is not therefore an entity; it, in fact, "designates *nothing.*" By bringing not only the temporal deferral of presence but the spatial distinction that places it in relation to an other, *différance* is what marks the impossibility for an identity to close in on itself. And it is in this sense that spacing becomes indissociable from the concept of alterity. As Derrida argues, "the irreducibility of spacing is the irreducibility of the other," but the other, in this case, functions not as an entity with a definable essence remaining outside the linguistic system, but as a movement of alterity that is inserted *in it,* thereby displacing all forms of identity including that of the system itself. If, then, Derrida shows a certain reticence with regard to Houdebine's insistence on the "materialist position," it is because alterity (or heterogeneity), in his view, can never be "posed" as such. Indeed, to do so would be not only to reinstate the traditional subject/object relation but to remain inattentive to the differential relations that constitute but also problematize the self-contained identity of both the subject and of the object that is "positioned" before it:

> If the alterity of the other is *posed,* that is, *only* posed, does it not amount to *the same,* for example in the form of the "constituted object" or of the "informed product" invested with meaning, etc.? From this point of view, I would even say that the alterity of the other *inscribes* in this relationship that which in no case can be "posed." Inscription, as I would define it in this respect, is not a simple position: it is rather that by means of which every position is *of itself confounded (différance):* inscription, mark, text and not only *thesis or theme*-inscription of the *thesis.* (P 95–96)

What is required then, according to Derrida, is both a rethinking of the "concept" of alterity and, perhaps more important, an interrogation of the idea of the "position" itself, and of the subject who "takes it," for these too are effects of *différance,* marked by the irreducibility of the other in the spacing relations that constitute them. To say, however, as Derrida does, that the subject cannot be conceived of in terms of a "pure self-presence" is not to indicate, as Kristeva has maintained, that *différance* "dissolves every thesis," or, in the words of Scarpetta, that for Derrida "the 'subject' of writing does not exist" (*P* 88). What *différance* marks is not the disappearance of the subject; it challenges instead a certain notion of the sovereign subject as master of its discourse and fully present to itself. Thus, the intentionality of the speaking or writing subject still has its place within the differing-deferring structure of *différance;* what is limited, however, is "the simplicity of [the subject's] features, its *undividedness.*"[18] Given that the subject does not precede *différance,* spacing, and iterability but is, in effect, dependent on them for the manifestation or ex-position of its "presence," the subject is caught up in a temporizing movement of deferral, constituted only as it is divided from itself. Consequently, there can be no opposition or contradiction between the subject and its heterogeneous "other," for heterogeneity and contradiction are already internal to its structure. As Derrida states in his interview with Kristeva, also published in *Positions,* "There is no subject who is agent, author, and master of *différance,* who eventually and empirically would be overtaken by *différance.*" The subject, like its object, has not, in this case, been eradicated; it is seen instead as "an effect of *différance,* an effect inscribed in a system of *différance.*"[19]

This means, however, that Derrida's notion of *différance,* which shows that the subject is always already a "subject in process/on trial," calls into question the principal assumptions structuring *Tel Quel*'s revolutionary project. For if Kristeva and Scarpetta object to the dissolution of the subject in Derrida's work, and if Houdebine tries to preserve heterogeneity by insisting on the difference between spacing and alterity (which can only be associated in his view as they confront one another as part of the "basic dialectical materialist contradiction"), it is because the two concepts serve *Tel Quel*'s political function, satisfying the need to preserve not only the identity of the subject to be transgressed but the subversive position of those "nonsymbolized," "nondeferred energy charges" that characterize instinctual heterogeneity.

If the members of the *Tel Quel* group thus refused to grapple with the questions raised by Derrida's essay, preferring instead to inscribe *différance* within what was becoming an increasingly reductive conception of the Marxist dialectic (through which the Marxist conception of contradiction initially embraced by Sollers in all its complexity was functioning as little more than a simple conflict between two opposing forces),[20] it was perhaps because Derrida's analysis of *différance* underscored the problematical nature of the hierarchizing oppositions upon which *Tel Quel*'s and indeed all conventional conceptions of the political depend. By showing that each element is always related to something other than itself, Derrida foregrounds the redundant (not to mention metaphysical) character of any concept of transgression that presumes the integrated status of an inside (in this case, of the subject and its mimetic representations) that has not yet been contaminated by that which presumably remains outside the subjective enclosure. In marking heterogeneity as an otherness that inhabits all forms of identity, the movement of *différance* indicates that the subversion of the self-present subject has always already taken place. *Différance* must be seen, then, not as a movement that completely dissolves subjectivity but as one that interrogates, in a way that went beyond *Tel Quel*'s own investigations of the subject, the very essence of subjectivity itself.[21] Had the politics at *Tel Quel* permitted them to remain open to the implications of Derrida's analysis, they would have seen that *différance* had no need of being "heterogenized" or radicalized.[22] While it works in service of no political program, and indeed calls into question such notions, *différance* marks an inscription of heterogeneity that is infinitely more radical, one that, in fact, allows for an examination of the very modes of thought that make politically repressive discourses possible.

That examination has been undertaken in its most explicitly political context by two important proponents of deconstruction, Philippe Lacoue-Labarthe and Jean-Luc Nancy, both of whom have written rather extensively in recent years on the mechanisms of fascism and its totalitarian logic. In claiming that traditional mimetic principles (manifested most directly in representational language but also evident in the sociopsychological identificatory mechanisms shaping psychic and communitarian identity) are at the very root of National Socialism, where the formative or fashioning power of the German myth is what strives to constitute national identity, they underscore the extent to which the deconstruction of traditional mimetic precepts and a more radical understanding of Derrida's notion of *différance* have important political ramifications by serving as a means of destabilizing the myths of the Aryan state and thereby of resisting the totalizing logic of which fascism is a possible outcome.

One could, in fact, argue that these writers' more penetrating analysis of the logic of mimesis presents possibilities for a reintegration of the political in a way that was in some respects envisioned by *Tel Quel* but that at the same time goes beyond the more doctrinaire aspects of *Tel Quel* theory and practice. That practice failed not only because of *Tel Quel*'s uncritical acceptance of Kristeva's notion of the semiotic as a disruptive space of pure drive existing outside the symbolic and its structuring representations, but also because of its unwillingness to embrace the more radical implications of *différance* itself, whose interrogation of traditional notions of the mimetic and whose confrontation with heterogeneity and otherness far exceed the limits of *Tel Quel*'s less penetrating critique. Although the members of the *Tel Quel* group were among the first to provide a comprehensive, critical analysis of the relationship between the political and language by focusing on the role of representational discourse in shaping cultural and political identity, they did not see that their own identification with a political group and its revolutionary ideal was governed by the very representational logic they set out to contest. For as Lacoue-Labarthe and Nancy show, such identifications take as their point of departure the structure of mimetic representation itself, which, when understood in its traditional sense, involves the subsumption of difference under a structure of sameness and identity and provides the basis, in its most extreme manifestations, for the formation of an exclusionary politics.

Indeed, as we move away from the practices of *Tel Quel* to deconstruction's interrogation of traditional notions of the mimetic, we come to recognize that the concept of mimesis itself takes on a different meaning. Limited by *Tel Quel,* in spite of its critique of traditional mimetic principles, to a more conventional notion of representation, whose unity of meaning and logic of identity must be undermined through the restoration of an excluded heterogeneity, mimesis emerges in the hands of those more closely linked to deconstruction as a process in which heterogeneity is "always already" inscribed. Here, the emphasis is placed on those processes of "depropriation" that have not been excluded by representational language but that are always supposed by the act of representation itself. This shift to a more profound recognition of the contradictions and duplicities that are an integral part of even the most normative discourses has, in my view, considerable political significance. Given that, as both Lacoue-Labarthe and Nancy have argued, the process of identification with a political group or national identity is in itself an act of *mimesis,* involving the mimetic appropriation of some predetermined political model or ideal, deconstruction's foregrounding, through the notion of *différance,* of the duplicities inherent in this mimetic relation to an other ultimately destabilizes the identificatory mechanisms that are essential to the formation of any political community (and this would include the rigidly ideological community formed by *Tel Quel*).[23] It exposes within the very processes that constitute community not the possibility of a closed, self-identical, totalitarian order, but the fundamental loss of the self-identical, the impossibility of closure that the duplicitous structure of mimesis necessarily implies.

Thus, one could argue that it is primarily through a rigorous interrogation of the mimetic on the cultural level, that is, of the identificatory mechanisms founding national identity, which is, according to both Jean-Luc Nancy and Lacoue-Labarthe, the mimetic mechanism par excellence, that provides us with a means not only of undoing the political program of fascism but of resisting the logic of identity upon which all forms of totalitarianism depend. For, if fascism never let up in its effort to exclude the heterogeneous elements undermining the cohesion of the social organization, it was because it carried to its ultimate conclusion the thinking that structures all dreams of political unity, a thinking that requires that the inherently intractable or disjunctive nature of community be forgotten so that the "phantasm of oneness and totality" can be affirmed. This idealized image of a closed and perfectly cohesive communality is, in fact, according to Nancy, one of the Western world's most ancient myths, and Nazism's reactivation and exploitation of its formative power is not only what allowed it to carry out, however imperfectly, its totalitarian objectives, but it exposed the totalitarian essence of myth itself, its desire for a never fully realizable psychological or social enclosure. And while Nancy insists that the thinker of myth is not necessarily responsible for Nazism, Nazi Germany's reconstruction of itself through its mythicizing of the Aryan race clearly shows to what extent the invention of myth "is bound up with the use of its power," allowing for the "staging and setting to work (*mise en oeuvre*) of a 'Volk' and of a 'Reich,' in the sense that Nazism gave to these terms."[24] As a fiction that fashions communitarian identity, and through which the community produces its own essence as its "work," myth presupposes the active adhesion of a people to the models it proposes, a total identification with the "dreamed image" through which the identity of the individual or of the state will find self-fulfillment.

It is thus because myth can be defined as the instrument of this identification (that is, as the instrument of a *mimesis,* as "*the* mimetic instrument par excellence") that German totalitarianism and its racist ideology became so caught up in its own mythic constructions. For it is the mimetic process alone, according to Nancy, that allows for the constitution of identity, and it does so, in this case, by attempting to hide, in accordance with the most traditional mimetology, any reference to its own constituting mechanisms; it tries to cover over, in other words, any reference to language (for the purity of the Aryan race was, as Nancy and Lacoue-Labarthe point out, linked to blood, not to language) as well as to the relationality that is implied in the very notion of community itself. This is why Lacoue-Labarthe claims that the conventional notion of mimesis is not simply a philosophical problem but a political problem as well. The philosophical condemnation of the mimetic is essential to any process of national identification. Insofar as the contradictions implied in the mimetic relation serve only to destabilize the identificatory mechanisms essential to the self-formation of a political community, people, or race, the "law of the proper" must prevail; there can be no admission of duplicity within the mimetic process itself. As Lacoue-Labarthe argues in *Heidegger, Art and Politics,* "mimetological law demands that *imitatio* rid itself of *imitatio* itself, or that, in what it establishes (or has imposed upon it) as a model, it should address something that does not derive from *imitatio.*" [25]

Thus, if Lacoue-Labarthe is right in saying that fascism is "the mobilization of the identificatory emotions of the masses" (*HAP* 95), it can be looked upon as one of the possible consequences of this attempt to overcome or erase mimetic paradoxality. It shows to what extent the traditional notion of imitation, which tries to eliminate the "improper" by presupposing a unifying and stabilizing return to the Same, can have monstrously political implications. Given that traditional notions of the aesthetic and of representational discourse are at the very root of the program of National Socialism, where the formative or fashioning power of the German myth is what constitutes national identity, then a notion of *différance,* which bears within it the traces of the nonpresent otherness, provides us with a means not only of destabilizing the political program of fascism but of resisting the logic of identity upon which all forms of totalitarianism depend. It challenges all of our most deeply embedded assumptions regarding the formation of a common political identity and points, as a result, to new ways of thinking community, where the political is not conceived in terms of a "fashioning of a people" but in terms of a "people" whose unraveling of the traditional models of fashioning gives rise to a community of an entirely different sort. It gives rise to something resembling Jean-Luc Nancy's notion in *The Inoperative Com-*

munity of the "unworked" or "unfashioned community" in which singular beings are exposed to their own limits. Here, we conceive of social structures not simply as repressive and exclusionary but more in terms of what emerges in the writings of a former member of the *Tel Quel* group, namely in Kristeva's *Strangers to Ourselves,* where community is seen as a gathering of finite beings whose very fragmented existence disrupts the traditional communo-political order. The disruption occurs not through a deliberate and willful act of transgression but by uncovering the heterogeneous "other" inhabiting all social (as well as representational) constructs and by countering even the most vicious attempts by the totalitarian apparatus to eliminate it through its countless purges, denunciations, and exterminations.

In this case, resistance does not come from the restoration of excluded heterogeneity which works to subvert a presumably stable social or linguistic order; it comes, as Nancy maintains, from the exposure of that order's inherently "disjunctive nature" through which society is revealed as "neither a work to be produced nor as a lost communion" but rather as a relational space of shared "singularities." It comes, in other words, from a world in which the gathering of finite beings destines community to its own "unworking," underscoring the impossibility of constituting itself as a "pure collective totality," calling into question the unifying function of myth itself.

This "unworking" of the identificatory mechanisms constituting community in the traditional sense thus responds to an exigency that goes far beyond a simple preoccupation with the textual or with the "nihilistic" refusal of one's ethico-political responsibility. For if, as a French poet has written, it was in the Nazi camps that "the resemblance of creatures [i.e., identification, mimesis] . . . reached . . . its zenith,"[26] if cultural and racial difference was exterminated within their barbed enclosures of hatred, then it is the recognition of this very otherness and of our shared state of incompletion that the Derridean notion of *différance* implies, that constitutes our ultimate defense against the political acts of exclusion and intolerance. Had the members of the *Tel Quel* group understood this, they would have recognized the limitations of their own project by acknowledging that heterogeneity, the specter of the excluded "other," was already inscribed within it. What is more, they would have seen that deconstruction's focus on the limitations of the discourses constructing national identity, together with its recognition of the very unattainability of the myth of absolute cohesion, are what open up the possibility for an engagement in real-world issues by allowing for the kind of political struggle that might possibly resist the appropriations, identifications, and propensity for closure to which the *Tel Quel* group, both in its theory and its practice, eventually succumbed.

Notes

1. A case for the political character of Derrida's thought was made as early as 1982 in Michael Ryan, *Marxism and Deconstruction: A Critical Articulation* (Baltimore: Johns Hopkins University Press). For a more recent study, see Drucilla Cornell, *The Philosophy of the Limit* (New York: Routledge, 1992).

2. Stressing the evasive tactics that deconstruction employs when it comes to dealing directly with concrete political issues, Nancy Fraser is particularly critical of Derrida's reticence with regard to Marxism in a *New German Critique* article of 1984. "Why," she asks,

> despite the revolutionary rhetoric of his ca. 1968 writings, and despite the widespread, taken-for-granted assumption that he is "of the left," has Derrida so consistently, deliberately and dextrously avoided the subject of politics? Why, for example, has he danced so nimbly around the tenacious efforts of interviews to pin him down on where he stands vis-à-vis Marxism? Why has he continued "to defer indefinitely" the encounter of deconstruction with "the text of Marx" which he has on occasion promised? (127–28)

Underscoring the "limitations of Derrideanism as an outlook seeking to confront the political," Fraser, whose article was published long before the appearance of Derrida's *Specters of Marx,* clearly viewed Derrida's refusal to declare his position on Marxism as another manifestation of deconstruction's avoidance of politics. See Nancy Fraser, "The French Derrideans: Politicizing Deconstruction or Deconstructing the Political," *New German Critique* 33 (Fall 1984): 127–54.

3. Simon Critchley, *The Ethics of Deconstruction: Derrida and Levinas* (Oxford: Basil Blackwell, 1992).

4. The distinction between the "responsibility to act" and the "responsibility to otherness" is elaborated by Stephen K. White in *Political Theory and Postmodernism* (New York: Cambridge University Press, 1991). Although White sees in Derrida's recent writings "a concerted attempt to explore the turn from the responsibility to otherness," as it was initially formulated by Heidegger, "to the responsibility to act," he claims that Derrida encounters "substantial impasses" in his effort to elaborate an acceptable approach to ethics and politics (76–84).

5.   In a 1981 interview with Shuhsi Kao in the journal *Sub-Stance,* Sollers states:

A collectivity consists of people who get together because they are rebelling against an established order. But as soon as this collectivity takes over, then it is no longer an interesting collectivity. *Tel Quel* was a collective up to the time when the movement threatened to become affirmative. If "Telquelism" were to prevail, it would have to be contested right away; I would even be the first to take command of a Liberation Front against Telquelism.

See Philippe Sollers, interview by Shuhsi Kao, *Sub-Stance* 30 (1981): 40.

6.   In one of his contributions to the journal, for example, Sollers was highly critical of a group of writers who banded together during the politically volatile events of May 1968. The Union of Writers (L'Union des Ecrivains), as it was called, was berated by Sollers for its "confusionist positions," for becoming an "amorphous crowd" (*foule vague*) governed by no overriding principle. Concluding his critique, he wrote: "We say simply that all the discourses that we just analyzed are absolutely contrary to the Marxist-Leninist line which, for us, is the only one that is scientifically founded." See Philippe Sollers, "De quelques contradictions," *Tel Quel* 38 (Summer 1969): 6–7; my translation. Unless otherwise indicated, all translations are my own.

7. Julia Kristeva, "From One Identity to an Other," in *Desire in Language: A Semiotic Approach to Literature and Art,* trans. Thomas Gora, Alice Jardine, and Leon S. Roudiez, ed. Leon S. Roudiez (New York: Columbia University Press, 1980), 135. Hereafter cited as *DL.*

8.   In *Strangers to Ourselves* (trans. Leon S. Roudiez [New York: Columbia University Press, 1991]), Kristeva no longer pits the modern, "polyphonic" literary text against the "monological" structure of traditional literature. She instead finds at the heart of the rationalist Enlightenment tradition manifestations of difference and heterogeneity that have not been repressed but that have been integrated into both the polyvalent discourses of Diderot's literary works as well as the "polyphonic community" of Montesquieu's philosophical texts.

9.   Criticizing Derrida for aligning himself, on the one hand, with the conservative position of the French Communist Party and the university system and, on the other hand, for refusing to accept "the more innovative aspects of Marxist theory," Sollers writes in *Tel Quel:* "As far as Derrida is concerned, let us say that he exploits to the hilt the classical situation where the French Party asks intellectuals to accept above all its party line without becoming involved in politics and least of all in Marxism." See Philippe Sollers, "Critiques," *Tel Quel* 57 (Spring 1974): 136–37. See also *Tel Quel* 66 (Summer 1976): 103–4, and *Tel Quel* 61 (Spring 1975): 5.

10. *Tel Quel* 61 (Spring 1975): 5 n. 1.

11. Julia Kristeva, *Revolution in Poetic Language,* trans. Margaret Waller (New York: Columbia University Press, 1984), 142. Hereafter cited as *RPL.*

12. See also Toril Moi's discussion of Kristeva's attempt "to account for the subject and the splitting (the *coupure* of the thetic) which produces it" in her introduction to *The Kristeva Reader,* ed. Toril Moi (New York: Columbia University Press, 1986), 16. Hereafter cited as *KR.*

13. Tilottama Rajan, in "Trans-Positions of Difference: Kristeva and Poststructuralism," confirms my view when she states that the "notion of a signifying material that operates outside the symbolic is crucial . . . to Kristeva's project of remobilizing as irruption and the heterogeneous what grammatology reduces to the trace and *différance.*" We differ, however, in that she appears to support Kristeva's effort to counter Derrida's "neutraliz[ation of] the political effectiveness of *différance*" by putting it back into the realm of "pre-symbolic immediacy." See Rajan's essay in *Ethics, Politics, and Difference* (New York: Routledge, 1993), 222, 225. *Ethics, Politics, and Difference* hereafter cited as *EPD.*

14. Jacques Derrida, "Positions: Interview with Jean-Louis Houdebine and Guy Scarpetta," in *Positions: Jacques Derrida,* trans. Alan Bass (Chicago: University of Chicago Press, 1981), 37–96. Hereafter cited as *P.*

15. Jacques Derrida, "La Différance," in *Théorie d'ensemble* (Paris: Editions du Seuil, 1968), 41–66.

16. An expression used by Geoffrey Bennington with reference to the *Tel Quel* position in Geoffrey Bennington and Jacques Derrida, *Jacques Derrida* (Paris: Editions du Seuil, 1991), 32.

17. In *P,* Derrida explicitly rejects the discourse of transgression by claiming that "even in aggressions or transgressions, we are consorting with a code to which metaphysics is tied irreducibly, such that every transgressive gesture reencloses us . . . within this closure" (12).

18. Jacques Derrida, *Limited Inc.* (Evanston: Northwestern University Press, 1988), 105.

19. Jacques Derrida, "Semiology and Grammatology: Interview with Julia Kristeva," in *P,* 28.

20. Philippe Sollers, "Sur la contradiction," in *Sur le matérialisme: De l'atomisme à la dialectique révolutionnaire* (Paris: Editions du Seuil, 1974), 121–57. The essay itself was written in 1971.

21. Judith Butler makes a similar case in an essay in *EPD* when she indicates that the failure of Kristeva's political strategy stems not only from her "uncritical appropriation of drive theory" (166) but also from an "exclusively *prohibitive* conception of the paternal law," which fails to "take into account the full complexity and subtlety of the law" itself: "If subversion is possible," she writes, "it will be a subversion from within the terms of the law, through the possibilities that emerge when the law turns against itself and spawns

unexpected permutations of itself." See Judith Butler, "The Body Politics of Julia Kristeva," in *EPD* 177–78.

22.   Thus, I would disagree with Suzanne Guerlac's endorsement of Kristeva's strategy to "'revolutionize' *différance*," which, in linking it to the transgressive movement of negativity (*le rejet*) that sets into motion the mechanisms pulverizing the speaking subject, perpetuates the illusion that such an unproblematized, unified, phenomenal subject actually exists. See Suzanne Guerlac, "Transgression in Theory: Genius and the Subject of *La révolution du langage poétique*," in *EPD* 242.

23.   Philippe Lacoue-Labarthe and Jean-Luc Nancy, "The Nazi Myth," trans. Brian Homes, *Critical Inquiry* 16, no. 2 (Winter 1990): 291–312.

24.   Jean-Luc Nancy, *The Inoperative Community*, trans. Peter Connor, Lisa Garbus, Michael Holland, and Simona Sawhney, ed. Peter Connor (Minneapolis: University of Minnesota Press, 1991), 46.

25.   Philippe Lacoue-Labarthe, *Heidegger, Art and Politics*, trans. Chris Turner (Oxford: Blackwell, 1990), 79. Hereafter cited as *HAP.*

26.   Edmond Jabès, *The Book of Resemblances*, vol. 1, trans. Rosmarie Waldrop (Middletown, Conn.: Wesleyan University Press, 1990), 47.

[T]here would be no gift at all if not the gift of what one does not have, under duress and beyond duress, in answer to an entreaty which strips and flays me and destroys my ability to answer, outside the world, where there is nothing save the attraction and the pressure of the other.
> —Maurice Blanchot, *The Writing of the Disaster*

Que désirez-vous donner
C'est le geste qui compte
> —Michel Deguy, "Donnant, donnant"

Ethical Figures of Otherness

Jean-Luc Nancy's Sublime Offering and Emmanuel Levinas's Gift to the Other

Dorota Glowacka

In *The Writing of the Disaster* (1980) Maurice Blanchot asks, "Why is the necessity of the gift so regularly expressed in our time, and yet assigned such different significance by thinkers as adverse and diverse as George Bataille, Emmanuel Levinas, Heidegger?"[1] What is the nature of this necessity, which has inspired the work of the "philosophers of the gift" cited by Blanchot, as well as of many others such as Jacques Derrida, Jean-Luc Nancy, and Jacob Rogozinski? For Emmanuel Levinas, the ethical relation with the Other precipitates the absolute gift of my world to the neighbor. On the other hand, Jean-Luc Nancy's rereading of Kant's aesthetic theory foregrounds the gesture of offering in the sublime as that which opens up the possibility of aesthetics. In this study, I will argue that the problematic of the gift traverses the borders between the philosophical categories of ethics and aesthetics, skirting the limits of the two realms and at the same time calling them into question.

The problematic nature of the relation between beauty and morality, good taste and good conduct, has been debated in the West since at least the time of Plato's *Republic*. The expulsion from the polis of poets—the imitative tribe, whose frolics had a negative effect on both morality and rational cognition—has become a symbol of the divisiveness between the two disciplines. Yet already Aristotle, Plato's most famous disciple, sought to rehabilitate mimesis and reasoned that art, tragedy in particular, is the foundation of moral education and a positive instrument of character formation. Ever since, the question of the interrelations between ethics and aesthetics has been suspended between the belief that art improves moral character and the view that it is self-sufficient and non-teleological, alienated from political, social, and ethical concerns.

The stricturing of the separation between the two philosophical realms punctuates Kant's inquiry into the nature of aesthetics in *Critique of Judgement*. Kant elevates aesthetic experience as surpassing every empirical standard and emphasizes its reliance on the free play of imagination, unbound by cognitive concepts and free from all guidance of rules. At the same time, the aesthetic experience of the sublime is said to allow man a glimpse of his higher destination in the realm of practical reason. This bridging, however, remains incomplete since, as Kant stresses repeatedly, the concurrence between beauty and morality works only by analogy, in the manner of "as if" (*als ob*).[2] Kant's placement of aesthetics as a philosophical centerpiece inaugurates aesthetic interpretations of other spheres of life, including morality. For instance, Schlegel proclaims that thought must aspire toward the truth and sublimity of the ultimate work of art, while Schelling fuses philosophical investigation with the contemplation of art when, in *The Philosophy of Art,* he refers to the universe as a work of art and to world history as a great poem. For Schopenhauer, aesthetic contemplation is the ultimate form of knowledge, epitomized in the art of music, which expresses the true meaning of things and "speaks of the will itself" (*The World as Will and Idea*). Nietzsche, in turn, sees art as the very expression of life, increasing the feeling of power (*The Birth of Tragedy*).

It is the moment of Dionysian frenzy in art, extolled by Nietzsche, that will lead the ethical philosopher Levinas to spurn aesthetics: "There is something wicked and egoist and cowardly in aesthetic enjoyment."[3] Mystical yearning for the Absolute, which suffuses art, sunders metaphysical desire for the absolutely Other. On a grand historical scale, Levinas's writings caution against the dire consequences of the growing aesthetization of ethics, reiterating Walter Benjamin's warning, in 1934, that "[a]ll efforts to render politics aesthetic culminate in one thing: war."[4] Certainly, it is no coincidence that war-making is usually referred to as an "art." In the preface to *Totality and Infinity*, Levinas writes: "The state of war suspends morality. The *art* of foreseeing war and winning it by every means—politics . . . is opposed to morality" (my emphasis).[5] The crusade against totality undertaken by Levinas involves realizing the dangers of an increasingly massive aesthetization of reality and the subsequent dissolution of the Other's alterity in aesthetic constructs and discursive practices. Aesthetics epitomizes the collusion of the Western politics of representation with power, and Levinas denounces the way in which it legitimates an arrogation of the Other's freedom. Yet, the arrival of the gift into Levinas's discourse problematizes his pronounced hostility toward aesthetics, just as Nancy's recasting of the Kantian sublime in terms of offering puts into question his apparent eliding of the ethical. The sublime, *sub-limitas,* always concerns itself with the limit and the possibility of transgressing the limit. It necessarily introduces the jargon of transcendence and destabilizes the borders traditionally considered to be indivisible and impermeable.

Contemporary philosophers of the gift point to a stubborn recurrence of the gift in the total economy of being. An unabsorbable remainder, the gift produces a disequilibrium in the system, destroying its homeostasis and interrupting the cycle of return. The gift has made a frequent appearance in Derrida's works, from *Donner le temps (Given Time)* and *Glas* to his more recent texts such as *Aporias* and *Donner la mort (The Gift of Death)*. Proceeding from the elucidation of Heidegger's *es gibt*—the structure of giving time and Being—Derrida elaborates the nonphenomenal character of the absolute gift; rather than belonging to a flow of objects, the gift occurs as the event of giving, which must not enter the symbolic order.[6] As a thing handed over and perceived as gift, it would only incur a debt and ultimately return to the giver: "*Oikonomia* would always follow the path of Ulysses" (*GT* 7). Conventional understanding of the gift as a present or presence within the structure of economic exchange, as discussed in Marcel Mauss's influential work, misses the radical nature of the gift altogether.[7] The gift must remain irreducible to presence; as Derrida remarks in *The Gift of Death,* "it demands a temporality of the instant without ever constituting a present."[8] As a gesture of giving, the gift is always already withdrawn or sacrificed as "object," and it never appears to the subject as the consequence of a volitional act. The gift disrupts representation because it signifies as giving before the subject engages in any self-identifying operations. The gift takes place outside the subject's Odyssean adventure, yet it functions as a structural necessity that opens up a rift between the subject and the economies in which it has always already been thrown. The gift dismantles the economimetic structuring of the world, but it is in view of this "impossibility inscribed in the promise of the gift" (*GT* 24) that the Western subject is constituted. It is worth noting that, so far, the problematic of the other remains as the absent pole of Derrida's own calculation. In his later writings, which were prominently influenced by Levinas's ethics, Derrida avers that the gesture of giving happens insofar as it is always oriented toward the other, exterior with respect to the self-absorbed, self-knowing subject.

According to Levinas, the self's journey toward the Other cannot take place as a consequence of *conatus,* which would only return the Other to the Same, but it is always provoked by the outer term that remains unthematized—incomprehensible and unmediated by concepts. The non-adequation of the Other and the Same is anterior to intentional consciousness, which, as in Husserl's scenario, can only construct the other by analogical appresentation, as a moment in the ego's self-perception. For Levinas, the Western representational paradigm amounts to a grand egological project, and aesthetics colludes in this emprise of the Other. Already in his essay on Leiris's *Biffures,* "The Transcendence of Words" (1949), Levinas refers to ethics as waking up from aesthetic experience,[9] and in *Totality and Infinity* he denounces aesthetics as "a determination of the other by the same, without the same being determined by the other" (*TI* 170). The image always arises within the horizon of the ego's self-reflective territory and relates to its object by resemblance; thus, it neutralizes or even murders the living, immediate relationship such as can be found in the face-to-face encounter with the Other (*Autrui*). The ethical relation with the Other is nonrepresentational; it imposes a suffocating proximity that leaves no room for mimetic distancing between the original and its copy; the self, out of breath in this encounter, is stripped of the power to reproduce the Other as the image of the Same or to adequately thematize it in language. Mimetic vision cannot pierce the opacity of the transcendent Other and scrutinize its enigma since the Other blocks schematism, that is, in Kant's vocabulary, it deflects imagination's effort to cast the incomprehensible manifoldness into the mold of the known.

In the essay "Aesthetic Totality and Ethical Infinity: Levinas on Art," Jill Robbins notes that, for Levinas, the work of art does not give access to the ethical. However, while examining the chapters of *Totality and Infinity* (1961) that center around the problematic of Work, as well as some of Levinas's earlier essays, Robbins notes an ambivalence in the philosopher's statements on representation and art, poetry in particular. The mark of uncertainty in Levinas's approach to the work of art forces us to rethink the apparent radical disjunction between the aesthetic and the ethical in the philosopher's work. Indeed, one cannot disregard Levinas's frequent excursions into literature, even if he often does not acknowledge these borrowings or downplays their belonging to the domain of aesthetics. For instance, in *Time and the Other,* he comments that the whole of philosophy is only a meditation on Shakespeare, and he frequently quotes Dostoevsky and Rimbaud, as in the famous opening sentence of *Totality and Infinity* (*TI* 33).[10]

In the present study, I seek the source of this ambivalence in the fact that Levinas's deprecating comments about aesthetics refer only to this category in its traditional formulation as the theory and practice of representations, indissociable in the West from the privileging of sight as the epistemological tool par excellence. Further, Levinas speaks of aesthetics solely in terms of the canons of the beautiful, which pronounce themselves as unconditional and universal, and denounces them as accomplices and perpetrators of a totality which always suppresses the Other (*TI* 22). On the other hand, the entire Levinasian project hinges on the problematic of representation and therefore cannot eschew bringing the question of aesthetics to bear upon the ethical. It poses the question about the possibility of testifying to the Other's existence without betraying him or her or lapsing into skepticism. Can there be an experience that would bear witness to the unpresentable Other without recuperating him or her in identification? Can ethics escape the lexicon of ontology and speak a language of the "otherwise than being"? I would like to propose an inquiry into this impasse of ethics through the lens of an "other" aesthetics, as developed in Jean-Luc Nancy's thought of the sublime offering.[11]

According to Nancy, the aesthetics of the sublime has always acknowledged itself to be in crisis, questioning aesthetics' essentialist claim to truthfulness. In his 1984 essay "The Sublime Offering," Nancy insists that the sublime has been a decisive moment in the thought of the beautiful and in art as such. At least since Nicholas Boileau's translation, in the seventeenth century, of the treatise on the sublime, *Peri Hypsos,* attributed to Longinus, the sublime has persisted on the margins of traditional aesthetics and has occasionally erupted as a fissure in the canons of the beautiful. Nancy proposes that, unlike philosophical speculation on art that sublates art into the presentation of truth, the sublime interrogates art in view of its proper destiny, as an offering. In the sublime offering, art suspends itself, incompletes itself, and trembles on its own border, yet it escapes the death sentence passed on art by philosophy. At the same time, the sublime is a critical essence of philosophy: "In the suspension of art, the task of thought is in question."[12]

Despite the high-winged bent of his own rhetoric, Levinas never deploys the concept of the sublime and, to the best of my knowledge, does not even mention the sublime as such. Yet the idiom of the sublime often permeates his powerful descriptions of the ethical relation with the Other. For example, he accentuates the dimension of verticality opened up by the metaphysical desire for the Other; the Other, the Most High, hovers over the Same, who is humbled by the greatness and mystery of what it cannot draw into its epistemological orbit. The metaphor of immense altitude, employed to convey the sense of imagination's failure to access the unpresentable, resonates in the thought of the sublime, from Longinus's examples of sublime rhetoric[13] to, most notably, Kant's account of the mathematical sublime as "absolutely great," that is, exceeding any standard of size. Inherent in these definitions is the notion of transport, the upward progression in which the finite is transcended. It is etymologically present in Kant's term *Erhabene* (from *erheben:* rise, lift, raise, get up), and it pervades Hegel's elaboration of the sublime in Hebrew poetry in the section on symbolic art in *Aesthetics: Lectures on Fine Art.* In opposition to the fixity of the beautiful object or image, the sublime has been defined in terms of ascending movement, in which the perceiving subject is both humbled and elevated. The transcendence of the Other, his or her exteriority, which is irreducible to mere opposition to immanence, points upward in "trans-ascendance," a term Levinas has borrowed from Jean Wahl. Levinas speaks of the Other's radical exteriority as "a fundamental movement, pure transport" ("Meaning and Sense," *CPP* 94); the face as the manifestation of the Other in the ethical encounter is not an immobile surface in which the gestures of my approach toward the Other are reflected. The infinite, the absolutely Other, coincides with *infinition,* that is, with the movement of its own production rather than with its end result.

In Kant's account of the mathematical sublime, infinity, an indeterminate concept of reason, is said to be necessarily unpresentable, unlike determinate cognitive concepts which can be accessed by imagination through schematism. The intensely affective experience of the sublime results from imagination's failure to grasp the idea of infinity, despite a tremendous effort to reach it across the abyss extending between the phenomenal and the noumenal. In the sublime, imagination stretches as if beyond its own limit, in a quasi-transcendent maneuver to which Kant refers as "overspilling." Levinas criticizes Kant's conceptualization of infinity as originating in the finite perceiving subject, which only reaffirms the supremacy of the Same and closes off the Other's positive infinity. Levinas draws instead on the idea of infinity in Descartes's third meditation, in *Meditations on First Philosophy:* for Descartes, the ideatum or "content" of the idea of infinity always exceeds the idea that corresponds to its "image" in the subject. Despite Levinas's bypassing of Kant, however, one should be alert to the language in which he attempts to designate transcendence: the movement of the Same toward the Other is said to be a strenuous and futile reaching-over, while the Other persists always in excess of the knowable, "a surplus over the inevitable paralysis of manifestation" ("Meaning and Sense," *CPP* 96). In the sublime, imagination strains itself to throw a bridge between the domain of understanding and legislating reason, infinitely disjointed from the sensible. For Levinas, despite the Other's suffocating proximity, the unbridgeable abyss separates the ego's territory and the world inhabited by the Other. The ego is bound to recover from the shock of its vain attempt to grasp the inaccessible by recoiling upon itself, into the security of the represented. Yet even the inevitable moment of recuperation is always subtended by the relation to the Other and effectuated as the infinite movement of traversing the distance, in which the Other overflows the boundaries demarcating "my world."

In "The Sublime Offering," Nancy points out that, in Kant's account of aesthetic judgment, the emphasis falls on the free play of imagination: an image does not truly represent its object, although we usually yield to the illusion that it does. Transcendental illusion, in the experience of the sublime in particular, causes the object itself to recede: "Therefore the feeling of the sublime in nature is respect for our own destination, which, by a certain subreption, we attribute to the object of nature (conversion of respect for the idea of humanity in our own subject into respect for the object)" (*CJ* 96). With the object in retreat, imagination does not present an image of something but the very fact that the presentation of an image is occurring. In the free operation of imagination, unbounded by determinate concepts, the faculty of presentation presents nothing but itself in free play, when it schematizes without concepts, prior to any determination. It shows itself as a mere gesture of figuring, which never enters into the finitude of form impressing itself upon the chaos of sensations.

Both Nancy and Jean-François Lyotard[14] note that, despite Kant's insistence on the autonomy, purposelessness, and disinterestedness of aesthetic judgment, in the domain of the beautiful, imagination operates in anticipation of the unity of presentation. It is this instance of presentation as if presenting itself to itself in the aesthetic experience that makes it possible for the subject to represent the world of phenomena to itself; thus, aesthetics is the anticipation of knowledge. In free presentation, reason prefigures itself; the ultimate, albeit recondite, goal of the aesthetic experience is the accord of the faculties and the unity of the subject. In the final calculation, therefore, reason takes possession of representation to make it a technique of self-presentation, and aesthetics turns out to be less autonomous than it is said to be. If it were not for this prehended unity, the unity which reason demands, how would one ever be able to trace a figure of anything? The beautiful then always secretly serves the unifying tendency of reason, and it is indeed complicit with the totality of reason, with the whole. The beautiful comes about as the accord of imagination with the form it presents and relies on the unity of the figure; it foregrounds the presented in the presentation. The pleasure of the beautiful lies in the discovery of the unity of the heterogeneous under the law, so its enjoyment is appropriative. The sublime, however, thwarts reason's stratagems and erodes the carefully wrought architectonics of the faculties. While the beautiful relies on delineation, the precise limit of the figure in accord with its design, the proper domain of the sublime is the formless (*die Formlosigkeit*), the unlimited; in the sublime, imagination is exposed to the outside. The sublime is no longer a matter of (re)presentation but of the outline itself. In the tracing out, setting off, and seizing of the limit, it signals that *there is* form, image, limit, that presentation is taking place. Nancy asserts that the stakes of the sublime lie in the movement of unlimitation (*die Unbegrenztheit*), a continuous removal of the limit, which "takes place on the border of the limit, and thus on the border of presentation" (*SO* 35). Before the sublime is seized in a figure and returned to the beautiful, it occurs as the syncopated tracing of the limit. This movement is radically opposed to the fixity of the figure, its immobility within a contour. The unlimitation is a motion of the limit, in which presentation appears as an endlessly recurring gesture.[15]

The sublime is not about the presentation or even nonpresentation of the infinite because then it would have to be construed analogously to the presentation of the finite. Nancy concludes that the sublime breaks with aesthetics since it is no longer a matter of (re)presentation, of whether something presents itself to the subject, but of the unbordering, dissipating, or splitting of the limit. Imagination plunges overboard, although at the same time it cannot step over the threshold of presentation. In the lexicon of Maurice Blanchot, this paradox of simultaneous separation and touching, the (non)passage to the other side, is designated as *pas-au-delà,* "step-(not)-beyond." The "step" cannot be completed since the gesture never becomes present to the perceiving mind. In that sense, it splits open the definitional line of the border, which alone allows for presentation to congeal into a figure. It also means that the sublime experience does not unfold as a moment in the temporal continuum, which could be apprehended by consciousness and retained as memory or even prehended in anticipation of a concrete shape. What gets re-moved in the movement of unlimitation is the beautiful, all form as such; what remains is syncopation itself, "the strict beating of the line against itself in the motion of its outline" (*SO* 41). In the sublime, the contour points only to itself or, rather, to its own interruption; instead of setting up a figure, it signals the incessant carrying away of all form through "this tiny, infinite pulsation, this tiny, infinite rhythmic burst that produces itself infinitely in the trace of the least contour and through which the limit itself presents itself . . . spasmodic vanishing of the limit along itself into unlimitedness" (*SO* 42).

It has been stated that Levinas continuously returns to the question of presentation in an attempt to elucidate what it means to "image" the face. The encounter with the Other in the face is not a "true" representation in which the Other would have to renounce his or her alterity; it signifies as expression, as that which attends representation but is never absorbed by it. To allow the face to enter into an image is to turn it into a petrified mask and imprison it in a caricature. A phenomenon present to self is always a mute, lifeless image that reclaims the exteriority of the Other for the Same, but from which the absolute Other has already absconded. The epiphany of the face, however, is alive, although it remains concealed by the image in which it is thematized. The Other, when becoming manifest in the face, casts off the dead shell, "like a being who opens the window on which his own visage is taking form."[16] The Other attests to his or her manifestation by vanishing from the visible sign, over and beyond form.

The face of the Other is eminently nonvisual; it is naked to the point of being stripped of the distinctive features that would make it recognizable as a person. Like the God of Mount Sinai, the face presents itself in hearing rather than vision, as a voice that cannot be ignored. As Levinas insists, the manifestation of the other in the face always takes place in language. Yet, the ethical language transcends the relational structuring of the symbolic order and calls the self's mastery into question. The Other evoked in language is not sublatable into the universality of concepts; he or she does not carry out a signifying function but persists expressively, as a singular, uniquely important appeal of the oppressed one. Speech that does not trap the Other in the system of meanings signifies as an interpellation, address, or supplication, in which the I has already been summoned to transcend its ipseity. Jean-François Lyotard, in his discussion of Levinasian ethics in *The Differend,* clarifies that in the discursive universe of the ethical relationship, in which the I is the addressee of the obligation issuing from the Other, the instance of the Other as the addressor of the plea is unmarked. The Other, who is absent from my world, is absolutely unpresentable within my "phrase universe." This is why in the relation with the Other as interlocutor, the silent call for help carries with it the impossibility to represent the visage of the other. Lyotard reminds us that this radical absence of the Other in my world echoes what Kant calls the most sublime passage, the biblical commandment "Thou shall not make graven images."[17]

Offering the gift of my world to the Other consists in speaking the world to the Other. Ethical speech, unmediated by cognition, is an infinite gesture of incision in the language of knowledge and communication, which transports its interlocutors beyond the immanence of conceptual speech. It is straightforward, and it eludes figuration, figures of speech in particular. Levinas, aware that, in systemic speech, the interruption of logos has to be carried out in the language of thematization, often insists on the nonfigurativeness of his own prose.[18] The unpresentability of the absolute Other is not even of the order of negative presentation: this rather awkward phrase, which, since Kant, has connoted the elusive nature of the sublime experience, still carries a promise of ineffable presence, even if it remains beyond the limit of the subject's conceptual grasp. Ethical language, however, invokes the Other without naming him or her, bearing witness to the neighbor's proximity without effacing the infinite distance or trying to fill in for the Other's complete nonexistence in my world. The mark of the Other's being there, the trace of his or her passage through language, invisible in representation, is Saying (*le dire*). Always overflowing the said (*le dit*), Saying, the ethical condition of language, is irreducible to the act or image that signifies. As an attitude of speech, expressing my readiness to respond to the call for help, Saying will have already opened language to the Other. The language in which my responsibility to and for the Other signifies before ever showing itself in the said cedes its desire to access the Other; yet it does not reduce him or her to repressive silence. When Saying signifies in the face, it overflows the Other's presentification in the coercive language of communication. However, it does not negate that language, since only by tracing invisible furrows in the ostensible can Saying attest that the Other is. Thus, it is possible to argue that, in a certain sense, Levinas's distinction between Saying and the said corresponds to Nancy's understanding of the beautiful and the sublime, although it would be reductive to insist on a simple parallelism.

The face-to-face encounter with the Other does not take place in a neutral, homogeneous space but in the world re-marked by the movement outside of oneself (*hors-de-soi*) and asymmetrically vectorized by the necessity to give. This irreversible trajectory toward the Other cannot be comprehended by logos that grasps the Other in knowledge. Thus, the ethical language is primarily dispossession rather than meaning, a donation of my world to the Other. As Levinas explains in his lectures on the Talmud, the absolute passivity of giving in response to the Other's supplication is like offering the Torah; one accepts it with blind obedience before knowing its content: "They act before they hearken!" (*Quatre lectures talmudiques,* quoted in *D* 98). The Other evicts the I from its dwelling in language, from the hearth of the native tongue. It paralyzes and contests all possession; the absolute gift to the Other takes away the I's *chez-soi,* its calm, primordial occupation of the site. Being, says Levinas in his critique of Heidegger's existential analytic of language, "requires man as a native land or a ground requires its autochthon" ("No Identity," *CPP* 144), while in the ethical relation the I is expelled from Being. Ethics requires that the *Da* of *Dasein*'s Being-in-the-world is interrogated because in being there it may usurp someone else's place.

In one of his frequent allusions to Rimbaud, Levinas writes: "'I am another,' but this is not the alienation Rimbaud refers to. I am *outside of any place*" (my emphasis). As Derrida has noted, the philosophy of totality and power always aligns itself with the language of the site and rootedness.[19] If in a site the Other falls under the power of the I, it follows that the recognition of the other must not occur in an empirical "here" but in a utopic non-place that cannot be reduced to a modality of distance. Thus, face-to-face is not a phenomenal encounter that would entail the co-appearance of the same and the Other in the present, but an event unfolding along the path toward the Other. The gesture of offering spatializes the already nonphenomenal *Lebensraum* of Being-in-the-world. The fact that the I's home is primordially open to the Other does not cancel its enjoyment of the hearth, but its privacy is already interrupted by the readiness to give it up for the sake of a needy stranger. In this sense, the I has to be a nomad so that it can greet the guest with due respect. This hospitality, a non-appropriative welcome, acknowledges the primacy of the guest over the host. In *The Gift of Death,* Derrida points out that the Other is not a guest who has been expected because this would imply my being an inviting power, secure in her home. Unlike a visitor who arrives upon an invitation, the Other is an *arrivant* who surprises the host. In the shock of the encounter on the threshold, the I's identity as host is called into question, and so is its ownership of the place. Only when the I is thus enabled to offer, however, is its possession made possible. The presence of objects in my world, the ways in which they are of use to me, presupposes their aptness for being donated to the Other. The asymmetry of the ethical relation, its lopsidedness toward the Other, interrupts *ego cogito*'s assumption that the I can only relate to the "yonder" of difference starting from the realm it claims as its own. The *au-delà* of absolute exteriority cannot be construed starting from "here" if the Other is to be encountered on his or her own terms.

According to Nancy, in the sublime, the dwelling in the image is relinquished to nomadism at the border, at the limit which is not a place since it comes about in the movement of interruption. In the *non-lieu* of the syncope, imagining takes place and does not take place in the "spacing and throbbing of the trace of figures" (*SO* 43). The presentation of the presented in the beautiful requires the delineated space of the figure, but the sublime is structured as a trace. The sublime offering will never converge with the three-dimensionality of the site since the "present" of the gift recedes from the offering but also exceeds the presence of its "present." As Nancy explains in his later text *The Experience of Freedom* (1988), "The gift is precisely that whose 'present' and presentation are not lost in a realized presence."[20] It seems that for both Nancy and Levinas, the "gifting" of the transcendent cannot occur in a locality since the gesture of offering is in itself spatialization or distancing, while space circumscribed by geometrical coordinates remains an appurtenance of the delineated and the immobile, the same and the immanent. The suffocating nearness of the Other does not leave the I space for turning back in self-reflection. As a result, in the ethical relation, the egological figure of "I-ness" is also undone. The I's subjectity presupposes servitude to the Other where, at every moment, the I suffers a fundamental impossibility to co-appear with the other in the world. Again, the ontological mode of existence in the world as *Mitsein* is revealed as ethically insufficient. It is on the issue of site that Nancy's predominantly Heideggerian idiom reverberates most distinctly with Levinas's language of destitute otherness. Let us listen to the following excerpt from Nancy's "Des Lieux Divins": "It is always in extreme destitution, in abandonment without shelter or protection, that man appears, waxes, or wanes before the face of the god. Whenever he presents himself or absents himself, God brings about destitution and denuding."[21]

The absolute gift falls outside presence in which the Other would exist as coterminous with the same. Outside the circle of exchange, the gift disallows the appropriation of the Other as an object; therefore, it entails the Other's ingratitude and excludes the possibility of remuneration. Opposed to the Odyssean itinerary of the ego, the gift to the Other is structured as the Abrahamic journey of no return.[22] The gesture of self-dispossession in the non-place, the act of giving, comes prior to the giving of something. Since in the ethical relation the I is always already bereft of its possessions, the I does not truly own what it donates: the I cannot will or choose to part with what is already beyond its disposal. As Maurice Blanchot has commented, the originary offering of my world to the other is the gift of what I do not have. Always already having offered, I am eternally deprived and disowned, bearing the burden of an accusation that I have not offered enough.

For Nancy, the sublime is an offering (*l'offrande*). What is being offered in the sublime is not just a receding object but totality itself; totality is put into question, interrupted and sacrificed. The offering retains of the "present" implied by the presentation of objects within the totality only the gesture of presenting. In Derrida's words, the gesture of giving, beyond the redistribution of "presents," is but "to give him the very giving of giving, a giving which might no longer even be an object or a present said."[23] Similar to Levinas's conceptualization of the absolute gift, the sublime offering is the giving up of the gift and of the present; it is offered to the possibility of the presentation to come, the infinite not-yet of the figure. This sacrifice will not be restituted in appearance if it is to remain the offering, but it *gives* the possibility of beginning the outline of the figure. In the sublime, as Kant already implied, the presentation of truth is no longer at stake but rather the presentation of freedom as the destination of art. Nancy contends that freedom, the emotion of the sublime, consists in the infinite recommencement of the figure. A contour or outline "arises in freedom, which is a freedom to begin, to incise, here and there, an outline, an inscription" (*SO* 52).[24] What the sublime "offers" is the freedom of breaking into inscription, into the infinite possibility of presentation insofar as it arises toward a contour. The gesture of sublime offering precedes freedom, or freedom is generosity before being freedom, which gives (*es gibt*) or offers freedom (*EF* 146). This is why the gift is a *free* gift; in the final reckoning of accounts, it is freedom that interrupts the economic calculation: the offering will not be returned to anyone or repossessed.

For Heidegger, *Dasein*'s freedom consists in its ability to interrogate its own relation to the meaning of Being. In his criticism of Heidegger's thought of Being, Levinas argues that an ontology that thinks being before existent, even if it is not a matter of temporal precession, always puts the I's freedom before justice, that is, before the irrecusable obligation toward the Other. Consequently, it is incapable of conceptualizing radical alterity and only proposes the freedom of thought which takes itself to be the origin of what it receives, thus remaining the same. For Levinas, freedom presupposes giving to the Other because it arises in absolute diachrony, always incommensurate with the present. As Derrida suggests in his tribute to Levinas, "At this very moment in this work here I am," responsibility has the proleptic structure of the phrase "*il aura obligé*" ("ATVM" 11). The gesture of offering my world to the Other offers freedom because the ethical relation with the Other allows me to exercise my freedom. Ethical freedom entails responsibility without the concept of owing something, without any determination grounded in knowledge. It is only against this infinite responsibility that a decision to act ethically will be undertaken. The gift is what endlessly initiates the ethical relation and what ensures that the I will always be ready to respond anew to the call of the Other, that its task is never fulfilled and its responsibility never ceases. Therefore, the way in which the face resists the I's efforts to "image" it does not limit the I's freedom but puts it into action. The crushing weight of the Other gives rise to the I's freedom: a being that expresses itself in Saying, the appeal of the destitute to which the I is unable to remain deaf, promotes the I's freedom by arousing its goodness. The gift to the Other, without a giver or a receiver, is not an act of sovereignty in which the I gives freely; the gift disempowers the I, which becomes divested of the power to give. The event of offering entails the donor's absolute passivity, prior to the volitional choice of whether to give or not to give. The will secures the self's autonomy, while the gift marks the I as heteronomous with respect to the donee.

Nancy mentions, in *The Experience of Freedom,* that the gift is the inessence of existence since it falls outside presence and interrupts the totality of being, while for Levinas, the absolute gift to the Other ejects the I outside being and essence. The economy of essences makes for very strict accounting that ensures perfect equivalence and allows for no loss or surplus. Yet, says Levinas, "Freedom is compromised in this balance of accounts. . . . Freedom in the genuine sense can be only a contestation of this book-keeping by a *gratuity*—as responsibility for another and ex-piation" ("Substitution," *LR* 115; my emphasis). Since no one is inherently good, it is a difficult freedom in which free enjoyment of my rights pre-supposes responsibility for the freedom of the Other. It is only in the name of this original responsibility that the free self can choose to act eth-ically.

Respect for the Other does not pass through the neutral element of the universal law or through any other mediating "third term" such as Spirit or Being, which, by inserting itself between the two poles of the ethical encounter, destroys its singularity. The unique, the personal, is indispensable for the infinite to maintain its absolute exteriority. The sin-gularity of the gesture of giving is cardinal in Levinas's phenomenology of the Other because it prevents the collapse of the ethical relation into an economic calculation of the Same and the mimicry of self-identity. Maintaining oneself in the ethical relation is tantamount to individual re-sponsibility for its infinite recommencement in every moment of time. For Nancy, the gesture of sublime offering, in which imagination tran-scends itself in striking against the limit, always arrives in a singular fash-ion. It cannot be conceptualized, yet it threatens the totality of the system because it eludes the grid of schematism. Freedom that arises in the sub-lime offering is never formulated as the idea of freedom, but it happens each time as a unique event of freedom. Thus, for both Levinas and Nancy, freedom, offered in the gift, is unique, occurring in the factuality of the singular, always "each time."

The question remains, what is the mode of (non)presentation at the limit? How does it (not) take place? For Kant, the "negative presentation" of the idea of reason occurs in the most intense, paradoxical feeling of pain and pleasure. Imagination senses itself at the limit and overexerts itself at the very instant of rupture. It can do no more than signal the frustration of its own incommensurability with the outside-the-limit. Sublime "presentation" arises in effort and produces shock, "the feeling of a momentary checking of the vital powers and a consequent stronger out-flow of them, so that it seems to be regarded as emotion" (*CJ* 82).

According to Levinas, the Other is sensed as an affective event: trau-matic and inescapable, sheer insistence of the absolutely unknowable, distant, and strange. The Other produces a shock that leaves the I non-indifferent, feeling the discomfort of being too tight in its skin. The suf-focating proximity produces a sensation of restlessness, "as though the atomic unity of the subject were exposed outside by breathing, by divest-ing its ultimate substance even to the mucous membrane of the lungs, continually splitting up" ("Substitution," *LR* 97). The Other is felt through the most vital, involuntary functions, in the "meanwhile" of breath being exhaled and inhaled again and of the heart beating against one's skin. It is in the intensity of this disquieting, inexpressible sensation that the I recognizes its capacity to be touched by the Other's plea for help. Levinas reproaches Heidegger for ignoring corporeity—bodily sensations of en-joyment and pain. As he observes in *Totality and Infinity,* "*Dasein* in Heidegger is never hungry" because Heidegger thinks of food in terms of equipmentality. For Levinas, one can think of food that way only "in a world of exploitation" that ignores the suffering of starvation (*TI* 134).

Nancy's rereading of Kant emphasizes that the experience at the limit, the sublime, is felt in the body as "[s]uspended life, *breath* cut off—the beating heart" (*SO* 46). Therefore, it *testifies to our capacity for being affected.*[25] It can be argued that, because of the emphasis on sensations, Nancy's thought inscribes itself in the tradition of empiricism. However, as Peter Feuves argues in the foreword to *The Experience of Freedom,* this empiricism leaves behind its classical incarnations with their empha-sis on positivist foundations. Nancy emphasizes that the feeling of the sublime, the *e-motion* of the limit, is a condition of possibility of beauty and knowledge, which falls outside thought and thus cannot be accessed or "touched" by philosophy. The sublime is the very limit of the Western thought at which the unity of the subject is being questioned and so is its possession of the realm it captures in knowledge. Derrida has noted that Levinas's insistence on the priority of the sensible experience and the primacy of the hurting existent is also a mark of empiricism. It is empiricism taken to the limit, where it hovers as a question mark over the disembodied Reason of the Western philosophical tradition ("VM" 151). Levinas himself speaks of "concretization" that departs from Hei-degger's hierarchization of the ontological over the empirical; "concrete" empirical acts are not grounded in an ontological condition of possibility, but they themselves perform an ontological role (*TI* 173). If Levinas calls to move beyond reason, he does not favor a passage into the irrational but calls for a different Reason that would go from one to the Other and acknowledge action without calculable results and rewards for self. There, ethics does not fall under reason's legislation but is its own sufficient reason.

Western thought has implicated the other in the scheme of mimesis, whereby the other returns as the reflection of the same. Thus, the search for a corrective must involve the recognition that representation is always an ethical issue. Levinas has argued that ethics is incompatible with mimetic representation, yet the way he uses the term "aesthetics," in its traditional formulation as the presentation of the presented, only perpetuates this classical model. If Levinas were indeed caught up in the labor of the negative against the mimetic understanding of representation, he would remain fettered by the Western representational thinking he condemns. It is possible to argue, however, that Levinas's writings betray a leaning toward a different conceptualization of aesthetics, if it is still to be called aesthetics.[26] This other aesthetics does not concern itself with revelation, representation, or dissimulation but with disturbance, interruption at the limit of the figure, where it opens up to the infinite. It purports to bear witness to the intensity of feeling when the event of breaking through the image is happening. Consequently, Levinas signals the possibility of a different kind of "signifyingness" that would let the I bear witness to the Other, even if he or she remains invisible, unable to appear in a theme. The unknowable, unpresentable Other can only attest to its existence as an incessant murmur behind the uttered word, an echo of what has always been forgotten because it has never been known, or a laceration in language that, at the same time, cuts deeply through my skin.

Perhaps the rapprochement of Levinas's thought with Maurice Blanchot's "writing of the disaster" indicates his orientation toward another aesthetics, although in his commentaries on Blanchot's work, especially in *Sur Maurice Blanchot,* Levinas no longer refers to literature in terms of aesthetics but as poetic language. Blanchot's "disaster," signaling a break with the bright light of the star that has illuminated the West at least since Plato, does away radically with every form of totality and proposes a way of thinking aesthetics in conjunction with ethics, on the hither side of the galaxy of Western metaphysics. Blanchot's writing of the disaster announces the arrival of "the era destined to the intermittence of a language unburdened of words and dispossessed, the silent halt of that to which without obligation we must nevertheless answer" (*WD* 34). Blanchot's poetic idiom surpasses the presentation of the actual and aims to undo the "sameness" perpetuated by language in which every word is brought into the totality of universal meanings. Levinas comments that in Blanchot's writing words defer the betrayal of the Other when they overflow their "saidness" and become aware of their condition. Only the language that erodes the prison walls of immanence and opens up to the Other may offer egress from totality.

The above counterpoint between the two thinkers indicates how Levinas's ethics necessarily transforms philosophical aesthetics. The opening up of the external limit onto the beyond-form in the sublime offering, where form appears only insofar as it is simultaneously interrupted and carried away, perhaps cannot be thought otherwise but as the very movement of unlimiting in the ethical relation to the Other. In this context, the task and obligation of art with respect to the other will be no longer formulated as representation but as bearing witness that the Other *is,* in his or her having affected the I. Aesthetic pleasure, as part of the self's proper enjoyment, presupposes the discomfort, even pain, of the ethical encounter. Under the weight of Levinasian ethics, the movement of unlimitation, the fading away of the subject in the sublime offering, becomes inflected by a vector from the same to the Other. Nancy contends that "[t]he sublime is that art should be exposed and offered" (*SO* 50). In *The Experience of Freedom,* which is a political text, he urges that aesthetics—the problematic of imagination, schematism, and presentation—cannot be allowed to remain divorced from the political because representation is tantamount to the impossibility of freedom. If the sublime is experienced as a feeling at the limit, which is "touching itself" at the instant of rupture, then this feeling doubles up. On one hand, it feels only through and by oneself and engenders the appropriative pleasure of the beautiful, but there is also feeling as exposition to the outside, through and by the other. Nancy's concern, ultimately, is not altogether dissimilar from Levinas's: he concludes that the question par excellence in the sublime is whether one can feel through the other, the outside, even if sensation depends entirely on the self as its means. The thought of the sublime offering then is important for man's comportment in the agora, in the space of my obligation to the community. The thought of the Other and the plurality of others, irreducible to a common denominator in either genus (man) or concept (humanity, State), necessarily enters Nancy's investigation. If the sublime offering gives freedom, it is also because my obligation to the Other is always greater than my rights to life, liberty, and the pursuit of happiness. For Nancy and Levinas, but also for Derrida, as becomes apparent in *The Gift of Death,* ethical responsibility extends to the third, thus making the plurality of society possible.[27] It can then be argued that the ethical already informs Nancy's examination of Kant's legacy. This ethics, as for Levinas, is understood as the obligation to the Other, anterior to morality as respect for the law or a system of moral values and principles.

Admittedly, the above discussion has facilitated an encounter between two philosophers who approach the problematic of the gift from two very different poles of philosophical investigation. Nancy's speculation on the offering stems from Heidegger's idea of the disclosedness of Being in *es gibt,* even if the French philosopher moves beyond the confines of thinking one Being. He would probably view as rash Levinas's rejection of Heidegger's thought of Being on ethical grounds, as an accomplice of totality. Nancy's thought of the sublime offering, moreover, seeks to overcome the dichotomy of immanence/transcendence that seems to pervade Levinas's phenomenology of the Other, and it situates the transcendent moment of the gift in the in-between of the limit that cuts through interiority. In the essay "The Unsacrificeable," Nancy argues that "[t]here is no 'outside.' . . . What we used to call 'transcendence' would signify rather that appropriation is *immanent.*"[28] The transcendence that Nancy has in mind traverses the limit; hence, the line that sets the finite and infinite apart is in itself infinitely divided. There is nothing beyond the limit: the contour does not point to a telos but only to its own tracing of itself, in the presentation of its own interruption. The beyond quivers on the limit, as the separating/uniting incision, an opening onto the unlimitedness of the outside.

It might appear that Levinas's reliance on the duality between the insidedness of the ego and the Other's absolute exteriority would make him incapable of radically stepping outside Western metaphysics. However, as becomes apparent in Levinas's later work, in *Otherwise Than Being* in particular, rather than reinstating the dichotomy of interiority and exteriority, which would amount to preserving the autonomous subject that relates to the world through knowledge, that is, power, Levinas shows that this relation is always put into question by the undeclinable request from the Other. It is important to note that the ethical relation, like the sublime offering, is nonteleological; the Other as "beyond" is not an absolute to be attained in transcendence. Just as being a host is made possible by an unexpected visitor, so does the subject arise in its subservient role only because it has to help. The I is made possible so that it can reach out and aid. Rather than preserving the limit that separates the subject from the outside, Levinas radically puts it into question. The ethical relation can never confer upon the I the uniqueness of impermeable interiority.

I have attempted to indicate the moments of confluence between Levinas and Nancy and the way this encounter could promote thinking ethics and aesthetics together. The thought of the gift, prominent in the work of both philosophers, points to a certain porousness of the border between the two domains. Surrendering the determinateness of the dividing line, this border is structured as an interruptive event in which the said, the presented, is continuously unsaid in the unpresentable Saying. For both thinkers, the gift, as a gesture of giving, a movement of infinition or unlimitation, respectively, is a condition of possibility of "there is." Freedom—of being for the Other—is offered in the interstices of being where it opens to the Other; this encounter is the event par excellence of breaking through the image and the dehiscence of form. For both thinkers the giving of the world is the primary giving of the word. They also recognize that the language of site and spatiality colludes with totality to oppress the Other but that this language is indelible from any account of exteriority, including their own.

By allowing the gift to interrupt the limit between ethics and aesthetics, I have attempted to indicate a possibility of their mutual penetration. As Nancy remarks, in a passage that will hopefully unlimit itself toward future investigation: "The sublime does not escape to a space beyond the limit. It remains at the limit and takes place there. This means further that it does not leave aesthetics in order to penetrate ethics. At the limit of the sublime, there is neither aesthetics nor ethics. There is a thought of the offering which defies this distinction" (*SO* 49).

Notes

1. Maurice Blanchot, *The Writing of the Disaster,* trans. Ann Smock (Lincoln: University of Nebraska Press, 1995), 108. Hereafter cited as *WD.*

2. See Immanuel Kant, *Critique of Judgement,* trans. J. H. Bernard (New York: Hafner Press, 1951), especially paragraph 59, "Of beauty as the symbol of morality." Hereafter cited as *CJ.*

3. Emmanuel Levinas, "Reality and Its Shadow," in *Collected Philosophical Papers,* trans. Alfonso Lingis (Dordrecht: Martinus Nijihoff, 1987), 142. Hereafter cited as *CPP.*

4. Walter Benjamin, "The Work of Art in the Age of Mechanical Reproduction," in *Illuminations* (New York: Schocken, 1969), 241.

5. Emmanuel Levinas, *Totality and Infinity*, trans. Alfonso Lingis (Pittsburgh: Duquesne University Press, 1994), 21. Hereafter cited as *TI*.

6. In the chapter "The Time of the King" in *Given Time*, Derrida retranslates Heidegger's expression *es gibt*, usually rendered in French as *il y a*, as *ça donne*. See Jacques Derrida, *Given Time*, trans. Peggy Kamuf (Chicago: University of Chicago Press, 1992). Hereafter cited as *GT*.

7. See Marcel Mauss, *The Gift: The Form and Reason for Exchange in Archaic Societies* (London: Routledge, 1990).

8. Jacques Derrida, *The Gift of Death*, trans. David Wills (Chicago: University of Chicago Press, 1995), 65.

9. Emmanuel Levinas, "The Transcendence of Words," trans. Alphonso Lingis, in *The Levinas Reader*, ed. Seán Hand (Oxford: Basil Blackwell, 1989), 88–125. *The Levinas Reader* hereafter cited as *LR*.

10. Emmanuel Levinas, *Time and the Other and Additional Essays*, trans. Richard A. Cohen (Pittsburgh: Duquesne University Press, 1987), 72; *Otherwise Than Being: Or Beyond Essence*, trans. Alphonso Lingis (The Hague and Boston: Martinus Nijhoff, 1991), 146.

11. The last chapter of Martin Jay's study on the primacy of sight in the Western tradition, *Downcast Eyes* (Berkeley: University of California Press, 1993), is titled "The Ethics of Blindness and the Postmodern Sublime: Levinas and Lyotard." To the best of my knowledge, this is the only text that situates Levinas in the context of the sublime. Jay, however, limits his discussion to tracing Levinas's influence on Lyotard and does not really focus on the relation between the thought of the sublime and Levinasian ethics.

12. Jean-Luc Nancy, "The Sublime Offering," in *Of the Sublime: Presence in Question*, trans. Jeffrey S. Librett (Albany: State University of New York Press, 1993), 27.

13. In *Peri Hypsos*, written in the first century A.D., Longinus writes: "For it is a fact of Nature that the soul is raised by true sublimity, it gains a proud step upwards." See Longinus, *On the Sublime*, trans. Arthur Octavius Prickard (Westport, Conn.: Greenwood Press, 1978; reprinted from 1926 edition published by Clarendon Press, London), 11–12.

14. See Jean-François Lyotard, "The Interest of the Sublime," in *Of the Sublime: Presence in Question;* and *Lessons on the Analytic of the Sublime*, trans. Elizabeth Rottenberg (Stanford: Stanford University Press, 1994).

15. See also Nancy's "Wild Laughter in the Throat of Death," *MLN* 102, no. 4 (September 1987): 719–36, and his "On Painting (and) Presence," in *The Birth to Presence*, trans. Brian Holmes et al. (Stanford: Stanford University Press, 1993), where he also argues that the ultimate stakes of the aesthetic experience are the presentation of the gesture of presentation.

16. Emmanuel Levinas, "The Trace of the Other," in *Deconstruction in*

Context, ed. Mark C. Taylor (Chicago: University of Chicago Press, 1986), 351.

17. Jean-François Lyotard, *The Differend: Phrases in Dispute,* trans. Georges Van Den Abbeele (Minneapolis: University of Minnesota Press, 1988), 115–16. Hereafter cited as *D.*

18. See John Llewelyn, *Emmanuel Levinas: The Genealogy of Ethics* (New York: Routledge, 1995), chap. 13.

19. Jacques Derrida, "Violence and Metaphysics," in *Writing and Difference,* trans. Alan Bass (Chicago: University of Chicago Press, 1978), 97. Hereafter cited as "VM."

20. Jean-Luc Nancy, *The Experience of Freedom,* trans. Bridget McDonald (Stanford: Stanford University Press, 1993), 147. Hereafter cited as *EF.*

21. Jean-Luc Nancy, *The Inoperative Community,* trans. Peter Connor, Lisa Garbus, Michael Holland, and Simona Sawhney, ed. Peter Connor (Minneapolis: University of Minnesota Press, 1991), 147; quoted in Hent de Vries, "Theotopographies: Nancy, Hölderlin, Heidegger," *MLN* 109, no. 3 (1994): 476.

22. In "The Trace of the Other," Levinas writes: *"A work conceived radically is a movement of the same unto the other which never returns to the same.* To the myth of Ulysses returning to Ithaca, we wish to oppose the story of Abraham who leaves his fatherland forever for a yet unknown land, and forbids his servant to even bring back his servant to the point of departure" (348).

23. Jacques Derrida, "At this very moment in this work here I am," in *Re-reading Levinas,* ed. Robert Bernasconi and Simon Critchley (London: Athlone, 1991), 15. Hereafter cited as "ATVM."

24. Jacob Rogozinski corroborates Nancy's insight into the sublime nature of freedom in his essay "The Gift of the World." He echoes Friedrich von Schiller's apology of the sublime as the shattering yet rapturous experience of "lofty demonic freedom." Although the subject always prefers to figure for itself a world in which it is assured of the familiar realm, "what erupts into distress of this time, what recalls the subject to its chance and convokes it into its freedom—that is sublime." See Jacob Rogozinski, "The Gift of the World," in *Of the Sublime: Presence in Question,* 156.

25. In "The Interest of the Sublime," Jean-François Lyotard draws far-reaching conclusions from his analysis of the preponderance of feeling in the sublime: "If the sublime occurs as a powerful sensation and if this affect alone allows us to intimate our higher nature, then it threatens to overthrow Kant's general economy of the faculties, and the sublime becomes a challenge to modernity's elevation of reason and its mastery over the realm of the not-I" (131).

26. John Llewelyn proposes the term "transcendental aesthetics."

27. Derrida develops his critique of Levinas's notion of "the third" as

related to "hospitality" in his most recent tribute to Levinas, *Adieu to Emmanuel Levinas,* trans. Pascale-Anne Brault and Michael Naas (Stanford: Stanford University Press, 1999).

28. Jean-Luc Nancy, "The Unsacrificeable," *Yale French Studies* 79 (1991): 37.

Part III

Modernity, Nationalism, and Cultural Difference

The man returned to the lower office and sat down again at his desk. He stared intently at the incomplete phrase: *In no case shall the said Bernard Bodley be . . .* and thought how strange it was that the last three words began with the same letter. The chief clerk began to hurry Miss Parker, saying she would never have the letters typed in time for the post. The man listened to the clicking of the machine for a few minutes and then set to work to finish his copy. But his head was not clear and his mind wandered away to the glare and rattle of the public house. It was a night for hot punches. He struggled on with his copy, but when the clock struck five he had still fourteen pages to write. Blast it! He longed to bring his fist down on something violently. He was so enraged that he wrote *Bernard Bernard* instead of *Bernard Bodley* and had to begin again on a clean sheet.

He felt strong enough to clear out the whole office single-handed. His body ached to do something, to rush out and revel in violence. All the indignities of his life enraged him. . . . Could he ask the cashier privately for an advance? No, the cashier was no good, no damn good: he wouldn't give an advance. . . . He knew where he would meet the boys: Leonard and O'Halloran and Nosey Flynn. The barometer of his emotional nature was set for a spell of riot.

—James Joyce, "Counterparts," in *Dubliners*

Counterparts

Dubliners, Masculinity, and Temperance Nationalism

David Lloyd

In this brief scene from the story "Counterparts," Joyce draws out the complex rhythms of alienated labor in early-twentieth-century Dublin, linking the repetitive functions performed by the legal clerk Farrington with his sensations of humiliation, frustration, and rage. Male rage and violence at the conditions of work in an office with which, apparently, his very bodily frame is at odds, are counterpoised with the heterotopic site of the public house, with its odors and sensations and the prospect of homosocial conviviality. In the larger course of the story, Farrington indulges in a brief witticism at the expense of the Northern Irish head of this clearly British firm, in consequence of which he is further humiliated by having to make public apology; later, in the pub, as the story is retold and circulated, the humiliation is erased and the scene becomes one in which Farrington figures as momentary hero. But as the evening progresses, Farrington is again humiliated, this time by an English actor whom the "boys" meet, who sponges off them and then defeats Farrington in an arm-wrestling contest: both his own and the "national honour" he is jocularly called on to defend are tarnished. Returning home, raging, his money spent, his watch pawned, his thirst unslaked, he finds the house dark, his dinner cold, and his wife out at chapel. The story concludes with him savagely beating his son, who pleads for mercy with the promise that he will "say a *Hail Mary*" for him.

This spare and desolate story, together with many others in *Dubliners,* is bitterly diagnostic of the paralysis of Irish men in colonial Ireland, of their alienation and anomie, which, so often, is counterpointed by drinking. As is so much of Joyce's work, it is also profoundly suggestive as to the disposition and practices of gendered social spaces in early-twentieth-century Dublin: spaces of work, leisure, domesticity, and religion. As much as anything, it is indicative of the troubled nature of the intersection of these spaces, of their antagonism and contradictory formations. In what follows, I want to situate "Counterparts" in relation to the gradual and complex emergence of modernity in late-nineteenth-and early-twentieth-century Ireland and to the sites of "countermodernity" that seem simultaneously to be engendered. In particular, I want to follow the story's suggestions in the exploration of the forms in which Irish masculinity was deliberately and programmatically being reconstituted by Irish nationalist movements at this moment and of the recalcitrance which the performance of masculinity in popular culture presented to such projects. Since this essay represents a small and early part of an ongoing project on the transformation of bodily practices in the modernization of Ireland and on the survival of "nonmodern" forms of cultural difference, I will from the outset make no apology for the speculative nature of the argument at many points. Much remains to be done by way of producing a "gender history" of Irish social spaces and their refiguration within nationalist as well as colonial projects of modernization. What I hope to do here is suggest the singularity and unevenness of the ways in which Irish culture enters modernity and the complexity of the historiographic project that we require in order to grasp the implications of such singularity.

The problematic status of the nationalist project of modernization is in evidence in Ireland as generally among third world nationalisms. It is evident both in relation to the philosophical foundations of modernity from which it largely derives and in relation to the cultural formations of the colonized society as these emerge in time with but yet athwart modernity. The problematic nature of nationalist projects has been more fully elaborated elsewhere and can be briefly summarized here. Nationalism is deeply informed, and yet simultaneously judged lacking or "secondary," by the twin concepts of autonomy and originality that furnish the regulative norms for virtually every level of the modern socius: for the individual; for culture, as this emerges as a separate or distinct sphere; and in turn for each of the increasingly differentiated social spaces of civil society. In its drive to produce or capture the modern state, the nationalist project in its turn must pass by way of the reproduction of such autonomous entities. At the same time, the legitimacy of the call for independent national statehood must be founded in the establishment of the cultural difference of the nation or people, a difference necessarily derived from the traditions of the people that are distinct from those of the dominant or colonial culture. In this way, the claim to autonomous statehood is founded in the originality of national identity, but in an identity whose configurations derive from the elements of society that have, in some sense, survived the inroads of colonial modernity, that are the formations of nonmodernity. Nationalism proceeds, furthermore, by the direct politicization of cultural institutions: that is, where it is the function of aesthetic culture in dominant societies discretely to form subjects for the state, under the conditions of insurgent nationalism, cultural forms are directly endowed with political significance. Culture cannot be either disinterested or autonomous but is openly subordinated to the political projects of the nationalist movement.

But nationalism's relation to tradition is no less refractive and problematic. For what, through a rigorous process of selection, canonization, and fetishization, gets called "tradition" in relation to modernity emerges as such in the very recalcitrance of popular practices to colonial modernity. These practices prove to be no less recalcitrant to nationalism insofar as it is itself devoted to modernization as the very condition of state formation. In particular, popular practices tend to be resistant to the cultural disciplines that seek to forge the formal citizen-subjects of political modernity that the nation state requires to constitute its people. Accordingly, in its drive to produce subjects to be citizens of the nation that has yet to come into being, nationalism seeks to refine its own version of national culture out of the heterogeneity of popular cultural practices, modernizing and regulating what survives in the form of cultural difference. This is understood, of course, as an attempt to overcome the damage inflicted by colonialism: it is the function of national culture to produce national subjects as empowered agents against the heteronomy and paralysis of the colonized culture and to restore the wholeness of a fragmented society. In this respect, the function of the icons selected as representative of tradition—whether national heroes or aestheticized natural or artifactual objects—is not merely inspirational. They are symbols which, by virtue of their participation in the original and—in its occluded depths— continuous life of the people, represent the virtual nation that has yet to be realized. Around these symbols the aesthetic formation of the citizen subject takes place. Tradition becomes, in this refined form, the means by which the nation accedes to modernity. But tradition itself, as Frantz Fanon vigorously argued in *The Wretched of the Earth*, thus becomes the paradoxical enemy of the popular culture wherein the cultural difference of the colonized persists in its embedded resistances, its unevennesses, and its perpetual transformative adaptations.[1] It is this problematic and doubled relation to its own modernity and its traditionalism that makes nationalism, in Partha Chatterjee's memorable phrase, at once "a different discourse, yet one that is dominated by another" (*NCW* 42).

A principal means by which nationalist movements declare their cultural distinctiveness from the dominant power and engage in the refinement of popular culture is manifest in a certain "transvaluation of values" undertaken generally in the early stages of anticolonial mobilization. This transvaluation involves the inversion of stereotypes by which the colonizer has marked as inferior the signs of the colonized's cultural difference. Perhaps the most famous instance of this process is that of the *negritude* movement among Francophone blacks, about which Fanon writes extensively and with some critical sympathy in *Black Skin, White Masks*, and with less sympathy in *The Wretched of the Earth*. Negritude, which begins by the inversion of such stereotypes as black "passion" or "primitiveness," or the propensity for rhythm, into the signs of a less alienated connection to the natural world than that of the European, of an essential fullness of life rather than the abstraction of modernity, eventually becomes for Fanon the index of a fetishizing fixation on the "native" and a consequent disavowal of the actual condition of the black intellectual. "I tested the limits of my essence," he remarks acerbically, "beyond all doubt, there was not much of it left."[2] In his later work on the dynamics of nationalist struggle, that fetishization becomes the sign of a hegemonic drive by bourgeois nationalists to arrest the decolonizing process by fixing the processes of popular culture into the form of traditions:

> The native intellectual who comes back to his people by way of cultural achievements behaves in fact like a foreigner. . . . The culture that the intellectual leans toward is often no more than a stock of particularisms. He wishes to attach himself to the people; but instead he only catches hold of their outer garments. And these outer garments are merely the reflection of a hidden life, teeming and perpetually in motion. The man of culture . . . will let himself be hypnotized by these mummified fragments which because they are static are in fact symbols of negation and outworn contrivances. Culture has never the translucidity of custom; it abhors all simplification. In essence it is opposed to custom, for custom is always the deterioration of culture. The desire to attach oneself to tradition or bring abandoned traditions to life again does not only mean going against the current of history but also opposing one's own people. (*WE* 223-24)

The critique of the *negritude* tendency is what enables Fanon to move beyond the prevalent perception of the paralyzed and historically fixed nature of popular culture under colonialism and toward an understanding of cultural difference rather than tradition as the foundation for an ongoing process of decolonization. As we shall see, this equally entails a different understanding of the temporal rhythms of colonialism than that which, on either side of anticolonial struggle, subsumes tradition within modernization.

Irish cultural nationalism at the turn of the century engaged in a reversal of stereotypes akin to and in anticipation of the *negritude* movement. Thus, for example, the notion of Irish factionalism, based in an inveterate attachment to clan or family rather than to the abstract forms of law and state, becomes the sign of an indomitable resistance and of a spirit of loyalty capable of attachment to the nation. It forms, no less, the foundations of a masculinity that would be transformed and disciplined through institutions ranging from sports to paramilitary movements. The famous quality of "sentimentality" is recast as the foundation for piety and for an empathetic moral identification with the oppressed, while even the stereotype of a racially determined backwardness becomes the sign of a distaste for mechanical English modes of modernity and the grounds for an alternative conception of the modern. It is important to emphasize this point, since it is rarely the case, even in such ardent defenders of Gaelic tradition as Douglas Hyde, that Irish nationalists seek to go against the current of history: it is an alternative modernity rather than the restoration of old forms that nationalists seek even as they appeal to traditions. The transvaluation of the stereotype at once recognizes it as a form of knowledge, predicated on the apprehension of a difference, and converts its meaning in relation to the possibility for modernization. A Celticist nationalism engages in a revalorization of social or cultural traits whose material conditions of possibility it in fact seeks to eradicate.

But in certain cases, both reversal and eradication are attended with peculiar difficulties. This is evidently the case with that most common and perdurable of stereotypes of the Irish, our propensity for drink and drunkenness. The reasons for the difficulty that nationalism found in dealing with the possibility that drinking represented an engrained ethnic trait are at once logical and cultural. Logically, it is difficult to conceive of a *reversal* of intemperance, though its eradication was all too readily advocable. For, though in different forms, drinking is the effect of a prior cause, whether that cause be seen, as we shall see, as colonialism or ethnic predisposition. Unlike sentimentality, it is not an essential characteristic whose valence only is in question; it is a metonym for Irishness which can be disavowed, suppressed, or denied, but not inverted or transvalued. Even where attempts were made to convert the phenomenon of drinking into a perversion of native "hospitality," drinking remains an ever possible effect of that trait, not its obverse: as Weathers, the English actor in "Counterparts," slyly remarks, "The hospitality was too Irish" (90). Culturally, it remains the case that drinking practices remain a critical site for the performance of Irish masculinity and ethnicity, an actuality so embedded that any national movement that attempted to overlook this phenomenon would have been obliged to disavow a profoundly significant popular mode of articulation of cultural difference. As I shall be suggesting, it is in the attempt to transform the terms of Irish masculinity rather than to transvalue the stereotype that nationalism backhandedly acknowledges the significance of this cultural trait while at the same time necessarily suppressing the countermodern implications of drinking practices themselves. But this may be because of a third difficulty that attaches to nationalism's relation to drinking, which is that drinking itself may be seen as an allegorical figure for nationalism itself. That is, like nationalism, drinking represents the imbrication of resistance with dependence: as a practice that rejects the values of the colonial economy, values of labor, regularity, or thrift in favor of an alternative mode of homosociality, drinking resists the incorporation of the colonized male into the colonial enterprise; as a practice that entails debt as well as psychic dependence, it is at once the cause and effect of an individual and national lack of autonomy. It is, to paraphrase Partha Chatterjee, a practice of difference, but a dependent one.

We will take up this line of argument again momentarily. But the acknowledgment that drinking practices constitute a mode for the performance of masculinity raises a second stereotype that proved difficult for nationalists to reverse, that is, the famous "femininity" of the Celt. The notion of an essentially feminine Celtic nature emerges in the writings of philologists and ethnographers in the nineteenth century and receives its clearest and most widely disseminated formulation in Matthew Arnold's *On the Study of Celtic Literature* (1867): "the sensibility of the Celtic nature, its nervous exaltation, have something feminine in them, and the Celt is thus peculiarly disposed to feel the spell of the feminine idiosyncrasy; he has an affinity to it; he is not far from its secret."[3] But it is important to note that the stereotype of the feminine Celtic nature is constituted within a matrix of stereotypes that intersects, on the one hand, with a corresponding set of stereotypes about the "feminine idiosyncrasy" and, on the other, with the set of stereotypes that constitute the "ungovernable and turbulent" Irish as the proper objects of Anglo-Saxon discipline within the empire. The femininity of the Celt is a function of his "receptivity," of a certain more or less passive submission to impulse, whether the impulse of unreflective personal inclination or the impulse of external influence of nature or society. It is the very foundation of Celtic sensibility, and Arnold's only wish is "that he [the Celt] had been more master of it" (85). The lack of self-mastery explains the possibility for the convergence of apparently incompatible stereotypes, of feminine sensibility with the violent turbulence that, especially in the proliferating caricatures of simian Irish terrorists that stemmed from the Fenian campaigns of the 1860s, dominated popular images of the Irish in late-nineteenth-century England.[4] An unmastered sentimentality founds the political servility of the Celt no less than his aesthetic hypersensitivity:

> The Celt, undisciplinable, anarchical, and turbulent by nature, but out of affection and admiration giving himself body and soul to some leader, that is not a promising political temperament, it is just the opposite of the Anglo-Saxon temperament, disciplinable and steadily obedient within certain limits, but retaining an inalienable part of freedom and self-dependence. (86)

The Celt's "unpromising political temperament" requires its complement in Anglo-Saxon rule just as, within the gradually consolidating domestic ideology of Victorian Britain, woman's private sentimental morality required regulation by male civic virtues.[5]

For an Irish nationalism seeking to restore a sense of agency to a colonized people, this is a no less unpromising stereotype to confront. Rather than a transvaluation, however, this stereotype requires eradication through a series of projects that are directed at the reconstitution of Irish masculinity. I use the term reconstitution advisedly, in order to suggest that what is at stake here is not merely assertions of Irish manliness in denial of the stereotype, but a more or less systematic attempt to reproduce in Ireland a modern division of gendered social spheres within which the image of a masculine civic or public sphere could be reframed in opposition to a privatized feminine space.[6] The nationalist modernization of Ireland is inseparable from its project of masculinization of Irish public culture and the regulation of a feminine domestic space, a project, as I shall suggest, that to a very large extent runs against the grain of both cultural and material popular practices. This is so because nationalism at once accepts the colonial stereotype of "turbulent" Irish masculinity and seeks to respond by transforming Irish masculinity into "governable" forms that would found an independent state formation.

In the first place, there seems little doubt that we are dealing here with the emergence of something new in Irish culture. For the apparent self-evidence of the assumption that masculinity is properly defined and differentiated in opposition to femininity was by no means predominant earlier in the century. For Young Ireland nationalists in the 1840s, "manliness" as an ethical and political disposition of the subject was properly opposed not to womanliness but to slavery as the ultimate index of subjection. The autonomy of the politically free citizen and nation was opposed to the absolute instantiation of heteronomy, the slave. Thus Thomas Davis, in an essay entitled "The Young Men of Ireland," addresses the problems of moral corruption in a colonized society:

A Frenchman, M. De Beaumont . . . has discussed the character of our People . . . and he has discussed it with severity and beauty. He has attributed the "dark vices" of the Irishman to that part of him which is the making of Englishmen—to that part of him which is a slave. If he be improvident and careless, it was because there was no use of accumulation under the eyes of English avarice; if he be "ireful" and vindictive, it is because "six hundred years of hereditary slavery, physical suffering, and moral oppression, have vitiated his blood and tainted his habits". . . . The vices of Irishmen are of English culture; their virtues are of the homegrowth of the heart—the nation's heart—"that recess where tyranny has vainly endeavoured to force an entrance; which has remained free from every stain; that part which holds his religion and his charities."[7]

A series of oppositions structures this passage: between slavery and moral manliness; between "English culture" and Irish nature; between the alien and tyrannical rule of the colonizer and the besieged home/body of the Irishman; between the healthy and the "vitiated" body. What now seems surprisingly undeveloped is an opposition between a distinctly feminine space for Irish culture that is to be protected or liberated by manly resistance. On the contrary, despite the implicit feminization of the inviolate "recess" that resists the invader, the Irishman is himself the site of division between a contingent outer world that is subject to slavery and an intimate and essential inner world in which the moral constitution of manliness itself is preserved. The project of Young Ireland is, in a sense, to expand that inner space in order to take back the "part" that is enslaved, to make the slave moral that he might be free. We can perhaps throw the distinctiveness of this formulation into greater relief by comparison with Partha Chatterjee's discussion of "the nationalist resolution of the woman question" in Bengal. There, in the context of the material domination of British colonialism, a discourse emerges which asserts the superiority of Indian *spiritual* values while acknowledging the *material* superiority of English civilization. While Indian men are obliged to function in the public world of the British Raj, the feminized domestic space is constructed as that of the preservation and reproduction of inviolate Indian spiritual values.[8] Clearly, Davis's formulations place the division rather within the Irish male body and psyche, at most foreshadowing the divide between the feminine domestic and the male public spheres

which, as we shall see, in any case emerges in Ireland in ways still different from those Chatterjee suggests to be the case for Bengal.

By the turn of the century, however, a fundamental shift has taken
place in nationalist discourse such that a major component of its rhetoric
involves the proper distribution of opposed male and female spaces and
practices, a distribution that is, as is well known, finally enshrined in the
constitution of 1937. The conditions for this shift are numerous, but we
can cite several relevant ones here. First is no doubt the simple fact of the
abolition of slavery, which made unavailable the very common analogy
between the conditions of the slave in the southern states of the United
States and those of the Irish poor. Second, the emergence into promi-
nence in the second part of the nineteenth century of a powerful Victorian discourse on domestic ideology had been made possible by the
productivity of British capitalism and the extension of the middle-class
domain of the private family home among the skilled working classes.
This ideology doubtless provides the model with which a modernizing
nationalism seeks to compete. Third, the intervention of a new racial
discourse on the Irish, which asserts their femininity as part of the set of
characteristics that makes them incapable of self-government, demands
a response in the form of a remasculinization of the Irish public sphere.

We can identify two distinct but interlocked modes of response to the
feminization of the Irish during this period. The first can be seen as a
celebration of those elements of Irish culture that could be identified in
certain ways as feminine. In general, the stereotype of femininity attaches
to those survivals of a Gaelic culture that are now seen as the domain of
folk or peasant society. As is well known, the Irish literary revival and the
Gaelic League's project to restore the Irish language are predicated on a
massive effort to collect, catalog, disseminate, and refunction Irish folk-
lore. This project required the translation of oral cultural elements into
the forms of a print culture, and in powerfully if inadmissible ways foregrounds the opposition between the modernity of the collectors and
their public and the premodernity of the folk. But the gathering and rationalization of a body of materials that include fairy tales and folktales,
superstition and rural religious practices, and records of medical and
other lore is shadowed equally by an implicitly gendered division. It is
not for nothing that, although many of the storytellers and informants
were men, the figure of the old woman as repository and transmitter
of folk culture dominates the folkloric imaginary. The space of the Irish
peasantry is at once premodern and feminine; in its conversion and refinement into a coherent body of tradition, it is subject to the labor of

modernizing nationalist men. At the same time, the tone of the collector
is elegiac: these are the records of a dying civilization that nationalism
itself has displaced, even though that cannot be acknowledged. In the
new dispensation, the feminine oral tradition has been absorbed into the
foundations of a virile Irish modernity. Yeats's famous distinction between the moon of folk culture and the sun of an aristocratic literary
culture is only the most notable expression of such an attitude.[9]

This ambiguous celebration of the "feminine" elements of Irish folk
culture is thus both counterpointed by and contained within a vigorous
project aimed at the reconstitution of Irish masculinity. Given the current
context, wherein it is all too often assumed that anticolonial violence
stems from the aberrant "hypermasculinity" of the Republican "physical
force" tradition, it is important to register that it is not only within the
tradition that lays claim to the right to take up arms that this project of
remasculinization is expressed. Not only in the paramilitary organizations
that found legitimation in the traditions of the United Irishmen, Young
Ireland, and the Fenians, but in a whole range of closely articulated civil
and paramilitary organizations, institutions, and practices did this project
emerge. For paramilitary displays constituted only one mode in a larger
effort to recapture the public sphere as the site for the performance of
Irish masculinity, and it belongs accordingly in the context of linked en-
deavors which seek to redefine the public sphere in relation to the production and protection of a distinctive Irish private or domestic sphere.
Their disciplinary formations are linked, similarly, to the attempt to transform the "turbulent" Irish male body, whose habits are the end result of
colonialism, into a disciplined and moral *laboring* as well as fighting body
on whose productivity the future prosperity of the nation must be predicated. These political and economic projects are triangulated and, at the
moment of the turn of the century, explicitly linked with the cultural
projects that found expression in the literary revival, the national theater,
and the Gaelic League. The emergent institutions of cultural nationalism
are no less concerned with the production of a new Irish masculinity and
have at their core the project of organizing Irish political desire around
feminized symbols of the nation which become the object of a heterosexual male devotion. There is, as I shall argue more fully later, a profound
connection between the symbolist poetic mode, no less present in Patrick Pearse than in the Yeats of about 1904, and the transformations and
regulation of social space that a modernizing nationalism requires.

The projects of this modernizing nationalism meet in every domain a
deep material and cultural resistance. The desire to produce an Ireland

whose foundations lay in a feminine domestic space was at best utopic in a country where a large proportion of the most exploited workforce was female, both in the industrialized and semi-industrialized cities of Belfast and Dublin and in rural areas where much female labor was unpaid and unacknowledged. It was utopic equally in a country where in urban centers there was a constantly acknowledged drastic shortage of dwellings, leaving whole families to inhabit single rooms in Dublin's notorious tenements, and where in rural society the stem family system continued to predominate over any emerging nuclear family unit. It also came up against an increasingly organized social resistance to the new post-Famine patterns of both industrial and agrarian labor, especially in the form of a syndicalist labor movement whose agenda was by no means always congruent with or subordinated to nationalist mobilization, and which forged its own version of engagement with capitalist modernity. These struggles and resistances, of course, produce the contestatory field within which Irish nationalism takes its shape. But there is another mode of resistance to official nationalism which I would term "recalcitrance," and which has less to do either with the difficulties of material conditions in the colony or with alternative modes of organization, and far more to do with cultural practices that are at once embedded in the popular imaginary and incompatible with nationalist canons of tradition and moral citizenship. They are problematic, as I have already suggested, precisely because they represent, alongside nationalism, significant sites for the performance of cultural difference that cannot simply be erased or disavowed.

In what follows, then, I want to focus on the cultural significance of drinking in Ireland and its rendering within nationalism as a problem of intemperance. The focus is not on what we would now call alcoholism, though that is ineradicably one aspect of an anomic culture within which dependence itself constitutes a form of resistance to incorporation by antipathetic social norms. I want rather to approach drinking practices more widely as these are embedded within a whole matrix of behaviors that are the recalcitrant effects of modernity. That is to say, Irish drinking is not to be seen as the residue of premodern, preindustrial practices, nor as in any simple way congruent with, for example, working-class drinking in modern industrial societies, but rather as itself transformed and reconstituted in relation to an emergent modernity as an element of unincorporated cultural difference.

Let us proceed by way of a brief history of temperance movements in nineteenth-century Ireland. Prior to the 1830s, temperance work was principally undertaken by Dissenting Protestants, whose campaigns were largely conducted against intemperance as an individual matter and without reference to the larger social conditions that might have contributed to excessive drinking in Ireland. In fact, to the contrary, their views tended to assume that the reputed turbulence of Irish society derived from intemperance rather than to understand that both drinking and unrest might stem from social conditions. In this connection, it is perhaps important to note that the evil was primarily understood as binge drinking, occasional excessive drinking at fairs or other social gatherings, rather than habitual drinking. Binge drinking was seen as the effective cause of riot and faction fighting, and it was generally assumed that the poverty of the Irish lower classes made habitual drinking impracticable. The problems caused by intemperance were thus associated with what might be called a "spasmodic" theory of social violence, whereby the Irish poor were understood to be reactive and effectively passive in relation to their conditions. We will see shortly how this understanding of intemperance seems to have shifted by the end of the century.

The first mass movement for temperance was instigated by the Capuchin Father Mathew in the 1830s and 1840s. This movement, which for the first time drew mass Catholic support, was nonetheless largely in accord with Protestant assumptions that the control of intemperance was a means to regulate and diminish social disorder. Father Mathew's work continued to emphasize individual reform rather than any genetic connection between intemperance and larger social ills. That connection was, however, directly made by the Young Ireland movement, which endorsed Father Mathew's campaign but did seek, in correspondence with their larger analysis of Irish society as a product of British rule, to connect the regulation of intemperance with its roots in the social and economic conditions of the Irish poor.[10] The abortive uprising of 1848 and the effective dissolution of Young Ireland interrupted the development of this understanding of intemperance, which was not to find full force till the end of the century.

By the 1880s and 1890s, a new convergence had become possible between the Irish Catholic church, the resurgent nationalist movement, and the cause of temperance. The increasingly unchallenged authority of the church, which may be seen to have gradually emerged as a kind of shadow civil society in nineteenth-century Ireland, made it possible for priests to articulate an ever more uncompromisingly nationalist position, one that supplanted an earlier sense of institutional dependence on the British state. The concern of the church with combating intemperance and with the general moral reform of the Irish accordingly coincided with a new political militancy. Within this new formation, an earlier concern with individual reform is linked to a vigorous rejection of English stereotypes of an essentially bibulous Irish race and an uncompromising attribution of intemperance to the effects of British rule:

> How many Englishmen ever reflect that England is responsible for [the] intemperance of the Irish? Our Celtic ancestors were a very temperate people before the English landed on our shores. . . . It was only after they had lost their independence that this vice broke out among the Irish; and when we take into consideration all that they suffered from English tyranny during the last seven hundred years, can we be astonished that they turned to drink?[11]

Intemperance is thus no longer to be seen as the symptom of an internal racial organization already given to modes of dependence that fit it only for the external discipline of British rule, but as a synecdoche for the larger effects of that rule on the Irish body and the Irish psyche. Colonialism is a kind of intoxication of which intemperance is one among many effects. Accordingly, intemperance and political dependence are seen to be in a reversible relation, such that the eradication of intemperance will lead to the eradication of British rule and vice versa. Hence emerges the celebrated slogan, "Ireland sober, Ireland free." In this respect, we may note again the difference from what Chatterjee analyzes in the Bengali context. For in Ireland, the assumption is that the Irish body and spirit are indeed both already contaminated by the effects of British rule, so that private no less than public life requires a process of "detoxification," a process which Douglas Hyde in another context termed "deanglicisation."[12]

Accordingly, the work of temperance nationalism becomes inseparable from the production and dissemination of a vigorous domestic ideology which seeks to establish the well-regulated feminized home and its counterpart, a reformed masculine labor, as the foundation of a reformed and independent nation state. Typical in its pedagogical insistence is the Reverend J. Halpin's *Father Mathew Reader on Temperance and Hygiene,* a text intended for school use, which makes quite explicit the connections between the reform of men for public duties and the feminine sphere of the domestic and the home as the foundations for society:

> For the homes make up the nation; and as are the homes, so will be the nation itself. Whatever wrecks the home wrecks

the nation as well. . . . Now, what destroys the home more surely and more quickly than intemperance? (7)

If intemperance unfits man for the discharge of his duties, how much more truly does it unfit woman for hers? What is to become of her home and her domestic duties—the care of her children, for instance, in the exercise of which so much depends for society itself as well as for the family? As the nation depends on the homes, the homes depend on the mothers that reign there. (14–15)

All women can, each in her own sphere, give good example. . . . We must be very practical here. In the first place our Irish women are blamed for their cookery, or rather for their ignorance of cookery. And it is said that a better knowledge of that "lost art" would half solve our drink question in Ireland.

Closely connected with this subject is another of hardly less importance. We have seen the woman as a cook; let us next see her as a druggist. (20–21)

Yet more than all this may woman do for temperance. She can make the home attractive and sanitary, and even beautiful; yes, beautiful, for even the humblest and poorest home may be made beautiful and attractive in its way and measure, and all that a home should be, by a tidy thrifty and intelligent woman. . . . Well, there is a rivalry between the home and the public-house; and if the home is to prevail it must have something attractive about it; something better than disorder and dirt, untidy children and an ill-tempered wife. (22–23)[13]

Halpin's linked concern not merely with temperance but with the inculcation of "domestic economics," with hygiene, cookery, and medical knowledge, marks this and texts like it as part of a larger project of modernization which, in its desire to regulate the feminine domestic sphere, establishes domestic economy as a foundation for the national or political economy. It is not so much a discourse about the repression of an evil, drunkenness, as it is about the reconstitution of the social formation and the establishment of the domestic sphere as the counterpart to an invigorated masculine public sphere of economic and political labor.

Inasmuch as "there is a rivalry between the home and the public-house," we can understand the public house to be no less a rival to the public sphere. It constitutes a third term whose very name marks its ambiguous location. It is a rival to the home in providing an alternative space for male conviviality, leisure, and community, one not yet subordinated to the regulations of private domesticity and accordingly "public." At the same time, it rivals the public sphere insofar as it constitutes a space for the dissemination of news and rumor, for the performance of a heterogeneous popular culture, and, indeed, for the organization and dissemination of dissent, sedition, and resistance. But it is no less a recalcitrant space, the site of practices that by their very nature rather than by necessary intent are out of kilter with the modern disciplinary projects. As a site that is irrevocably a product of modernity in its spatial and its temporal demarcations and regulations, in its relation to the increasingly disciplined rhythms of work and leisure, it is nonetheless a site which preserves and transforms according to its own spaces and rhythms longstanding popular practices that will not be incorporated by discipline: treating or the round system; oral performance of song, story, and rumor; conversation itself, which becomes increasingly a value in a society ever more subject to the individuation and alienation of the worker within the system of production.[14] It may be seen as a crucial site of countermodernity.

In this respect, then, the pub is no less a rival to the linked set of national institutions which came into being alongside and in relation to temperance nationalism, and often under the auspices of the same figures: the Gaelic Athletic Association, the Gaelic League, the Irish literary movement, the national theater, and the various paramilitary movements. At the same time as such institutions often expressly sought to provide an alternative to drinking as the predominant form of male recreation, they sought to produce a public sphere cleansed of the intoxicating influence of English culture and commodities. As Archbishop Croke, first patron of the Gaelic Athletic Association, put it: "England's accents, the vicious literature, her music, her dances, and her manifold mannerisms . . . [are] not racy of the soil, but rather alien, on the contrary to it, as are for the most part, the men and women who first imported and still continue to patronise them."[15] Yet it is clear that these various institutions sought equally and no less importantly to constitute an alternative, nationalist civil society alongside the institutions of the colonial state, in the anticipation of an independent national state with its own civic institutions. Their function is not only to propagandize and disseminate nationalist ideology; it is also to produce *formally* a counterhegemonic set of articulated but autonomous spheres that will perform the modernizing functions of education, recreation, political organization, and opinion formation and through which the national citizen will be formed.

The public house not only rivals such institutions, then, it troubles their intents. It is a site of the performance of a profoundly heterogeneous popular culture, one inflected, as the "Sirens" chapter of *Ulysses* alone might suggest, by Italian opera, English music hall, nationalist balladry, gossip, irreverence, and humor, all of which is intrinsically recalcitrant to nationalist refinement. At the same time, it is, even in its demarcation as a distinct space, internally resistant to differentiation: it is a crucial site not only for the mixing of cultural elements but for the intersection of functions—leisure and work, politics and religion, literature and orality, public life and a kind of domesticity. It is the locus of cultural differences with which nationalism must intersect but which it cannot fully incorporate.

Nationalism, as we have seen, requires the establishment of cultural differences from the colonial power in order to legitimate its own claims to statehood, but the cultural difference it requires must, in order to fit with its modernizing drives, be a difference contained and refined into the canonized forms of tradition. The civil institutions of national modernity work off but also against the grain of popular cultural practices through which the heterogeneous, unrefined, and recalcitrant modes of cultural difference are continually constituted and transformed. What is intended here is not the ideal form of pure and originary difference toward which an extreme traditionalist and separatist nationalism might tend; it is rather that mode of constant differentiation, refraction, and refunctioning that occurs in the encounter between the evolving institutions of colonial modernity and the adaptive spaces of the colonized culture. What determines cultural difference is not its externality to modernity nor the persistence of a premodern irrationality, but rather the mutually constitutive relation between the modern and the countermodern. The temporal structure within which the colonized culture emerges in its difference is not that of a movement from an origin which is interrupted by and then assimilated into a more developed, more powerful state, nor that of the recuperation of an authentic and ultimately unbroken tradition within the revivalist logic of nationalism. It is rather the structure of the eddy by which Walter Benjamin redefines the processes of origination:

> Origin (*Ursprung*), although an entirely historical category, has, nevertheless, nothing to do with genesis (*Entstehung*). The term origin is not intended to describe the process by which the existent came into being, but rather to describe that

which emerges from the process of becoming and disappearance. Origin is an eddy in the stream of becoming, and in its current it swallows the material involved in the process of genesis.[16]

The cultural forms of the colonized do not simply disappear; in the turbulence of the encounter with colonization, they become something other, which retains the traces of the violence of that encounter, preserving it in the form of a persistent damage, and yet survives. Survival in this sense is a mode of adaptation that is often more resistant to than acquiescent in domination, a "living on" that is not about the preservation or fetishization of past forms but nonetheless refuses incorporation. This unevenly distributed relation of damage and survival forges the recalcitrant grain of cultural difference.

We can situate Irish drinking as one element in a matrix of such historically shifting cultural differences, differences of practice and social form that prove unincorporable either by colonial or by nationalist modernity and that remain accordingly ungathered by history, as a kind of dross or irregularity of which neither sense nor use can be made. At this juncture, I want to touch speculatively on a number of instances through which we might come to understand more fully what survives in the countermodernity of Irish drinking. It is, for example, well known that both the Land League and the Fenians customarily used pubs as sites for meeting, recruiting, and organizing, a fact by no means neglected in the temperance advocates' attempts to introduce stricter licensing hours throughout the latter nineteenth century. Publicans, indeed, seem to have made up a high proportion of the Fenians' local organizers, and the pub itself represented a crucial locus for congregation and dissemination.[17] What remains unclear is how the location itself may have inflected the forms and practices of these populist movements and even retained a persistent if officially unacknowledged influence on later nationalist and republican mobilizations. It is at least certain, however, that the use of the pub as a principal organizing center signals ways in which the space of the political was not rigorously differentiated from other social spaces in Irish popular culture.

In fact, the problematic status of Irish drinking has over and again to do with what seems to the modernized eye the improper confusion of spaces and practices. One instance of this is evident within the arguments for the licensing and regulation of drinking in order to separate work time from leisure or drinking time and to end such practices as paying workers in public houses. This was, as Roy Rosenzweig points out, a ubiquitous concern of industrial societies, but it may be that the uneven penetration of rationalized capitalist modes of labor in Ireland permitted the persistence of mixing labor and pleasure to a greater degree than elsewhere ("RS" 121–26). Similarly, particularly in rural districts, the overlap between public and domestic drinking, between the shebeen and the private dwelling, and the persistence of customs like the wake and the *ceilidh*, spelled a culture spatialized in ways not only different from those that were coming to be regulated by state law and religious dictate but in ways increasingly seen to be improper. These spaces of popular drinking were clearly not gendered and indeed could involve whole communities: there is little to suggest the homosociality of drinking practices at least prior to the Famine. At the same time, these were spaces often regarded as giving material expression to the fluctuations of Irish "sentimentality": wakes, in particular, which had always been suspected by English observers, were the object of increasing censure by the Catholic church as the century progressed, not least because of their improper display and mixing of lament and keening, laughter, social criticism, and satiric, often impious, invective, all under the influence of drinking.[18]

What each of these instances figures is the persistence and complexity of a culture of orality, in the fullest sense, alongside, inflecting, and inflected by a modern state and print culture. What orality here signifies is not so much the modes of transmission of a nonliterate society—it would be hard to point to any moment at which Gaelic culture was not already chirographic at the least, and nineteenth-century Ireland was saturated with writing—as the modes of sociality and bodily practice.[19] Indeed, it would perhaps not be entirely fanciful to suggest that the persistence of forms of orality in Irish culture represents the sublimation and survival of the non-nucleated settlements of pre-Famine Ireland, whose patterns and social relations furnish a material map of contiguity rather than differentiation, a map that underlies like a palimpsest the actual and psychic landscapes of modernized Ireland.[20] What disturbs the modernizing mentality is the confusion of spaces, emotions, and functions that are signified in Irish orality. The improperly differentiated functions of the mouth and the tongue are the indices of that disturbing cultural difference—mouths that imbibe drink and utter sedition, nonsense, lament, and palaver are the figure for an absence of distinction and for the borderless contiguity of social and psychic or emotional spaces. Looseness of the tongue makes of it an insubordinate and virtually separable autonomous organ, one that is closely associated in "Counterparts" with the recalcitrance and pleasures of the drinker:

> . . . almost before he was aware of it, his tongue had found a felicitous moment . . . (87)
>
> He had made a proper fool of himself this time. Could he not keep his tongue in his cheek? (88)
>
> The bar was full of men and loud with the noise of tongues and glasses. (90)

Within the emergent modernity of early-twentieth-century Dublin, the pubs that Farrington repairs to constitute heterotopic sites within which drinking is articulated with a whole set of other cultural practices that functions as an Irish mode of countermodernity. It is precisely this fact that makes the public house an alternative space for homosocial conviviality that operates outside the norms and rhythms of alienated labor or the hierarchies of the work space that impinge on Farrington's daily life—outside, but nonetheless constrained and defined in relation to those rhythms and norms as a transgressive negation. The public house as alternative space is already defined by licensing hours as a space of leisure that no longer intersects with the rhythms of work: the consumption of alcohol during the day has become marked as the sign of indiscipline and anomie; its pleasures are tainted and secretive. The public house, with its traditions of treating and oral exchange, abuts the theater that has become marked as the domain of English incursions and commodification. The figure of Weathers condenses that displacement and contamination of Irish male pleasure by its rivalrous counterpart, and the English actor's victory over Farrington is doubly humiliating, expressing not only a breach in his performance of masculinity but his inferiority within a colonial hierarchy and the consequent endangerment of his spaces of pleasure. Within the unforgiving laws of commodity exchange, drinking is only notionally a space of reciprocity: defiant of the logic of the cash nexus as a cultural survival like treating may be, modernity makes of it an accumulation of debt. Pawning his timepiece to subvent the evening's drinking, as if in revolt against the clock that has marked his entrapment, Farrington nonetheless ends his evening penurious and on the edge of a fatal economic dependence that matches as it is produced by his alcoholic dependence. His outlet is to bring home the violence he could not express at work: the story concludes with a violence that, for all its vigor, is no less paralyzed insofar as it is issueless and doubtless the source of its own repetition, generation after generation.

Read in this way, "Counterparts" stages drinking as a dangerous and unstable instance of damage and survival within and athwart the terrain of modernity. To be sure, drinking represents the recalcitrance of an Irish orality against the alienating rhythms of labor, against the regulation and division of time and space characteristic of modernity. It is no less opposed in this to the domestic than to the work spaces of modernity, and is by no means the site of a sentimental celebration of hearth and home against economic rationality and calculation that structures domestic ideology as a function of capitalist modernity. Yet its containment within the spaces of modernity makes of it the locus of a damaged masculinity, predicated on the recalcitrance of an anomie that constantly swallows up any articulation of resistance that might emerge there. Shot through with the paralysis of anomie, drinking repeats, at the level of the individual, the violent colonial apparatus of humiliation, with its system of economic and cultural dependence. In this, I have already suggested, drinking is, as Joyce clearly grasped it, the shadowy figure of nationalism's own articulation of resistance and dependence: drink, not temperance, is nationalism's counterpart.[21]

And yet, as so often in Joyce, something escapes the dismal sobriety of this logic.

Let us return to the scene from "Counterparts" with which we opened. It is a scene of writing in which, as Farrington repetitively, absently, copies over a document, the materiality of the letters ("B . . . B . . . B") separates out from the sense of the phrase. In his very frustration and alienation, and in his mild inebriation, something detaches itself from sense. In this scene, Farrington is copying a document known in legal parlance as a *counterpart:* a copy torn off from the original in such a way that, when the two are brought together, the copy authenticates the original. The counterpart of the title refers, then, not only to rivalry but to secondariness, imitation, but in a way that disturbs the hierarchies of originality. If we consider nationalism as a rival of the imperial state, it is also its counterpart in the second sense, its dependent or secondary copy. But its repetition constitutes not simply a difference, capable of rehierarchization, but a deviation of sense. This deviation is, I shall argue, into the space of a cultural difference that is not caught in the logic of opposition.

This deviation is no less a deviation from what were, around 1900, the givens of nationalist aesthetics, with its emphasis on the representative function of the symbol. The counterpart as document is identical to the symbol in its etymological derivation, from the Greek *symbolon:*

> *Symbola* were pledges, pawns or covenants from an earlier understanding to bring together a part of something that had been divided specifically for the purpose of later comparison. . . . A coin could be a *symbolon.* Indeed, *symbola* were often "halves or corresponding pieces of (a bone or) a coin, which the contracting parties broke between them, each keeping one piece."[22]

But this etymological derivation highlights the extent to which the contemporary meaning of the symbol deviated from its original. The *symbolon,* like the counterpart, is an allegory: it is in a relation of contiguity to what it represents rather than being a part of it. But precisely what activates the nationalist political possibilities of a post-Romantic definition of the symbol is its conceptualization as a representation that participates in what it represents, as a particular that is part of the whole for which it stands. The landscape may be a symbol of nature or natural process because it is already a part thereof; the national martyr or poet is the symbol of the nation for whose virtual existence he stands. The temporality of symbolism entails the transformation of a merely contingent relation to the nation into a representative function. We might describe this as a series of rhetorical transformations: from the metonymic (Leopold Bloom's "I'm Irish; I was born here") to the synecdochic ("I participate in the nation as a particular instance or member of the whole body politic") to the metaphoric ("I represent the nation because my qualities are those with which an Irish subject should identify"). It is a movement which educes generality out of particularity and contingency and its mechanism is desire, in the sense that Yeats understood his early cultural nationalist work to have sought to "organize" the desire of the nation around certain symbols.[23] In its effort to mobilize a unifying desire, nationalist symbolism is directed against the fragmentation and dispersal of the body and the social space of modernity and toward a suturing of the individual body in itself and with the nation as a whole.

Joyce's *Dubliners* is structured rather around what he describes as the epiphany, an epiphany secularized beyond the account that Stephen Dedalus gives of it in *Stephen Hero.* There, the epiphany appears as a still auratic translation of the religious epiphany, the moment of the manifestation of the divine in the worldly; in effect, as a symbol in which the particular undergoes a transubstantiation into an illumination of the transcendent:

> By an epiphany he meant a sudden spiritual transformation, whether in the vulgarity of speech or of gesture or in a memorable phrase of the mind itself. . . .
>
> First we recognize that the object is *one* integral thing, then we recognize that it is an organized composite structure, a *thing* in fact: finally, when the relation of the parts is exquisite, when the parts are adjusted to the special point, we recognize that it is *that* thing which it is. Its soul, its whatness, leaps to us from the vestment of its appearance. The soul of the commonest object, the structure of which is so adjusted, seems to us radiant. The object achieves its epiphany.[24]

But even within this description, saturated as it is with the young Joyce's Aquinian aesthetic vocabulary, something moves beyond the symbolic, auratic register and closer to the form of the profoundly secular epiphanies that he collected in his notebooks and which came to inform the work of *Dubliners*. For the epiphanies of Joyce's work, as opposed to those of Stephen's theory, are dedicated less to the symbolization of the real, its transumption into representation, and rather to a certain metonymic singularity. They are dedicated to a presentation of the "whatness" of the thing that is achieved by way of what this passage intimates, an extreme degree of internal intensification that ensures their detachment from rather than their representation of that of which they are a part. The intensified moment, like Gabriel Conroy's glimpse of his wife standing on the stairs listening to distant music, in fact refuses to be a symbol of something and embeds instead a profound resistance to incorporation, a recalcitrant particularity that refuses to be subsumed into the narrative of representation.[25] It is, as a diagnostic moment structured around its internal relations, closer to the "alienation" of Bertolt Brecht's later tableau or *gestus*.

In Stephen's analogy, what is emphasized in the epiphany is its effulgence of spiritual radiance: an auratic light emanates from and detaches itself from the transubstantiated object. As Joyce writes of the effect of *Dubliners*, it is not so much an aura that detaches itself from the object as an odor: "It is not my fault that the odour of ashpits and old weeds and offal hangs around my stories. I seriously believe that you will retard the course of civilisation in Ireland by preventing the Irish people from having one good look in my nicely polished looking-glass."[26] Odor is for

Joyce the aura that escapes the representation of the object, that is suspended above it as its ineffable trace. Insofar as it is also distasteful, it implies the status of a counteraesthetic. What is implied here is the inseparability of the odor from a project of rigorous mimesis, the juxtaposition of a project of specular revelation, predicated on visibility and illumination, with an unprojected effect of that mimesis, its countersense. The celebrated "scrupulous meanness" of the style of *Dubliners* invokes a naturalism that refuses the incorporative desire of either symbolism or realism that would be the privileged modes of a bourgeois nationalism. It is devoted to the mimesis of a paralysis which suspends action outside the teleological drive of representation: it refuses to redeem colonial paralysis by subordinating it to a transformative sense of history. Instead, the diagnostic mimesis of paralysis produces a suspension of sense which issues in this odor that hangs around these stories. The odor is a countersense made possible by the very rigor of the sense on which Joyce's mimesis of colonial Dublin insists.

We can understand the relation between odor and mimesis as constituting a double track of signification. Within the track of mimesis, which is still subject to a moral and formative intent, narrative itself becomes over and again suspended in paralysis. In that paralysis, we are to decipher the dysfunctional contours of colonial Dublin, the ineluctable determination of material and psychic conditions, repetition and the inhibition of the will. The sense of the narratives in this register is overwhelmingly that of the vacuity of narrative itself where nothing moves. And yet that very suspension of narrative in paralysis releases an odor whose sense has nothing to do with paralysis, which does not even seek to effect or justify things in the registers of moral or political agency. Odor is a trace which survives the passing of the body as the circulation of stories in the public house detaches itself from the violence and repetition of the narrative to constitute less a determinate engagement with the real than a repertoire and a rehearsal of alternatives. This realm of possibilities is not legitimated by its realization in the actual but sets off eddies in the forward-moving stream of a historicized temporality. Joyce suggests to us, as does Fanon, that in the sites of an apparent suspension of historical motion are the grounds for possible counterhistories. For with the countersenses that these eddies preserve, a materialist historiography must go to work, tracing over and again the alternative resources that are the emanations of the damage taken up in every living on.

Notes

1. Since the literature on nationalism from which I have drawn here is so voluminous, let me cite those sources from which I have drawn most closely: Frantz Fanon, *The Wretched of the Earth,* trans. Constance Farrington (New York: Grove Press, 1968), esp. 223–24, hereafter cited as *WE;* Partha Chatterjee, *Nationalism and the Colonial World: A Derivative Discourse?* (London: Zed Books, 1986), hereafter cited as *NCW;* Luke Gibbons, "Identity without a Centre: Allegory, History and Irish Nationalism," and, indeed, the whole book in which this essay is collected, *Transformations in Irish Culture. Critical Conditions: Field Day Essays,* vol. 2 (Cork: Cork University Press, 1996), 134–37. My own explorations of the discrepancies between official nationalism and popular culture are in *Anomalous States: Irish Writing and the Post-colonial Moment* (Dublin: Lilliput Press, and Durham, N.C.: Duke University Press, 1993).

2. Frantz Fanon, *Black Skin, White Masks,* trans. Charles Lam Markmann, foreword by Homi Bhabha (London: Pluto, 1986), 130. The chapter translated as "The Fact of Blackness" is Fanon's reckoning with the subjective implications of the stereotype and its inversion.

3. Matthew Arnold, *On the Study of Celtic Literature,* in *On the Study of Celtic Literature and Other Essays,* intro. Ernest Rhys (London: Dent, 1910), 86.

4. On the Victorian representation of the Celt, see L. P. Curtis, *Anglo-Saxons and Celts: A Study of Anti-Irish Prejudice in Victorian England* (Bridgeport, Conn.: Conference on British Studies at the University of Bridgeport, 1968), and *Apes and Angels: The Irishman in Victorian Caricature* (Washington, D.C.: Smithsonian Press, 1971).

5. Indeed, Arnold's aesthetic appreciation of the sentimentality of the Celts, which finds expression in the propensity to elegiac poetry lamenting their perpetual defeats, finds a precise correlative in John Ruskin's highly popular text on male and female dispositions, *Sesame and Lilies,* where one of woman's principal functions is to mourn: "she is to extend the limits of her sympathy . . . to the contemporary calamity, which, were it but rightly mourned by her, would recur no more hereafter." See John Ruskin, *Sesame and Lilies,* in *Works,* ed. E. T. Cook and Alexander Wedderburn (London: George Allen, 1905), vol. 18, p.126.

6. I use the term also by analogy with KumKum Sangari and Sudesh Vaid's conception of the "reconstitution of patriarchies" that takes place continually both under the British Raj and in the context of Indian nationalism. See their introduction to *Recasting Women: Essays in Colonial History,* ed. KumKum Sangari and Sudesh Vaid (New Delhi: Kali for Women, 1989), 1, 25, and passim.

7. Thomas Osborne Davis, "The Young Men of Ireland," *Nation*, 15 July 1843, 32.

8. Partha Chatterjee, "The Nationalist Resolution of the Woman Question," in *Recasting Women*, 232-53.

9. See W. B. Yeats, "Gods and Fighting Men," in *Explorations* (New York: Macmillan, 1962), 24-26. Marjorie Howes has explored in detail the ways in which Yeats responded to the Arnoldian stereotype by setting his own masculinity over against the femininity of folk culture in *Yeats's Nations: Gender, Class, and Irishness* (Cambridge: Cambridge University Press, 1996), 18-43. I have discussed Douglas Hyde's need to refine and purify the Irish songs he collected in order to produce a coherent sense of the Irish "spirit" in "Adulteration and the Nation," in *Anomalous States*, 101-4.

10. Elizabeth Malcolm remarks:

> The Young Irelanders took up and supported his [Father Mathew's] call for self-discipline, thrift and education, but as only one part of a much broader movement. To them major political reform was essential; teetotalism of itself was not adequate to achieve the desired ends. Only when Irishmen substantially controlled their own government would the country's problems be solved. The Young Ireland programme for political reform and social advancement shows all the hallmarks of a modernising urban radicalism, but at the same time it highlights the very limited and simplistic nature of Father Mathew's philosophy.

See Elizabeth Malcolm, *'Ireland Sober, Ireland Free': Drink and Temperance in Nineteenth-Century Ireland* (Dublin: Gill and Macmillan, 1986), 147. I have drawn extensively on Malcolm's work for this essay. For a briefer but no less valuable overview of temperance work in the period, see her "Temperance and Irish Nationalism," in *Ireland under the Union: Varieties of Tension,* ed. F. S. L. Lyons and R. A. J. Hawkins (Oxford: Clarendon, 1980), 69-114.

11. Fr. C. J. Herlihy, *The Celt above the Saxon* (1904), cited in Luke Gibbons, "Race against Time: Racial Discourse and Irish History," *Oxford Literary Review* 13 (1991): 103. On the emergence and spread of such views in temperance nationalism, see Malcolm, "Temperance and Irish Nationalism," 101-8.

12. See Douglas Hyde's influential essay, "The Necessity for Deanglicising Ireland," in *Language, Lore, and Lyrics: Essays and Lectures,* ed. Breandán Ó Conaire (Blackrock: Irish Academic Press, 1986), 153-70.

13. Rev. J. Halpin, P. P., *The Father Mathew Reader on Temperance and Hygiene* (Dublin: M. H. Gill, 1907); pages given in text.

14. Surprisingly, there has been little historical or anthropological work

done on the Irish pub or on Irish drinking practices. But for a very suggestive analysis of the cultural significance of the pub, or saloon, which has considerable insight to offer on Irish practices despite examining the context of Massachusetts, see Roy Rosenzweig, "The Rise of the Saloon," in *Rethinking Popular Culture: Contemporary Perspectives in Cultural Studies,* ed. Chandra Mukerji and Michael Schudson (Berkeley: University of California Press, 1991), 121–56. Hereafter cited as "RS."

15.   Quoted in Kevin Rockett, "Disguising Dependency: Separatism and Foreign Mass Culture," *Circa* 49 (January/February 1990): 22.

16.   Walter Benjamin, *The Origin of German Tragic Drama,* trans. John Osborne, intro. George Steiner (London: Verso, 1985), 45.

17.   See, for example, Malcolm, "Temperance and Irish Nationalism," 84–90, 98, and *'Ireland Sober, Ireland Free,'* 192–93. One might say that the largely teetotal Fenian leaders knew well how to swim in the water of the people, even if, like fish, they abstained from drinking it.

18.   I have discussed this more fully in "The Memory of Hunger," in *Irish Hunger,* ed. Tom Hayden (Boulder, Colo.: Roberts Rinehart, 1997), 32–47.

19.   On the imbrication at any historical moment, and especially in modernity, of past and emergent modes of cultural transmission and practice, see Donald A. Lowe, *History of Bourgeois Perception* (Chicago: University of Chicago Press, 1982), 14–16.

20.   On the pre-Famine landscape and the social forms of the rural Irish poor, see Kevin Whelan, "Pre- and Post-Famine Landscape Change," in *The Great Irish Famine,* ed. Cathal Poirteir (Cork and Dublin: Mercier Press, 1995), 19–33.

21.   This is perhaps also allegorized in *Dubliners* through the fate of Jimmy in the story "After the Race," whose attempt to emulate the representatives of more powerful modern nations—England, France, and the United States—leads him into drunkenness and enormous gambling debts. See Vince Cheng, *Joyce, Race and Empire* (Cambridge: Cambridge University Press, 1995), 101–9.

22.   See Mark Shell, *The Economy of Literature* (Baltimore: Johns Hopkins University Press, 1978), 32–33. Internal citation from H. G. Liddell and Robert Scott, *A Greek-English Lexicon* (Oxford: Oxford University Press, 1940).

23.   See W. B. Yeats, *Autobiography* (New York: Macmillan, 1953), 119. I have discussed Yeats and the conception of nationalist symbolism more fully in "The Poetics of Politics: Yeats and the Founding of the State," in *Anomalous States,* 70–74.

24.   James Joyce, *Stephen Hero,* ed. Theodore Spencer (New York: Granada, 1977), 188.

25.   See James Joyce, "The Dead," in *Dubliners* (New York: Viking Press, 1993), 211: "There was grace and mystery in her attitude as if she were a

symbol of something. He asked himself what is a woman standing on the stairs in the shadow, listening to distant music, a symbol of?"

"The Dead," of course, is set at the Feast of the Epiphany, and this passage represents, as it were, Joyce's metacommentary on the relationship between the secular epiphany and the urge to symbolization, an urge that is directly associated with the formation of male heterosexual desire that Gretta seems to elude. For further commentary on this story and its understanding of male desire, see Luke Gibbons, "Identity without a Centre," 134–47.

See also Terence Brown's introduction to *Dubliners,* xxxiv–xxxv, and his citation of C. H. Peake: "there could hardly be a more emphatic assertion that an epiphany was an apprehension of the thing's unique particularity, and not a symbol of something else." I have learned much from this excellent introduction.

26. James Joyce, *Letters,* ed. Stuart Gilbert (New York: Viking Press, 1966), 63–64.

Lacan with Adorno?

The Question of Fascist Rationalism

Gilbert Chaitin

REASON AND VIOLENCE

In June 1964, Jacques Lacan concluded his seminar on *The Four Funda-mental Concepts of Psycho-Analysis*[1] with the claim that his teaching was meant to counteract the prevalence of Kant's morality, which he held responsible for the mentality that led to the Nazi genocide of the Jews and, by implication, to modern totalitarianism. From a certain standpoint there was nothing unusual about the assertion of such a connection: con-servatives from Burke to Barrès had been railing against the universality, the abstraction, and thus the deadening inhumanity of Enlightenment ideals since the end of the eighteenth century. Moreover, at least since Blake, the same charge of inhumanity has also been leveled at the Enlight-enment by thinkers of the left, including the same Barrès in his left-socialist period, but usually for the opposite reason: they saw it as the cover for rampant particularism, for the ideology of the autonomous, bourgeois subject with his lack of communal sense and his lust for exploitation and domination.[2]

It nevertheless seems strange at first sight that Lacan should concur with these condemnations, and even extend them to the point of laying Auschwitz at the feet of the Enlightenment, for he had always opposed obscurantism wherever he found it and repeatedly asserted that whatever is rational is real. One key to this apparent contradiction is found in the distinction he draws in 1964 between two versions of Enlightenment, the ethics of Spinoza and the moral imperative of Kant. Lacan regrets that Spinoza's "intellectual love of God," which allows the philosopher to detach himself from human passions by loving the universal within the individual, is *no longer* a tenable stance. The Kantian notion of conscience is truer *for us* now, and that, he goes on to say, is why he wrote the article entitled "Kant with Sade."[3] His implication is that the categorical imperative gave a sadistic twist to the otherwise benign project of Enlightenment, and thus that it is as great a mistake to attribute the source of Nazism to irrationalism, as was usually done during the 1930s and 1940s, as to rationalism, as has often been the case in recent years, especially with poststructuralism. Indeed, the conception of love he proposes as the goal of psychoanalysis in these same closing pages of the 1964 seminar is a modified version of the Spinozan ideal: "in you more than you," the Lacanian phrase that the editor (Jacques-Alain Miller) uses as the heading for this chapter, indicates the remainder of that universal which Spinoza claimed we should love in each individual.

In "Kant with Sade," Lacan explicitly states that he will show that Sade is the "truth" of Kant, by which he means that Sade both agrees with Kant and completes the latter's thought by bringing out into the open what had remained hidden in the philosopher's text. Such a consolidation of the standard criticisms of the Kantian version of Enlightenment via the divine marquis might seem to be just another one of Lacan's typical outlandish enterprises, or perhaps the stroke of genius for which he seems to give himself credit when he boasts that "Sade is the inaugural step of a subversion, of which . . . Kant is the turning point . . . [a fact] never noted, to our knowledge, as such" ("KS" 55), were it not for the fact that Horkheimer and Adorno had already explored the same juxtaposition in their chapter on "Juliette or Enlightenment Morality" in *Dialectic of Enlightenment*,[4] which dates from the 1940s (first circulated in New York in 1944 under the title "Philosophische Fragmente" and published in Amsterdam in 1947).

There is, to be sure, no evidence to date either to substantiate or to contradict the hypothesis that Lacan was already acquainted with the Frankfurt School work which preceded his first discussion of the question in the 1959–60 seminar on *The Ethics of Psychoanalysis*[5] as well as the later journal and *Ecrits* treatments,[6] but the Adorno essay has not escaped the attention of Lacanians entirely. In her biography of the psychoanalyst, Roudinesco credits it as a primary inspiration of his *écrit,* but without comparing the two treatments of the comparison, and Žižek mentions it in a note to an article on ideology written in French which appeared in *Ornicar?* in 1985.[7] After summarizing the argument in a brief paragraph, he concludes that Lacan's interpretation is the exact opposite of Adorno's, for the latter makes the sadistic tormentor into the subject whose object is the victim, Justine; whereas for Lacan, the tormentor is the *object,* while the victim is precisely not reduced to the status of object but is the so-called split subject who is both fascinated and repelled by the object ("PPMI" 59).

To anyone who has compared the two texts, however, it is clear that their affinities are far-reaching and significant, and deserve more serious scrutiny than they have received until now. Moreover, the harshness of the critiques leveled at the Enlightenment in both essays would seem to manifest a shared sense of pain and betrayal by a formerly cherished ideal. These essays thus raise, in acute form, the question so often repeated in contemporary critical debate of the value of Enlightenment rationality in the modern, and postmodern, worlds.[8] The following juxtaposition of Lacan with Adorno is designed to throw light on the intellectual ancestry and mass appeal of fascism, just as that of "Kant with Sade" is meant to uncover the hidden tendencies in the formal reason of the Enlightenment.

KANT, SADE, AND THE ETHICS OF FORMALISM

The starting point for both essays is Kant's purely formal definition of reason. Adorno and Horkheimer point out that in Kant's *Critique of Pure Reason* the salient characteristics of reason are unity, consistency, and system, so that its ultimate principle is the purely logical one of noncontradiction (*DE* 81). The unity of rationality is thus the agreement of the general and the particular; more specifically, "reason is the 'faculty . . . of *deducing the particular from the general'*" (*DE* 82, my emphasis; inner quote from *Critique of Pure Reason*). The industrial society that has developed in consonance with this principle of Enlightenment reason makes the individual into a mere example, or representative, of a social type: "It allows no determination other than the classifications of the societal process to operate" (*DE* 84). The Frankfurt School writers argue that by its exclusion of any "content," this "formalization of reason" opens the way for its "instrumentalization": indifferent to goals, to social or human considerations such as pity or solidarity, reason can be used for any goal whatsoever, becoming a mere tool for the cold, calculating manipulation of physical nature or of other people for one's own pleasure, self-interest, power, and domination. In similar fashion, they observe, Sade's tormentors must learn to suppress their qualms and human feelings, so that their search for pleasure becomes, as it were, a technical matter. Despite Kant's beliefs and intentions, they argue, this possibility is inherent in his position. Like so many of Kant's nineteenth-century critics, they see a fundamental opposition between Kantian morality, which enjoins us to treat people as ends rather than means, and Kantian science, which reduces people to being means in the service of domination: the lust for domination is "in contradistinction to the categorical imperative and all the more in accordance with pure reason" (*DE* 86). It is in this sense that Sade can be seen retrospectively as Kant's "truth." Retrospectively, because it is only in light of bourgeois dominance in the nineteenth century and fascism in the twentieth that the implications of technological domination over nature and humanity have played themselves out politically. In philosophy, the main butt of their critique is logical positivism, which, by its formalism, technologizes science and logic, making them the willing tools of the powers that be, and thus depriving reason of its fundamental function, that of critique.[9]

Far from tracing the sadistic potential of Kantian ethics to the domination of the formalism of speculative reason over the ineffectual humanism of his practical reason, Lacan's point of attack is the formalism of Kant's categorical imperative itself. "Act on the maxim which can at the same time be made a universal law."[10] A maxim (a rule of behavior) must not lead to a contradiction when universalized, that is, when extended to all possible cases of application, in order to be considered truly moral; but also in order to impose itself on the rational subject as an absolute duty, the categorical imperative. So anxious is Lacan to pinpoint logic, the principle of noncontradiction, as the source of the evil contained in Kant's ethics, that he goes so far as to assert: "Let us recall that this does *not* mean that this right [of logic, universalizability] imposes itself *upon everyone*, but that it is valid for all cases" ("KS" 57; my emphases). Lacan interprets Kantian universalization to mean exclusively that the maxim must be applicable to all possible cases, whereas in fact Kant understands universalization to mean that the maxim must be valid *both* for all cases *and* for all people, indeed for "all rational beings," and he seems to take it for granted that the one necessarily entails the other.[11] But Kant does insist that moral judgment must be purely "analytic," that is, it must pay no attention to what he calls the field of the "pathological"—consideration of the empirical effects of the application of the maxim, the good, or harm, that it may procure the agent or society. For if ethical judgments were "synthetic," if they combined aspects of experience with purely logical considerations, then they could never be made universal. The maxims that derive from sensuous experience, from the world of nature, are all potentially self-contradictory, for they pertain to self-interest, and clearly what promotes the interests of one person or group may easily injure those of others (*CPR* 36–37). In short, and here the pertinence of Lacan's claim becomes manifest, however exaggerated it may be, "[p]ractical universal laws [are such] . . . because of their form and not because of their matter. . . . nothing remains except the mere form of giving universal law" (*CPR* 26). For Kant as for the entire European rationalist and theological tradition, the world of experience is the world of the contingent, of that which is always subject to internal contradiction, unless it be subjected to a principle that is beyond or before experience.

Lacan introduces his discussion of the defect in formalized reason in his own characteristic way, by quoting Ubu the King's famous last words: "Long live Poland, for if there were no Poland, there would be no Poles."[12] This definition of "Polishness" is of course purely "analytic" in the Kantian sense of the term; that is, it relies solely on qualities inherent in the concept of the subject rather than seeking its predicates in the empirical world, as a Kantian "synthetic" judgment would do. Making no attempt to take into account the realities of concrete history, Ubu's pronouncement illustrates the absurdity of such formal definitions, for he utters it just as the existence of the Polish state is once again being swallowed up into Russia. In a very real sense, the less there is a Poland, the more Polish the Polish people become.

Having illustrated the negative effects of ignoring historical reality, Lacan follows up his attack on the dangers of ethical formalism with the attempt to prove that Sade's *Philosophy in the Bedroom* contains a universalizable maxim whose consequences are even more perilous. The gist of Sade's sarcastic exhortation to his fellow citizens during the Revolution, "Frenchmen, yet another effort if you want to be republicans [that is, true citizens of the Republic]," which is contained in the Fifth Dialogue of *Philosophy in the Bedroom,* is that the Declaration of the Rights of

Man has as a logical consequence that everyone has the right to enjoy the body parts of anyone else, regardless of the other's wishes. Why? Because the new dignity of the citizen precludes ownership of human beings; their freedom being inalienable, no one can legitimately claim possession of another, for instance of a wife, or even of one's own body. "Never may an act of possession be exercised on a free being; it is as unjust to possess a woman as it is to possess slaves; all men are born free, all are equal before the law."[13] In order to demonstrate the logical connection between Kant's formalization and sadism, Lacan constructs a universalizable maxim for this "right," which functions as a parody of Kant's formal reason: "I have the right of enjoyment over your body, anyone can say to me, and I will exercise this right, without any limit stopping me in the capriciousness of the exactions I might have the taste to satiate" ("KS" 58). If we stick to the purely formal level of the rule, of the Law as a matter of universalizability alone, then there is no way to distinguish between Kant's morality and Sade's "principles."

One might be tempted to reject this maxim as un-Kantian, on the grounds that if everyone tried to put it into practice, its concept would annihilate itself, for I cannot coerce your will at the same time that you coerce mine. Having foreseen this objection, Sade, and Lacan after him, insist that the lack of reciprocity does not prevent universality, for it suffices that each person who has been victim of another's exactions can then use another person in turn. Thus Sade provides for a place where women can exercise the same "freedom" as men, subjecting them to their own sexual wishes (*PB* 212–14). Indeed, Lacan goes even farther than Sade, asserting that this asymmetry is a fundamental characteristic of the relation of the subject to moral law (the superego) and that the Sadian formulation reveals the lack of reciprocity the latter entails ("KS" 59).

Sade anticipated a similar but more radical objection: one might argue that his notion of the right to enjoyment cancels out the very concept of freedom conferred by the Declaration of the Rights of Man, which he alleged to be its basis. To this he replies:

> Let no one say that I contradict myself here, and that, after establishing above that we had no right to bind a woman to ourselves, I am destroying those principles by saying now that we have the right to compel her; I repeat that it is only a matter of enjoyment, not of property; I have no right of property over

this fountain that I encounter along my path, but I certainly do have the right to enjoy it. (*PB* 232 n. 1)[14]

Sade's defense thus depends on the notion of time contained in the distinction between lasting ownership (*propriété,* property) and temporary use (*jouissance,* enjoyment) which was so often deployed in eighteenth-century debates about natural law, the ostensible basis of the Rights of Man, as Sade repeatedly emphasizes. The "constraint" involved is only temporary, much like conscription into military service, and, since once released the victim may now exercise the same "right," it does not limit the basic freedom of the citizen. Of course the brunt of Sade's defense is carried as much by the double meaning of the word *jouissance* as it is by the logical or legal argument, and Lacan is well aware that this right to enjoyment is a caricature of the Kantian ethic. He nevertheless emphasizes that the formal criterion alone is not sufficient to distinguish the model from its grimacing image ("KS" 59).

A more compelling criticism would seem to be the one emphasized by Horkheimer and Adorno, that the suffering imposed on the victim and the utter disregard for her integrity contradict Kant's formulation of the categorical imperative as the injunction to treat people as ends rather than merely as means. Kant himself undermines this argument, however, and exposes the potential contradiction between the two aspects of his moral imperative, in his response to the criticism leveled against his concept by Jacobi and then Constant. The latter protested, it will be recalled, that in certain cases it is one's duty to lie, as when a murderer asks you whether your friend has taken refuge from him in your house;[15] to which Kant retorted that even in this case the duty to tell the truth is absolute and brooks no exceptions. In the *Groundwork of the Metaphysic of Morals,* he had maintained that an "*absolutely good will*," one which "cannot be evil," is precisely one which "can never be in conflict with itself" because its maxims are universal (*GMM* 104). He therefore responds to Constant that we still have the duty to tell the truth, no matter what harm may befall us or others as a result, for in lying I would be acting to undermine belief in statements, and this would harm mankind in general.[16] "Mankind in general" (*die Menschheit überhaupt*) thus takes absolute precedence over particular men and women, as the Frankfurt School and their many nineteenth-century predecessors had emphasized. One could use the same logic to argue that the interest of mankind in general in the right of enjoyment takes absolute precedence over the harm which might be done to individuals in the exercise of that right. In fact, just this line of argument was often taken in eighteenth-century attacks on property rights (without the sadistic component of course), and it is these that Sade is aping.

Now, as Lacan indicates in "Kant with Sade," when Sade justifies the absolute nature of his "right to enjoyment," he employs exactly the same type of formalistic argument to prove the claim that what Kant calls the "pathological" must be excluded from matters of principle ("KS" 59). To the objection that men's sexual practices might cause physical damage to very young girls, Sade's pamphlet replies that such empirical considerations are irrelevant:

> This consideration is devoid of any value; as soon as you grant me the right of property over enjoyment, that right is *independent of the effects produced* by enjoyment; from that point on it becomes indifferent whether that enjoyment be *advantageous or harmful* to the object who must submit to it . . . disregarding all selfish feelings. (*PB* 234; my emphases)[17]

In sum, the rejection of the pathological, of the good of the individual in the name of a formally defined universal principle, is the second bond that links Kant to Sade.

Once it is conceded that Kant's formal machine for ascertaining the moral validity of a maxim cannot distinguish between beneficence and cruelty, then it is only a short step to the conclusion that the universality derived from the principle of noncontradiction is not only indifferent to the suffering or murder of the actual person but is capable of justifying a general principle of evil as well as of good. This step was in fact taken, well before Adorno or Lacan, by nineteenth-century critics of Kant's system of moral law. In volume 2 of his *Essais de critique générale* (1859), the French neo-Kantian philosopher Charles Renouvier, well known at the time but since fallen into obscurity, tempers his admiration of Kant's concept of absolute duty with the caveat that "pathological" elements, "moral feeling, passionate ties, the love of people,"[18] are necessary to the foundation of genuine law. Otherwise, one could make evil (*le mal*) into the general principle of a universal legislation. In that case, there would be only two possibilities, both of which lead to contradictions:

> [Such a] consciousness should . . . either have not the slightest notion of the conditions necessary for maintaining human society nor of the very existence of others, or else aim purposely

at the destruction of the universe. In the first case, such a high degree of idiocy is assumed that consciousness no longer exists, and yet we are assuming that it does when we speak of it generalizing and legislating. In the second case, perfect wickedness would find no obstacle in an abstract law of which, precisely, it would not be aware, since by its nature it *could will* that which, according to Kant, one *cannot will.* (*ECG* 228–29; emphases in text)[19]

In thus concluding that natural feelings and an empirical experience of community are required in order to bring Kant's formal principle into agreement with his description of a totally good will, Renouvier demonstrates that without such considerations the logic of Kant's ethic does indeed support total wickedness (*la parfaite scélératesse*), which Renouvier describes in the terms used by Sade, and which Lacan will take over in order to characterize the Freudian death drive beyond the pleasure principle: the conscious aim of destroying the universe.

HAPPINESS IN EVIL

What distinguishes psychoanalytic explanations of social phenomena from purely political or sociological interpretations is the former's insistence on the motivating force of more or less hidden desires. Sadism of course involves more than simple indifference to suffering; it craves and enjoys the suffering it can impose. Starting from the first page of "Kant with Sade," Lacan argues that the link he has uncovered between the two—the exclusion of any empirical object and the consequent acceptance of the imposition of suffering in the name of a universal principle—is at the root of what he calls the theme of "happiness in evil," which, becoming more and more widespread throughout the nineteenth century, acts as the bond which joins the Enlightenment, Sade, and psychoanalysis ("KS" 55). On one level, this expression means that starting with Kant and continuing through Freud's assertion of his pleasure principle, one can no longer claim that it is possible to reconcile the striving for happiness with morality, that there is no consonance between the search for pleasure, however broadly defined, and the striving for "the good." The more significant point, as in Renouvier's interpretation of Kant, is that evil can bring satisfaction for its own sake, without any empirical gain to the subject,[20] and, as Freud so clearly demonstrated, that morality and its agency, the superego, operate according to this principle, deriving sadistic enjoyment from the suffering of the ego.

Let us return for a moment to Lacan's humorous quote about the essence of Polishness from *Ubu the King*. Anyone the least bit familiar with the tragedies of Polish history will recognize that in this case as so often, humor is no laughing matter. In fact, according to Freud's analysis, on one level humor is never a laughing matter, precisely because it involves the superego. In this context, the notes to the translation of "Kant with Sade" point out that Freud's prime example of humor involves consolation for inevitable suffering: a fellow being led to the gallows one Monday morning says, "Well, this week's beginning nicely!" What is at stake here is, first of all, the heightened recognition of the "pain of living" captured in *Oedipus at Colonus*'s "It is better not to have been born," which Lacan often cited. This pain is unavoidable, according to Lacan, because the symbolic system of a culture is always violently imposed from without onto the person, and it is this very imposition that gives rise to the subject as such. The superego inevitably involves the exacerbation of the distinction between the subject of the statement—the one who says, "without Poland there would be no Poles" or "this week's beginning nicely"—and the subject of the enunciation—the one who means, "there's more to being a Pole than being the citizen of a Polish state" or "the week's just beginning for everyone else, but for me. . . ."

The ethical dimension of this split subject in its relation to the superego appears most clearly in one of Kant's illustrations of the moral law. He supposes that someone has entrusted a valuable object to another and wonders whether the obligation to return the valuable on request is a universalizable, and therefore valid, maxim. He answers that it is, regardless of any personal motives of the trustee or of particular empirical conditions affecting either party at the time (*CPR* 27).[21] Lacan criticizes Kant for this stance because the philosopher has thereby reduced the subject to the mere subject of the statement, the one who is completely and entirely defined analytically, that is, by the concept of trustee, and such an elimination of the unconscious dimension of the subject is precisely what Lacan terms "alienation." This reproach echoes in Lacanian language Horkheimer and Adorno's protest that, in the industrial society which has developed from the Enlightenment, the particular individual has been reduced to a mere instance of the general social type.

If we smile at humor nevertheless, it must be because the superego has a hidden face of enjoyment, of enjoyment in suffering. Indeed, Lacan's general argument is that the superego somehow commands both the prohibition of desire and the paradoxical obligation of enjoyment at the same time: Kant *with* Sade. Desire, as he puts it in another passage, is the flip side of the Law. The key to understanding this paradox and its relation to Kant's categorical imperative is the notion of the lost object. Kant's most powerful formulation of the rule that all pathological considerations must be eliminated from the moral law states that morality can have no empirical object, no end outside itself whose acquisition would represent the good (*GMM* 82). On the contrary, through its universality and autonomy from experience, the moral law creates its own object (*CPR* 71). It is this new creation which becomes the object of what Lacan calls a "chaste desire," to which Kant alludes in *Groundwork:* "To behold virtue in her proper shape is nothing other than to show morality stripped of all admixture with the sensuous and of all the spurious adornments of reward or self-love" (*GMM* 94).[22] In *Practical Reason,* and even more forcefully in *Religion within the Limits of Reason Alone,* Kant presents God as the object of the love of the moral person.[23] For Kant then, the loss of the (empirical) object, the institution of the moral law, and the substitution of a nonphenomenal object of desire all coincide.

In psychoanalytic terms, the lost object, which promises total enjoyment, appears only in retrospect, the nonphenomenal mother, who is created precisely by her "loss," that is, by the imposition of the Law, in the form of the incest taboo. Acknowledging, like Kant, that the subject must have some object of desire, the modern superego of the industrialized world orders the subject to enjoy the substitute goods it creates in place of the lost object.[24] Of course, there never was an empirical object which could serve as the good, just as there never was a mother who could entirely satisfy the child's desire for complete and entire existence. It is therefore the prohibition of something that was impossible in the first place which institutes both the superego and the illusory ultimate object of desire, of complete enjoyment. And it is this same imposition which alienates the subject from his "originary" self, that natural being which also surfaces only in the retrospective view of the subject who has been created by his or her induction into the non-natural cultural system. The nucleus of the superego is at once a prohibition and a command to enjoy, both of which lack any rational justification and must therefore remain equally incomprehensible to, and unintegrated by, the subject.

It would seem that Lacan has taken us a long way from the instrumentalization of reason identified by Horkheimer and Adorno as the common ground between Kant and Sade. Indeed, when Žižek later returned to the question of the relation between the Frankfurt School's appropriation of psychoanalysis and Lacan's teachings, he asserted that the weak spot in Adorno's analysis of postmodern societies was precisely the lack of an adequately developed concept of the superego, one that could account for the unintegrated quality of its commands combined with its obscene order to enjoy.[25] While there is a good deal of truth in Žižek's argument, which relies on "The Relation between Sociology and Psychology" and "Freudian Theory and the Pattern of Fascist Propaganda" rather than on the Sade chapter of *Dialectic of Enlightenment,* I would assert that, without using the term "superego," Horkheimer and Adorno do propose a theory of alienation and enjoyment similar to, and prior to, that of Lacan.

> Nature does not feature enjoyment as such. . . . It originates in alienation. Even when . . . enjoyment lacks any knowledge of the interdiction against which it offends, it owes its origin to civilization, to the fixed order from which it longs to return to nature. . . . Men sense the magic of enjoyment only in that dream which releases them from the pressure of work and the bond which joins the individual to a specific social function. . . . Thought originated in the course of liberation from a terrifying nature. . . . Pleasure is, so to speak, nature's vengeance. In pleasure men disavow thought and escape civilization. (*DE* 105)

> [With sufficient enlightenment, however,] enjoyment becomes the object of manipulation, until, ultimately, it is entirely extinguished in fixed entertainments. (*DE* 106)

Substituting Lacan's "symbolic order" and "Law" for Horkheimer and Adorno's "civilization," and his "signifying chain" for their "thought," we can see that they have already formulated a theory of enjoyment based on the alienation of the subject and the need for transgression, although they attribute to "nature" a preexisting reality which Lacan holds to be a retrospective illusion. And once enjoyment, removed from the hands of a nature thirsting for revenge, has become the object of social manipulation, something very similar to Lacan's notion of the modern superego is born, the one that commands the subject to enjoy.[26]

The other major difference Žižek mentions, that concerning the role of the tormentor—subject for the Frankfurt School, object for Lacan— is also not quite so distinct as first appears. The main point of Lacan's interpretation here is that the sadist tortures the victim in order to preserve her own status as "brute subject," that is, as a whole, substantial, autonomous being who refuses to renounce the desire for wholeness, for the unity of the precultural self supposedly at one with nature. Inflicting pain involves enjoyment, the attempt to gain control over the will of the

Other.[27] But, as in the Hegelian struggle for pure prestige, the enjoyment disappears when it succeeds too well, since the Other then faints or dies, and thus cannot ratify the existence of the tormentor and, in fact, escapes the control of his will. In short, he wants to throw all the pain of living onto the victim, who thus plays the part of the split subject resulting from the imposition of the symbolic Law—which ostensibly prohibits the enjoyment of the originary object—so as to maintain the fiction that he, the tormentor, is spared that loss of object Lacan calls symbolic castration. It is for this reason that the tormentor can perform the function of the fantasized object of desire, that which restores wholeness and plenitude.

As Žižek rightly observes, Horkheimer and Adorno consider that it is the victim who has lost all autonomy, having become the mere instrument of the sadist's quest for pleasure. Nevertheless, they do make a point very similar to Lacan's. The first sentence of their chapter quotes Kant's famous definition of Enlightenment as the emergence of a mature subject who can use her understanding without the guidance of any other person or authority; that is, of a subject whose intellectual independence from the symbolic system strongly resembles the autonomy of Lacan's "brute subject" (the S without the bar in the graphs Lacan inserts into the text of "Kant with Sade"), which the pervert is striving to conserve at all costs. Of course, Kant later makes this autonomous subject subject to itself in the form of the moral Law; and Lacan therefore equates his brute subject to Kant's "pathological" subject of empirical pleasure. For the Frankfurt School writers, however, it is this liberation of the subject from all traditional social bonds that makes the formalization of reason so dangerous: by removing all concern for the good, for the welfare and happiness of the members of society, formalization makes reason into a mere instrument at the disposal of any goal, thereby giving free rein to cruelty and domination. They criticize Spinoza, for instance, who was, of course, along with Kant and various empiricists, the favorite philosopher of the partisans of science in the nineteenth century, for his rejection of pity and remorse in the name of a stoic ataraxia, pointing out with glee the presence of the same apathy in Sade's criminals. They thus leave the impression that ataraxia is always at the disposal of the criminal as much as the sage,[28] and that the reason of Kantian Enlightenment serves the enjoyment of the autonomous bourgeois subject, thereby assimilating the intellectually autonomous Enlightenment ego to the ego of pleasure and domination, although, as mentioned above, they attribute this possibility to Kant's speculative rather than his practical reason.

Moreover, like Horkheimer and Adorno, Lacan also uses the term "instrument" repeatedly in his essay, both to characterize the role of the sadist ("KS" 62–63) and to describe his own use of Sade to illuminate the hidden recesses of Kant's practical reason ("KS" 63). Lacan's version of instrumental reason makes the Kantian good will the agency whereby the alienated subject is reconstituted as whole; that is, the will serves the same function in Kant's fantasy of practical reason as the tormentor does in the Sadian phantasm, that of object, of instrument:

> It is thus indeed the will of Kant which is encountered in the place of this will [represented by the letter V, for *volonté*, in Lacan's schema] which can be called the will to enjoy only by explaining that it is the subject reconstituted from alienation at the price of being no more than the instrument of enjoyment. ("KS" 63; translation modified)

The will, listening solely to the voice (*voix* in French, another sense of the V in Lacan's diagram) of reason, in fact acts so as to please the noumenal Other ("KS" 60–61).

KANT AND FASCIST THEORY

It is one thing to point to possible implications of Kant's moral philosophy and quite another to attribute real political effects to his thought. From the time of the French Revolution, in Britain, France, and Germany, conservative and reactionary thinkers generally associated him with Robespierre and the radical left of the Terror. During the anti-Jacobin reaction in the Germanic states and Austro-Hungary in 1794, Kant's works were banned and burned in the Hungarian capital because he was widely thought of as a Jacobin, due to his continued support of the principles of the Revolution even after the Terror, as can be seen in his essay on "The Contest of the Faculties" (1794), when other German intellectuals had turned against them.[29] Given these repeated assaults on Kant from the right, it might seem incongruous for an Adorno or a Lacan to make him the source of fascism and even to lay major responsibility for the Nazi genocide at his feet! In a broad sense, it is the possibility of state terror that many thinkers find to be the common characteristic of the French Revolution and of fascism. Burke and his many imitators, such as Taine, asserted that the attempt to impose abstract "metaphysical" principles on society led to unprincipled government violence by undermining respect for all principles of established custom and law. Heine also

satirized Kant's passionless abstraction and discovered fundamental simi-
larities between Robespierre and Kant in that the French politician killed
a king while the German philosopher executed God himself in his first
Critique, but he attributed their parallel "terrorism" to their shared
narrow-minded bourgeois mentality, their talent for distrust, whether of
ideas or of people, and, above all, to their "inexorable, trenchant, sober
honesty, utterly devoid of poetry."[30] Hegel was probably the first, however, to link Kant's ethical principles directly to the Terror. He incorporated the gist of Burke's attacks on Enlightenment politics into his own
more philosophical indictment of Kant, the tenor of which was that the
pure free will exalted by Kant's moral philosophy leads to the kind of
"frightful tyranny" instituted during the Reign of Terror, since it subordinated the lives and interests of the majority of real people to the assertion
of the abstract principle of a subjective "virtue," adherence to which
could be judged only by divining people's inner feelings (*Gesinnung*), as
Kant maintains, rather than on objectively available legal forms.[31] Moreover, he saw a connection between the "empty formalism" of the categorical imperative and the Reign of Terror, arguing that Kant's ethics constituted an internalization of Rousseau's political principle of the rule of the
"general will," for both lacked any specific content and thereby eliminated the possibility of objective judgments of the "virtue," whether civic
or private, of an action. Ethics were reduced to a matter of gauging inner
sincerity and the purity of motives, opening the way during the Revolution for the arbitrary persecution of alleged "hypocrites," those who
strove to fulfill private ends under the guise of serving the common good.
Blind obedience to duty regardless of the content, far from inaugurating
true freedom, simply transferred the old master-slave relation to the new
planes of the general will to the citizen and of conscience to subject.[32]
During the Nazi period, this same relation was played out between the
Führer and his followers. For instance, when Hans Frank took control of
the Nazi government bureaucracy in East Prussia in 1942, he exhorted
his charges to rationalize their procedures by adopting the technological
version of Kant's categorical imperative: "The categorical imperative of
action in the Third Reich says: Act in such a way that if the Führer learned
of your action, he would approve of this action."[33] And of course, in his
trial in Jerusalem, Adolf Eichmann justified his part in the mass extermination of the Jews with a similar reference to Kant's moral imperative.[34]

There was, however, a more direct connection between Kant and fascist thought, whose source was precisely the distinction he draws between the realm of speculative, scientific reason, and that of practical,

moral reason. This distinction allowed Houston Stewart Chamberlain, son-in-law of Richard Wagner, to confer a veneer of philosophical and scientific profundity on the Bayreuth racial theories in his enormously successful *Grundlagen des XIX. Jahrhunderts*.[35] History became a Manichaean struggle between God, the principle of light, represented by the Aryans, the Germanic race; and the Devil, the principle of darkness, embodied in the Semitic race. At first sight it may seem difficult to imagine how Kant's thought could be invoked to support such drivel. But invoked it was. Probably the most widespread interpretation of the significance of Kant's critique during the nineteenth century, in Germany as in France, contended that by restricting the sphere of application of (speculative) reason to empirical phenomena, Kant had preserved the realm of the noumenon, of the *Ding an sich,* for religion. Now in Chamberlain's scheme of things, the major contribution of the Teutonic peoples to history was the addition of the "metaphysical element" to the legacy they had taken over from Greek and Roman civilizations. By virtue of its capacity for mystical contact with the cosmos, members of the Aryan race alone were capable of knowing, and hence saving, the world.

At the same time, however, in a neo-Kantian fashion, Chamberlain insisted on the equal importance of empirical science, which for him was of course "German" science. The main political significance of this rehabilitation of the natural sciences was its influence on the real National Socialist program a few decades later, in that the Nazis could remain faithful to the racial ideology of other neo-Romantic groups while abandoning the latter's more nostalgic rejection of modern industry and technology in the name of a xenophobic peasant traditionalism. Once science and technology were used in the service of the spiritual regeneration of the Germanic race, future society could incorporate the supposed virtues of the idyllic past and enter into the "new, splendid, and light-filled" future of Kant's "pure ideal."[36] For Chamberlain, then, it was Kant's radical dualism—the absolute separation of phenomenon from noumenon, combined with the retention of both—that supported the racial, historical, and social theories the National Socialists, and Hitler in particular, would find so appealing.

Lacan's criticism of the Kantian ethic focuses on precisely the same aspect of his thought. Just as the Germanic race can attain a metaphysical knowledge of the world order that will help it achieve the pure ideal, so the Kantian good will, by virtue of its faith in reason, can claim to know how to reach the "Kingdom of God," the combination of morality and happiness (*CPR* 129–31). By limiting the range of the understanding to the phenomenal world, reason both justifies the necessity of deterministic natural laws and protects its own noumenal domain from the encroachment of critique. Despite, but also as a result of, the pure formalism of his moral law and the resulting autonomy of his good will, Kant had reinstated God and immortality as transcendent ideas which are nevertheless necessary to the goal that the good will holds before itself in order to justify its adherence to the law. In spite of Kant's repeated disclaimers, the logic of his argument requires that, in order to act in conformity with the universal moral law, the subject must claim to know the tenor of these transcendent ideas; that is, to comprehend, by virtue of what Kant calls "rational faith," the desire of God (*CPR* 129). In subsection V of "The Dialectic of Pure Practical Reason," Kant argues that, although happiness is neither the ground nor the incentive of morality (the moral law is), happiness may follow morality as a result, provided there be an omnipotent, rational, and omniscient God who will harmonize nature with morality, natural law with the laws of freedom (*CPR* 117, 130–40). It is thus the principle of universality, of formal reason, which allows the subject to know "the perfect volition of an omnipotent rational being" (*CPR* 117). As we shall see, for Lacan it is this power to control the desire of the Other which forms the most powerful link between Kant and Sade.

Chamberlain's theories appealed to no one more than Alfred Rosenberg, who proclaimed him to be the "creator and founder of a German future."[37] It was Rosenberg, along with Dietrich Eckhart, who most probably introduced Hitler to Chamberlain's theories and who has been credited with giving ideological coherence to Hitler's visceral race-hatred. A member of the Nazi Party from 1920, editor of its chief journal from 1921, head of the party during Hitler's imprisonment in 1924, founder and leader of the *Kampfbund für deutsche Kultur* from 1929, Rosenberg was Hitler's chief ideologist until 1934, and he still retained some influence while holding various important government positions until the end of the war. His magnum opus, *Der Mythus des 20. Jahrhunderts* (1933),[38] continues the strain of Chamberlain's "scientific" history of the evolution of races and his violent anti-Semitism, and while it is not overtly based on an interpretation of Kant's thought, it does cite him as a culture hero of German "race-history" more than any other figure except Luther. The most significant function of this work was to give Nazism the idealistic and utopian patina that earned it acceptance among the bourgeois public by allowing the latter to maintain the fiction of promoting culture and decency while pursuing or ignoring the torture and murder of millions.[39]

CONCLUSION: SACRIFICE AND THE ETHICS OF DESIRE

For psychoanalytic social critique, however, idealist ideology is not simply a cover for base motives nor just a dangerous departure from the world of empirical reality. Horkheimer and Adorno claim that fascist racial ideology is totally irrational, a mere pretext designed to hide the actual motive for committing racial or ethnic violence. In their scenario, the victims are scapegoats onto whom the racist has projected the natural satisfactions which he himself has had to renounce in order to participate in modern society. The fascist leader manipulates the rage and frustration of the ordinary citizen, inciting him to sacrifice the members of the race which supposedly enjoys all the fruits of modern civilization without having had to pay the price in instinctual renunciation. The sacrifice of the victims thus reenacts the very sacrifice of natural instincts which has cost the potential racist his own enjoyment.

For Lacan also, the Nazi genocide was a matter of sacrifice. That is why he purposely used the term "holocaust" in his seminar of 1964 to indicate the sacrificial core of that event along with its reference to age-old religious practices. He too notes the prevalence of the type of experience the Frankfurt School writers invoke to explain the effectiveness of fascist anti-Semitic ideology. He sees this effect of narcissistic identification, however, as an indicator of something that lies beyond the narcissistic plane of goods: it is a "reference of the dialectic of the good to a beyond that . . . [he] will call 'the good that mustn't be touched'" (*FFC* 237). The key to understanding the sacrificial aspect of genocide in its relation to ideology, the primary element that connects Kant, Sade, and fascism, is the role of the third party which "mustn't be touched," the Other whose presence, whether hidden or overt, controls the process of perversion. Lacan adds another, crucial twist to the theory of sadism, absent from the Frankfurt School interpretation, as Žižek emphasizes in his note on the "Juliette" chapter: without knowing it, the sadist makes himself into the object for the benefit of that third party, that Other whose enjoyment he is out to ensure. Thus it is not their own lost enjoyment which the fascist followers sacrifice again in the victim; rather, it is the enjoyment of the Other, and first of all that of the Führer, which the fascist *refuses* to sacrifice and hence feels impelled to guarantee by the sacrifice of the victim. Nothing better illustrates the fundamental lack of reciprocity inherent in the categorical imperative than this fascist version in that the one who announces duty is not bound by the duty he announces; despite the explicit content of the philosopher's assertions, Kantian ethics announce the freedom of the Other, not of the subject ("KS" 60).

In support of this interpretation of sacrifice for the benefit of the Other, Lacan refers to the constant blasphemy of Sade's characters and the imprecation that the sufferings of the victim should endure in hell through all eternity, which show that on some level they have not freed themselves from the belief in a God for whom they perform their cruelties and crimes ("KS" 64), just as Kant had reinstated God and immortality as transcendent ideas necessary to the goal which the good will holds before itself in order to justify its adherence to the law. The idea of justice in the afterlife presupposes a subjective presence who keeps score of our good and bad deeds; that is, an Other for whose enjoyment we exercise our practical reason (*EP* 317). Lacan suggests that Sade is more honest about this matter than Kant. While the latter pretends that the voice of practical reason is in fact that of the subject herself, Sade openly recognizes that the voice which commands the sadistic sacrifice comes from outside the self. That is why Lacan concocts such a convoluted formula for Sade's right to enjoyment: by embedding the expression of that right within a framing quote, he indicates that the enunciating subject (*le sujet de l'énonciation*) is actually the Other who addresses me, the one who first says "I" within the quotation rather than the "me" to whom the quote is addressed, who is merely the subject of the statement ("DL" 235).

In part, then, fascist ideology is the deceptive mask of the sadistic superego which demands sacrifice for its own enjoyment. Yet, paradoxically—and here he clearly parts company with the Frankfurt School writers—for Lacan the indifference to considerations of happiness, of the good, recommended by various forms of stoicism and crystallized in Kant's purification of the moral law, connotes the remedy for, as much as the source of, the danger which ultimately led to the fascist genocide. Lacan's own maxim, expressed in his seminar on *The Ethics of Psychoanalysis,* is that one should not give up on one's desire. Desire being the flip side of the Law, this is tantamount to saying that you should not allow considerations of the good, Kant's pathological, to interfere with your desire. In fact, he argues, desire is an even better counterweight to the pathological than is the Law. In the second *Critique,* Kant introduces an example in order to demonstrate the power of the Law to outweigh the demands of the pathological, and thus to establish that it is moral duty which first leads us to the concept of freedom. Suppose a subject were ordered by his prince, on pain of death, to bear false witness against an innocent person the ruler wanted to ruin. The subject might not be sure what he would do if actually faced with this situation, but, Kant argues, he would certainly acknowledge that it would be *possible* for him not to obey this order. He thinks he could do something because he is aware that he *should* do it (*CPR* 30). Lacan's response is, typically, oblique: what if the tyrant ordered his subject to tell the *truth* instead of to lie, about a Jew to a Nazi tribunal, about an atheist before the Inquisition, or about a "deviationist" in Stalin's purge trials ("KS" 69–70)? Here Lacan is of course echoing Constant's objection and pointing to the implicit sadism of Kant's universal Law. Lacan then suggests that perhaps a better maxim would be: "Thwart the desire of the tyrant, if a tyrant is one who arrogates to himself the power to enslave [control] the desire of the Other" ("KS" 70). In that case, the desire to resist the desire of the tyrant would be just as effective as Kant's moral imperatives (always telling the truth) in discovering one's freedom from the "pathological," and with greater right, since sometimes telling the truth is the coward's way of giving in to his "pathological" wishes (to live, to prosper). His conclusion is that, when it comes to balancing out the claims of the pathological, "desire can not only have the same success [as the Law], but can obtain it with greater legitimacy" ("KS" 70).

Now it may seem that this agreement with the Kantian principle— that ethics and freedom begin only where the pathological leaves off— would contradict the position from which we began, Lacan's assertion that Kant's philosophy opened the way for fascism. But the question is, "What desire does Lacan have in mind?" As we have seen, according to him, the Kantian moral Law derives from a fantasy in which the autonomy of the subject is asserted for the benefit, for the enjoyment, of an Other; specifically, for the subjectivity entailed by Kant's arguments for the immortality of the soul as a place of pure justice, a possibility only if there were someone to tot up the punishments and rewards. Unlike Sade, however, Kant does not acknowledge the enjoyment of the Other in the moral Law, for this might suggest the malignity of God, since moral action always involves some degree of suffering; he contends, on the contrary, that the voice of conscience is in fact the subject himself, thus sustaining the fantasy of autonomy, the lack of any object of desire. "The moral law represent[s] desire in the case when it is not the subject, but the object that is lacking" ("KS" 67; translation slightly altered). And this is what Lacan calls "pure desire."

It is tempting to align the purity of this desire with the intransigence of Lacan's prime example of heroic desire in *The Ethics of Psychoanalysis,* Antigone, as some commentators have done. But intransigence is not identical to purity, and Lacan explicitly rejects that assimilation in the same passage at the end of *Concepts* with which we began: "The analyst's desire is *not* a pure desire" (*FFC* 276; my emphasis). And he does so precisely because that pure desire is the very danger against which analysis is meant to protect:

> [Kant's] theory of consciousness, when he writes of practical reason, is sustained only by giving a specification of the moral law which . . . is simply desire in its pure state, that very desire which culminates in the *sacrifice* . . . of everything that is the object of love in one's human tenderness . . . not only in the rejection of the pathological object, but also in its *sacrifice and murder.* That is why I wrote *Kant avec Sade.* (*FFC* 276; my emphases)

It is this willingness to surrender the object in the name of the pure (moral) law in order to appease a god that differentiates Kant from Spinoza and aligns him with Sade. What makes us susceptible to the fascination of sacrificial murder "is that, in the object of our desires, we try to find evidence for the presence of the desire of this Other that I call . . . the dark God" (*FFC* 275). All religions, Lacan argues in *Ethics,* aim to recover the phallus, and, as Joseph De Maistre insists in his anti-Enlightenment diatribe *On Sacrifices,* the purpose of sacrifice, and the reason for its universal practice among religions, is that it allegedly offers the only possibility of paying for, and thereby cleansing us of, our guilt.[40] The sad irony that Lacan points to is that the Enlightenment itself, in the categorical imperative of Kant, with Sade, gives a renewed justification for the ancient practice of assuaging the superego by means of sacrifice.

But psychoanalytic experience has shown, as Freud explains eloquently in *Civilization and Its Discontents,* that appeasing the superego only increases its thirst for bloody propitiation. It is the very irrationality of pure practical reason that constitutes the danger. Here Lacan once again rejoins Adorno and Horkheimer when they argue that the mathematical formalism of a Kant, as of logical positivism, renounces the reason of reason, the essential function of mediating critique, and reverts to the mythical thinking it strives to overcome, thereby abandoning the whole claim of knowledge.

As the history of the West since the eighteenth century has shown, the practical consequence of this lack of mediation has been the utterly irrational growth in the power of the social system over its subjects in direct proportion to their increased liberation from that of natural forces (*DE* 38-39). In Lacan's terms, the liberation of the "Other" from all constraints of meaning—where this Other is understood as the signifier both linguistic and mathematical, the pure symbolic, and therefore social, system which must be accepted in order for a subject to come into existence, and hence the set of rules which constitute the superego—may lead to the utter objectification of the subject.

But while Lacan's diagnosis of the malady coincides with that of Adorno and Horkheimer, and while they share the goal of using critical reason to "dissolve domination" (*DE* 42), the specific method and point of attack he recommends differ from theirs. On the social level, one must reject any political discourse that would propitiate the Other by sacrificing the object. As Lacan puts it, one must take as a maxim: resist the tyrant, the tyrant being anyone who, like the sadist, claims to know, and therefore to be able to control, the desire of the Other ("KS" 70). That is why one should not meekly accept one's "absolute duty" but maintain one's desire. However, this desire, like that of the analyst or of Antigone, is not the pure desire of the "law without limits" represented by Creon (*EP* 259) but one that is "outside the limits of the law" (*EP* 276). For Lacan's ultimate objective is not to depsychologize the subject as Adorno proposes but to provide a place beyond the Law where the subject can exist. Where Horkheimer and Adorno aim to use knowledge to counteract domination (*DE* 42), he will assert that it is only the preservation of a region of lack of knowledge, of an unconscious, and thus of a desire that is outside the Law which can support the freedom of the subject.[41] Unlike Constant, Lacan does place responsibility for the Terror on the shoulders of the universal Rights of Man; the new factor introduced by the Revolution, Lacan claims, is not the politics of happiness, which has ever existed, but the (universal) freedom to desire ("KS" 71). But the latter also wills the Law to be free, free of any object, à la Kant, and of any restraint by custom, à la Burke, and thus, as Hegel declares, leads to the guillotine ("KS" 71). By removing all prior constraints in the name of reason, the new law gives free rein to the death drive, to the urge to destroy everything that exists and start life all over from scratch, as Sade describes his desideratum ("KS" 64-65; *EP* 260). Yet Lacan agrees with

Constant that, with certain qualifications, it is necessary to maintain some general principles and that the freedom to desire is worth fighting for. But at the site of Constant's "intermediate principles" or Kant's noumenon, Lacan places the void of being, that nothingness which constitutes the residue of Spinoza's universal within the particular. Interestingly, Horkheimer and Adorno cite a concept which bears a close resemblance to Lacan's "in you more than you," that of "mana" developed by Marcel Mauss, the French anthropologist, in order to account for the combination of divinity and individuality that nonindustrial societies find within particular objects. Similarly, as Lacan explains in his analysis of Antigone's relation to Polynices, the brother she insists on burying according to traditional rites, the signifier, and especially the proper name, both imprisons the subject within a general system of classification and confers upon him or her a unique value beyond that system (*EP* 279).

In sum, for Lacan the subject cannot exist without the law, whose prohibition makes desire possible, but in order to escape the complete reification implicit in either the rationalist or the irrationalist conception of the relation of the phenomenal to the noumenal, she must preserve a nonknowable component, a zero term, that is beyond the reach of the law. It is precisely the tension between the universal and the particular, the splitting of the subject between the imposition of symbolic prohibition and individual desire, which alone can avoid the temptation of sacrifice to the dark god of fascism.

Notes

1. Jacques Lacan, *The Four Fundamental Concepts of Psycho-Analysis,* trans. Alan Sheridan, ed. Jacques-Alain Miller (New York: W. W. Norton, 1977). Hereafter cited as *FFC.*

2. See Blake's bitter attack on the classicist and thus class-based universalism of Reynolds, in his "Annotations to *The Works of Sir Joshua Reynolds,*" in *The Complete Poetry and Prose of William Blake,* ed. David V. Erdman and Harold Bloom (Berkeley: University of California Press, 1982), 635–62. For Barrès's early socialist period, see Zeev Sternhell, *Maurice Barrès et le nationalisme français* (Paris: Armand Colin, 1983), 150–225.

3. Jacques Lacan, "Kant with Sade," trans. James B. Swenson, *October* 51 (Winter 1989): 55–75. Hereafter cited as "KS."

4. Max Horkheimer and Theodor Adorno, *Dialectic of Enlightenment,* trans. John Cumming (New York: Continuum, 1972). Hereafter cited as *DE.*

5. Jacques Lacan, *The Seminar of Jacques Lacan, Book VII, The Ethics*

of Psychoanalysis, trans. Dennis Porter, ed. Jacques-Alain Miller (New York: W. W. Norton, 1992). Hereafter cited as *EP.*

6. It is a little disconcerting, however, that, as far as I can tell, the excellent annotations to the English translation, which cite a host of sources from Jacob Boehme to Charlie Chaplin and from the Bible to Sade's mother-in-law, give no hint of the existence of the "Juliette" chapter. And it should be noted that, precisely in 1959, the spring (2ᵉ Trimestre) issue of the French Communist journal *Arguments* included a short article on "Adorno et l'école de Francfort," which mentions *Dialektik der Aufklärung* in a note. The passage from that work included in the subsequent selection of excerpts from Adorno's writings does not, however, come from the "Juliette" chapter.

7. Slavoj Žižek, "Sur le pouvoir politique et les mécanismes idéologiques," *Ornicar?* 34 (July–September 1985): 41–60. Hereafter cited as "PPMI." Although much of that article appeared in English in Žižek's *The Sublime Object of Ideology* (London: Verso, 1989), as far as I can tell his note on the "Juliette" chapter has not been translated.

8. The recent flap about Sokal's hoax in *Social Text* is simply one of the more farcical offspring of this deadly serious debate. To dismiss theories of the social construction of reality as "subjectivist thinking," "epistemic relativism," and lack of concern for "internal logical consistency," in short, as a kind of irrationalism, as Sokal does in "A Physicist Experiments with Cultural Studies," *Lingua Franca* (May–June 1996): 62–64, is no more rational a move than to castigate all rationalism as "fascist" or "totalitarian." To claim that "for most of the past two centuries, the Left has been identified with science and against obscurantism" (64) is to ignore those very "facts and evidence" Sokal claims "*do* matter" (63; his emphasis), for in fact science has *also,* and often at the same time, been associated with the right. Social Darwinism in the United States and Britain, the positivism of the later Comte, Renan, and Taine in France, are the most glaring and well-known examples.

9. See especially Max Horkheimer, *Eclipse of Reason* (New York: Oxford University Press, 1947).

10. Immanuel Kant, *Groundwork of the Metaphysic of Morals,* trans. H. J. Paton (New York: Harper and Row, 1964), 104. Hereafter cited as *GMM.*

11. Immanuel Kant, *Critique of Practical Reason,* trans. Lewis White Beck (New York: Macmillan, 1993), 24. Hereafter cited as *CPR.* See also *GMM* 81, 89.

12. Lacan has altered Ubu's maxim slightly by adding the words "Long live Poland." The exclamation contains the last words of *Ubu the King,* but of course Ubu the character appears in subsequent plays.

13. "Jamais un acte de possession ne peut être exercé sur un être libre; il est aussi injuste de posséder une femme qu'il est de posséder des esclaves; tous les hommes sont nés libres, tous sont égaux en droit." The Marquis de Sade, *La Philosophie dans le boudoir* (Paris: Editions 10/18, 1972), 209.

Hereafter cited as *PB*. This and all further translations from this work are mine.

14. "Qu'on ne dise pas ici que je me contrarie, et qu'après avoir établi plus haut que nous n'avions aucun droit de lier une femme à nous, je détruis ces principes en disant maintenant que nous avons le droit de la contraindre; je répète qu'il ne s'agit que de la jouissance et non de la propriété; je n'ai nul droit à la propriété de cette fontaine que je rencontre dans mon chemin, mais j'ai des droits certains à sa jouissance. . . ."

15. Benjamin Constant, *Des réactions politiques, Écrits et discours politiques,* ed. O. Pozzo di Borgo (n.p.: Jean-Jacques Pauvert, 1964), 21–91. I have purposely truncated this one point from its context in order to make Lacan's argument as clear as possible. But Constant's assertion of this duty not to tell the truth to the potential murderer occurs as part of a larger dispute, written in the heat of the Thermidor reaction (An V, 1797), in which Constant was trying to defend the Republic against both the forces of political reaction—the royalists and constitutional monarchists who had won important victories in recent elections—and the Jacobins, whose alleged "excesses" had led to widespread public support for the reactionaries. The main brunt of his argument is directed overtly against Burke, through whom of course he is attacking the French counterrevolutionaries. For this reason, he devotes most of the section to justifying the political necessity and value of universal principles, in agreement with Kant (although Kant rejected Constant's inductive rationale for them). It is not the principles of the Revolution, nor the Declaration of the Rights of Man, that were responsible for the Reign of Terror, but their imposition without due regard for what he terms the proper "intermediate principles." If the application of general principles based on the common interest often causes disorder, as a Burke would claim, it is because the intermediate principles have not been found. As a result, only their immediate, destructive effects have surfaced, whereas the "prejudices" of particular (class) interests, constituting the basis of current institutions, are well adapted to sustaining communal life. Once institutions are built on the common interest, however, then it is prejudices which will appear harmful and the general principles that represent the common good will be considered beneficial.

Constant was equally fearful that, under the threat of counterrevolution, the Directory would resort to arbitrary and brutal repression of its reactionary enemies, thus beginning again the cycle of violence the country had experienced under Robespierre during the Reign of Terror. His example of the murderer at the door, while ostensibly designed to show the necessity of intermediate principles in the realm of ethics, no doubt had the primarily political motivation of demonstrating the disastrous results of the supposed Jacobin practice of treating principles as absolutes, with no consideration for particular circumstances. There is in fact good evidence that the example is based on real events that occurred during the Terror, when Mme de Staël (with whom Constant had fallen in love in 1795 and who was probably responsible for his conversion away from his earlier Jacobinism and strict Kantism in the realm of ethics) lied to the spy who asked her whether Mathieu de Montmorency was in her townhouse. He argues, then, that in such a case Kant's assertion of the absolute duty to tell the truth is not only preposterous but unethical. But the elimination of the injunction against lying would be just as harmful. What is needed is an intermediate principle which makes it possible to know when and how to apply the universal principle. In this case, it is the idea that one has duties only to those who have rights, and a murderer does not have the right to the truth (64–71). Kant was of course aware of the specific arguments marshaled by Constant and strove to refute them directly in his response.

16. Immanuel Kant, "Über ein vermeintes Recht aus Menschenliebe zu lügen" (1797), in *Kant's Werke* [*Erste Abteilung, Kant's Gesammelte Schriften*, ed. Königlich Preußische Akademie der Wissenschaften], vol. 8, *Abhandlungen nach 1781* (Berlin: Georg Reimer Verlag, 1912), 426.

17. "Cette considération est sans aucune valeur; dès que vous m'accordez le droit de propriété sur la jouissance, ce droit est indépendant des effets produits par la jouissance; de ce moment il devient égal que cette jouissance soit avantageuse ou nuisible à l'objet qui doit s'y soumettre. . . . abstraction faite de tout sentiment égoïste."

18. Charles Renouvier, *Essais de critique générale,* vol. 2 (Paris: A. Colin, 1912), 229. Hereafter cited as *ECG.* All translations from this work are mine.

19. "[une telle] conscience devrait . . . ou n'avoir pas la moindre notion des conditions nécessaires du maintien de la société humaine et de l'existence même des êtres, ou viser sciemment la destruction de l'univers. Dans le premier cas, l'idiotisme est supposé à ce degré où la conscience n'existe plus, et cependant on la suppose, en parlant pour elle de généraliser et de légiférer. Dans le second cas, la parfaite scélératesse ne trouverait point un obstacle dans une loi abstraite que précisément elle ne connaîtrait pas, puisque de sa nature elle *pourrait vouloir* ce que, selon Kant, on *ne peut pas vouloir.*"

20. See Jacques-Alain Miller, "A Discussion of Lacan's 'Kant with Sade,'" in *Reading Seminars I and II: Lacan's Return to Freud,* ed. Richard Feldstein, Bruce Fink, and Maire Jaanus (Albany: State University of New York Press, 1996), 213. Hereafter cited as "DL."

21. Note that Kant sets himself in opposition here to Socrates' argument at the beginning of the *Republic;* the latter maintains that under certain circumstances—for instance, if the first person had gone mad in the interval—the trustee should not return his weapon, for he might then use it to harm himself or others (331c–d).

22.   See Julia Saville, "Of Fleshly Garments: Ascesis and Desire in the Ethic of Psychoanalysis," *American Imago* 49, no. 4 (1992): 452–53, for an illuminating discussion of this "negative object."

23.   Immanuel Kant, *Religion within the Limits of Reason Alone*, trans. Theodore M. Greene and Hoyt H. Hudson (Chicago: Open Court, 1934).

24.   Rousseau seems to have been the first to describe the process leading to contemporary commodity lust, in his *Discourse on the Origin of Inequality.*

25.   Slavoj Žižek, *The Metastases of Enjoyment: Six Essays on Woman and Causality* (London: Verso, 1994).

26.   Of course the Frankfurt School and Lacan had common predecessors in addition to Freud himself, from Rousseau and the European Romantics through Hegel and Marx to Nietzsche and the French schools of sociology, including Durkheim, Mauss, Bataille, and Caillois, the latter of whom Adorno quotes in this very context.

27.   See also the descriptions of the sadistic perversion in Jacques Lacan, *The Seminar of Jacques Lacan, Book I, Freud's Papers on Technique*, trans. John Forrester, ed. Jacques-Alain Miller (New York: W. W. Norton, 1988), 214–19.

28.   Foreseeing just such an objection, Kant wrote in *Groundwork:*

> Moderation in affections and passions, self-control, and sober reflexion . . . are far from being described as good without qualification. . . . For without the principles of a good will they may become exceedingly bad; and the very coolness of a scoundrel makes him, not merely more dangerous, but also immediately more abominable in our eyes than we should have taken him to be without it. (61–62)

29.   Georges Lefebvre, *La Révolution française* (Paris: Presses Universitaires de France, 1989), 306; Immanuel Kant, "The Contest of the Faculties," in *Kant: Political Writings*, trans. H. B. Nisbet, ed. Hans Reiss (Cambridge: Cambridge University Press, 1991), 176–90.

30.   "unerbittliche, schneidende, poesielose, nüchterne Ehrlichkeit." Heinrich Heine, *Zur Geschichte der Religion und Philosophie in Deutschland*, in *Heinrich Heine Werke*, Vierter Band (Frankfurt am Main: Insel Verlag, 1968), 124; my translation.

31.   G. W. F. Hegel, *Vorlesungen über die Philosophie der Weltgeschichte*, ed. Georg Lasson, Vierter Band, *Die Germanische Welt* (Leipzig: Felix Meiner, 1944), 922–30.

32.   G. W. F. Hegel, *Phenomenology of Spirit*, trans. A. V. Miller (Oxford: Oxford University Press, 1977). See also Steven B. Smith, *Hegel's Critique of Liberalism* (Chicago: University of Chicago Press, 1989), 52.

33.   "Der kategorische Imperativ des Handelns im Dritten Reich lautet:

Handle so, daß der Führer, wenn er von deinem Handeln Kenntnis hätte, dieses Handeln billigen würde." Hans Frank, *Die Technik des Staates* (Krakau: Burgenverlag, 1942), 15-16; my translation.

34. Hannah Arendt, *Eichmann in Jerusalem: A Report on the Banality of Evil* (New York: Viking, 1964), 135-37.

35. Houston Stewart Chamberlain, *Die Grundlagen des XIX. Jahrhunderts* (Munich: F. Bruckmann, 1962).

36. Quoted in George L. Mosse, *The Crisis of German Ideology: Intellectual Origins of National Socialism* (New York: Grosset and Dunlap, 1964), 97.

37. "den 'Verfünder und Begründer einer deutschen Zukunft'" (my translation), quoted in the advertising blurb to Georg Schott's collection of two hundred excerpts from Chamberlain's works published at the height of the Nazi period, *Houston Chamberlain Der Seher des dritten Reiches: Das Vermächtnis Houston Stewart Chamberlains an das Deutsche Volk,* ed. Georg Schott (Munich: F. Bruckmann, 1936). In an introductory essay entitled "Houston Stewart Chamberlain as Prophet," Schott explains that the heart of Chamberlain's thought was Kant's "critical idealism," which allowed him to grasp the importance of having a spiritual *Weltanschauung* that brought about a Third Reich in philosophy, producing a revolution in thought parallel to that of Hitler in politics (3).

38. Alfred Rosenberg, *Der Mythus des 20. Jahrhunderts: Eine Wertung der seelisch-geistigen Gestaltenkämpfe unserer Zeit* (Munich: Hoheneichen-Verlag, 1935).

39. Robert Pois, introduction to *Race and Race History, and Other Essays by Alfred Rosenberg,* ed. Robert Pois (New York: Harper and Row, 1970), 31.

40. Joseph De Maistre, *Eclaircissement sur les sacrifices,* in *Oeuvres complètes,* vol. 5 (Geneva: Slatkine Reprints, 1979), 283-360.

41. Cf. Joan Copjec, *Read My Desire: Lacan against the Historicists* (Cambridge, Mass.: MIT Press, 1994), 139.

Das Denken ist fast wie ein Mitdichten
—Martin Heidegger, "Hölderlins Hymne 'Andenken'"

Of National Poets and Their Female Companions

Herman Rapaport

Among the central issues in German idealism to which contemporary German philosophers like Dieter Henrich and Manfred Frank have been returning is the so-called original insight of Johann Gottlieb Fichte, which concluded that the self cannot be understood apart from its being self-posited or self-asserted. Fichte, of course, was quite well aware that the act of self-assertion explicitly raised questions of self-presentation, self-construction, self-reflection, self-objectification, and self-transcendence, in other words, a battery of problems that organize themselves under the general rubric of positing, or posure. Fichte himself put the question of positing or posure in an almost Heideggerian way when he wrote, "Thus the first question would be: how does the self exist for itself? The first postulate: Think of yourself, frame the concept of yourself; and notice how you do it." However, emphasis upon enframing was quickly sub-sumed by reflection theory. "Everyone who does no more than this [pose the question of the self] will find that in the thinking of this concept [one's] activity as an intelligence reverts into itself and makes itself its own object."[1]

In *Einführung in die frühromantische Ästhetik: Vorlesungen,* Man-fred Frank provides some detailed historical accounts of how the German idealists developed the question of positing. He notices, for example, that Novalis had already begun to question positing of the self in terms of the relationship between being and reflection in the following citation. "Des Wesen der Identität läßt sich nur in einem Scheinsatz aufstellen."[2] Yet, if the question of identity and being is mediated by the posure of reflective representations, for Novalis there nevertheless was a transcendental and unifying notion of Being which was not to be questioned in the same sense that in reflection a certain feeling unified and stabilized the sub-ject's "Vertrautheit mit dem Selbst." No doubt, Frank's probing into the relationship between ontology and reflection theory is a historical follow-up to Martin Heidegger's late essay "Kants These über das Sein" (1962), which more aggressively reconceptualizes self-positing by means of cit-ing passages in Kant's *Critique of Pure Reason* that provide an oppor-tunity to question the subject-object relation which reflection theory presupposes.

Heidegger argues that already in Kant there may be an awareness that the Object cannot be divorced from the question of the difference be-tween Being and beings and that thinking is not, in fact, grounded in what Heidegger terms the *Ich-Subjekt* but is posited or posed in relation to how Being is positioned; thinking is in no way to be considered en-tirely independent of being but, quite to the contrary, must be under-stood in terms of how being is posited, posed, or positioned with respect to how subjects apprehend objects. Whereas the subject-object relation takes priority in much of reflection theory, Heidegger argues that, in fact, this relation is only the consequence of an ontological orientation or posi-tioning that shows itself more or less explicitly from time to time in Kant's writings. Fundamental to Heidegger's analysis is the insight that being may not be a fixed category which is identical to itself, nor posited or positioned in a determinate manner with respect to what Kant, in the *Critique of Pure Reason,* called *Sein und Denken.* Whereas reflection theory drove Kant, Fichte, Schelling, and Hegel toward a dialectical mode of analysis, Heidegger's ontological considerations offer the possibility that the *Ich-Subjekt* can be thought of within a structure that does not give priority to the dialectical circularity of the reflection model developed in, say, Fichte's "Deduction of Presentation," which, as Jean Hippolyte tells us, was fundamental to Hegel's *Phenomenology of Spirit.* Indeed, it was Edmund Husserl who had already attacked the Kantian comprehension of *Sein und Denken.* In *Ideas I* Husserl argued that the positing of intentionality—an already existing attitude presupposing the experience of something perceived as "there" or "on hand"—can be negated or called into question. Methodologically one can simply "parenthesize it." In so doing, Husserl suggested that one could interrogate the question of being, which may well be foundational for an understanding of how intentionality (but more generally, consciousness) is posited. Husserl spoke of this parenthesis or *epoché* as a means to acquire "a new region of being never before delimited in its own peculiarity."³ But Heidegger, who was quite aware of Husserl's critique, thought that this "new region" should not be thought of as proper to consciousness, intentionality, or the object but as a place (*Ort*) cleared by Being. In the essay on Kant, Heidegger calls this place an *Ortsnetz,* a "network," or, more colloquially, a "telephone exchange." Oddly, it is in terms of such a telecommunications system that "das Sein als Position gehört." In short, the *Ortsnetz* (as opposed to the Kantian faculties) is the manifold of open relationships in the world as such, within which we have to rethink Kantian reflection, and particularly as it concerns a subjectivity which in Heidegger has been exteriorized or drawn out of the self.

It is in this sense that the following passage on reflection radicalizes Kant. Indeed, Heidegger focuses on a reflective movement back to the *Ich-Subjekt* that breaks with the circularity of Kantian reflection thanks to the intercession of the *Ortsnetz im Ort des Seins,* which I translate as "telecommunications network in the neighborhood of Being."

> Die Betrachtung geht nicht mehr geradezu auf das Objekt der Erfahrung, sie beugt sich zurück auf das erfahrende Subjekt, ist Reflexion. Kant spricht von 'Überlegung.' Achtet nun die Reflexion auf diejenigen Zustände und Verhältnisse des Vorstellens, dadurch überhaupt die Umgrenzung des Seins des Seienden möglich wird, dann ist die Reflexion auf das Ortsnetz im Ort des Seins eine transzendentale Reflexion.⁴

> *Reflection is a way of thinking that is not directed immediately on the object of experience but arches back to the experiencing subject. Kant speaks of 'deliberation.' Provided reflection heeds the situations and conditions of presentation, through which above all the delimitation of the Being of be-*

*ings would be made possible, reflection would be transcen-
dental in terms of a communications network in the neighborhood of Being.*

No doubt, one could read this back into Heidegger's own writing on poetry. For example, one could begin to explore how a term like *Gespräch* is mediated by a conception closer to the *Ortsnetz* than, say, mere conversation or dialogue. In fact, I imagine this kind of radical interpretation of *Gespräch* is what the philosopher Véronique Fóti had in mind when she translates the term into English as "destinal interlocution." In *Heidegger and the Poets,* Fóti purposely avoids the word "conversation" because it does not reflect the openness or indetermination of Being which is fundamental to its Heideggerian call. In short, the term "interlocution" is used to denote something other than dialogue, or, to put it another way, speculative reflection. Thanks to an interlocution, as opposed to mere dialogue, the poet achieves a subjectivity of the *Ortsnetz,* a tele-communication, which suggests that there is always more than one subjectivity on the line. Hence the interlocution with Being takes into account a subjectivity that is by no means solitary but, rather, brought into relation with Being by means of an other (*Mitsein*). Indeed, Heidegger himself pointed to this potential in poetry when he said of Hölderlin's hymn "Andenken," "das Denken ist fast wie ein Mitdichten."

In terms of Dorothy Wordsworth and Susette Gontard—the respective female companions of William Wordsworth and Friedrich Hölderlin—this remark broaches questions of how the poet's self-positing may be internally divided or shared with an other who is the poet's friend or companion. In particular, it raises the question of how a self-positing can be conceptualized from the standpoint of a "destinal interlocution," which I take to be a fateful speaking given (or "destined") alongside that of the poet and in which is manifest a positing, positioning, or posure that is not self-identical or present to itself and, as such, cannot be constituted or objectified through self-reflection per se. Such positing or posure would not be totalizable or unifiable, but characterized by a rupture, which I would like to call a caesura of difference that preserves an alterity even as it denies separability. It is this caesura that we will see figured in the abysses of the poets and their companions.

In May 1800 Dorothy Wordsworth began *The Grasmere Journals,* a text influential for her brother's most important lyrics. In her first entry in the journal, Dorothy Wordsworth addresses the departure of her brother on a trip that will separate them for some days. "My heart was so full that I could hardly speak to W. when I gave him a farewell kiss," she wrote.

> I sat a long time upon a stone at the margin of the lake, and after a flood of tears my heart was easier. The lake looked to me I knew not why dull and melancholy, and the weltering on the shores seemed a heavy sound. I walked as long as I could amongst the stones of the shore. The wood rich in flowers. A beautiful yellow, palish yellow flower, that looked thick round and double, and smelt very sweet—I supposed it was a ranunculus—Crowfoot, the grassy-leaved Rabbit-toothed white flower, strawberries, Geranium—scentless violet, anemones two kinds, orchises, primroses. The heckberry very beautiful as a low shrub. The crab coming out. Met a blind man driving a very large beautiful Bull and a cow—he walked with two sticks.

There are no gods in the passage, no longing for ancient Greece, no commemorative greetings, no heroes, and, moreover, no national poet. Instead the sister, having bade the poet farewell, sits behind by the margin of the lake where one day she will see a raft of daffodils flashing beneath the darkness of thunder. And though her mood has clearly altered the aspect of the landscape, it is clear that she is concentrating so strongly that she has forgotten herself at the moment she encounters the melancholy and dullness of the water. Yet, given this withdrawal of nature into dullness, she does not make depressive pronouncements such as the following, which can be found in Hölderlin's *Hyperion:* "es gibt ein Vergessen alles Dasein, ein Verstummen unsers Wesens" (there is a forgetting of all being, a muting of our essence). The extrapolation from particularized moments of experience to the destiny of historical epochs is simply not made. Instead we are told the wood is rich in flowers and that the heckberry is very beautiful. In place of a meeting with a demigod, Dorothy encounters a blind man driving a large bull and cow. The blind man is treated as if the most remarkable thing about him were the two beautiful animals with whom he seems so out of place. If there is nothing mythic about this blind man, there isn't anything ordinary about him, either. And Dorothy Wordsworth will come back to such wanderers in a place called Rydale, because without explicitly making the connection she has unself-consciously associated her brother's journey with the wanderings of destitute people.

"At Rydale," she writes,

> a woman of the village, stout and well dressed, begged a half-penny—she had never she said done it before—but these hard times!—Arrived at home with a bad headache, set some slips of privet. The evening cold had a fire—my face now flame-coloured. It is nine o'clock. I shall soon go to bed. A young woman begged at the door—she had come from Manchester on Sunday morn with two shillings and a slip of paper which she supposed a Bank note—it was a cheat. She had buried her husband and three children within a year and a half—All in one grave—burying very dear—paupers all put in one place—20 shillings paid for as much ground as will bury a man—a stone to be put over it or the right will be lost—11/6 each time the ground is opened. Oh! that I had a letter from William![5]

As far as history is concerned, the two beggar women exemplify a world in decline. As such, they reflect a condition of being that is threatening to Dorothy Wordsworth. The first woman is still well dressed and is at the beginning of what will be her ruin; the second woman is beyond what one would ordinarily consider ill fate. She had buried her husband and three children in the same grave and may not be able to pay for the cost of a stone with which to ensure the plot's sanctity. Narratively positioned between these two female figures is Dorothy herself, who arrived at home with a bad headache and who, with steadfast heart, plants some slips of privet. The evening is cold and she builds a fire. And only then, for the slightest moment, does she come into self-appearance with the phrase "my face now flame-coloured." That, of course, is the extent of her Cartesian awakening, her figuring the self as a being-in-the-world. "I burn, therefore I am." One wonders: Is it around nine o'clock that the second beggar woman has come to the door? Or does the memory of the beggar woman and her dead only occur to her just then? It's as if the flames had consumed time, as if in the moment of self-awareness time got slightly derailed. In that moment where she has figured herself, one suspects that where there should have been a moment, an abyss had opened in which the difference and identity between Dorothy and the unfortunates on the road undergoes disequilibrium, a kind of vertigo, which is only arrested by recollecting the poet, her brother: "Oh! that I had a letter from William!" (*GJ* 15–16).

This line, of course, has the status of a lost object whose absence has only been temporarily forgotten or displaced, only to return, without warning, to stabilize the abyss where thoughts are swirling, as well as to mark the painful break around which the entire day's events have been circulating. In the *Grasmere Journals,* such a lapse or failure to remember is not uncommon. It is noticeable in terms of small temporal slippages, narrative inconsistencies, sudden fade-outs, and the force of displaced recollections which mark openings or abysses of disequilibrium in which the temporality of everyday life is disturbed. We should not be surprised, therefore, that the sudden exclamation that Dorothy would like a letter from her brother is not only expressed *après coup* but is, at the same time, irrationally premature. After all, William has just left some seven or eight hours earlier than the moment at which the wish is narratively introduced. Arriving both too late and too soon, the remark intensifies even as it stabilizes the very disequilibrium it addresses. This is further troubled because the wish for a letter or word from the poet immediately follows remarks about the reopening of mass graves and the deaths of husbands and children, suggesting further that we're still in some kind of opening, caesura, or abyss.

Coincidentally, in the same year and month, May 1800, a banker's wife, Susette Gontard, is writing the German poet Friedrich Hölderlin in Homburg. Hölderlin, who is no longer a tutor living in the Gontard household, is still in love with this passionate young woman with the Athenian profile. "Are you returning?" she writes to him in her last letter dated Thursday morning, May 1800.

> The whole region is silent and deserted without you and I am in such agony. How will I be able to keep to myself those strong feelings for you if you don't come back? And should you return, it will also be difficult to maintain my balance and not experience even more violent feelings. Promise me you will not come back and that you will leave peacefully; deprived of this certitude, I will perpetually remain in a tense and disturbed state at my window every morning. And in the end we will be calm again, therefore pursue your way with confidence and let us be happy even in the depths of our pain and hope that it will ever ever be so for us since we want the affirmation of the perfect nobility of our feelings. . . . Adieu! Adieu! blessings . . . be with you.[6]

Here, again, we notice a text by a woman whose love is illicit to the poet, and a poet who is not just any poet but a national poet, though, as in the case of William Wordsworth, at a time before his significance as such has been definitively established. Moreover, in both instances, we notice how the writing is meant to calm what is clearly a very emotional and agitated state of mind following upon the poet's departure. Like Dorothy Wordsworth's journal entry, Gontard's letter to Hölderlin correlates mood to place—the silent and deserted country—and proceeds with a number of rather abrupt shifts marked by contrary desires: the desire for him to be with her and the desire for him to go away. Deprived of the certitude of knowing he is gone forever, she says she will always be anxious. Yet in the end they will both find peace. In their despair they will find happiness. Nobility of feeling will be achieved and, in the end, she even anticipates that calm nobility of mind as she blesses the poet, even to the point of anointing him in an act so selfless and giving that the entire letter undergoes an enormous sea change reminiscent of various moments in *Hyperion,* which, Gontard tells Hölderlin elsewhere, she admires, even though her nervous temperament isn't well suited to the reading of serious literature. What is quite noticeable as well is that just as Dorothy Wordsworth's journal approaches the kind of natural and social observations associated with the poetry of her brother, Gontard's letters are reminiscent of the dialectics of the philosophical circles in which Hölderlin moved. For example, the dialectics of nearness and distance suggested in the letter ends in an elevated and noble resolution in which the poet receives benediction or sanctification. Her letters also invoke philosophical terminology, as in the following example in which she argues that her spirit and soul are mirrored in his. "Mein Geist, meine Seele spiegeln sich in Dir, Du giebst was sich geben läßt, in so schöner Form, als ich es nie könnte." Nowhere in Dorothy Wordsworth's journals do we hear such elevated language. Conversely, nowhere in Gontard's letters are we given any sense of the immediate experiences through which the passions are at once dampened and intensified. Indeed, Gontard herself points out that despite the fact that the passion of Hölderlin's letters has given her the idea to start a diary, she is so agitated that she can never find the right words to express herself:

> Ich bin nur so wenig ungestöhrt, wenn ich es verstohlen tun muß, ist eine Art von Angst in mir, die mich hindert die rechten Worte zu finden, so oft werde ich aus meinen Gedanken gerissen und werde dann leicht verdrüßlich, doch, will ich es versuchen, und jede ruhige Minute nutzen, nur mußt Du auf keinen Zusammenhang rechnen. (March 12, 1799)

> *I am but so agitated, and when writing in secret I feel an anxiety which keeps me from finding the right words, so of-*

ten am I cut off from my thoughts and then easily discouraged; however, I will attempt it and use every quiet moment, but you must not count on any coherence.

If one thinks of Hölderlin's later poetry especially, these words strike an uncannily sympathetic accord between the poet and his beloved, as if her attitude about writing had disclosed something essential about the destiny of his poems. To put this a bit more sharply, I would like to say that this destinal anticipation is not just relayed by means of Gontard's empathic appropriation of certain German Idealist manners of philosophical expression, but is given or destined by means of what is "so wenig ungestöhrt," that is to say, of a disequilibrium of mind that has its abysses or rifts. Gontard frequently broaches these abysses, for example, in a letter of early fall 1798 when she tells Hölderlin that her mind is always elsewhere and that she cannot stabilize her thoughts. "When I want to dream," she says, "even my fantasy won't serve me." And "when I want to read, my thoughts stay still." She says she feels apathetic, beside herself, unable to express the right words. Courage and activity fail her. All of these feelings relate to a moment analogous to that in the *Grasmere Journals,* the departure of the poet. Gontard writes, "I have often regretted having advised you, at the moment of our separation, to distance yourself in another place." And she tells the poet that she did not understand what feeling had compelled her to do that. "I believe, though, that it was fear, of the whole sensation of our love, which became too intense for me in this powerful break" (Ich glaube aber, es war die Furcht, vor der ganzen Empfindung unserer Liebe, die zu laut in mir wurde bei diesem gewaltigen Riß). This is the break, encouraged by Gontard, which, unpredictably, has opened as an abyss in her being that cannot be stabilized, despite her meticulous instructions about how Hölderlin is supposed to secretly make his way to her bedroom, as if these elaborate rituals could somehow compensate for the *Riß* that has opened. It is a *Riß* that Gontard tries to figure even as her text holds it back in disequilibrium as part of an experience that is properly speaking hers and that sets her apart from Hölderlin, the poet, who is himself so often being pushed away by these abysses, these lapses in which Gontard says she cannot pose herself in relation to him. Yet, in the very holding-back of these abysses by not only Gontard but by Dorothy Wordsworth, who so carefully hides them as so many secrets in the seams of her sentences, there is, nevertheless, a destinal or fateful effect which is perceptible in the poetry of Gontard's and Wordsworth's companions.

How, then, do these abysses in being figure in the poetry of poets who only much later will be strongly identified within their respective cultures as national poets? If we turn to Heidegger's examination of Hölderlin in the 1934 seminar on the poem "Germanien" ("Germania"), we will immediately notice that he has sighted abysses, not to say abyssal structures. "Des Gedicht ist Sprache. Aber wer spricht nun eigentlich im Gedicht?"[7] If poetry is speech, who or what is speaking? It is not Hölderlin simply, but, according to Heidegger, language itself that keeps shifting levels and introducing new voices and tonalities whose sources are concealed. In "Germania," for example, the stanzas are not all spoken by the same subject, and the "I" who announces itself for the last time in line 29 cannot, according to Heidegger, be considered the origin or source for the poem. For "dieses Sprachgefüge ist in sich ein *Wirbel*, der uns irgendwohin reißt" (*HH* 45). That is, the speaking is constellated such that it delimits a tourbillon or whirling movement that rips and pulls us—sweeps us away—in some unspecified direction. In "Germania" this disequilibrium drags us to no one else than the virgin woman, the mother of all things who is said to be the upholder of an abyss. This abyss is a particularly odd one that I want to exploit in that if one looks at drafts A and B of "Germania," one notices that the phrase "und den abgrund trägt" is missing from the B manuscript. Heidegger himself makes quite a bit of this, and in the Hamburger translation, one notices that in the German the phrase is left out, while in the translation it is supplied. Hamburger too sees that in Hölderlin's B manuscript the abyss has been evacuated or emptied in the place of its having been posited in the A manuscript. Which is to say, the abyss has literally fallen into itself and disappeared. Hence it could be said to be present in its very absence.

> Die Mutter ist von allem, und den abgrund trägt
> Die Verborgene sonst genannt von Menschen,
> So ist von Lieben und Leiden
> Und voll von Ahnungen dir
> Und voll von Frieden der Busen.[8]

> *The Mother of all things, upholder of the abyss,*
> *Whom men at other times call the Concealed,*
> *Now full of loves and sorrows*
> *And full of presentiments*
> *And full of peace is your bosom.*[9]

In these lines particularly, an allusion to Diotima—Hölderlin's name for Susette Gontard—is made with respect to the notion of concealment. In all of the poems entitled "Diotima," it is quite explicit that Diotima is in decline and that she is becoming increasingly concealed in the earth: "seine Sonne, die schönere Zeit, ist untergegangen" (Your sun, of a lovelier time, has descended). This is why she blooms "verschlossen," or is concealed in a fallen world that cannot fully sustain her. In "Germania," the traces of this Diotima survive in that other feminine presence, the upholder of the abyss. Like that abyss, however, she is both appropriated and expropriated by the poem, gathered and dissipated. Indeed, such an appropriation and expropriation could be said to be the destiny of other texts that are always being held in reserve outside the poem, namely, the letters of Susette Gontard with their numerous small breakdowns and intimate shocks. We could put this another way by saying that thematically encrypted in her divinization in the poem "Germania" is an abyss into which she disappears, though it is an abyss that is itself a sublation of those abysses of her prose that have been destined to take on national significance with respect, in this case, to a poem about the fatherland and its people. This co-determination of companion texts, held in reserve outside the poem, which nevertheless achieve their destiny within the poem, bears on what Heidegger calls *Gespräch,* or "destinal interlocution." In the case of Hölderlin and Gontard, this interlocution is precisely that of how the woman's disequilibrium has been put at the disposal of the poet even as it has been held back within Gontard's experience as a woman, not to say within her writings, which are prejudicially deemed, at the time, to be of lesser significance because of her gender. Yet it is in the everydayness of her experiences that a certain comportment has been disclosed that involves the construction of an *Ab-grund,* a zone of disequilibrium where the poet is posed or posited as a figure that cannot stabilize or hold together the *Wirbel* that is sweeping the text away from its moorings or supports—the stable relationships of everyday life. At the same time, these texts are engaged in a destinal interlocution where the *Ab-grund* of female experience will not only require itself to be divinized or spiritualized by the poet, but, much more radically, will also require that such experience become a co-determining force of disruption or rupture within a national poetry *as yet to come,* say, in the twentieth century, that will not only speak to the piety of the fatherlandish but, by extension, to the *calling into Being* of that fatherland's people as a distinctively German people. It is here, of course, that the turning from the private relationship between poet and female companion—their destinal cohabitation—to that of the public relationship between poet and a national people or *Volk* occurs by means of a destinal interlocution or *Orts-*

netz im Ort des Seins from which women's writings are not to be so easily excluded (as, for example, by Heidegger himself, who does not consider the possibility of a fateful significance of Gontard's writings for the destiny of the German people).

For it is in the writing of Susette Gontard that something is concealed, reserved, held back, or set aside, a disequilibrium in which the self has lost itself in the transport of conflicting moods, motivations, desires, fantasies, or somatic symptoms which point to a hole, gap, or rupture that cannot be repaired by any ecstasy whatsoever, least of all Gontard's brief ecstasies with Hölderlin in her bedroom. It is in this woman's letters, then, that we see to what extent a destructive tear is guarded or vouchsafed for the sake of a destinal interlocution through which she gives herself over to the destinal arrival of a national poet, a giving or positing that holds something back that cannot be posed. It is in that positing/ nonpositing by the poet's companion that a destructive poetic rupturing becomes visible—the tornado or *Wirbel*—through which the fatherland as homeland of Being is posed as the proper place (*Ort*) for a national German identity, though, of course, this place is precisely what the destinal interlocution has called into question as something that is essentialistically posed or posited by the poet(s).

In the case of the Wordsworths, where we might think an English temperament would avoid the sort of nationalistic political horizon imaginable in the case of Hölderlin, it has to be said that something not entirely dissimilar is at work. If we look at the famous poem "Lines, Composed a Few Miles above Tintern Abbey on Visiting the Banks of the Wye During a Tour. July 13, 1798," we will see that William has divinized his sister and that she has been put in the role of a spiritual guide and, in anticipating the keen poetic perceptions of the *Grasmere Journals,* of a muse. Yet, as in the journals, there is temporal distortion as well, for William has projected their lives forward to such an extent that he is recovering the present companionship with his sister from an undetermined future point from whose perspective the walk with Dorothy by the Wye River is itself but a stabilizing moment whose purpose is to assuage the violence of an abyss—the approach of death which will inevitably sunder one from the other. Hence the walk a few miles above Tintern Abbey will be posed or set up by William for Dorothy as a remembrance which pays homage to her from the perspective of the future anterior, a temporal perspective which, when compared to the present, delimits a very curious caesura that in divinizing the sister also points to the evanescence or the forgettableness of the moment which is supposed to be salvific, as if that moment were swallowed up into itself in the very same way that the abyss in Hölderlin's "Germania" disappears into its own absence. In fact, it is this disappearance or fading of the scene within a temporality of the future anterior that makes the closing lines of "Tintern Abbey" extremely emotional and brings them quite close to the Diotima poems of Hölderlin, where the very flowering of Diotima characterizes the decline of her sun. Like Diotima, William's sister is sacralized or recovered even as from the future anterior she is destroyed or lost in advance. And the abyss which delimits this recovery and loss is that within which a figure is constructed and dismantled, or, in Heidegger's terms, appropriated and expropriated. But, of course, it is this division or difference between appropriation and expropriation that we saw reflected in the everyday events of the sister herself, events that are already recorded in the *Alfoxden Journal* of the year 1798, the very same year the poem "Tintern Abbey" was composed in tranquillity. It is in her comments on this journal that Virginia Woolf was especially sensitive to Dorothy Wordsworth's reticence or holding back. Commenting on the passage about having received Mary Wollstonecraft's biography, Woolf notices that there is no comment about Wollstonecraft's life as such, just a caesura. And yet, a day later "an unconscious comment" is dropped. "Quaint waterfalls about, about which Nature was very successfully striving to make beautiful what art had deformed—ruins, hermitages, etc. etc. In spite of all these things, the dell romantic and beautiful, though everywhere planted with unnaturalised trees. Happily we cannot shape the huge hills, or carve out the valleys according to our fancy."[10] Whereas Wollstonecraft wanted to dramatically revolutionize the world, Dorothy Wordsworth argues for a conservation or abiding relation wherein attention to the minute details of the landscape discloses the *Ab-grund* or abyss which is, in fact, revolutionary in a different way from Mary Wollstonecraft's fulgurations. For the abysses of Dorothy Wordsworth are, in fact, the destabilizing co-determinants of a destiny that will work itself out in the poetry of her brother, an *Ortsnetz im Ort des Seins* that brings the countryside of England into the place of Being as homeland or perhaps even as fatherland to a people who are called into assembly by an intimate company. In their place she accepts the com-posure of brother and sister, a com-posure or conversation that for all its correspondences resists intersubjectivity. As such, they are not posited in terms of a Fichtean reflection theory, wherein the subject's striving toward determination through the positing of the self in relation to an object is to be occupied or taken over, merely, by an other. Rather, Dorothy and William

Wordsworth reflect what in the context of *Andenken* Heidegger calls *der Zurückbleibende,* the ones who in staying back have achieved a composure that enables them to encounter their land as fatherlandish—not subject to the feminist challenge of one like Wollstonecraft—and to hear the call of its holiness as a call to *das Eigene.* Yet, as in the context of Heidegger, this *Eigene* is nothing but the staying-back of the poet and of the poetic word, which keeps to itself as inter-locution rather than conversation: the silence in which the truth is concealed and disclosed, a truth which is the truth in art.

Toward the end of *The Prelude,* William Wordsworth points us in the right direction when he speaks of a humbler destiny in contrast to the revelation of a divine spirit on the peak of Mount Snowdon: "A humbler destiny have we retraced, / And told of lapse and hesitating choice, / And backward wanderings along thorny ways." It is in this humbler destiny with its lapses, hesitating choices, and backward wanderings that the holding-back of the sister comes to appearance as the "trait" of the national poet, if not that of the fatherland itself. In that sense, the sister is the trait without which the fatherland could not disclose itself as Being, or what Heidegger in the context of Hölderlin calls the holy. That this trait is destined in the interlocution between sister and brother speaks to the divisibility and noncoincidence that persists even in the disclosure of the natural world as *das Eigene,* a natural world that will come to be identified more and more strongly with nation. On Wednesday, October 2, 1800, Dorothy Wordsworth wrote in her journal: "A fine morning—a showery night. The lake still—in the morning in the forenoon flashing light from the beams of the sun, as it was ruffled by the wind. We corrected the last sheet."

THEORETICAL POST-SCRIPT

In an essay entitled "Sauf le Nom," Jacques Derrida cites the following lines of Angelus Silesius's *Cherubinic Wanderer:* "Friend, let this be enough; if you wish to read beyond, / Go and become yourself the writ and yourself the essence." Commenting on these lines, Derrida writes, "The friend, who is male rather than female, is asked, recommended, enjoined, *prescribed* to render himself, by reading, beyond reading; beyond at least the legibility of what is currently readable, beyond the final signature—and for that reason to write." Derrida's point is that the friend is at once prescribed and rendered by the poet's reading and simultaneously situated "beyond the final signature." Both Susette Gontard and Dorothy Wordsworth are, in my view, situated in precisely this way as friends whose own writings fall outside the writing of national poets despite the fact that they are, as Silesius might put it, "the writ" and "the essence." Derrida summarizes this as follows:

> Not to write this or that that falls outside his writing as a note, a *note bene* or a *post-scriptum* letting writing in its turn fall behind the written, but for the friend himself to become the written or Writing, to become the essence that writing will have created. (No) more place, starting from there, beyond, but nothing more is told us beyond, for a *post-scriptum*. The *post-scriptum* will be the debt or the duty. It will have to, it should, be reabsorbed into a writing that would be nothing other than the essence that would be nothing other than the being-friend or the becoming-friend of the other. The friend will only become what he is, to wit, the friend, he will only have become the friend at the moment when he will have read that, which is to say, when he will have read beyond—to wit, when he will have gone, and one goes there, beyond, to give oneself up, only by becoming writing through writing. The becoming (Werden), the becoming-friend, the becoming-writing, and the essence (Wesen) would be the same here.[11]

My account of the poets and their female companions adds a biographical dimension to Derrida's claims about friendship in which the presence of the friend is always already prescribed as arche-trace or, more precisely, arche-voice.[12] That the friend is writ is something I have attempted to show in terms of how the female companions are themselves what one might call the post-scriptum or PS of the text—what in earlier writings Derrida was calling the "supplement," in this case, a supplement that precedes or comes in advance of a national poetry. That the relation between the poet and the friend escapes a binding or tangible connection is, of course, why one necessarily speaks of a caesura wherein there is both a turning toward and turning away from an other. Indeed, it is because of the undecidable logic of this caesura that the post-scriptum calls to us from "beyond the ear," an unheard of intimacy. Here, of course, one encounters the peculiar possibility that a national poetry will come to pass not because a poet was necessarily attuned to a people or *Volk*, but because he participated in what we could call an "unheard of intimacy" with a woman that escapes objectification as a concrete relation. What comes to pass in this "unheard of intimacy," however, is the destinality of an interlocution that expresses itself over time (that is, historically) as the recognition of a national poet whose work is fatherlandish to the extent that it grounds the destinal interlocution by means of asserting a male poetic voice that is heard by others as if it were the voice of a people or nation.

Now it is true that Derrida has alerted us to the fact that in terms of a Heideggerian understanding of *Mitsein* one is always going to encounter what Heidegger himself called *Kampf*. "*Kampf* belongs to the very structure of *Dasein*. It belongs to its historical structure and thus, this must also be explicitly stated, to the subjectivity of the historical subject" ("HE" 177). In our context, this *Kampf* obviously relates to the question of gender and the prioritization of a male voice. No doubt, we can think of this as reflecting a subjectivity that is itself the consequence of a national *Kampf* or inter-locution that implicitly or unconsciously organizes itself around an idea of there being a fatherland—a national *paysage* grounded in terms of the priority of a man's poetic voice, that is to say, a voice that determines the writ of the female companion to be postscriptive, despite its essential significance as a voice that makes legible a determining caesura without which a certain poetry could not have come to pass. In the case of the Wordsworths, this is evident in the relation between Dorothy's *Grasmere Journals* and William's *Prelude*. In the case of Hölderlin, the *Kampf* can be detected in the subsuming of Gontard's turbulence within the lyricism of works like "Germania."

In *Being and Time* Heidegger asks, "To what extent and on the basis of what ontological conditions does historiality belong, as an essential constitution, to the subjectivity of the 'historial subject?'"[13] If the prioritization of the fatherlandish voice of the national poet could be said to fulfill those metaphysically oriented ontological conditions upon which historiality depends, is it not, in fact, the case that this fatherlandish voice is always already constituted by the caesura of an interlocution to which a female voice is quite essential? After all, is it not to this post-scriptum that the fatherlandish is largely indebted insofar as the writ of the female companions is an engendering of something other than themselves? In "Sauf le Nom," Derrida thinks of this sort of engendering in terms of a logical breakdown between the possible and the impossible, since a becoming-self engenders a becoming-other if not a becoming-nothing that is, strictly speaking, impossible even if it is inevitable. This surplus, beyond, or hyper "introduces an absolute heterogeneity in the order and in the modality of the possible. The possibility of the impossible, of the 'more impossible' that as such is also possible ('more impossible than the impossible'), marks an absolute interruption in the regime of the possible that nonetheless remains, if this can be said, in place" (43). The trace or trait of this possibility/impossibility, which may exceed hearing points to the peculiarity of a destinal interlocution that characterizes the fate of a poetry which over considerable time will be recognized as having national significance. It is inevitable that reflection theory will eventually install itself at the very point where the two genders face off over the question of who speaks for a people, something that feminists notice more often than not. Important for us, however, has been the prehistory of this *Kampf* in terms of a caesura and *Mitdichten* that undermines the conceptions of self-positing upon which a nationalized battle of the sexes may be founded.

Notes

1. J. G. Fichte, *The Science of Knowledge* (London: Cambridge University Press, 1982), 33.
2. Manfred Frank, *Einführung in die frühromantische Ästhetik: Vorlesungen* (Frankfurt am Main: Suhrkamp, 1989), 251.
3. Edmund Husserl, *Ideas Pertaining to a Pure Phenomenology and to a Phenomenological Philosophy. First Book: General Introduction to a Pure Phenomenology*, trans. F. Kersten (The Hague: Martinus Nijhoff, 1982), 63.
4. Martin Heidegger, "Kants These über das Sein," in *Wegmarken* (Frankfurt am Main: Klostermann, 1967), 300.
5. Dorothy Wordsworth, *The Grasmere Journals* (Oxford: Oxford University Press, 1991), 1–2. The entry I've quoted is the first to appear in the journals. Hereafter cited as *GJ.*
6. All entries from the letters appear in *Hölderlins Diotima Susette Gontard: Gedichte, Briefe, Zeugniss,* ed. Adolf Beck (Frankfurt am Main: Insel, 1980), 32–90.
7. Martin Heidegger, *Hölderlins Hymnen 'Germanien' und 'Der Rhein,'* vol. 39 of *Gesamtausgabe* (Frankfurt am Main: Klostermann, 1980), 45. Throughout Heidegger's various seminars on Hölderlin during the 1930s and early 1940s, the main strategy is to jettison authorial and formalist readings while allowing the words to speak poetically in ways that further philosophical thinking about man's relation to the world and to the divine. Central to Heidegger's thinking is a notion of openness, of which the *Abgrund* or "abyss" is but one. Hereafter cited as *HH.*
8. See Friedrich Hölderlin, *Hölderlin, Sambliche Werke, Zweiter Band,* ed. F. Beissner (Stuttgart: Kohlhammer, 1951), 739, for complete variants.

9. Friedrich Hölderlin, "Germania," in *Poems and Fragments: A Bilingual Edition*, trans. Michael Hamburger (London: Cambridge University Press, 1980), 400–1.

10. Virginia Woolf, *The Second Common Reader* (New York: Harcourt Brace, 1960), 149.

11. Jacques Derrida, "Sauf le nom," in *On the Name*, ed. Thomas Dutoit (Stanford: Stanford University Press, 1995), 41–42.

12. Also see Jacques Derrida, "Heidegger's Ear: Philopolemology," in *Reading Heidegger: Commemorations*, ed. John Sallis (Bloomington: Indiana University Press, 1993), 174. Hereafter cited as "HE."

> Dasein's opening to its ownmost potentiality-for-being, as hearing the voice of the other as friend, is absolutely originary. This opening does not come under a psychology, a sociology, an anthropology, an ethics, or a politics, etc. The voice of the other friend, of the other as friend, the ear that I prick up to it, is the condition of my own proper being. But this voice nevertheless defines the figure of an originary sharing (*partage*) and an originary belonging, of a *Mitteilen* or of everything that is, as Heidegger says in this passage, 'shared' (*geteilt*) with the other in the *Mitsein* of discourse, of address and response.

13. Martin Heidegger, *Being and Time*, quoted in ibid., 177.

Suis-je encore trop moderne . . . ?
—Jean-François Lyotard, *Histoire*

Postmodern Investments

Lyotard and Rorty on Disenchantment and Cultural Difference

Andreas Michel

The writings of Jean-François Lyotard pose an interesting conundrum: one never quite knows where to locate him on the divide that he helped define between modern and postmodern sensibilities. In the early formulations from *The Postmodern Condition,* his condemnation of the modern metanarratives was so strong that there ought to be no doubt as to his partiality for the postmodern.[1] Yet already in his 1984 foreword to the English translation of the same volume, Fredric Jameson saw in Lyotard a representative of high modernism.[2] Even if we take Jameson's use of the term "high modernism" to refer to the artistic reaction against modernity, that is to say, the attempt launched by the aesthetic avant-garde to reject the economic, social, and political changes brought about by the process of modernization, the question still remains as to whether this reaction itself ought to be classified as modern or postmodern. The difficulties that one encounters in strictly locating Lyotard's writings stem, I believe, from the fact that he entertains a deeply ambivalent relationship to what seems to me the fundamental issue of modernity, namely the functional differentiation of Western societies into semiautonomous subsystems, such as science, law, politics, economy, or art. The stress here is on semi-*autonomous* subsystems, as, for instance, those conceived by the German social theorist Niklas Luhmann.[3] In Luhmann's theory, social subsystems are organized as autopoietic, semiautonomous structures that enact their own independent forms of reproduction. The thrust of such a description is that, in modern Western societies, social subsystems are no longer bound into an overarching metanarrative that would define the subsystems' field of action and supply their grounds of legitimation.

Lyotard's ambivalence with respect to this state of affairs brings him into an antagonistic relationship to modernity as well as into conflict with his own pronouncements about the end of metanarratives in *The Postmodern Condition.* However, his ambivalence is also instructive, for it points to an unresolvable dilemma not only in his own thought but in the moral fiber of modern Western societies. In the following, I propose to approach this issue via a comparison of the treatment of the question of cultural difference in an exchange between Lyotard and Richard Rorty. Before embarking on this comparison, however, I would like to briefly introduce the other term of my title, namely, the notion of disenchantment, in order to set the stage for the discussion to follow.

It seems to me that the basic issue in the modern/postmodern debate is not whether we are dealing here with a period style or with a modality of modernity, as Lyotard has more recently tried to refine his position.[4] Rather, I believe, the central issue consists in what importance one grants to what Max Weber called *Entzauberung,* or disenchantment. As is well known, Weber defined *Entzauberung* as the modern outcome of a centuries-long process of intellectualization and rationalization, of which modern science and technology are the most characteristic examples. In his 1918 speech "Science as a Vocation," Weber asks himself what this process of intellectualization means. And he arrives at the following, famous, diagnosis:

> The [process of] increasing intellectualization and rationalization do[es] *not* . . . indicate an increased and general knowledge of the conditions under which one lives.
> It means something else, namely, the knowledge or belief

that if one but wished one *could* learn it at any time. Hence
it means that principally there are no mysterious incalculable
forces that come into play, but rather that one can, in principle, master all things by calculation. This means that the
world is disenchanted. One need no longer have recourse to
magical means. . . . Technical means and calculation perform
the service. This above all is what intellectualization means.[5]

Weber's central concern here is to define modernity in contrast to premodern societies. The difference he finds consists in modernity's belief
"that if one but wished one *could*" explain everything. This "disenchantment of the world" is the result of the scientific attitude which takes
on the role previously held by religion and myth. The point of Weber's
speech, however, must be seen in his insistence that, contrary to religion
and myth, modern science *cannot* function as overarching (transcendent) meaning (*Sinn*), as *Weltanschauung*, which would ground and legitimate all aspects of social action. In the structural place that religion
held in premodern societies, all modernity offers is an empty space.

At the same time, Weber's speech is a passionate *defense* of the limitations of science, because modern science fosters a radically *immanent*
approach to the issues it addresses. For the process of intellectualization
can provide at least this much: it discusses openly its methodological
assumptions and furnishes proofs so that its conclusions, which are always provisional, can be modified by future research. To the extent that
Weber defends the limitations of science, he implicitly accepts the division of modern society into different functional spheres: science adminis-
ters knowledge (*Wissen*), while religion and other *Weltanschauungen*
offer meaning (*Sinn*). The important point, however, is that, in modernity, religion and other *Weltanschauungen* no longer serve in the overarching structural position they had held in premodern societies. They
too have become semiautonomous functional systems that, rather than
legitimate all social systems in general, serve specific ends and needs.

As I intimated before, Lyotard seems to be troubled by this *modern*
state of affairs. Not, to be sure, by the fact that religion serves no longer
as foundation for the social whole. But rather than subscribe to Weber's
interpretation of the disenchanted state of modernity and to accept the
loss of transcendence, if in tragic spirit, Lyotard fears that the spirit of
performance, the essence of the logic of capitalism, has usurped the
structural place once held by religion. This view is, of course, familiar—
not least from Marxist, neo-Marxist, and Frankfurt School traditions—
for it echoes the revolutionary counterdiscourse that has accompanied

modernity ever since Schiller's aesthetico-political writings. For two hundred years, this radical tradition combated the ill effects brought on by the processes of intellectualization and rationalization by promising different avenues to the reenchantment of the world.

In Lyotard's view, this enlightened trust in the spirit of reenchantment exhausted itself in the course of the twentieth century. One factor contributing to this loss of faith was the emergence, after World War II, of postcolonial liberation movements in the course of which the ideological presuppositions of the West, such as the notion of universal history and the Enlightenment view of the human subject, were radically questioned. Political philosophers, especially those who, like Lyotard in the French-Algerian War, had taken the side of the former colony, took note and revised their philosophical premises in the attempt to come to terms with cultural difference. Thus during the 1950s and 1960s, the issue of cultural difference rose to the center of philosophical reflection, where it has stayed to this day. It is of such interest because a radical formulation of cultural difference potentially disables the very foundations of Western politico-philosophical thought.

If, then, cultural difference presents a potential rupture for philosophical thought, who better to account for that rupture than Lyotard? On some level at least, his entire oeuvre seems to be one long critique of philosophy as Eurocentric geopolitics, that is, a decidedly *local* version of the human ability for metaphysical speculation and the founding of scientific knowledge. Thus, when Lyotard speaks about cultural difference, one may justifiably expect a critical account of Western philosophy's universalist aspirations. Interestingly enough, as I would like to show, this is not necessarily the case. Lyotard seems to want to hold on to at least one aspect of the universalism of philosophical thought, namely, when it comes to the question of human emancipation. This represents, however, *at the very least* a theoretical problem for the philosopher who more than any other has decried the universalist aspirations of modern Western thought. Thus, it seems to me, the proclaimed end of metanarratives stands in striking contrast to—and this is what I would like to interrogate here—Lyotard's pursuit of justice in universal terms, that is, in terms of the metanarrative of the universal subject. The scope of my analysis is necessarily limited to a number of texts. I hope, however, that it will suggest, beyond its limited range, a wider explanation for the structure of feeling which underlies Lyotard's descriptions of the decline of the modern metanarratives.

If it is true, then, that the recognition of cultural diversity hastened along the end of metanarratives of universal history, such as that of the project of emancipation and of the notion of a universal subject as ground for sociopolitical engineering, one might expect that this fact ought to have quenched Lyotard's desire, at least in terms of his own theory, for a universalist approach to history. However, I believe, this is clearly not the case. As a first step, I would like to concentrate on Lyotard's explicit appeal to the universal subject—and, implicitly, to the metanarrative of human emancipation—in order to (and this is my second step) compare it to Richard Rorty's antifoundationalist pragmatism, which, while defending the Western "first-order narrative" of political liberalism, is wholly unconcerned with claims for human nature. My guiding questions are, first, whose account of cultural difference is more convincing, and, second, what are the implications of these two different accounts of dealing with cultural difference and the issue of human emancipation?

Lyotard's essay "Missive on Universal History" explores the following question: "Can we today continue to organize the mass of events coming from the human and nonhuman world by referring them to the Idea of a universal history of humanity?" (*PE* 24).[6] In its original version, Lyotard's article bears the title "Histoire universelle et différences culturelles," thus indicating more clearly than the English translation the concern with cultural difference at the heart of the inquiry into universal history under postmodern conditions. Richard Rorty's reflections on the consequences of cultural diversity for philosophy were conceived as a direct response to Lyotard's presentation and appeared in the same volume of the French journal *Critique*.[7]

The issue of universal history is thus intimately linked to the emergence of cultural diversity and the questions arising from the relativizing of Western universalist modes of legitimation. The question is one of ultimate legitimation for political action in a postmodern world, that is, in a world in which the modern narratives of legitimation have been exhausted. Thus, the premise of "Missive" as well as *The Postmodern Condition* is that the project of modernity has failed. More precisely, the political history of the last two centuries does not warrant any further belief in the legitimating power of the modern metanarratives, the various philosophies of history that were supposed to legitimate the implementation of the modern project. Modernity has failed to bring about its own most cherished goal of universal freedom.

> The Christian narrative of the redemption of original sin through love; the *Aufklärer* narrative of emancipation from ignorance and servitude through knowledge and egalitarianism; the speculative narrative of the realization of the universal Idea through the dialectic of the concrete; the Marxist narrative of emancipation from exploitation through the socialization of work; and the capitalist narrative of emancipation from poverty through technoindustrial development. Between these narratives there are grounds for litigation and even for differends. But in all of them, the givens arising from events are situated in the course of a history whose end, even if it remains beyond reach, is called universal freedom, the fulfillment of all humanity. (*PE* 25)

This fulfillment, as we know, has not come about. The fact that the narratives of emancipation have not succeeded in bringing about emancipation is reason enough for Lyotard (in opposition not only to Habermas but also, in a different manner, to Rorty) to doubt the modern project of universal freedom as a whole. And he speculates that the reason for the failing of modernity lies in the nature of the Western *kind* of legitimation. The modern metanarratives derive their legitimation from the fact that they are *cosmopolitan* narratives that enjoin everyone (humanity) to participate in their promise. They are open toward the future, that is, they locate their moment of authenticity, the fulfillment of their ideal, in the future rather than in the past. "Emancipation" and "human freedom" remain *ideas* for which no ultimate, or true, representation can be found as long as these ideals have not been realized. By contrast, in traditional cultures—so Lyotard's argument goes—legitimation is not derived from an idea to be fulfilled in the future. Rather, it arises from an original story, a mythic narrative, which encompasses and anchors past, present, and future in a set of definite representations and regulations. In addition, traditional narratives are not cosmopolitan but rather *local* manifestations of a particular culture.

Now, according to Lyotard, the failure of modernity is due, at least in part, to the fact that the cosmopolitan narratives of Western modernity were unable to convince the adherents of traditional cultures of its innate superiority and desirability—despite, or rather because of, extensive imperialist and proselytizing efforts. In other words, the West's narratives of panhuman liberation, along with their "social and political institutions and practices, forms of legislation, ethics, modes of thought, and symbolics" (*PE* 50), failed to gain support in non-Western cultures. On the contrary, post-World War II history has seen a resurgence of liberation movements as well as wars of liberation that are decidedly ethnic, nationalist, and noncosmopolitan.

> It is as though the enormous effort, marked by the name of the Declaration of Rights, seeking to deprive peoples of their narrative legitimacy (shall we say lying upstream in the course of time) and make them take up the Idea of free citizenship (lying downstream) as the only legitimacy—it is as though that effort, which has taken so many different paths over the last two centuries, had failed. A premonitory sign of this failure might be seen in the very designation of the author of this declaration of universal import: "We, the French people." (*PE* 34–35)

With the last words of this passage Lyotard intimates that the story of universal emancipation, along with the manner in which such liberation is to be achieved, has from its inception been a Western narrative and that this narrative might not necessarily be applicable to all of humanity. The "failing of modernity" is thus directly linked to the "insurmountable diversity of cultures" (*PE* 30–31). In addition, he seems to argue that the recognition of cultural difference necessarily entails the renunciation of Western metanarratives of emancipation. The failing of modernity is then directly attributable to two incompatible kinds of legitimation ("archaic legitimation" [*PE* 46] versus the idea of free citizenship) that are separated by a *differend*.

The interesting thing now is that, in "Missive," Lyotard does not celebrate the activity of bearing witness to the *differend* as in some of his other, more famous writings.[8] Nor does he elevate traditional narrative legitimation over its modern alternative. One might even say that the opposite is the case. For when it comes to the question of justice, Lyotard's sympathies lie, in this piece at least, with the universal (modern, Western) rather than the local approach to this issue. This comes to the fore when Lyotard explores the modalities of the word "can" in the question structuring his essay: "Can we today continue to organize . . . ?" "Missive" is organized around three prefatory clarifications that inquire into the terms "continue," "we," and "can." Lyotard's third clarification discusses the modalities of "can," which are *possibility, capacity* (strength, competence), and *having the right*. It is in the context of the last modality of "can," the deontic dimension, that Lyotard lays down his cards when he describes the contemporary situation in the following terms:

Many believe this is the moment for religion, a moment to re-
build a credible narration where the wounds of this fin de siècle will be healed. They claim that myth is the originary genre;
that in myth the thought of origin is present in its originary
paradox; and that we must raise myth from the ruins to which
it has been reduced by rational, demythologizing and positivistic thought. (*PE* 29)

And he adds: "These few remarks [*i.e.*, his essay] are simply meant to
indicate the anti-mythologizing direction I think we should take in 'working [through]' the loss [*perte*] of the modern *we*" (*PE* 30).

In this declaration of intention, the deontic marker "should" is combined with the demythologizing attitude of the modern *Aufklärer*. Lyotard here expressly states his intention not to retreat from the project of
Aufklärung after and despite the decline of the metanarratives of emancipation and the loss of the modern *we*. While the question of the *exact
nature* of this *Aufklärung* remains to be explored, it is clear from this
remark that Lyotard does not intend to give up the memory and the possibility of the metanarrative of human emancipation. The entire "Missive"
is written in the spirit of mourning the decline of a common *we*—the
linguistic marker of the possibility of universal history. But there is an
equivocation in Lyotard's argument which finds a parallel on the semantic
level. On the semantic level, he speaks at times of the failing (*défaillance*)
of modernity, as if of an event in process, and, at other times, of the loss
(*perte*) of the modern *we,* as if referring to a final state of affairs. This
equivocation, I believe, reflects Lyotard's own ambivalence with respect
to the project of modernity. Only the notion of a failing or a decline,
however, rather than the finality of "loss," makes it reasonable to still
pursue, as Lyotard does, the possibility of the *we*. "What, finally, is this
we that tries to reflect on this predicament of failing [*défaillance*], if it is
no longer the core, minority, or avantgarde that anticipates today what
liberated humanity might be tomorrow?" (*PE* 36). Although Lyotard does
not answer his own question, the very fact that the question persists
(as Rorty also notes in his response) indicates an attachment to the old
metanarrative that Lyotard has at other times pronounced obsolete. Despite the decline, in other words, the desirability of the human metanarrative remains powerful and intact. And Lyotard returns to this issue in the
final words of his essay when he writes: "After the age of the intellectual,
the age of the party, it would be interesting if on each side of the Atlantic,
without presumption, we could begin to trace [*commence à se tracer*] a
line of resistance to the failing of modernity" (*PE* 37). Although the *we*

of the final clause appears only in the English translation—the French original preferring to leave the subject unnamed—I believe it is safe to assume that Lyotard's appeal is addressed—at the very least—to the room filled with professors and students where he gave his presentation. Very likely, however, it refers also to the community of like-minded intellectuals the world over, and probably even to enlightened humanity at large. Thus an incarnation of the modern subject, the subject of the emancipation narrative—even if it remains unnamed and without identity—controls his discourse. Which amounts to saying that the Idea of the universal subject, the very idea that he had pronounced dead, is alive and well. Phrased in a more provocative manner, one might say that Lyotard, far from erecting a tomb for the intellectual, here makes the case that after the age of the intellectual comes . . . the age of the intellectual.[9] For how else to describe the status of the reflections in "Missive"?

Lyotard *Aufklärer,* then? Not if one means by that the modern trust in the project of emancipation that characterizes the work of Jürgen Habermas.[10] And yet, there is an affinity between the two that is greater than either one would have it. For Habermas as for Lyotard, the *we,* the possibility to think the universal human subject, is a necessity of practical reason: only the human subject in universal rather than local terms can guarantee the idea of human liberation.[11]

This, I believe, is a provocative conclusion at which to arrive. It challenges the prevalent image of Lyotard as a postmodern thinker for whom the emergence of cultural diversity is held to signal the end of Western hegemony, including, in particular, the end of the universal aspirations of philosophical reflection. In this reading, to the contrary, it appears as if, in the case of human emancipation, and maybe only *ex negativo,* Lyotard, not unlike Habermas, relies upon the notion of a universal subject of history: the human being whose nature it is that he or she needs to be emancipated. In order to further clarify the stakes of the issue, I would like to turn to Richard Rorty's reply to Lyotard.

Rorty's reply to Lyotard's presentation lends itself particularly well for this purpose. For Rorty immediately points to the difference that divides the two thinkers. The manifestolike title of his presentation has the ring of a battle cry, a clear drawing of the line: "Cosmopolitanism without Emancipation." In the course of the elaboration of this theme, he gives a rather different account of how to address the problems posed by the emergence of cultural difference than Lyotard.

Rorty agrees with Lyotard about the description of the present as the end of metanarratives—provided one thinks of metanarrative in terms of the traditional enterprise of philosophical foundationalism, of metaphysics in short. Philosophical pragmatism, after all, came into being as a theory that propounded the end of metaphysics. For Rorty, therefore, the entire project of modernity, as foundational enterprise, is not simply outdated but inherently dubious. And he espouses wholeheartedly the political vision of his teacher John Dewey. "Dewey thinks that muddle, compromise, and blurry syntheses are usually less perilous, politically, than Cartesian clarity." Rorty's espousal of Dewey's antifoundationalism includes the rejection of the idea of a human essence which, once ascertained, verified, and implemented, would lead to the liberation of humanity. Thus "Dewey spent half his time debunking the very idea of 'human nature' and of 'philosophical foundations' for social thought. But," and here lies the germ of Rorty's disagreement with Lyotard,

> he [Dewey] spent the other half spinning a story about universal history—a story of progress according to which contemporary movements of social reform within the liberal democracies are parts of the same overall movement as the overthrow of feudalism and the abolition of slavery. He offered a historical narrative in which American democracy is the embodiment of all the best features of the West, while at the same time making fun of what Jean-François Lyotard, in his *The Postmodern Condition,* has called "metanarratives." . . . Like Lyotard we want to drop *meta*narratives. Unlike him, we keep on spinning edifying first-order narratives. (*ORT* 211)

Rorty thus seems to be keen on establishing a distinction between the pragmatists' first-order narrative of universal history and Lyotard's metanarratives of legitimation. The distinction consists in the fact that the pragmatists' narrative of human history is self-consciously *ethnocentric: that is to say, it recognizes and celebrates* its local origin. In other words, like Lyotard, Dewey and Rorty take leave from modernity's attempt at self-grounding through narratives of legitimation. At the same time, however, the pragmatists celebrate the Western history of progress, according to which the general direction of Western history tends toward ever greater participation of the people in their own fates. To stand up for this view, leads, according to Rorty, to the pragmatist's defense of political liberalism and to reformist, rather than revolutionary, politics. This story of progress and of political liberalism, however, is a Western story, not a universal story: it is "our" ethnocentrism, the essence of the

West. "This sort of ethnocentrism is," according to Rorty, "inevitable and unobjectionable."

> We Deweyans have a story to tell about the progress of our species, a story whose later episodes emphasize how things have been getting better in the West during the last few centuries, and which concludes with some suggestions about how they might become better still in the next few. But when asked about cultural difference, about what our story has to do with the Chinese or the Cashinahua, we can only reply that, for all we know, intercourse with these people may help modify our Western ideas about what institutions can best embody the spirit of Western social democracy. (*ORT* 212)

As his smug use of ethnocentrism (or anti-anti-ethnocentrism, as he calls it at other times)[12] demonstrates, Rorty's defense of the Western story of progress stands in marked contrast to the thought of Lyotard, since it knows no guilt.[13] Rorty has no problem at all championing a local *we* that claims the superiority of the Western social democratic tradition over alternative traditions. His claim is, however, different from that of the Enlightenment tradition of human emancipation. The difference consists in the fact that Rorty's community of pragmatist liberal intellectuals argues its case *on the basis of conviction, or interest, alone,* rather than, and this is crucial, on the basis of human nature or with a view toward establishing a legitimate basis for human history. The ground of legitimation, in other words, is local. Its claim to exhibit a superior model of the progress of history, a model that everyone should be able to enjoy, rests on nothing but the instituted will of the majority of the community who accept it as expression of their desire. Thus, Rorty's cosmopolitan agenda acknowledges its local roots, without either guilt or the claim to universal necessity. This resonates with the title of his essay: "cosmopolitanism," *i.e.,* the continuation of the "ethnocentric" agenda, "without emancipation," *i.e.,* without a conception of human essence to legitimate the agenda.

> We [pragmatists] want narratives of increasing cosmopolitanism though not narratives of emancipation. For we think that there was nothing to emancipate, just as there was nothing which biological evolution emancipated as it moved along from the trilobites to the anthropoids. There is no human nature which was once or still is in chains. (*ORT* 213)

In this close alliance of nature and culture, pragmatism reveals its roots in the discourse of nineteenth-century science, more precisely in the theories of evolution, which supplant the eighteenth-century paradigm of reason as ultimate legitimating instance. This, however, is precisely the crux of the matter. Theories of biological evolution have no room for a notion such as legitimation, since legitimation is essentially a moral category. Thus, in the eyes of Dewey and Rorty, political and social actions have no need of ultimate legitimation in the universal sense of the Enlightenment. For the pragmatists, the very project the *Aufklärer* of modern enlightened humanity struggled to conceive on the basis of a purportedly universal Reason, namely the foundation, justification, and legitimation of everyday practice in higher moral and theoretical principles, is precisely what is wrong with Enlightenment rationality. Since the pragmatists do not engage in metaphysical speculations about ultimate legitimation but, instead, formulate rules for actions within well-defined, local, and spatiotemporally limited bounds, the modern project of human emancipation never comes into view.

Where does this leave the issue of cultural diversity, which had been one of the touchstones for Lyotard's postmodern critique of modern metanarratives? Rorty's argument on ethnocentrism suggests that cultural diversity is no problem at all since "cultural differences are not different in kind from differences between old and ('revolutionary') new theories propounded within a single culture" (*ORT* 214). Consequently, the manner of dealing with cultural difference is in no way different from the way in which one treats different points of view within the same culture. In other words, the pragmatist believes that a culture's—any culture's—ethnocentric way of dealing with difference is the ineluctable *condition of possibility of communication* in general regardless of whether it is a question of inner or intercultural communication.

Rorty's and Lyotard's positions on the meaning of the emergence of cultural difference for Western philosophy are thus, from one perspective at least, diametrically opposed. Where Lyotard records the foundering of the politico-philosophical project of modernity, Rorty sees no reason to withdraw his support for the Western narrative of progress:

> We see no reason why either recent social and political developments or recent philosophical thought should deter us from our attempt to build a cosmopolitan world-society—one which embodies the same sort of utopia with which the Chris-

tian, Enlightenment, and Marxist metanarratives of emancipation ended. (*ORT* 213)

In order to properly understand this statement, it is important to re-
place "metanarrative" by "first-order narrative" in the sense in which I
commented on it above. For it should have become clear, despite the
choice of words in this passage, that Rorty does not mean metanarrative
in the sense that Lyotard gave it in *The Postmodern Condition*. Still, the
differences between their positions are profound, and I believe quite
clearly stated. On the one hand, a "tragic" Lyotard[14] holds on to the possibility of a universal history of emancipation after the exhaustion of
the modern metanarratives which embodied that very possibility. On the
other hand, an optimistic Rorty gives up the idea of a human essence
underlying all of Western metaphysics including the modern metanarratives, trusting instead that from "our" point of view, the cosmopolitan
vision of the Western first-order narrative of progress will make possible
give-and-take negotiations with other cultures.

What are Lyotard's problems with a position such as Rorty's? As we have
seen, Lyotard holds that the emergence of cultural diversity invalidated
the philosophical and political presuppositions of the modern narratives
of emancipation: "There is nothing in the savage community to lead it
to transform itself dialectically into a society of citizens" (*PE* 34). This
conclusion on the part of the Western intellectual means, however, that
there is no longer any raison d'être for the claims of the modern narratives of human emancipation. Then why not simply recognize the notion
of universal history as a Western construct and leave metaphysics, in Rorty's words, "one of the less important sideshows of Western civilization"
(*ORT* 218), behind? Lyotard's resistance to such a solution indicates that
he insists on thinking the place that has been left empty by the demise
of the metanarratives. He insists, in other words, on *thinking* the metaphysical foundations of a possible *we*. This insistence, I believe, is *the
postmodern expression of the modern desire for ultimate legitimation.*
It is postmodern only to the extent that, for Lyotard, the modern project
of legitimation has failed once and for all. This is reconfirmed when Lyotard, with reference to Habermas's claim that postmodernity abandoned
the project of modernity, maintains:

> It is not a case of "abandoning" the project of modernity, as
> Habermas has said with regard to postmodernity, but of the

liquidation of that project. With this annihilation, an irrepara-
ble suspicion is engraved in European, if not Western consciousness: that universal history does not move inevitably "toward the better," as Kant thought, or rather, that history does
not necessarily have a universal finality. (*PE* 51)

As is clear from the passages quoted from Rorty's essay above, this "irrep-
arable suspicion" distinguishes Lyotard's tragic genre of discourse from
Rorty's optimism. Yet despite this situation he persists. What are the reasons for Lyotard's insistence on metaphysical inquiry, and how exactly
does he intend to think the place left empty by the failing of modernity?
In "Missive," Lyotard provides hints, not much more, for a possible answer
to such questions when, in his second clarification to the question "Can
we perpetuate the grand narratives?" he advances some speculations of
what it would take to think the *we* after the exhaustion of the modern
narratives of legitimation.

It would be a matter of elaborating the status of the *we*, the
status of the subject—that is, of escaping both an unrevised
renewal of the modern subject and its parodical or cynical
repetition (tyranny). Such elaboration, I believe, can only lead
to an immediate abandonment of the linguistic structure of
communication (I/you/he), which the moderns, whether consciously or not, held up as their ontological and political
model. (*PE* 27)

This, then, the "immediate abandonment of the linguistic structure
of communication (I/you/he)" prevalent in modernity is Lyotard's most
concrete suggestion, at least in "Missive," on how to develop a postmodern mode of elaborating the *we*. This fairly radical suggestion has to be
seen in the context of the linguistic pragmatics of legitimation. In the
modern narratives of emancipation the knowing subject, whether it be
conceived as consciousness, spirit, proletariat, or avant-garde, combined
in its *we* the linguistic positions of the personal pronouns *I, you,* and
they. In the contemporary demise of modernity

the *we*, it seems, will be condemned (but a condemnation only
in the eyes of modernity) to remain particular, to be you and
me (perhaps), to leave many third parties on the outside. But,
since this *we* has not forgotten (yet) that third parties were
once potential and even promised first persons, it will have to
resign itself to the loss of unanimity and find another mode of

thought and action, or else sink into incurable melancholy for
this lost "object" (or impossible subject): liberated humanity.
(*PE* 26)

The mention of "third parties" refers us back to the issue of cultural
difference at which these deliberations are directed. And again, a comparison with Rorty imposes itself. For Rorty, respecting cultural difference
would mean to accept the "linguistic structure" of modernity, the pragmatics of *I, you,* and *they,* and not to claim to speak for third parties.
Indeed, one feels compelled to remind Lyotard that the idea according to
which third parties are potentially first persons is exactly what he has
himself been arguing against, namely the presumption of universal human essence, or at least of the narrative of universal emancipation. But,
as we have seen, Lyotard wants to think in the wake of universal thought.
What, then, does he mean by "another mode of thought or action"? Or
to put it in terms of the final appeal of "Missive" already referred to, what
does the "line of resistance to the failing of modernity" (*PE* 36) consist of?

I would like to suggest that this other mode of thought consists in the
elaboration of a *metaphysics of community* that will respect the modern
idea according to which "the *we* has not forgotten (yet) that third parties
were once potential and even promised first persons." Lyotard will attempt to think the essential sameness of the *we* in terms of a metaphysics
of the event. This mode of thought will take him far beyond the pale of
political praxis. However, this is a price Lyotard is not only willing but
eager to pay. For in his view both traditional (myth, religion) and modern
forms of political legitimation (narratives of emancipation based on the
Idea of freedom) enable, invite, and practice terror.[15] Both despotic and
republican forms of government ultimately rule by a politics of terror. In
short, any political activity, including wars of liberation, is highly suspect
because it employs terror without ultimate legitimation on its side.

> A war of liberation does not indicate that humanity is continu-
> ing to emancipate itself. Nor does the opening of new markets
> indicate humanity's increasing wealth. Schooling no longer de-
> livers citizens; at best it delivers professionals. So what legiti-
> mation could we put forward for the pursuit of development?[16]

In this passage from an essay entitled "Gloss on Resistance," the tragic
aspect of Lyotard's thought comes to the fore. It is concerned with the
state of delegitimation that comes "with the collapse of metaphysics, and
particularly with the decline of an idea of politics" (*PE* 96). Since, for

Lyotard, the very idea of politics has been delegitimated, the only alternative consists in abandoning modernity's "linguistic structure of communication." He thus turns to a reflection on the universal conditions of human communication in order to lay bare the conditions of possibility of a thought that remembers the loss of the human subject. I understand his essay "Sensus communis: The Subject in *statu nascendi*" to represent his most successful attempt at elaborating the status of the *we* that he called for in "Missive."[17] Although I can hardly do justice to the scope of this essay here, I would like to indicate the general direction of the essay in the context of my guiding questions.

As we have seen, the emergence of cultural difference imposes upon Lyotard a turn toward a mode of thought that tries to locate the moment of the *we,* the moment of human community, *anterior to the universal concepts of emancipation,* prior to conceptual thought as such. He argues his case via a strong reading of Kant's third *Critique,* in particular by way of the notion of aesthetic feeling. On the basis of the third *Critique,* Lyotard develops a notion of aesthetics that, de jure, precedes the conception of aesthetics as it is laid out in the transcendental aesthetic of the first *Critique.* This is to say that what Lyotard calls *sensus communis* refers to a universal *affection of the subject that precedes the transcendental forms of intuition for sensibility,* namely, space and time. Thus, this affect cannot be registered *in the terms of conceptual thought.* It can thus also not be properly exhibited in terms of critical philosophy.

> So all philosophy can do . . . is register that the concept, my concept, does not manage to touch the *sensus communis.* . . . This *sensus* is indeed not situated in that space and time that the concept uses to know objects, neither in the space-time of knowledge, nor in the space-time that sensibility in the first *Critique* prepares precisely for knowledge by means of the schemata. For if there is a *sensus communis* it is made necessary by another necessity, another universality, and another finality than those that knowledge requires. (*SC* 218)

The model for Lyotard's community of *feeling,* as opposed to the *cognitive* community, is Kant's delineation of the judgment of taste. "The aesthetics of the beautiful is not the aesthetics of truth. Taste teaches nothing about the object, it has no object, no referent" (*SC* 219). The judgment of taste is one of pleasure, a judgment about the state of the subject only. Nevertheless, it is a judgment, a synthesis that is being rendered. But according to Lyotard, this synthesis is not a cognitive one.

A kind of *nondenotative* synthesis, not turned toward the object, and thus called strictly subjective, that is exclusively felt (there's the *sensus,* which is feeling). This sentimental synthesis, this judgment that is feeling, deserves to be attributed to a *sensus,* unlike good sense. For with this sensus we are sent back to the most humble, the most "common," level of judgment, in a "state of mind" that as yet owes nothing (nothing as yet, or already nothing) to knowledge and its intrigues. (*SC* 219)

Without following all the twists and turns of Lyotard's argument, it must suffice here to say that this feeling, which precedes the cognitive apparatus, is described in terms almost indistinguishable to Kant's transcendental delineation of the claim to universality in singular aesthetic judgments. Similar to Kant, Lyotard derives the universality of aesthetic feeling from the fact that the subject, or rather the presubject (*SC* 235), is constituted in the "euphony [of the faculties of the mind] singularly felt in the pleasure of the beautiful or the judgment of taste" (*SC* 232). In short, Kant's delineation of the aesthetics of the beautiful serves Lyotard for a purpose similar to that of Kant. Both strategies are designed to safeguard the unity of the subject (*in potentia*) at the very threshold of its heterogeneous disintegration. In other words, the condition of possibility of difference (different empirical judgments about what is beautiful) is at the same time, as aesthetic feeling, the guarantor of the universal constitution of the subject, and as such it represents a point of community anterior to diversity. In the case of Kant, the unified nature of judgment (and thus of knowledge) had been endangered by the apparent arbitrariness of empirical aesthetic judgments, so that a transcendental ground had to be found in the potential euphony of the faculties. In the case of Lyotard, cultural difference challenged the notion of a universal subject, universal history, and thus of a commonality of human experience. Lyotard thus uses the Kantian model in order to establish, in terms of *sensus communis,* the universality of the human subject prior to the heterogeneity of cultural difference.

The *sensus communis* . . . is a sensible analogue of the transcendental euphony of the faculties, which can only be the object of an Idea, and not of an intuition. This *sensus* is not a sense, and the sentiment that is supposed to affect it (as a sense can be affected) is not common, but only in principle communicable. There is no assignable community of senti-

ment, no affective consensus in fact. And if we claim to have
recourse to one, or a fortiori to create one, we are victims of
a transcendental illusion and we are encouraging impostures.
(*SC* 235)

This caution at the end of his article serves two purposes: on the
one hand, Lyotard clearly states that any politics that tries to act on this
community of sentiment encourages impostures because it uses concepts of knowledge and will on a subject matter that precedes these
regimens and is forever only promised, in *statu nascendi.* The universal
subject Lyotard delineates here, in other words, is a fiction of the imagination. This realization leads to the second consequence implicit in *sensus
communis:* only the experimentations of art can be open to the moment
of subject constitution. Art can bear witness to the presubject, the as yet
un-mediated, the im-mediate, through an experimentation with time and
space before they become pure forms of sensible intuition. Only art, because it is not determined by the will to know or the will to will, can
register the event of the subject in *statu nascendi, the sensus communis,
that which is common to* all human beings, yet never in the form of any
representation, or any politics.

Thus, my contention is this: through the metaphysical elaboration of
the *sensus communis,* Lyotard has located the point from which he can
once again, legitimately—and thus in modern fashion—call on "us" to
participate, if not in a politics, at least in an "artistics" of human liberation. This aspect of his work is paramount in some of the writings uncon-
sidered in this essay.[18] In these he enjoins the reader to participate in the
work of anamnesis, the work designed to remember the aesthetic feeling
before "knowledge and its intrigues." This appeal to the reader—if it be
legitimate—must be performed on a ground which he found in aesthetic
feeling, in the common which "is not common but only in principle communicable." This, "in principle," however, functions in the same manner
as did the promise of emancipation, that is, it represents the moment of
legitimation. At the same time, this promise can be pursued only as the
work of anamnesis, in the form of heeding the call to bear witness in
primarily artistic forms. The promise of emancipation has thus retreated
from its role as guarantor of political action to the realm of contemplation. Yet, and this is the mark of its descendancy, *it still carries the force
of a moral injunction when it enjoins us all* to bear witness. Thus,
while legitimation may have changed in *kind,* Lyotard's investment in the
universal Idea of emancipation remains as strong as ever.

We should now have a clearer picture of what I called the conundrum of Lyotard's thought at the beginning of my essay. The sense of ambiguity in Lyotard's writings stems from the contradictory relation to the project of human emancipation which informs his thought. On the one hand, he rejects emancipation as the failed project of modernity, while on the other, he holds on to the promise of human liberation through the metaphysical elaboration of the *sensus communis, which makes it possible* to still think the universal nature of subject constitution.

Since Lyotard does not give up the promise of emancipation, he has to develop a *modus vivendi* which will allow him to reverse the legitimation deficit that the project of modernity has incurred. There are basically two avenues open to deal with this situation. One possibility is that legitimation comes from the inside, that is, in the form of a ruler, a constitution, or a social system charged with establishing the rules for human conduct and the parameters of human freedom. What is described here is usually referred to as legality rather than legitimation—for there is no authority to legitimize the process itself. The other possibility consists in locating legitimation in some outside, such as where Lyotard finds it: aesthetic feeling functions as just such an outside. As we saw early on, this outside is, however, not conceived in terms of the transcendence of myth or religious belief. Rather, we are here dealing with an immanent outside, that is, one that is conceived in terms of something which, though immanent to the world, is external to *representation* and *communication,* these being the modes and models of immanence. Something has been *felt* to be real, but it eludes communication and therefore representation. The notion of the aesthetic feeling signals this paradox of the presentation of the unrepresentable.

What my reading suggests, then, is that Lyotard's discourse, even though it is postmodern and against politics, is closely tied to the modernist project of human emancipation. This is the place where Lyotard meets Habermas, and where their mutual difference from another discourse on modernity, the discourse of disenchantment, becomes all important. Disenchantment, as mentioned in the beginning, accepts the immanence of modernity, the loss, not just the demise, of metanarratives, that is to say, of the Idea of human nature and a common human history. This discourse does not rely upon what I described above as the outside within. It is therefore apposite to distinguish, when talking about modernity, between the proponents of a disenchanted version of modernity (Kant, Weber, Luhmann, and, albeit in a slightly different manner, Rorty) and those who mourn the demise of the utopia modernity had promised (Schiller, Marx, Habermas). Lyotard is one of the latter.

Disenchantment is thus the other discourse of modernity, the one most clearly articulated in German and American sociological traditions. Max Weber, and even more so Niklas Luhmann, accept the immanence and limited range of social constructions of modernity. Rorty's pragmatics also accepts this state of affairs. Indeed, it is quite surprising that although Lyotard is the one to speak against imperialism and in favor of respecting cultural difference, Rorty's smug anti-anti-ethnocentrism seems to outline a far more convincing picture of a politics grounded on the recognition of cultural difference. For Lyotard, despite his protestations to the contrary, wants to think human history in universalist fashion rather than in terms of cultural difference, a strategy which has to resort to a fiction of human nature or to a utopia rather than to actual historical and cultural formations already in place.

This is not, however, the whole story. Lyotard's desire for some form of ultimate legitimation, be it as a metaphysics of community, is not a gesture to be dismissed out of hand. On the contrary. As I indicated at the outset of my essay, the ambiguity of his writings need not necessarily be considered a flaw. Rather, his holding on to the promise of emancipation indicates what is lost in a disenchanted world. What is lost is the promise of redemption, of ultimate justice. Without legitimation from any outside authority, the world is a place of competing discourses, values, opinions, and perspectives, as well as more violent manifestations of difference. In this state of affairs, Lyotard's stress on the *differend,* the necessity to bear witness to the differences and distinctions that are lost in representation and negotiation, remains a powerful reminder not to blithely assume that modernity and liberalism have achieved "truth and justice for all."

For a position such as Rorty's, especially in the manner in which he presents it, does not address the question of power relations. It takes them for granted. Lyotard can argue that such a position is smug and self-serving since it leaves everything up to the goodwill of the stronger partner in conversation. As convincing as Rorty's position is on an epistemological level, it is disturbing because it abdicates the idea of justice on a human scale. While Rorty has powerful arguments for his position, the question of justice does not go away. Conversation, Rorty's answer to cultural difference, does not address the actuality of negotiation. Can we really assume that we are just in our negotiations with others simply because this is part of our tradition, as Rorty suggests? How do we know we are not *simply* dealing in power? How do we decide what is to be done if one partner in the conversation feels overpowered not by argument but by the *force* of argument? Rorty cannot address these questions because his gaze is deliberately, and for good reason, restricted. Lyotard stubbornly, persistently, keeps that kind of thought, the thought of the *differend,* open. He wants to locate a "place" from where it would be possible to think the *we* that seems to have gotten lost in the struggle for recognition of cultural differences. I believe that *we* (!?) are here in the presence of the unresolvable dilemma, the conundrum, that represents the center of the postmodern or, better yet, the modern situation, since it has been this way since the beginning of secular modernity, that is, since the beginning of disenchantment.

In this perspective, Lyotard's espousal of the promise of emancipation makes him a critic of modernity, an antimodernist radical, even if his radicalism has evaporated into an attitude of cautionary contemplation. For the radical pursuit of human liberation is at odds with the functional organization of modern society and seeks to overcome it. This is the reason why Lyotard's every essay, at least in *The Postmodern Explained,* is conceived in terms of resistance to modernity. Such radical resistance, however, in contrast to reform, is possible only on the basis of a belief in the necessity of emancipation on a human scale.

Notes

1. Jean-François Lyotard, *The Postmodern Condition,* trans. Geoff Bennington and Brian Massumi (Minneapolis: University of Minnesota Press, 1984). Hereafter cited as *PC.*

2. Fredric Jameson, foreword to *The Postmodern Condition,* xvi.

3. Niklas Luhmann, *Social Systems,* trans. John Bednarz Jr. with Dirk Baecker, foreword by Eva M. Knodt (Stanford: Stanford University Press, 1995).

4. Jean-François Lyotard, *The Postmodern Explained: Correspondence 1982-1985,* trans. and ed. Julian Pefanis and Morgan Thomas (Minneapolis: University of Minnesota Press, 1993), 24. Hereafter cited as *PE.*

5. Max Weber, "Science as a Vocation," in *From Max Weber: Essays in Sociology,* ed. Hans H. Gerth and C. Wright Mills (New York: Oxford University Press, 1946), 139.

6. Lyotard's essay "Missive on Universal History," which now appears in *The Postmodern Explained* (23-37), was first published as "Histoire universelle et différences culturelles" in the French journal *Critique* 41 (May 1985): 559-68. It was part of the conference "A French-American Collo-

quium: The Case of the Humanities," held at Johns Hopkins University on November 15-16, 1984.

7. Richard Rorty, "Le Cosmopolitisme sans émancipation," *Critique* 41 (May 1985): 569-80. The English version, "Cosmopolitanism without Emancipation: A Response to Jean-François Lyotard," was published in Richard Rorty, *Objectivity, Relativism, and Truth* (Cambridge: Cambridge University Press, 1991), 211-22. Hereafter cited as *ORT.*

8. I am thinking of passages like the last lines of Lyotard's essay "An Answer to the Question, What Is the Postmodern?" which read: "War on totality. Let us attest to the unpresentable; let us activate the differends and save the honor of the name" (*PE* 16). In "Missive," Lyotard in fact values the opposite of the name (which stands for the local), namely justice, as idea. The distinction between name and idea parallels that between mythic and modern legitimation. See also Lyotard's "Memorandum on Legitimation" (*PE* 39-59) for a similar treatment of this issue.

9. See Lyotard's quite different pronouncements in "Tomb of the Intellectual": "There ought no longer to be 'intellectuals,' and if there are any, it is because they are blind to this new fact in Western history since the eighteenth century: there is no universal subject-victim, appearing in reality, in whose name thought could draw up an indictment that would be at the same time a 'conception of the world.'" See Jean-François Lyotard, *Political Writings,* trans. Bill Readings and Kevin Paul Geiman (Minneapolis: University of Minnesota Press, 1993), 6-7.

10. In direct reference to Habermas's notion of the incomplete project of modernity, Lyotard writes: "I would argue that the project of modernity (the realization of universality) has not been forsaken or forgotten but destroyed, 'liquidated.' There are several modes of destruction, several names that are symbols for them. 'Auschwitz' can be taken as a paradigmatic name for the tragic 'incompletion' of modernity" ("Apostil on Narratives," *PE* 18).

11. As already suggested by the previous note, I do not attempt to minimize Lyotard's profound differences with Habermas, although these differences tend to be reduced to the all too neat distinction between dissensus (Lyotard) and consensus (Habermas) as the ultimate purpose of social interaction. (See especially chapter 14 of *The Postmodern Condition* in this context.)

12. See for instance Rorty's "On Ethnocentrism: A Reply to Clifford Geertz," in *Objectivity, Relativism, and Truth,* 203-10.

13. Lyotard's sense of "guilt" is twofold. On the one hand, clear enough, it stems from the *geopolitics* of Western metanarratives (imperialism). On the other hand, however, it is based on a more fundamental distrust of politics in general, including democratic republicanism. In point 6 of his comments on Rorty's presentation, Lyotard refers to this aspect:

We French cannot think politics, philosophy, literature, without remembering that all of this, politics, philosophy, literature, occurred in modernity under the sign of a crime. A crime was committed in France in 1792. A fair king [*brave roi*], entirely lovable, was killed who was the incarnation of legitimacy (in Hegel's sense when he says that legitimate power has to be incarnated in a living individual). We cannot not remember that this crime was horrible. This means that when we try to think politics we know that the question of legitimacy can be posed at any moment.

Critique 41 (May 1985): 583.

14. It is in these terms that Lyotard refers to his own genre of discourse in his reply to Rorty: "There exists a differend between Richard Rorty and me. I do not believe that there is (reason for) litigation since I believe we are almost in agreement. But there is a differend. My genre of discourse is tragic. His is conversational. Where is the court that could decide which of these two genres of discourse is the more accurate (just) one [*le plus juste*]?" (ibid., 581).

15. See Lyotard's "Memorandum on Legitimation" (*PE* 39-59), as well as "Postscript to Terror and the Sublime" (*PE* 67-73). Lyotard here argues that despotism and democratic republicanism are different forms of totalitarianism: "the totalitarianism that turns its back on modern legitimation through the Idea of freedom and the totalitarianism that, on the contrary, issues from that Idea" (*PE* 51).

16. Lyotard, "Gloss on Resistance," in *The Postmodern Explained,* 96.

17. This essay was first published in the journal *Paragraph* 11 (1988): 1-23. It was also included in the essay collection *Who Comes after the Subject,* ed. Eduardo Cadava, Peter Connor, and Jean-Luc Nancy (New York and London: Routledge, 1991), 217-35. The latter publication is hereafter cited as *SC.*

18. I am thinking of all those moments in Lyotard's *Just Gaming,* trans. Wlad Godzich (Minneapolis: University of Minnesota Press, 1985), and *The Postmodern Condition* when he calls on his readers to assist in "multiplying and refining language games" (*JG* 49) or in "invent[ing] allusions to the conceivable which cannot be presented" (*PC* 81). In similar fashion, the following appeal seems to be reasonable only once the ground of legitimation has been secured: "That is why it is important to increase displacement in the games, and even to disorient it, in such a way as to make an unexpected 'move,' a new statement" (*PC* 16; see also n. 7).

Bibliography

Acker, Kathy. *Blood and Guts in High School.* New York: Grove Weiden-
feld, 1978 (first published London: Pan Books, 1984).
———. *Empire of the Senseless.* New York: Grove, 1988.
———. "A Few Notes on Two of My Books." *Review of Contemporary Fic-
tion* 9, no. 2 (Summer 1989): 31–36.
———. Interview. In *Varieties of Violence,* special issue of *2gz* (formerly
Two Girls Review) 1, no. 1 (Spring 1995; http://www.2gz.com/acker.
html): 1–12.
———. Interview by Rebecca Deaton. *Textual Practice* 6, no. 2 (Summer
1992): 271–82.
———. Interview by Lisa Palac. *On Our Backs* (May/June 1991): 19.
———. *Kathy Goes to Haiti in Literal Madness.* New York: Grove, 1988
(first published by Rumor Publications in 1978).
———. *My Mother: Demonology.* New York: Pantheon, 1993.
———. *Pussy, King of the Pirates.* New York: Grove, 1996.
———. "A Conversation with Kathy Acker." Interview by Benjamin Bratton.
Speed (http://www.arts.ucsb.edu:80/~speedPast/1.1/acker.html): 1–5.
———. "A Conversation with Kathy Acker." Interview by Ellen G. Fried-
man. *Review of Contemporary Fiction* 9, no. 2 (Summer 1989): 12–22
———. "Devoured by Myths." With Sylvere Lotringer. In *Hannibal Lecter,
My Father.* New York: Semiotext(e), 1991.
Adorno, Theodor W. *Aesthetic Theory.* Trans. Robert Hullot-Kentor. Minne-
apolis: University of Minnesota Press, 1997.
Arendt, Hannah. *Eichmann in Jerusalem: A Report on the Banality of
Evil.* New York: Viking, 1964.
Arnold, Matthew. *On the Study of Celtic Literature and Other Essays.* Lon-
don: Dent, 1910.
Barrès, Maurice. *Les déracinés: Maurice Barrès: Romans et voyages.* Ed. Vi-
tal Rambaud. Paris: Robert Laffont, 1994.
Barthes, Roland, *A Lover's Discourse: Fragments.* Trans. Richard Howard.
New York: Hill and Wang, 1978.
Behar, Ruth, and Deborah Gordon, eds. *Women Writing Culture.* Berkeley:
University of California Press, 1996.
Beissner, Friedrich, ed. *Hölderlin, Sambliche Werke, Zweiter Band.* Stutt-
gart: Kohlhammer, 1951.
Benjamin, Walter. *The Origin of German Tragic Drama.* Trans. John Os-
borne. London: Verso, 1985.
———. "The Work of Art in the Age of Mechanical Reproduction." In *Illu-
minations.* New York: Schocken, 1969.

Bennington, Geoffrey, and Jacques Derrida. *Jacques Derrida*. Paris: Éditions du Seuil, 1991.

Bergson, Henri. *Creative Evolution*. Trans. Arthur Mitchell. New York: Random House, 1944.

———. *The Creative Mind: An Introduction to Metaphysics*. Trans. Mabelle L. Andison. New York: Citadel Press, 1992.

———. *Matter and Memory*. Trans. N. M. Paul and W. S. Palmer. New York: Zone Books, 1988.

Bernasconi, Robert. *Heidegger in Question: The Art of Existing*. Atlantic Highlands, N.J.: Humanities Press, 1993.

Blake, William. *Annotations to Reynolds' "Discourses." The Poetry and Prose of William Blake*. Ed. David V. Erdman and Harold Bloom. New York: Doubleday, 1965.

Blanchot, Maurice. "Notre compagne clandestine." In *Textes pour Emmanuel Lévinas*. Ed. François Laruelle. Paris: Editions Jean-Michel Place, 1980. 79-87.

———. *The Writing of the Disaster*. Trans. Ann Smock. Lincoln: University of Nebraska Press, 1995.

Brennan, Karen, "The Geography of Enunciation: Hysterical Pastiche in Kathy Acker's Fiction." *boundary 2* 21, no. 22 (1994): 243-68.

Butler, Judith. "The Body Politics of Julia Kristeva." In *Ethics, Politics and Difference*. New York: Routledge, 1993.

Cacciari, Massimo. *Gewalt und Harmonie: Geo-Philosophie Europas*. Trans. G. Memmert. Munich: Carl Hanser, 1995.

Capek, Milic. "Microphysical Indeterminacy and Freedom: Bergson and Peirce." In *The Crisis in Modernism: Bergson and the Vitalist Controversy*. Ed. Frederick Burwick and Paul Douglass. Cambridge: Cambridge University Press, 1992. 171-89.

Castricano, C. Jodey. "If a Building Is a Sentence, So Is a Body: Kathy Acker and the Postcolonial Gothic." In *American Gothic: New Interventions in a National Narrative*. Ed. Robert K. Martin and Eric Savoy. Iowa City: University of Iowa Press, 1998.

Chaloupka, William. *Knowing Nukes: The Politics and Culture of the Atom*. Minneapolis: University of Minnesota Press, 1992.

Chamberlain, Houston Stewart. *Die Grundlagen des XIX. Jahrhunderts*. Munich: F. Bruckmann, 1962.

Chatterjee, Partha. *Nationalism and the Colonial World: A Derivative Discourse?* London: Zed Books, 1986.

———. "The Nationalist Resolution of the Woman Question." In *Recasting Women: Essays in Colonial History*. New Delhi: Kali for Women, 1989.

Cheng, Vince. *Joyce, Race and Empire*. Cambridge: Cambridge University Press, 1995.

Christian, Barbara. "Being the Subject and the Object: Reading African

American Women's Novels." In *Changing Subjects: The Making of Feminist Literary Criticism.* Ed. Gayle Greene and Coppélia Kahn. New York: Routledge, 1993.

Cixous, Hélène. "The Laugh of the Medusa." Trans. Keith Cohen and Paula Cohen. In *New French Feminisms: An Anthology.* Ed. Elaine Marks and Isabelle de Courtivron. New York: Schocken, 1981. 245-64.

Clifford, James. "On Ethnographic Allegory." In *The Predicament of Culture: Twentieth-Century Ethnography, Literature, and Art.* Cambridge, Mass.: Harvard University Press, 1988.

Constant, Benjamin. *Des réactions politiques: Écrits et discours politiques.* Ed. O. Pozzo di Borgo. N.p.: Jean-Jacques Pauvert, 1964. 21-91.

Copjec, Joan. *Read My Desire: Lacan against the Historicists.* Cambridge, Mass: MIT Press, 1994.

Cornell, Drucilla. *The Philosophy of the Limit.* New York: Routledge, 1992.

Critchley, Simon. *The Ethics of Deconstruction: Derrida and Levinas.* Oxford: Basil Blackwell, 1992.

Curtis, L. P. *Anglo-Saxons and Celts: A Study of Anti-Irish Prejudice in Victorian England.* Bridgeport, Conn.: Conference on British Studies at the University of Bridgeport, 1968.

————. *Apes and Angels: The Irishman in Victorian Caricature.* Washington, D.C.: Smithsonian Press, 1971.

Dane, Gabrielle. "Hysteria as Feminist Protest: Dora, Cixous, Acker." *Women's Studies* 23 (1994): 231-56.

Davis, Angela Y. "Afro Images: Politics, Fashion, and Nostalgia." *Critical Inquiry* 21 (Autumn 1994): 27-45.

Davis, Thomas Osborne. "The Young Men of Ireland." *Nation* (15 July 1843): 32-33.

Dawkins, Richard. *The Blind Watchmaker.* New York: W. W. Norton, 1986.

Deleuze, Gilles. *Bergsonism.* Trans. Hugh Tomlinson and Barbara Habberjam. New York: Zone Books, 1988.

————. *Cinema 2 : The Time-Image.* Trans. Hugh Tomlinson and Robert Galeta. Minneapolis: University of Minnesota Press, 1989.

————. *Difference and Repetition.* Trans. P. Patton. New York: Columbia University Press, 1994.

————. "Mediators." Trans. Martin Joughin. In *Incorporations.* Ed. Jonathan Crary and Sanford Kwinter. New York: Zone Books, 1993. 281-94.

Deleuze, Gilles, and Félix Guattari. *What Is Philosophy?* Trans. Hugh Tomlinson and Graham Burchell. New York: Columbia University Press, 1994.

Deleuze, Gilles, and Claire Parnet. *Dialogues.* Trans. Hugh Tomlinson and Barbara Habberjam. London: Athlone Press, 1987.

De Maistre, Joseph. *Eclaircissement sur les sacrifices.* In *Oeuvres complètes,* vol. 5. Geneva: Slatkine Reprints, 1979. 283-360.

Deren, Maya. *Divine Horsemen: The Living Gods of Haiti.* Kingston, N.Y.: Documentext, 1970.

Derrida, Jacques. *Adieu to Emmanuel Levinas.* Trans. Pascale-Anne Brault and Michael Naas. Stanford: Stanford University Press, 1999.

———. *Aporias.* Trans. Thomas Dutoit. Stanford: Stanford University Press, 1993.

———. "At this very moment in this work here I am." In *Re-reading Levinas.* Ed. Robert Bernasconi and Simon Critchley. London: Athlone Press, 1991.

———. "Before the Law." In *Acts of Literature.* Trans. Avital Ronell and Christine Roulston. Ed. Derek Attridge. New York: Routledge, 1992.

———. "Des Tours de Babel." In *Difference in Translation.* Trans. and ed. Joseph F. Graham. Ithaca: Cornell University Press, 1985.

———. "La Différance." In *Théorie d'ensemble.* Paris: Éditions du Seuil, 1968. 41–66.

———. *Dissemination.* Trans. Barbara Johnson. Chicago: University of Chicago Press, 1981.

———. *The Ear of the Other: Otobiography, Transference, Translation.* Trans. Peggy Kamuf. Ed. Christie McDonald. Lincoln: University of Nebraska Press, 1988.

———. *Edmund Husserl's "Origin of Geometry": An Introduction.* Trans. John P. Leavey Jr. Stony Brook, N.Y.: Nicholas Hays, 1978.

———. "En ce moment même dans cet ouvrage me voici." In *Textes pour Emmanuel Lévinas.* Ed. François Laruelle. Paris: Editions Jean-Michel Place, 1980. 21–60.

———. *The Gift of Death.* Trans. David Willis. Chicago: University of Chicago Press, 1995.

———. *Given Time.* Trans. Peggy Kamuf. Chicago: University of Chicago Press, 1992.

———. "Heidegger's Ear: Philopolemology." In *Reading Heidegger: Commemorations.* Ed. John Sallis. Bloomington: Indiana University Press, 1993.

———. *Limited Inc.* Trans. Samuel Weber. Evanston: Northwestern University Press, 1988.

———. *The Other Heading: Reflections on Today's Europe.* Trans. P.-A. Brault and M. Naas. Bloomington: Indiana University Press, 1992.

———. *Points . . . Interviews, 1974–1994.* Ed. Elisabeth Weber. Stanford: Stanford University Press, 1995.

———. *Positions: Jacques Derrida.* Trans. Alan Bass. Chicago: University of Chicago Press, 1981.

———. "Psyché: Inventions of the Other." In *Reading de Man Reading.* Trans. Catherine Porter. Ed. Lindsay Waters and Wlad Godzich. Minneapolis: University of Minnesota Press, 1989.

————. "Sauf le nom." In *On the Name.* Ed. Thomas Dutoit. Stanford: Stanford University Press, 1995.

————. "Signature Event Context." In *Margins of Philosophy.* Trans. Alan Bass. Chicago: University of Chicago Press, 1982.

————. *Signéponge/Signsponge.* Trans. Richard Rand. New York: Columbia University Press, 1984.

————. *Specters of Marx.* Trans. Peggy Kamuf. London: Routledge, 1994.

————. *Speech and Phenomena.* Trans. David B. Allison. Evanston: Northwestern University Press, 1973.

————. "'This Strange Institution Called Literature': An Interview with Jacques Derrida." In *Acts of Literature.* Trans. Geoffrey Bennington and Rachel Bowlby. Ed. Derek Attridge. New York: Routledge, 1992.

————. "The Time of a Thesis: Punctuations." Trans. Kathleen McLaughlin. In *Philosophy in France Today.* Ed. Alan Montefiore. Cambridge: Cambridge University Press, 1983.

————. "Violence and Metaphysics: An Essay on the Thought of Emmanuel Levinas." In *Writing and Difference.* Trans. Alan Bass. Chicago: University of Chicago Press, 1978. 79-153.

Docherty, Thomas. "Tragedy and the Nationalist Condition of Criticism." *Textual Practice* 10, no. 3 (1996): 479-505.

DuCille, Ann. "The Occult of True Black Womanhood: Critical Demeanor and Black Feminist Studies." *Signs* 19, no. 3 (Spring 1994): 591-629.

Echols, Alice. *Daring to Be Bad: Radical Feminism in America, 1967-1975.* Minneapolis: University of Minnesota Press, 1989.

Emmeche, Claus. "Life as an Abstract Phenomenon: Is Artificial Life Possible?" In *Toward a Practic of Autonomous Systems.* Ed. Francisco J. Varela and Paul Bourgine. Cambridge, Mass.: MIT Press, 1992.

Engebretsen, Terry. "Primitivism and Postmodernism in Kathy Acker's *Kathy Goes to Haiti.*" *Studies in the Humanities* 21, no. 2 (December 1994): 105-19.

Evans, Sara, ed. "SNCC Position Paper (Women in the Movement)." In *Personal Politics: The Roots of Women's Liberation in the Civil Rights Movement and the New Left.* New York: Vintage, 1980.

Fabian, Johannes. *Time and the Other: How Anthropology Makes Its Object.* New York: Columbia University Press, 1983.

Fanon, Frantz. *Black Skin, White Masks.* Trans. Charles Lam Markmann. Foreword by Homi Bhabha. London: Pluto, 1986.

————. *The Wretched of the Earth.* Trans. Constance Farrington. New York: Grove Press, 1968.

Fichte, Johann Gottlieb. *The Science of Knowledge.* London: Cambridge University Press, 1982.

Foucault, Michel. "The Discourse on Language." In *The Archaeology of*

Knowledge. Trans. A. M. Sheridan-Smith. New York: Harper Colophon, 1972.

Frank, Hans. *Die Technik des Staates.* Krakau: Burgenverlag, 1942.

Frank, Manfred. *Einführung in die frühromantische Ästhetik: Vorlesungen.* Frankfurt am Main: Suhrkamp, 1989.

Fraser, Nancy. "The French Derrideans: Politicizing Deconstruction or Deconstructing the Political." *New German Critique* 33 (Fall 1984): 127-54.

Freud, Sigmund. *Civilization and Its Discontents.* Trans. Joan Riviere. London: Hogarth, 1963.

Friedman, Ellen G. "'Now Eat Your Mind': An Introduction to the Works of Kathy Acker." *Review of Contemporary Fiction* 9, no. 2 (Summer 1989): 37-49.

———. Review of *My Mother: Demonology* by Kathy Acker. *Review of Contemporary Fiction* 14, no. 1 (Spring 1994): 213-14.

Ferguson, Frances. "Nuclear Sublime." *Diacritics* 14, no. 2 (Summer 1984): 4-10.

Gallop, Jane. *Around 1981: Academic Feminist Literary Criticism.* New York: Routledge, 1992.

Gasché, Rodolphe. *The Tain of the Mirror: Derrida and the Philosophy of Reflection.* Cambridge, Mass.: Harvard University Press, 1986.

Geertz, Clifford. "Us/Not-Us: Benedict's Travels." In *Works and Lives: The Anthropologist as Author.* Stanford: Stanford University Press, 1988.

Gibbons, Luke. "Identity without a Centre: Allegory, History and Irish Nationalism." In *Transformations in Irish Culture, Critical Conditions: Field Day Essays,* vol. 2. Cork: Cork University Press, 1996.

———. "Race against Time: Racial Discourse and Irish History." *Oxford Literary Review* 13 (1991).

Giddings, Paula. *When and Where I Enter: The Impact of Black Women on Race and Sex in America.* New York: William Morrow, 1984.

Gilbert, Nigel, and Rosaria Conte, eds. *Artificial Societies. The Computer Simulation of Social Life.* London: University College of London Press, 1995.

Goodrich, Chris. Review of *Pussy, King of the Pirates* by Kathy Acker. *Los Angeles Times Book Review* (24 March 1996): 10.

Gordon, Deborah A. "Conclusion: Culture Writing Women: Inscribing Feminist Ethnography." *Women Writing Culture.* Ed. Ruth Behar and Deborah A. Gordon. Berkeley: University of California Press, 1996.

Grosz, Elizabeth. "The Labors of Love, Analyzing Perverse Desire: An Interrogation of Teresa de Lauretis's *The Practice of Love." differences* 6, nos. 2-3 (Summer-Fall 1994): 274-95.

Grünbaum, Adolf. *Philosophical Problems of Space and Time.* Dordrecht and Boston: R. Reidel, 1973.

Guerlac, Suzanne. "Transgression in Theory: Genius and the Subject of *La révolution du langage poétique*." In *Ethics, Politics and Difference*. New York: Routledge, 1993.

Halpin, Rev. J., P. P. *The Father Mathew Reader on Temperance and Hygiene*. Dublin: M. H. Gill, 1907.

Hansen, Christian, Catherine Needham, and Bill Nichols. "Pornography, Ethnography, and the Discourse of Power." In Bill Nichols, *Representing Reality: Issues and Concepts in Documentary*. Bloomington: Indiana University Press, 1991. 201–28.

Hegel, G. W. F. *Phenomenology of Spirit*. Trans. A. V. Miller. Oxford: Oxford University Press, 1977.

———. *Vorlesungen über die Philosophie der Weltgeschichte*. Ed. Georg Lasson. Vierter Band. *Die Germanische Welt*. Leipzig: Felix Meiner, 1944.

Heidegger, Martin. *Basic Writings*. 2d ed. Ed. and intro. David Farrell Krell. New York: HarperCollins, 1993.

———. *Being and Time*. Trans. J. Macquarrie and E. Robinson. London: SCM, 1962.

———. *Beiträge zur Philosophie: Vom Ereignis*. Vol. 65 of *Gesamtausgabe*. Frankfurt am Main: Klostermann, 1989.

———. *Hölderlins Hymnen 'Germanien' und 'Der Rhein.'* Vol. 39 of *Gesamtausgabe*. Frankfurt am Main: Klostermann, 1980.

———. "Kants These über das Sein." In *Wegmarken*. Frankfurt am Main: Klostermann, 1967.

———. "The Origin of the Work of Art." In *Poetry, Language, Thought*. Trans. Albert Hofstadter. New York: Harper and Row, 1971.

———. *What Is Philosophy?* Trans. W. Kluback and J. T. Wilde. Estover: Vision Press, 1989.

Heine, Heinrich. *Zur Geschichte der Religion und Philosophie in Deutschland. Heinrich Heine Werke*. Vierter Band. Frankfurt am Main: Insel Verlag, 1968. 44–165.

Hölderlin, Friedrich. "Germania." In *Poems and Fragments: A Bilinqual Edition*. Trans. Michael Hamburger. London: Cambridge University Press, 1980.

———. *Hölderlins Diotima Susette Gontard: Gedichte—Briefe—Zeugniss*. Ed. Adolf Beck. Frankfurt am Main: Insel, 1980.

Horkheimer, Max. *Eclipse of Reason*. New York: Oxford University Press, 1947.

Horkheimer, Max, and Theodor Adorno. *Dialectic of Enlightenment*. Trans. John Cumming. New York: Continuum, 1972.

Howes, Marjorie. *Yeats's Nations: Gender, Class, and Irishness*. Cambridge: Cambridge University Press, 1996.

Hulley, Kathleen. "Transgressing Genre: Kathy Acker's Intertext." In *Inter-*

textuality and Contemporary American Fiction. Ed. Patrick O'Donnell and Robert Con Davis. Baltimore: Johns Hopkins University Press, 1989. 171–90.

Hunter, Ian. "Aesthetics and Cultural Studies." In *Cultural Studies.* Ed. Lawrence Grossberg, Cary Nelson, and Paula A. Treichler. New York and London: Routledge, 1992.

Husserl, Edmund. *The Crisis of Euopean Sciences and Transcendental Phenomenology.* Trans. D. Carr. Evanston: Northwestern University Press, 1970.

———. *Ideas Pertaining to a Pure Phenomenology and to a Phenomenological Philosophy. First Book: General Introduction to a Pure Phenomenology.* Trans. F. Kersten. The Hague: Martinus Nijhoff, 1983.

Hyde, Douglas. "The Necessity for Deanglicising Ireland." In *Language, Lore, and Lyrics: Essays and Lectures.* Ed. Breandán Ó Conaire. Blackrock: Irish Academic Press, 1986.

Irigaray, Luce. *An Ethics of Sexual Difference.* Trans. Carolyn Burke and Gillian C. Gill. Ithaca: Cornell University Press, 1993.

———. *Speculum of the Other Woman.* Trans. Gillian C. Gill. Ithaca: Cornell University Press, 1985.

———. *This Sex Which Is Not One.* Trans. Catherine Porter. Ithaca: Cornell University Press, 1985.

Jabès, Edmond. *The Book of Resemblances.* Vol. 1. Trans. Rosmarie Waldrop. Middletown, Conn.: Wesleyan University Press, 1990.

Jameson, Fredric. Foreword to *The Postmodern Condition* by Jean-François Lyotard. Minneapolis: University of Minnesota Press, 1984.

Jarry, Alfred. *Ubu Plays.* Ed. Simon Watson Taylor. London: Methuen, 1968.

Jay, Martin. *Downcast Eyes.* Berkeley: University of California Press, 1993.

Jordan, June. "On Richard Wright and Zora Neale Hurston: Notes on a Balancing of Love and Hatred." *Black World* (August 1974).

Joyce, James. *Dubliners.* New York: Viking Press, 1993.

———. *Letters.* Ed. Stuart Gilbert. New York: Viking Press, 1966.

———. *Stephen Hero.* Ed. Theodore Spencer. New York: Granada, 1977.

Kant, Immanuel. "The Contest of Faculties." In *Kant: Political Writings,* trans. H. B. Nisbet, ed. Hans Reiss. Cambridge: Cambridge University Press, 1991.

———. *Critique of Judgement.* Trans. J. H. Bernard. New York: Hafner Press, 1951.

———. *Critique of Practical Reason.* Trans. Lewis White Beck. New York: Macmillan, 1993.

———. *Groundwork of the Metaphysic of Morals.* Trans. H. J. Paton. New York: Harper and Row, 1964.

———. "On a Newly Arisen Superior Tone in Philosophy." In *Raising the Tone of Philosophy: Late Essays by Immanuel Kant, Transformative*

Critique by Jacques Derrida. Trans. and ed. Peter Fenves. Baltimore: Johns Hopkins University Press, 1993.

————. *Religion within the Limits of Reason Alone.* Trans. Theodore M. Greene and Hoyt H. Hudson. Chicago: Open Court, 1934.

————. "Über ein vermeintes Recht aus Menschenliebe zu lügen" (1797). In *Kant's Werke.* [This is the first section (*Abteilung*) of *Kant's Gesammelte Schriften,* ed. Königlich Preußische Akademie der Wissenschaften.] Vol. 8, *Abhandlungen nach 1781.* Berlin: Georg Reimer Verlag, 1912. 423–30.

Katz, Jakob. *Wagner et la question juive.* Trans. (from German) Pierre Rusch. Paris: Hachette, 1986.

Kearny, Richard. "Jacques Derrida: Deconstruction and the Other." In *Dialogues with Contemporary Continental Thinkers: The Phenomenological Heritage.* Manchester: Manchester University Press, 1984.

Kennedy, Colleen. "Simulating Sex and Imagining Mothers." *American Literary History* 4, no. 1 (Spring 1992): 165–85.

Kincaid, Jamaica. *A Small Place.* New York: Plume, 1988.

Klein, Richard. "The Future of Nuclear Criticism." *Yale French Studies* 77 (1990): 77–78.

Kristeva, Julia. *About Chinese Women.* Trans. Anita Barrows. New York: Marion Boyars, 1977.

————. *Desire in Language: A Semiotic Approach to Literature and Art.* Trans. Thomas Gora, Alice Jardine, and Leon S. Roudiez. Ed. Leon S. Roudiez. New York: Columbia University Press, 1980.

————. *Revolution in Poetic Language.* Trans. Margaret Waller. New York: Columbia University Press, 1984.

————. *Strangers to Ourselves.* Trans. Leon S. Roudiez. New York: Columbia University Press, 1991.

Lacan, Jacques. *The Four Fundamental Concepts of Psycho-Analysis.* Trans. Alan Sheridan. Ed. Jacques-Alain Miller. New York: W. W. Norton, 1977.

————. "Kant avec Sade." In *Ecrits.* Paris: Le Seuil, 1966. 765–90.

————. "Kant with Sade." Trans. James B. Swenson. *October* 51 (Winter 1989): 55–75.

————. *The Seminar of Jacques Lacan. Book I. Freud's Papers on Technique.* Trans. John Forrester. Ed. Jacques-Alain Miller. New York: W. W. Norton, 1988.

————. *The Seminar of Jacques Lacan. Book VII. The Ethics of Psychoanalysis.* Trans. Dennis Porter. Ed. Jacques-Alain Miller. New York: W. W. Norton, 1992

Lacoue-Labarthe, Philippe. *Heidegger, Art and Politics.* Trans. Chris Turner. Oxford: Basil Blackwell, 1990.

Lacoue-Labarthe, Philippe, and Jean-Luc Nancy. "The Nazi Myth." Trans. Brian Homes. *Critical Inquiry* 16, no. 2 (Winter 1990): 291–312.

Lacoue-Labarthe, Philippe, and Jean-Luc Nancy, eds. *Les Fins de l'homme: A partir du travail de Jacques Derrida.* Paris: Galilée, 1981.

Langton, Chris. "Artificial Life." In *Artificial Life,* vol. 4. Redwood City, Calif.: Addison-Wesley, 1989.

Lefebvre, Georges. *La Révolution française.* Paris: Presses Universitaires de France, 1989.

Levinas, Emmanuel. *Difficult Freedom: Essays on Judaism.* Trans. Seán Hand. Baltimore: John Hopkins University Press, 1990.

———. "Meaning and Sense." In *Collected Philosophical Papers.* Trans. Alphonso Lingis. Dordrecht: Martinus Nijhoff, 1987. 75-107.

———. "No Identity." *Collected Philosophical Papers.* Trans. Alphonso Lingis. Dordrecht: Martinus Nijhoff, 1987. 141-51.

———. *Otherwise Than Being: Or Beyond Essence.* Trans. Alphonso Lingis. The Hague and Boston: Martinus Nijhoff, 1991.

———. "Reality and Its Shadow." In *The Levinas Reader.* Ed. Seán Hand. Oxford: Basil Blackwell, 1989. 129-43.

———. "Substitution." Trans. Alphonso Lingis. In *The Levinas Reader.* Ed. Seán Hand. Oxford: Basil Blackwell, 1989. 88-125.

———. *Sur Maurice Blanchot.* Paris: Fata Morgana, 1985.

———. *Time and the Other and Additional Essays.* Trans. Richard A. Cohen. Pittsburgh: Duquesne University Press, 1987.

———. *Totality and Infinity.* Trans. Alphonso Lingis. Pittsburgh: Duquesne University Press, 1994.

———. "The Trace of the Other." In *Decontruction in Context.* Ed. Mark C. Taylor. Chicago: University of Chicago Press, 1986.

———. "The Transcendence of Words." Trans. Alphonso Lingis. In *The Levinas Reader.* Ed. Seán Hand. Oxford: Basil Blackwell, 1989.

Llewelyn, John. *Emmanuel Levinas: The Genealogy of Ethics.* New York: Routledge, 1995.

———. "Responsibility with Indecidability." In *Derrida: A Critical Reader.* Ed. David Wood. Oxford: Basil Blackwell, 1992.

Lloyd, David. *Anomalous States: Irish Writing and the Post-colonial Moment.* Dublin: Lilliput Press, and Durham, N.C.: Duke University Press, 1993.

———. "The Memory of Hunger." In *Irish Hunger.* Ed. Tom Hayden. Boulder: Roberts Rinehart, 1997. 32-47.

Longinus. *On the Sublime.* Oxford: Clarendon Press, 1964.

Love, Courtney, and Hole. "Softer, Softest." On *Live Through This.* BMI, 1994.

Lowe, Donald A. *History of Bourgeois Perception.* Chicago: University of Chicago Press, 1982.

Luhmann, Niklas. *Social Systems.* Trans. John Bednarz Jr. with Dirk Baecker. Stanford: Stanford University Press, 1995.

Lyotard, Jean-François. *The Differend: Phrases in Dispute.* Trans. Georges
Van Den Abbeele. Minneapolis: University of Minnesota Press, 1988.

———. "Histoire universelle et différénces culturelles." *Critique* 41 (May
1985): 559–68.

———. "The Interest of the Sublime." In *Of the Sublime: Presence in Question.* Trans. Jeffrey S. Librett. Albany: State University of New York
Press, 1993. 109–32.

———. *Just Gaming.* Trans. Wlad Godzich. Minneapolis: University of Minnesota Press, 1985.

———. "Matter and Time." In *The Inhuman.* Trans. Geoffrey Bennington
and Rachel Bowlby. Stanford: Stanford University Press, 1991.

———. *Political Writings.* Trans. Bill Readings and Kevin Paul Geiman. Minneapolis: University of Minnesota Press, 1993.

———. *The Postmodern Condition.* Trans. Geoffrey Bennington and Brian
Massumi. Minneapolis: University of Minnesota Press, 1984.

———. *The Postmodern Explained: Correspondence 1982–1985.* Trans.
and ed. Julian Pefanis and Morgan Thomas. Minneapolis: University of
Minnesota Press, 1993.

———. "Sensus communis: The Subject in *statu nascendi.*" In *Who Comes
After the Subject.* Ed. Eduardo Cadava, Peter Connor, and Jean-Luc
Nancy. New York and London: Routledge, 1991. 217–35.

Malcolm, Elizabeth. *'Ireland Sober, Ireland Free': Drink and Temperance
in Nineteenth-Century Ireland.* Dublin: Gill and Macmillan, 1986.

———. "Temperance and Irish Nationalism." In *Ireland under the Union:
Varieties of Tension.* Ed. F. S. L. Lyons and R. A. J. Hawkins. Oxford:
Clarendon, 1980.

Massumi, Brian. *A User's Guide to Capitalism and Schizophrenia: Deviations from Deleuze and Guattari.* Cambridge, Mass.: MIT Press, 1992.

Mauss, Marcel. *The Gift: The Form and Reason for Exchange in Archaic
Societies.* London: Routledge, 1990.

McDowell, Deborah E. "Transferences: Black Feminist Discourse: The 'Practice' of 'Theory.'" In *Feminism Beside Itself.* Ed. Diane Elam and Robyn
Wiegman. New York: Routledge, 1995.

Miller, Jacques-Alain. "A Discussion of Lacan's 'Kant with Sade.'" In *Reading
Seminars I and II: Lacan's Return to Freud.* Ed. Richard Feldstein,
Bruce Fink, and Maire Jaanus. Albany: State University of New York
Press, 1996. 212–37.

Miller, Nancy K. "Decades." In *Changing Subjects: The Making of Feminist
Literary Criticism.* Ed. Gayle Greene and Coppélia Kahn. New York:
Routledge, 1993.

———. *Getting Personal: Feminist Occasions and Other Autobiographical Acts.* New York: Routledge, 1991.

Minkowski, Eugene. *Lived Time: Phenomenological and Psychopathologi-*

cal Studies. Trans. Nancy Metzel. Evanston: Northwestern University Press, 1970.

Moi, Toril, ed. *The Kristeva Reader.* New York: Columbia University Press, 1986.

———. *Sexual/Textual Politics: Feminist Literary Theory.* London: Methuen, 1985.

Moya, Andrés, Esteban Domingo, and John J. Holland. "RNA Viruses: A Bridge between Life and Artificial Life." In *Advances in Artificial Life.* Ed. F. Moran, A. Moreno, J. J. Mereko, and O. Chacón. Berlin: Springer-Verlag, 1995.

Mosse, George L. *The Crisis of German Ideology: Intellectual Origins of National Socialism.* New York: Grosset and Dunlap, 1964.

Nancy, Jean-Luc. *The Birth to Presence.* Trans. Brian Holmes et al. Stanford: Stanford University Press, 1993.

———. *The Experience of Freedom.* Trans. Bridget McDonald. Stanford: Stanford University Press, 1993.

———. *The Inoperative Community.* Trans. Peter Connor, Lisa Garbus, Michael Holland, and Simona Sawhney. Ed. Peter Connor. Minneapolis: University of Minnesota Press, 1991.

———. *The Muses.* Trans. Peggy Kamuf. Stanford: Stanford University Press, 1996.

———. "L'Offrande sublime." In *Du Sublime.* Ed. Jean-François Courtine. Paris: Belan, 1988. 37-75.

———. "The Sublime Offering." In *Of the Sublime: Presence in Question.* Trans. Jeffrey S. Librett. Albany: State University of New York Press, 1993. 25-54.

———. "The Unsacrificeable." *Yale French Studies* 79 (1991): 20-38.

———. "Wild Laughter in the Throat of Death." *MLN* 102, no. 4 (September 1987): 719-36.

Norris, Christopher. *Derrida.* Cambridge, Mass.: Harvard University Press, 1987.

———. *Uncritical Theory: Postmodernism, Intellectuals and the Gulf War.* London: Lawrence and Wishart, 1992.

Peters, Greg Lewis. "Dominance and Subversion: The Horizontal Sublime and Erotic Empowerment in the Works of Kathy Acker." In *State of the Fantastic: Studies in the Theory and Practice of Fantastic Literature and Film.* Selected Essays from the Eleventh International Conference on the Fantastic in the Arts, 1990. Westport, Conn.: Greenwood Press, 1992. 149-56.

Plato. *Republic.* Trans. G. M. A. Grube. Indianapolis: Hackett, 1974.

Rajan, Tilottama. "Trans-Positions of Difference: Kristeva and Poststructuralism." In *Ethics, Politics and Difference.* New York: Routledge, 1993.

Reiter, Rayna R., ed. *Toward an Anthropology of Women*. New York and London: Monthly Review Press, 1975.

Renouvier, Charles. *Essais de critique générale*. Vol. 2. Paris: A. Colin, 1912.

Robbins, Bruce. *Secular Vocations: Intellectuals, Professionalism, Culture*. London and New York: Verso, 1993.

Robbins, Jill. "Aesthetic Totality and Ethical Infinity." *L'Esprit créateur* 35, no. 3 (Fall 1995): 66–79.

Rockett, Kevin. "Disguising Dependency: Separatism and Foreign Mass Culture," *Circa* 49 (January/February 1990).

Rogozinski, Jacob. "The Gift of the World." In *Of the Sublime: Presence in Question*. Trans. Jeffrey S. Librett. Albany: State University of New York Press, 1993. 133–56.

Rorty, Richard. "Cosmopolitanism without Emancipation: A Response to Jean-François Lyotard." In *Objectivity, Relativism, and Truth*. Cambridge: Cambridge University Press, 1991.

———. "Le Cosmopolitisme sans émancipation." *Critique* 41 (May 1985): 569–80.

———. "On Ethnocentrism: A Reply to Clifford Geertz." In *Objectivity, Relativism, and Truth*. Cambridge: Cambridge University Press, 1991.

Rosenberg, Alfred. *Der Mythus des 20. Jahrhunderts: Eine Wertung der seelisch-geistigen Gestaltenkämpfe unserer Zeit*. Munich: Hoheneichen-Verlag, 1935.

———. *Race and Race History, and Other Essays by Alfred Rosenberg*. Ed. Robert Pois. New York: Harper and Row, 1970.

Rosenzweig, Roy. "The Rise of the Saloon." In *Rethinking Popular Culture: Contemporary Perspectives in Cultural Studies*. Ed. Chandra Mukerji and Michael Schudson. Berkeley: University of California Press, 1991.

Ross, Andrew. *Strange Weather: Culture, Science and Technology in the Age of Limits*. London and New York: Verso, 1991.

Rousseau, Jean-Jacques. *Discourse on the Origin of Inequality*. Trans. Franklin Philip. New York: Oxford University Press, 1994.

Rubin, Gayle. "Sexual Traffic." *differences* 6, nos. 2–3 (Summer–Fall 1994).

———. "The Traffic in Women: Notes on the 'Political Economy' of Sex." In *Women, Class, and the Feminist Imagination: A Socialist-Feminist Reader*. Ed. Karen V. Hansen and Ilene J. Philipson. Philadelphia: Temple University Press, 1991.

Ruskin, John. *Sesame and Lilies*. In *Works*. Ed. E. T. Cook and Alexander Wedderburn. London: George Allen, 1905.

Ryan, Michael. *Marxism and Deconstruction: A Critical Articulation*. Baltimore: Johns Hopkins University Press, 1982.

Sade, Marquis de. *La Philosophie dans le boudoir*. Paris: Éditions 10/18, 1972.

Sangari, KumKum, and Sudesh Vaid. "Introduction." In *Recasting Women: Essays in Colonial History.* New Delhi: Kali for Women, 1989.

Saville, Julia. "Of Fleshly Garments: Ascesis and Desire in the Ethic of Psychoanalysis." *American Imago* 49, no. 4 (1992): 445–65.

Sciolino, Martina. "Kathy Acker and the Postmodern Subject of Feminism." *College English* 52, no. 4 (April 1990): 437–45.

Schwenger, Peter. *Letter Bomb: Nuclear Holocaust and the Exploding Word.* Baltimore: Johns Hopkins University Press, 1992.

Shell, Mark. *The Economy of Literature.* Baltimore: Johns Hopkins University Press, 1978.

Siegle, Robert. *Suburban Ambush: Downtown Writing and the Fiction of Insurgency.* Baltimore: Johns Hopkins University Press, 1989.

Simondon, Gilbert. "The Genesis of the Individual." Trans. Mark Cohen and Sanford Kwinter. In *Incorporations.* Ed. Jonathan Crary and Sanford Kwinter. New York: Zone Books, 1992.

Smith, Steven B. *Hegel's Critique of Liberalism.* Chicago: University of Chicago Press, 1989.

Smith, Valerie. "Black Feminist Theory and the Representation of the 'Other.'" In *Changing Our Own Words: Essays on Criticism, Theory, and Writing by Black Women.* Ed. Cheryl A. Wall. New Brunswick: Rutgers University Press, 1989.

Sollers, Philippe. "Critiques." *Tel Quel* 57 (Spring 1974): 136–37.

———. "De quelques contradictions." *Tel Quel* 38 (Summer 1969): 6–7.

———. "Sur la contradiction." In *Sur le matérialisme: De l'atomisme à la dialectique révolutionnaire.* Paris: Editions du Seuil, 1974.

———. *Tel Quel* 61 (Spring 1975): 5.

———. *Tel Quel* 66 (Summer 1976): 103–4.

Sokal, Alan. "A Physicist Experiments with Cultural Studies." *Lingua Franca* (May/June 1996): 62–64.

Spafford, Eugene H. "Computer Viruses—A Form of Artificial Life?" In *Artificial Life II.* Ed. C. Langton, C. Taylor, J. D. Farmer, and S. Ramussen. Redwood City, Calif.: Addison-Wesley, 1992.

Spivak, Gayatri Chakravorty. "Can the Subaltern Speak?" In *Marxism and the Interpretation of Culture.* Ed. Cary Nelson and Lawrence Grossberg. Urbana: University of Illinois Press, 1988.

———. "French Feminism in an International Frame." In *Other Worlds: Essays in Cultural Politics.* New York: Routledge, 1988. 134–53.

Sternhell, Zeev. *Maurice Barrès et le nationalisme français.* Paris: Armand Colin, 1983.

Trinh T. Minh-ha and Judith Mayne. "From a Hybrid Place." In Trinh T. Minh-ha, *Framer Framed.* New York: Routledge, 1992. 137–48.

Vries, Hent de. "Theotopographies: Nancy, Hölderlin, Heidegger." *MLN* 109, no. 3 (1994): 445–77.

Washington, Mary Helen. "Black Women Image Makers." *Black World* (August 1974).

Weber, Max. "Science as a Vocation." In *From Max Weber: Essays in Sociology.* Ed. Hans. H. Gerth and C. Wright Mills. New York: Oxford University Press, 1946.

Whelan, Kevin. "Pre- and Post-Famine Landscape Change." In *The Great Irish Famine.* Ed. Cathal Poirteir. Cork and Dublin: Mercier Press, 1995.

White, Stephen K. *Political Theory and Postmodernism.* New York: Cambridge University Press, 1991.

Wilson, Kate. Review of *My Mother: Demonology* by Kathy Acker. *Entertainment Weekly* (1 October 1993): 50.

Woolf, Virginia. *The Second Common Reader.* New York: Harcourt Brace, 1960.

Wordsworth, Dorothy. *The Grasmere Journals.* Oxford: Oxford University Press, 1991.

Yates, F. Eugene. "Quantumstuff and Biostuff." In *Self-Organizing Systems: The Emergence of Order.* Ed. F. E. Yates. New York and London: Plenum Press, 1987.

Yeats, W. B. *Autobiography.* New York: Macmillan, 1953.

———. "Gods and Fighting Men." In *Explorations.* New York: Macmillan, 1962.

Žižek, Slavoj. *The Metastases of Enjoyment: Six Essays on Woman and Causality.* London: Verso, 1994.

———. *The Sublime Object of Ideology.* London: Verso, 1989.

———. "Sur le pouvoir politique et les mécanismes idéologiques." *Ornicar?* 34 (July–September 1985): 41-60.

Notes on Contributors

Joan Brandt teaches French in the Cooperative Program in Modern Languages and Literatures at the Claremont Colleges. Her publications include *Geopoetics: The Politics of Mimesis in Poststructuralist French Poetry and Theory* (Stanford, 1997) and articles on twentieth-century French literature and theory. She is currently editing a special issue of *L'Esprit Créatur* on the legacy of May '68 in France.

Gilbert Chaitin is a professor of French and comparative literature at Indiana University (Bloomington). His publications include *The Unhappy Few: A Psychological Study of the Novels of Stendhal* (Indiana, 1972), *Romantic Revolutions* (co-editor, Indiana, 1990), and *Rhetoric and Culture in Lacan* (Cambridge, 1996) as well as articles on Stendhal, Hugo, Renan, Zola, Camus, theory of narrative, psychoanalysis and literature, and Lacan.

Seamus Deane is Keough Professor of Irish Studies at the University of Notre Dame. His most recent works are *Reading in the Dark* (Knopf, 1997), a novel, and *Strange Country: Modernity and Nationhood in Irish Writing since 1790* (Clarendon, 1997).

Alice Gambrell teaches in the English Department at the University of Southern California, where she is also affiliated with the Program in American Studies and Ethnicities and the Gender Studies Program. Her book *Women Intellectuals, Modernism, and Difference* was published in 1997 by Cambridge University Press.

Rodolphe Gasché is Eugenio Donato Professor of Comparative Literature at the State University of New York at Buffalo. His books include *Die Hybride Wissenschaft* (Metzler, 1973), *System und Metaphorik in der Philosophie von Georges Bataille* (Lang, 1978), *The Tain of the Mirror: Derrida and the Philosophy of Reflection* (Harvard, 1986), *Inventions of Difference: On Jacques Derrida* (Harvard, 1994), *The Wild Card of Reading: On Paul de Man* (Harvard, 1998), and *Of Minimal Things: Studies on the Notion of Relation* (Stanford, 2000). Currently, he is working on book-length study of Kant's aesthetics.

Dorota Glowacka teaches critical theory, contemporary literature, and Holocaust literature in the Contemporary Studies Programme at the University of King's College in Halifax, Canada. She has published essays on Continental theory and American, French, and Polish literature. She is the editor of *Between Ethics and Aesthetics: Crossing the Boundaries* (SUNY). Her current work focuses on Holocaust literature and art in the context of contemporary philosophical debates. She is working on a book titled *The Shattered Word: Writing of the Fragment and the Holocaust Testimony.*

Elizabeth Grosz teaches English and comparative literature at the State University of New York at Buffalo. Her publications include *Space, Time and Perversion: Essays on the Politics of Bodies* (Routledge, 1995), *Volatile Bodies: Toward a Corporeal Feminism* (Indiana, 1994), *Jacques Lacan: A Feminist Introduction* (Routledge, 1990), and *Sexual Subversions: Three French Feminists* (Allen and Unwin, 1989). She has edited several collections (*Becomings: Explorations in Time, Memory, and Futures* [Cornell, 1999]; *Sexy Bodies: The Strange Carnality of Feminism* [with Elspeth Probyn; Routledge, 1995]; *Crossing Boundaries: Feminism and the Critique of Knowledges* [with Barbara Caine and Marie de Lepervanche; Allen and Unwin, 1988]) and special journal issues of *Hypatia, Diacritics,* and *Australian Feminist Studies.*

Joseph Kronick is a professor of English at Louisiana State University and the author of *American Poetics of History: From Emerson to the Moderns* (LSU, 1984) and *Derrida and the Future of Literature* (SUNY, 1999).

David Lloyd is Hartley Burr Alexander Chair in the Humanities at Scripps College, Claremont. He is the author of *Nationalism and Minor Literature: James Clarence Mangan and the Emergence of Irish Cultural Nationalism* (California, 1987), *The Nature and Context of Minority Discourse* (Oxford, 1990), *Anomalous States: Irish Writing and the Post-Colonial Moment* (Lilliput, 1993), and *Ireland after History* (Cork, 1999).

Marilyn Manners teaches in the Department of Comparative Literature at the University of California, Los Angeles. She has published on Sylvia Plath and Hélène Cixous in the journal *Comparative Literature,* on Cixous in *French Forum* and in the book *Hélène Cixous: Critical Impressions,* on Madonna and Courtney Love in the book *Reading Rock and Roll: Authenticity, Appropriation, Aesthetics,* and on posthuman romance and feminist sexualities at the end of millennium in the journals *Discourse* and *Strategies.* Her current research examines irony and parody in contemporary feminism.

Andreas Michel is an associate professor of German and European studies in the Department of Humanities and Social Sciences at Rose-Hulman Institute of Technology. He has published articles on literary theory, cultural studies, media theory, (post)modernity (Lyotard), primitivism (Carl Einstein), and exoticism (Victor Segalen). He is presently finishing a book-length study on the German expressionist writer and art critic Carl Einstein (1875–1940). He is also the co-translator of Jean-François Lyotard's *Heidegger and "the Jews"* (Minnesota, 1990) and the co-editor and co-translator of *Theory as Practice: A Critical Anthology of Early German Romantic Writings* (Minnesota, 1997).

Herman Rapaport is a professor of English at the University of Southhampton. He is the author of *Heidegger and Derrida: Reflections on Time and Language* (Nebraska, 1989), *Between the Sign and the Gaze* (Cornell, 1994), *Is There Truth in Art?* (Cornell, 1996), and *Theory Mess: Deconstruction in Eclipse* (Columbia, 2000).

Krzysztof Ziarek is an associate professor of English at the University of Notre Dame. He is the author of *Inflected Language: Toward a Hermeneutics of Nearness. Heidegger, Levinas, Stevens, Celan* (SUNY, 1994) and *The Historicity of Experience: Modernity, the Avant-Garde, and the Event* (Northwestern, 2001).